mass
media
issues

Articles & Commentaries

Edited by

Leonard L. Sellers
San Francisco State University

William L. Rivers
Stanford University

Prentice-Hall, Inc.
Englewood Cliffs, New Jersey 07632

Library of Congress Cataloging in Publication Data

Main entry under title:

Mass media issues.

Includes index.
1. Mass media—United States—Addresses, essays,
lectures. I. Sellers, Leonard L. (date)
II. Rivers, William L.
P92.U5M3   301.16'1'0973   76-30802
ISBN 0-13-559500-2

For Carolyn and Sarah

"It's the Sound that Does It," by John P. Robinson and Paul Hirsch, copyright © 1969
Ziff-Davis Publishing Company. Reprinted by permission of *Psychology Today Magazine*.

Prentice-Hall International, Inc., *London*
Prentice-Hall of Australia Pty. Limited, *Sydney*
Prentice-Hall of Canada, Ltd., *Toronto*
Prentice-Hall of India Private Limited, *New Delhi*
Prentice-Hall of Japan, Inc., *Tokyo*
Prentice-Hall of Southeast Asia Pte. Ltd., *Singapore*

contents

newspapers 189

Social Force *190*

magazines 255

film 287

contents

by categories

news

economics

ix

regulation

structure and process

affect and effect

preface

As far as we have been able to determine, this is the first anthology that carries commentaries. At the beginning, we thought we would publish "debates" between writer and editor. Hardly had we begun choosing articles than the idea of a debate seemed silly. Had we identified the pros and cons, according to our own biases, the reader might be bewildered. The writer would say Yes, the editor would say No—and he has the last word. The reader could also ask: If the editor disagrees, why did he pick the article to begin with?

So instead we chose the articles that would present a broad view of mass media issues and would give the reader something to think about. You may disagree with certain points made in various articles, and you will find that we take issue with many individual paragraphs and some whole articles. But we should make it clear that we *like* everything in this book.

Moreover, casting our replies as commentaries gives us the latitude to respond in still another direction. Although we are enthusiastic about these articles, how much more could be said! The writer of any article finds that he is limited severely. When he writes on a theme, he thinks regretfully of how much more he could do if he were not limited by space or editorial focus. For example, even Leo Rosten, in writing his admirable "The Intellectual and the Mass Media," must narrow the scope of his argument. He hasn't the space to spread out his argument and attack the counterpoints he can foresee. So it is that the writers have opened vast territories that invite our commentaries.

Although we have limited our responses to approximately 1,500 words, we have ample space to bring up other related points. For example, after Gary Atkins has presented a careful analysis of the history of objectivity, we are free to explore the methods of the objective story, interpretive reporting, and finally, an example of Atkins's method. We believe that these commentaries will do much more for our readers than a simple set of pro and con arguments. They will invite the reader to explore closely related ideas.

Each of the mass media—television and cable, radio, newspapers, magazines, film, and advertising—is first explored as a social force. Then, we examine the inevitable constraints on the media, not all of them legal; we find ethical constraints too, as well as the restraining forces of commercialism. These opposing forces also have considerable power.

You will find only a few articles from academic journals in this book. We decided to choose the best and most embracing articles wherever we could find them—and we found them in many places. We also required that the articles be interesting to students and to scholars and be written recently. There is only one exception regarding currency, Leo Rosten's excellent article. With these rules in mind, it is remarkable how few of these articles are likely to change with passage of time. Nearly everything in this book, we think, is likely to stand up for years.

We are indebted to many people for their help with this book, especially Kimberly Vergez, whose work from beginning to end was invaluable. We would also like to thank Janet Collom, Sharron Fien, Carolyn Nelson-Sellers, and Mary Sellers for their expert editorial assistance, and Richard Dangerfield, Jon G. Donhoff, Pamela deDeugd, and Yves Gagnon for their aid and comments. Also, we are indebted to Gail Rivers, who compiled the index.

1 intro-
duc-
tion

introduction
an overview

"I don't have any attitudes of my very own. The media has shaped all of my attitudes!"

Leo Rosten

The Intellectual and the Mass Media: Some Rigorously Random Remarks

Most intellectuals do not understand the inherent nature of the mass media. They do not understand the process by which a newspaper or magazine, movie or television show is created. They project their own tastes, yearnings, and values upon the masses—who do not, unfortunately, share them. They attribute over-simplified motivations to those who own or operate the mass media. They assume that changes in ownership or control would necessarily improve the product. They presume the existence of a vast reservoir of talent, competence, and material which does not in fact exist.

A great deal of what appears in the mass media is dreadful tripe and treacle; inane in content, banal in style, muddy in reasoning, mawkish in sentiment, vulgar, naïve, and offensive to men of learning or refinement. I am both depressed and distressed by the bombardment of our eyes, our ears, and our brains by meretricious material designed for a populace whose paramount preferences involve the narcotic pursuit of "fun."

Why is this so? Are the media operated by cynical men motivated solely by profit? Are they controlled by debasers of culture—by ignorant, vulgar, irresponsible men?

Many intellectuals think so and say so. They think so and say so in the face of evidence they either do not examine or cannot bring themselves to accept: that when the public is free to choose among various products, it chooses—again and again and again—the frivolous as against the serious, "escape" as against reality, the lurid as against the tragic, the trivial as against the serious, fiction as against fact, the diverting as against the significant. To conclude otherwise is to deny the data: circulation figures for the press, box-office receipts for the movies and the theater, audience measurement for radio and television programs.

The sad truth seems to be this: that relatively few people in any society, not excluding Periclean Athens, have reasonably good taste or care deeply

Reprinted by permission of Leo Rosten from *Daedalus,* Spring 1960.

about ideas. Fewer still seem equipped—by temperament and capacity, rather than education—to handle ideas with both skill and pleasure.

The deficiencies of mass media are a function, in part at least, of the deficiencies of the masses. Is it unfair to ask that responsibility for mental laziness and deplorable taste be distributed—to include the schools, the churches, the parents, the social institutions which produce those masses who persist in preferring pin-ball games to anything remotely resembling philosophy?

Intellectuals seem unable to reconcile themselves to the fact that their hunger for more news, better plays, more serious debate, deeper involvement in ideas is not a hunger characteristic of many. They cannot believe that the subjects dear to their hearts bore or repel or overtax the capacities of their fellow citizens. Why this is so I shall try to explore later. At this point, let me remark that the intellectual, who examines his society with unyielding and antiseptic detachment, must liberate himself from the myths (or, in Plato's term, the royal lies) by which any social system operates. It is ironic that intellectuals often destroy old myths to erect and reverence special myths of their own. A striking example is found in the clichés with which they both characterize and indict the mass media. Let us consider the principal particulars in that indictment.

"The mass media lack originality."

They certainly do. Most of what appears in print, or on film, or on the air, lacks originality. But is there any area of human endeavor of which this is not true? Is not the original as rare in science or philosophy or painting as it is in magazines? Is not the original "original" precisely because it is rare? Is it not self-evident that the more that is produced of anything, the smaller the proportion of originality is likely to be? But is the absolute number of novel creative products thereby reduced? Are we dealing with Gresham's Law—or with imperfect observation?

The mass media are not characterized by endless inventiveness and variation. But they are considerably more varied and inventive, given their built-in limitations, than we give them credit for. Consider these limitations: neither life nor truth nor fiction offers infinite choices: there is only a limited number of plots or stories or themes; there is only a limited number of ways of communicating the limited body of material; audiences develop a cumulative awareness of resemblances and an augmented resistance to the stylized and the predictable; and even the freshest departures from routine soon become familiar and routine. Besides, originality is often achieved at the price of "balance" or proportion: the most arresting features in, say, *The New Yorker* or *Time* often incur the displeasure of scholars precisely because they prefer vitality to a judicious ordering of "all the facts."

The artist, of course, wrests freshness and new insight from the most familiar material; but true artists, in any field at any given time, are so rare that their singularity requires a special word—"genius."

The mass media are cursed by four deadly requirements: a gargantuan amount of space (in magazines and newspapers) and time (in television and radio) *has* to be filled; talent—on every level, in every technique—is scarce; the public votes, i.e., is free to decide what it prefers (and it is the deplorable results of this voting that intellectuals might spend more time confronting); and a magazine, paper, television or radio program is committed to periodic and unalterable publication. Content would be markedly improved if publications or programs appeared only when superior material was available. This applies to academic journals no less than to publications or programs with massive audiences.

"The mass media do not use the best brains or freshest talents."

Surely the burden of proof is on those who make this assertion. The evidence is quite clear that talent in the popular arts is searched for and courted in ways that do not apply in other fields: seniority is ignored, tenure is virtually nonexistent, youth is prized. In few areas is failure so swiftly and ruthlessly punished, or success so swiftly and extravagantly rewarded.

And still—talent is scarce. It is a woeful fact that despite several generations of free education, our land has produced relatively few first-rate minds; and of those with first-rate brains, fewer have imagination; of those with brains and imagination, fewer still possess judgment. If we ask, in addition, for the special skills and experience involved in the art of communicating, the total amount of talent available to the media is not impressive.

"The best brains" in the land do not gravitate to the media—if by brains we mean skill in analyzing complexities, or sustaining abstract propositions for prolonged intellectual operations. But the best brains would not necessarily make the best editors, or writers, or producers, or publishers —at least they would not long survive in a competitive market.

The media are enterprises, not IQ tests. They feed on inventiveness, not analytic discipline. They require creative skills and nonstandardized competences. Their content has, thus far at least, resisted the standardized and accumulative statement of propositions of a Euclid or an Adam Smith.

"The mass media do not print or broadcast the best material that is submitted to them."

To edit is to judge; to judge is, inevitably, to reward some and disappoint others.

The assumption that a vast flow of material pours into the editorial offices of the media—from which publishers or producers simply select the worst—is simply incorrect. A huge proportion of what finally appears in magazines, radio, and television was "dreamed up" inside the media offices, and ordered from the staff or from free-lance writers. And as often as not, even when the best talent is employed, at the highest prices, and given complete freedom, the results disappoint expectations. Excellence is not necessarily achieved because it is sought.

"The mass media cannot afford to step on anyone's toes."

The following recent articles in popular magazines most conspicuously stepped on quite powerful toes: What Protestants Fear About Catholics; Cigarettes and Lung Cancer; Birth Control; The Disgrace of Our Hospitals; Fee-Splitting by Doctors; Agnosticism; Financial Shenanigans and Stock Manipulations; A Mercy Killing; The Murder of Negroes in the South.

The movies and television recently offered all but the deaf and blind these scarcely soporific themes: miscegenation; adultery; dope addiction; white-Negro tensions; the venality of television; the vulgarity of movie executives; the cowardice of a minister, a banker; hypocrisy in business and advertising; big business and call girls; the degeneracy of Southern whites.

It was long assumed that the most sacred of sacred cows in a capitalist society is the Businessman or Big Business as an institution. But in recent years we have been exposed to a striking number of revelations about Business. Advertising men and methods, presumably too "powerful" to expose, much less deride, have been raked with coals of fire—in media which depend upon advertisers and advertising. "The Man in the Grey Flannel Suit" became a symbol of conformity to the masses, no less than the intellectual, through the mass media.

It is worth noticing that the sheer size of an audience crucially influences the content of what is communicated to it. Taboos, in movies or television, are not simply the fruit of cowardice among producers (though their anxiety is often disproportionate, and their candor unnecessarily hampered by pessimistic assumptions of what public reaction will be). Taboos are often functions of audience size, age-range, and heterogeneity. Things can be communicated to the few which cannot be communicated (at least not in the same way) to the many.

Books, magazines, and newspapers can discuss sex, homosexuality, masturbation, venereal disease, abortion, dope addiction, in ways not so easily undertaken on television or film. The reader reads alone—and this is a fact of great importance to those who write for him.

"The mass media do not give the public enough or adequate information about the serious problems of our time."

Never in history has the public been offered so much, so often, in such detail, for so little. I do not mean that Americans know as much as intellectuals think they ought to know, or wish they did know, about the problems which confront us. I do mean that the media already offer the public far more news, facts, information, and interpretations than the public takes the trouble to digest. I find it impossible to escape the conclusion that, apart from periods of acute crisis, most people do not want to be *involved,* in precisely those areas which the intellectual finds most absorbing and meaningful. . . .

Do intellectuals find it unnoteworthy that, year after year, four to five times as many citizens in New York City choose the *Daily News* as against the New York *Times* . . . ? Or that for decades the citizens of Chicago have preferred the Chicago *Tribune* to competitors closer to the intellectuals' heart? Or that for decades the people of Los Angeles have voted in favor of the Los Angeles *Times,* at the expense of less parochial competitors?

"The aesthetic level of the mass media is appalling: truth is sacrificed to the happy ending, escapism is exalted, romance, violence, melodrama prevail."

The mass media do not attempt to please intellectuals, on either the aesthetic or the conceptual plane. Some commentators believe that if the media offered the public less trivia, the taste of the public would perforce be improved. But if the media give the public too little of what they want, and too much of what they don't want (too soon), they would simply cease to be mass media—and would be replaced by either "massier" competitors or would drive the public to increased expenditures of time on sports, parlor games, gambling, and other familiar methods of protecting the self from the ardors of thought or the terrors of solitude.

The question of proportion (how much "light stuff" or staple insipidity to include as against how much heavy or "uplifting" material) is one of the more perplexing problems any editor faces. It is far from uncommon to hear an editor remark that he will run a feature which he knows will be read by "less than 5 per cent of our readers."

I suspect that intellectuals tend to judge the highbrow by its peaks and the nonhighbrow by its average. If we look at the peaks in both cases, how much do the mass media suffer by comparison? . . .

In my opinion, some of the more insightful work of our time can be found in the mass media, for example, the comic strip *Peanuts,* which throws an original and enchanting light on children; the comic strip *Li'l Abner,* which is often both as illuminating and as savage as social satire should be; the movies of, say, William Wyler, George Stevens, Jules Dassin, John Huston, David Lean, Delbert Mann.

Intellectuals generally discover "artists" in the popular arts long after the public, with less rarefied aesthetic categories, has discovered them. Perhaps there is rooted in the character structure of intellectuals an aversion, or an inability, to participate in certain sectors of life; they do seem blind to the fact that the popular can be meritorious. This changes with time (e.g., consider the reputations of Twain, Dickens, Dumas, Balzac, Lardner). And a Jack Benny or Phil Silvers may yet achieve the classic dimension now permitted the Marx Brothers, who—once despised as broad vaudevillians—have become the eggheads' delight.

"The mass media corrupt and debase public taste; they create the kind of audience that enjoys cheap and trivial entertainment."

This implies that demand (public taste or preference) has become a spurious function of manipulated supply. Here the evidence from Great Britain is illuminating: for years the government-owned BBC and the admirable Third Program offered the British public superior fare: excellent music, learned talks, literate discussions. For years, the noncommercial radio defended the bastions of culture. Yet when the British public was offered choices on television, it dismayed Anglophiles by taking to its heart the same silly quiz shows, panel shows, Westerns, melodramas, and "situation comedies" which the critics of daily newspapers deplore both in London and New York. . . .

Doubtless the mass media can do more, much more, to elevate what the public reads, sees, and hears. But the media cannot do this as easily or as rapidly as is often assumed. Indeed, they cannot get too far in front of their audiences without suffering the fate of predecessors who tried just that.

There is considerable evidence to support the deflating view that the media, on the whole, are considerably *ahead* of the masses—in intelligence, in taste, in values, e.g., the vocabulary in almost any popular journal, not excluding fan magazines, is often too "highbrow" for its readers.

It seems to me a fair question to ask whether the intelligence or taste of the public is really worse today than it was before the mass media came along.

"The mass media are what they are because they are operated solely as money-making enterprises."

Publishers and producers are undoubtedly motivated by a desire for profits. But this is not *all* that motivates them. Publishers and producers are no less responsive than intellectuals to "ego values"; they are no less eager to win respect and respectability from their peers; they respond to both internalized and external "reference groups"; they seek esteem—from the self and from others.

Besides, producers know that a significant percentage of what they present in the mass media will not be as popular as what might be substituted—but it is presented nonetheless. Why? Partly because of nonpecuniary values, and partly because of what critics of the crass profit-motive seem blind to: the fact that part of the competitive process involves a continuous search for products which can win favor with audiences not attracted to, or satisfied by, the prevailing output. New and minority audiences are constantly courted by the media, e.g., the strictly "egghead" programs on television, the new magazines which arise, and flourish, because they fill a need, as *Scientific American, American Heritage.*

Whenever profits, used as either a carrot or a stick, are criticized, it is tacitly assumed that reliance on other human impulses would serve man better. Is this so? Do virtue, probity, self-sacrifice guarantee excellence? It seems to me that most of the horrors of human history have been the work not of skeptical or cynical or realistic men, but of those persuaded of their superior virtue.

To replace publication for profit by publication via subsidy would of course be to exchange one set of imperfections for another. The postal system offers scant support to those who assume that nonprofit enterprise is necessarily better than private competition (I hasten to add that in some fields, e.g., public health, it clearly is).

It should be noted, parenthetically, that anyone who enters the magazine or newspaper field in the expectation of high profits is either singularly naïve, extremely optimistic, or poorly informed: few areas of American business show so high a mortality rate, are plagued by such unpredictabilities, promise so many headaches, and return so low a net profit. Successful magazines earn as modest a profit as three percent on invested capital. To the purely profit-minded, business has long offered innumerable opportunities outside of publishing which far surpass it in profitability, security, or potential.

"The mass media are dominated—or too much influenced—by advertisers."

The influence of advertising is often too great—even if that influence is one-tenth as potent as many assume it to be. The editorial function should be as entirely free of non-editorial influences as possible.

But publishers, producers, and editors would respond to power or influence *even if all advertising were abolished.* It is an inescapable fact of human organization that men adjust to power (that, indeed, is one of power's attributes); that men consider, or try to anticipate, the effect of their acts on those who hold most of whatever is most prized in a society.

There is a reverse and paradoxical angle to advertising: when a newspaper or magazine, a radio or television station becomes successful, the advertiser needs it as much as the other way around. Revenues from many advertisers increase the capacity to resist pressure from individual advertisers. Organs which can be "bought" nearly always decline in prosperity and influence.

Purely professional calculations often override vested interest. Some news or stories are so significant that it is impossible to prevent their publication.

The instance of the cigarette industry, mentioned above, is worth notice. Tobacco companies represent one of the largest and most consistent sources of national advertising revenue. Yet within an hour after medical reports appeared linking cigarette smoking to lung cancer, they were fully and dramatically presented to the public—not only on the front pages of newspapers but in radio and television reporting as well. The news was simply too big, too "newsworthy" to be suppressed (even though several discussion programs shied away from the subject). The deficiencies of automobiles, where safety is concerned, have been analyzed in magazines which receive huge advertising revenues from automobile companies.

This is not to say that all truths which threaten power—in business, in the arts, even in the groves of academe—always gain as swift and public an airing as they deserve. They often do not. They do not because men, even men in power, are often timid, or weak, or frightened, or avaricious, or opportunistic, or unwise, or short-sighted. Some media operators, like some politicians, some clergymen, some labor leaders, some economists, are overly sensitive to the side on which their bread is buttered. . . .

"The mass media do not provide an adequate forum for minority views—the dissident and unorthodox."

Producers and publishers give more space and time to minority views (which include the *avant-garde*) than numerical proportions require. They feel that it is the function of specialized journals to carry specialized content. The popular media carry far more material of this kind than anyone would have predicted two decades ago.

The democratic society must insure a viable public forum for the dissenter—in politics, morals, arts. That forum will never be as large as the dissenters themselves want. But I know of no perfect way to determine who shall have what access to how many—at the expense of whom else —except to keep pressing for as free a market as we can achieve.

It may seem to some readers that I have substituted an indictment of the masses for an indictment of the mass media; that I have assigned the role of villain to the masses in a social drama in which human welfare and public enlightenment are hamstrung by the mediocrity, laziness, and indifference of the populace. I hope that detachment will not be mistaken for cynicism.

I should be the first to stress the immensity of the social gains which public education and literacy alone have made possible. The rising public appreciation of music, painting, ballet; the growth of libraries; the fantastic sales of paperback books (however much they are skewed by . . . the works of Mickey Spillane), the striking diffusion of "cultural activities" in communities throughout the land, the momentous fact that popular magazines *can* offer the public the ruminations of such nonpopular minds as Paul Tillich or Sir George Thomson—the dimensions of these changes are a tribute to the achievements of that society which has removed from men the chains of caste and class that hampered human achievement through the centuries. I, for one, do not lament the passing of epochs in which "high culture" flourished while the majority of mankind lived in ignorance and indignity.

What I have been emphasizing here is the inevitable gap between the common and the superior. More particularly, I have been embroidering the theme of the intellectual's curious reluctance to accept evidence. Modern intellectuals seem *guilty* about reaching conclusions that were once the *a priori* convictions of the aristocrat. It is understandable that twentieth-century intellectuals should dread snobbery, at one end of the social scale, as much as they shun mob favor at the other. But the intellectual's snobbery is of another order, and involves a tantalizing paradox: a contempt for what *hoi polloi* enjoy, and a kind of proletarian ethos that tacitly denies inequalities of talent and taste.

The recognition of facts has little bearing on motivations and should surely not impute preferences. The validity of an idea has nothing to do with who propounds it—or whom it outrages. The author is aware that he is inviting charges of Brahminism, misanthropy, a reactionary "unconscious," or heaven knows what else. But is it really heresy to the democratic credo for intellectuals to admit, if only in the privacy of professional confessionals, that they are, in fact, more literate and more skillful—in diagnosis, induction, and generalization, if in nothing else—than their fellow-passengers on the ship of state?

Perhaps the intellectual's guilt, when he senses incipient snobbery within himself, stems from his uneasiness at being part of an elite, moreover, a new elite which is not shored up by ancient and historic sanctions. For intellectualism has been divorced from its traditional *cachet* and from the majesty with which earlier societies invested their elites: a classical education, Latin or Greek (in any case, a language not comprehensible to the untutored), a carefully cultivated accent, the inflection of the well born, the well bred, or the priestly. One of the painful experiences spared intellectuals in the past was hearing Ideas discussed—with profundity or insight—in accents which attest to birth on "the other side of the tracks."

It may be difficult for shopkeepers' sons to admit their manifest superiority over the world they left: parents, siblings, comrades. But the intellectual who struggles with a sinful sense of superiority, and who feels admirable sentiments of loyalty to his non-U origins, must still explain why it was that his playmates and classmates did not join him in the noble dedication to learning and the hallowed pursuit of truth. The triumph of mass education is to be found not simply in the increment of those who can read, write, add, and subtract. It is to be found in a much more profound and enduring evolution: the provision of opportunities to express the self, and pursue the self's values, opportunities not limited to the children of a leisure class, or an aristocracy, or a landed gentry, or a well-heeled bourgeoisie. The true miracle of public education is that no elite can decide where the next intellectual will come from.

Each generation creates its own devils, and meets its own Waterloo on the heartless field of reality. The Christian Fathers blamed the Prince of

Darkness for preventing perfectible man from reaching Paradise. Anarchists blamed the state. Marxists blame the class system. Pacifists blame the militarists. And our latter-day intellectuals seem to blame the mass media for the lamentable failure of more people to attain the bliss of intellectual grace. This is a rank disservice to intellectuals themselves, for it dismisses those attributes of character and ability—discipline, curiosity, persistence, the renunciation of worldly rewards—which make intellectuals possible at all. The compulsive egalitarianism of eggheads even seems to lure them into a conspicuous disinterest in the possible determinism of heredity.

Responsibility increases with capacity, and should be demanded of those in positions of power. Just as I hold the intellectual more responsible than others for the rigorous exploration of phenomena and the courageous enunciation of truths, so, too, do I ask for better and still better performance from those who have the awesome power to shape men's minds.

---

to the student: a commentary

Leo Rosten is one of the few intellectuals who writes so clearly that almost anyone can understand the points he's making. It is not surprising that he is a Ph.D. in sociology and a former writer for *Look* magazine. Rosten is also the author of such books as *H*y*m*a*n K*a*p*l*a*n* (a humorous delight) and *Captain Newman, M.D.,* which was made into a fine movie. Although he is an intellectual, here Rosten defends the mass media against the intellectuals' attacks.

Rosten's article is, by all odds, one of the most approving essays of the media from an intellectual. In fact, it seems throughout that he is speaking solely to the intellectuals. Is he too defensive? Perhaps. Here and there Rosten sounds a bit like an intellectual on a soapbox, seeking to convince his readers even though he seems to elevate his argument to a shrill note.

How would he have argued before, say, the proprietors of the media? Certainly his essay would have presented a much more negative view of the media, expressing the intellectual's disaffection for them. Here, Rosten makes a sound argument, skillfully anticipating the response of his intellectual audience because he too is an intellectual.

But Rosten, whether writing for the intellectual or for the publishers and broadcasters, must narrow the scope of his argument; he hasn't the space of a book within which he can spread out his argument and attack the counterpoints he foresees. Nor have I such space. But it seems apparent that a few other points must be made.

One of the most telling comments about the stance of the intellectual in the United States comes from David Manning White in his book *Mass Culture:*

The xenophilic critics who discuss American culture as if they were holding a dead vermin in their hands seem to imply that in some other, better age the bulk of people were fair copies of Leonardo Da Vinci. No critic shudders more audibly when discussing the vulgarities of American life than T. S. Eliot. Yet it is only realistic to note that in the England which became Eliot's haven, one of the most popular of diversions for nearly 700 years was bear-baiting. I do not cite this to demean the contributions to our world culture of a Chaucer, a Reynolds, a Thomas Tallis, or any English artist who added to the world's treasury, but only to draw the point that art was no more important to the mass of the people of their day than the goings-on at Paris Garden in Southwark, the chief bear-garden in London. When the Londoners got tired of seeing chained bears torn to pieces by the dogs they had other diversions.

Of all the many kinds of criticism that was published in *Mass Culture,* to students this was the most memorable paragraph: bear-baiting. For although the intellectuals at the earlier time were haughty of all the mass culture, they were lured by bear-baiting. At once, the lust for bear-baiting embraced nearly everyone of every description, whether intellectual or lowbrow.

So much of the intellectual attitude toward entertainment is negative that we must consider it from the other way around. Few have defended it more pointedly than Dr. Charlene Brown of Indiana University:

Entertainment is necessary to provide the relief to enable human beings to face the demands of modern life—or maybe just life in general. Not all of us have the same sensibilities. The highbrows prefer their entertainment in different forms from the lowbrows, but it's still entertainment no matter how arty or how heavy with message. People need to relax. The sad scene is the culture vulture who feels compelled to seek out art but doesn't enjoy it. In fact, he's punishing himself. He's miserable but he feels he's accomplished something. The experience has been good for him, he tells himself. I recognize that when I go to the movies I want to be entertained. I don't need to go to the movies in order to be depressed by the cares of the world. Even from that point of view, most of what is on television does not entertain me. But I don't want to let television give entertainment a bad name.

One way of deciding what is entertainment is to bypass the content itself and to consider its effect, which a number of social researchers have done. Some define entertainment as an escapist activity, which relieves tensions by affording the media user relief from his personal problems. Joseph T. Klapper in *The Effects of the Mass Media* has reviewed the different meanings that social scientists have given to the term *escapist,* and fashioned a common-denominator definition: "that communication which provides emotional release by diverting the reader from his own problems or anxieties."

What is escapist for one person, then, is not necessarily so for another. If one uses media content primarily for pleasure, it is escapist no matter what else it is. Thus a businessman who relaxes with a magazine article about science or a scientist who takes refuge in the sports page of the newspaper is using the mass media for diversion. Under that concept all media fare is potentially entertainment. Whether it is or not depends on the use to which the reader, viewer, or listener puts it.

More pointedly, essayist Dwight Macdonald identified three different cultures in the United States: *high culture, mass culture,* and *folk art,* which are roughly analogous to the division into highbrows, middlebrows, and lowbrows. Macdonald praised high culture: the painstaking work of rich talent and genius carried to the ultimate degree for the sake of high art. Mass culture, in which most of us probably are, is the art of the marketplace—appealing and not quite genuine because it aims at mass consumption rather than at perfection. Folk art is the natural talent, usually of one who would be classified as a lowbrow on an intellectual scale, expressed in folk songs, spirituals, and primitive drawings. Can you place yourself in one of these three categories? Perhaps. But then in the course of pursuing a college degree you may change.

Finally, if you're acidly negative of the media, you can at least understand the struggles and gyrations the media proprietors and managers go through. Consider the almost impossible situation in which they find themselves. What is "bad" in one culture is not necessarily so in another; so, the wider the audience the more cultures it will embrace, and the more kinds of behavior that must be avoided. Stories that would be all right in a traveling salesmen's or luncheon club's culture are not all right in the home culture into which television enters. The treatment of cows which is perfectly acceptable in American movie theaters is taboo in India, where Hollywood wants to sell the same films. A treatment of divorce which might be suitable in an American Protestant culture is not so in an American Catholic culture. And so the wider the audience, the fewer the kinds of behavior that popular art may teach without violating the mores of some important group within the audience.

Whether you're delighted with one or more of the instruments of the mass media or whether you're repelled by all they offer, you have no escape. You are *surrounded* by the media—even immersed in them. Perhaps in the end you will find that Leo Rosten has written an article that you must ponder again. It is worth rereading.

WLR

William L. Rivers

Another Government:
The News Media

Commenting on the trial of Bruno Richard Hauptmann, who was charged with the kidnaping and murder of the infant son of Charles Lindbergh, Walter Lippmann argued in 1936 that "there are two processes of justice, the one official, the other popular. They are carried on side by side, the one in the courts of law, the other in the press, over the radio, on the screen, at public meetings." Lippmann went on to argue that there are two pursuits of the criminal, two trials, and two verdicts, and that the official verdict often becomes confused with the popular verdict, sometimes in the court itself, and almost always in the public mind.

It seems evident that Lippmann's observation is quite true, but those who end the discussion with the court verdict and the popular verdict are limiting themselves severely. For the basic question is not just whether we have two legal systems, but whether we have two governments. Do we have an official government, and another government that exists only in the public mind? Indeed we do. Another Government, in sharp contrast to the official government, is made up of the reports of more than 2,000 correspondents in Washington. Only when we think of more than 215 million Americans—more than *215 million*—can we focus sharply on our needs for information. What can we know about the actions of government? In our daily lives, we trace a path from home to work and back. Without the media, we know almost nothing beyond our own sphere of activity.

There is little doubt that the public's knowledge of government depends not on experience and observation, but rather on the news media, which set the agenda for public discussion. We get only occasional firsthand glimpses of government: seeing a president or a presidential candidate in the flesh for a moment, or on a televised news conference, shaking hands with a congressman (or talking with one while he absent-mindedly shakes hands with another voter), or doing piddling business with government agencies.

We learn more about government secondhand—from friends, acquaintances, and lecturers on hurried tours, especially those who have been near the seats of power and are eager to impart what they consider, perhaps erroneously, to be the real story of what is going on there. Such stories add only a small patch to the fabric of our knowledge. Most of what we know about the workings of government must come to us from the news media; we have no practical alternatives.

To learn about the national government from the news media, it is as though we are watching a play by a director who commands the performance. He brings in the president at some length, the leading congressmen briefly, a quick picture of the justices of the Supreme Court, and finally a fleeting glimpse of a few of the president's cabinet members. There are not many more. Meanwhile, many publications such as *Aviation Week* or *Broadcasting* are plumbing the depths of government, but their reporting is a kind of very small sideshow. Publications such as the *New York Times,* the *Washington Post,* the *Los Angeles Times,* and several others including magazines let us see the leaders of the national government at a length that is almost paralyzing, but they show us very few of the highly placed employees of the national government: there are three *million* employees. But our effort to move beyond the play to see the reality is of no avail. We must understand this: the government *appears* to be shown through the news media. In essence, the reality is quite different. Those journalists reporting public affairs are, in fact, the creators of an image of government.

It would seem that division of labor would help us to learn about everything: radio and television rapidly reporting the action; newspapers putting many stories in context; and the magazine writers and book authors reporting them more fully, and with more grace and flavor.

But the range of public affairs reports, however carefully some may be fashioned, seem to be a faulty mirror. The mirror is first held this way, then that way, but how narrowly it is focused! The presidency, the congressional leaders, the Department of State, the Department of Defense, and sometimes, the Department of Health, Education, and Welfare are in view. Only occasionally is mention made of the Department of Transportation, which figures in our everyday lives although we cannot see it, or the Department of Agriculture. Only a few officials or agencies ever appear on the front page, the television set, or the radio program.

At root are the newsworthy actions that appeal powerfully to correspondents. Journalistic concepts of newsworthiness, the structures and purposes of the media, and the human failings of journalists drive most reporters to focus on the presidency, the congressional leaders, and a few executive department secretaries. And how distorted the picture is! Consider what occurs:

1. Something happens in government.
2. Government officials decide how to announce or present this occurrence. This may differ from (1).

3. Through a press secretary, the news media are presented with this government announcement. This may differ from (1) and (2).

4. A reporter produces a story of the occurrence. This may differ from (1), (2), and (3).

5. The media organization processes the reporter's story for presentation to the public, either directly or through its client newspapers and broadcast stations. This may differ from (1), (2), (3), and (4).

6. The public receives an image of the occurrence. This may differ from (1), (2), (3), (4), and (5).

From the beginning of an occurrence in the federal government until it is presented as an image, it must hurdle four crucial obstacles. First, the responsible official has winnowed an announcement from the work of many subordinates—which may displease them. Nonetheless, the official contracts the announcement, which is necessary, in a way that will please *him or her.* Next, ordinarily the official relies on a press secretary (or one known as a public information specialist) who may think well of the announcement or not. The press secretary submits the announcement to a journalist and then fulfills the rather unusual role of answering questions. If questioned perceptively, the press secretary has an unusual opportunity to suggest that the journalist check with the higher official—or the secretary may simply answer the questions, or even guide the journalist to an unhappy subordinate. In many cases, however, the journalist is in a hurry —or lazy—and will print or broadcast the information given. Increasingly, though, one encounters adversary journalists, who question closely and look beyond the announcement. When that journalist finds apparent lying or corruption—or the beginnings of it—he or she faces a high obstacle: the editor. Because editors usually pass the bland story as it is written, journalists may not be encouraged to look for unethical or illegal behavior. But more and more often, a vision of fame and prizes increases the journalist's ardor. The editor, however, has final authority. And whatever decisions are made when an occurrence is finally presented to the public, it will be merely an image, certainly not reality, after passing through the hands of officials, press secretaries, journalists, and editors.

It must be clear that the difference between the real government and the media image of government begins with the deliberate action by most officials to insert the image they desire into the media process. The government nearly always tries to create an image of itself, and whether it is successful depends on the reporter. In some cases, the image of the officials vies with the reporter's own concept of the image.

Ben Bagdikian, the most powerful media critic in the United States, commented upon the interrelationships between government image-making and press image-making in his study of the newspaper columnist ten years ago. He talked to many assistant secretaries for public affairs about how they briefed their bosses on how to break government news. Assistant secretaries were heavily influenced by what they saw in the news media, accepted this as what the media would respond to, and as a result, fashioned their output to serve what they perceived to be the media interest. The work of the columnists, Bagdikian speculated, "includes guessing what the government is doing." This produces a double-mirror effect, each side responding to what the other is doing, while at the same time adjusting itself to the other side's anticipated needs. Thinking about the mirrors of politics, John Kenneth Galbraith commented wryly:

Nearly all of our political comment originates in Washington. Washington politicians, after talking things over with each other, relay misinformation to Washington journalists who, after further intramural discussion, print it where it is thoughtfully read by the same politicians. It is the only completely successful closed system for the recycling of garbage that has yet been devised.

Viewed in the rawness of this circus of political reporting, government news seems very complicated—and dangerous. Since the Vietnam War and the Watergate crisis, however, Washington correspondents are much more suspicious of the announcements of government officials. More and more correspondents every year are asking sharp questions of officials, and increasing numbers of reporters are gaining the specialized training necessary to ask pointed questions. The gaps in most reporters' economic training became obvious, for example, when the United States went off the gold standard in 1933. Vainly trying to explain what happened, the generalist reporters appealed to the White House, and a government economist was sent over to help. Then the reporters tried to explain the new facts of economic life using the economist's idiom, with poor results.

Not long ago, when Lyndon Johnson was president, the chairman of the Council of Economic Advisers was Gardner Ackley. Vexed by sloppy reporting, he suggested that the economics reporter be required to meet two standards: First, that the reporter had taken an introductory college course in economics. Second, that he had passed it.

More recently, the large bureaus of Washington correspondents have become much more sophisticated in economics reporting; some of the other bureaus now have specialists who, like Edwin Dale of the *New York Times,* can discuss the meaning of money with the most elevated bankers and can translate it. And of course, some of the smaller bureaus, like the large ones, are trying to hire someone who is a specialist *and* a generalist, which is difficult.

But even the specialists must be adrift today, however talented they are. For example, when I was working for the now-defunct *Reporter,* I was writing about a powerful congressman named John J. Rooney of Brooklyn, who headed the House of Representatives subcommittee that controlled the budget of the Department of State. He savaged its budget request every year by speaking against "booze money for those striped-pants cookie-pushers."

I interviewed the assistant secretary of state who had the task of arguing for the budget the department thought reasonable. In the subcommittee hearings Rooney conducted, the assistant secretary experienced Brooklyn politics firsthand. Congressman Rooney's mildest adjective for him was "self-serving."

I asked him how much Rooney's attacks crippled the budget request. Why, not at all, he said. In fact, Congressman Rooney was the best friend the Department of State had. By berating the so-called cookie-pushers on the floor of the House even as he was pushing a generous budget, Congressman Rooney persuaded the Representatives who abhorred striped pants that he had the State Department's number. Rooney's strong words were a facade, the assistant secretary said, that enabled the congressman to sneak more money into the budget than Congress would have granted.

That sounded to me like double-talk. But no matter how many people I interviewed, they were almost evenly split. In the end, I decided that Congressman Rooney wasn't a friend of the State Department, and so reported that he was budget-slasher. But it *could* have been that he was a clever ally. I was proud of my Ph.D. in political science, but like most specialists, I could be convinced at times that Machiavelli is alive and advising congressmen.

If it sometimes seems that neither the reporter nor the public can know the truth, it is somehow comforting to think of Another Government in the United States in comparison to the Russian system. For example, Hedrick Smith wrote of Moscow:

In early August 1972, Moscow was enveloped for days in a mysterious blue haze. It hung motionless over the city. The big domestic airport at Domodedovo, south of Moscow, had to divert flights because of poor visibility. Muscovites were coughing terribly, wiping tears from their eyes. Streetcars and automobiles were forced to use headlights. People were alarmed by rumors that fires in the fields around Moscow were menacing populated areas. Yet for nearly a week, the press said nothing. Finally, one skimpy back-page article mentioned a peat-bog fire near Shatura, about 60 miles east of Moscow. It turned out that some fires were extinguished no more than 15 or 20 miles from the Kremlin, very close to populated suburbs of Moscow. Yet most of the press printed practically nothing and *Pravda,* the party's flagship newspaper, ran not a word.

Smith, who had been in Moscow for the *New York Times,* also wrote:

A scientist friend told me of a young woman who flew from Karaganda to Moscow to take entrance examinations for Moscow State University. She was scheduled to spend a week in Moscow, he said. Her parents waited 10 days and became concerned at hearing nothing from her or from friends in Moscow. After two weeks, the father flew to Moscow to try to find her. When he got to the university, he was told that his daughter had never appeared for the exams and people knew nothing about her. He called on family friends with whom she had thought of staying but they had not seen her. He went to the police. At one precinct station, an officer suggested trying the airport police detachment. There, as everywhere, he appealed for help in locating his daughter. Only then was he informed confidentially— and instructed to keep the information confidential—that her plane from Karaganda to Moscow had crashed and she had been killed with the other passengers. He was stunned: it was the first he or his friends had heard of the plane crash.

In contrast, many of the Washington correspondents are trying to dredge up the roots of the real government in order to present an image that is much closer to the reality. As the government becomes more complex, the correspondents are working with more suspicion and greater certainty. Some, however, are showing up at the congressman's door with, "Have you got any news today?" With the increasingly sophisticated reporters, we can rely with more assurance on Another Government, the news media. Sometimes.

---

to the student : a commentary

William Rivers's concept of Another Government—that particular image of our government we all carry in our minds, as opposed to the reality—is a refined slice of a problem articulated at least as far back as Plato. The Greek philosopher presented a case: If people were raised in a cave, chained so that they faced the back wall, and all that they saw of the real world were the shadows on that wall, would not that be their "reality"? And wouldn't they, if freed, reject the real world as mere shadow?

The basic theme of Rivers's article is the discrepancy between image and reality. Yet his discrepancy is part of a natural and normal human phenomenon. The fact that we are all victims, in some sense, of the standard filtering caused by selective exposure and selective perception, separates each of us some distance from "reality." That the media supply most of our information does not mean that they are entirely responsible for shaping our opinions. We have developed mental processes that enable us to reject information that does not square with our individual views of the world. It has been demonstrated often, for example, that one's senses are likely to be exposed primarily to information that will reinforce, rather than oppose, prior opinions. This reaction is what is called *selective exposure.*

We also tend to register what we want to register—*selective perception* —a process that psychologists have demonstrated so often that many are now no more interested in proving its existence than a mathematician is interested in proving that two-plus-two equals four. Many people go to extravagant lengths to perceive "facts" that will support their prejudices. For example, it has been shown that some people who are strongly anti-Semitic can look at an editorial cartoon that plainly ridicules religious bias and see it in reverse—as a glorification of Anglo-Saxon lineage.

Through *selective retention,* many of us remember bits of information that enhance our own views and conveniently forget opposing facts. One experiment, for instance, had a group of college students list both pleasant and unpleasant experiences encountered during the Christmas break. When they were asked to recreate the list weeks later the number of unpleasant experiences decreased markedly. Similarly, another professor has for years conducted classroom experiments in which his students read highly laudatory articles about whatever president is in office at the time. Most of the students who favor the incumbent president not only learn the laudatory material sooner than do the others, they also remember it longer.

Mass communication researchers use the term *gatekeeper* to identify those who sit astride the channels of communication, exercising their power to stop, alter, or simply let pass the information sent through the channels. Each of the individuals described by Rivers in his step-by-step process— government officials, government press secretary, reporter, editor—are gatekeepers. And so, finally, are we all. We individually decide to ignore or attend, agree or disagree, accept or reject, the wide range of information provided us about our government.

The crucial point in Rivers's article is that we live in a synthetic environment. What most of us know about the world is based mainly on secondhand information. We don't *know* the president, or our senators, or probably even the mayor. We haven't been at the center of each world crisis, nor in the policy-making councils of government. What we do know about events around us, local or international, is almost always based on information provided us by the news media.

Yet most of us seldom acknowledge that fact. We act as though our view of the world were based on direct, firsthand experience; as if our information were naturally accurate and trustworthy. We rarely, if ever, consider the methods by which information is *processed,* and therefore often altered. The very structure of the mass media, with their machines, technicians, gatekeepers, and constraints of time and space, affects the substance of what is transmitted. But we respond to that end product as if it were a pristine re-creation of reality, mainly because we know so little about the process in between.

The extent of our ignorance about the media is highlighted by a story told by the manager of a television station. A viewer kept calling him to complain about some of the programs being broadcast. After many polite explanations, the frustrated station manager finally solved the problem. "Look," he told the viewer, "if you call here once more I'm going to unplug your set from this end." The viewer never called again.

The news media have often called themselves the "mirror on the world." Rivers has likened the process to a double mirror, and selectively narrow at that. Both concepts may be too simple. If you will briefly allow an elaborate metaphor, the complexity of the news media may be better understood if it is thought of, not as a mirror, but a prism. Let's say that this prism, twisting in the wind of events, picks up light (information) from all directions and refracts it, bends it, before sending it out again. The light may be sent out in different directions, to the many audiences for information, or back toward the original source (where you can have the case of the politician responding to the media image of himself). Each facet of the media—television, newspapers, magazines—has its own particular angle on events. Refracting according to structural limitations (time, space, film, deadlines), each medium sends out its uniquely altered message.

So what you hear on the five-minute radio news will not, of course, be the same as what you see on television. Neither is it precisely the same version you'll get in the newspaper, and all will differ from the account offered by magazines.

It is important—very important—that we recognize that the information we receive about government is not quite the same as the government itself. While we are not often deliberately deceived, as in Rivers's example of Russian "no news," we must be wary of our tendency to respond to the image rather than reality. To put it simply: when we vote are we electing people according to what we really know—or are our ballots cast according to brief bits of film on the 6 o'clock news? When we decide to support—or reject—our government's foreign policy, is the decision made on the basis of solid information, or an article in a weekly news magazine?

The first step in reducing the discrepancy between the image and the reality, between the real government and another government, is to acknowledge that there is a difference. The next time you digest political information, you might try to chew slowly.

LLS

Gary Atkins

In Search of New Objectivity

"The tradition of objectivity is one of the principal glories of American journalism."—Alan Barth, *Washington Post,* 1950

"We can do a good job . . . as long as we keep the flag of objectivity flying high. That will give a more honest and more accurate view of this imperfect world than trusting a latter day Trotsky, or any other partisan on any side, to tell us what's what."—Herbert Brucker, *Saturday Review,* 1969

"The trouble with reporting today, and the trouble with writing . . . is this philosophy of objectivity. Walter Cronkite was quoted as saying 'The supreme pursuit is objectivity.' Well, this is patent bullshit."—Jann Wenner, *Rolling Stone,* 1971

Seldom has the concept of objectivity been at peace in its journalistic home. Since it became the dominant ideology of newspaper reporting a century ago, the debate about what the word means, and whether it should be an ideal or not, has been almost continuous.

Yet, for all the words written, those persons most concerned with the debate—the journalists themselves—have rarely tried to learn about their own argument, and about the concept of objectivity itself, by studying similar quarrels in other fields. Rather, they have chosen to argue about objectivity as if both they and it exist in a vacuum. They quote each other and rely solely on their own experiences in their arguments about old journalism versus new, objectivity versus subjectivity, straight reporting versus interpretation, and they do not raise questions about the origin of their concept of objectivity.

Yet, in that origin, and in the debates in other fields, is a key to understanding what the journalistic disagreement is about and a key to moving journalistic theory beyond the circular, often superficial, quarreling of the past.

In returning to the origins, journalism textbooks and histories are little help. Although they point out that objectivity has not always been the

Reprinted by permission of Gary Atkins.

journalistic ideal it became in the twentieth century—the press was born and nurtured in partisanship—they usually give only passing treatment to the rise of the ideal. Their explanation is an economic one: that the wire services, which became the primary exponents of objective reporting, had to serve newspapers with different political leanings and so, to survive, had to develop a colorless, inoffensive style of reporting that would replace the more personal reports of highly partisan correspondents. At the same time, newspapers were being transformed from their status as personal extensions of editors or publishers into more faceless corporations.

The economic explanation is not wrong in itself, but it is hardly adequate to explain why an economic necessity and an uncontroversial method of writing should come to be considered an ideal and the "highest moral concept ever developed in America and given to the world."

In the early 1900s, the form an "ideal" journalism should take was a topic well discussed in magazines and books. One article, written by Erman Ridgeway in 1910, is worth noting since its description of the desired style of journalism and objectivity was close to that which was to become the common ideal. "I am persuaded," Ridgeway wrote, "that the ideal newspaper is an emotionless machine; that the function of this machine is solely to give the news; that it attains its maximum usefulness when every wheel in the gigantic machine runs smoothly, grinding out its daily grist of facts without emotion, dispassionate, unswerving, relentless."

Even editorials were to be subjected to this machine-like ideal: they were not to propound personal opinions, but were to "line-up today's effects with yesterday's causes."

This idea of dispassionate detachment became the foundation of objective journalism, and what it implied in news coverage was spelled out in 1924 in a text written for journalism students by Casper Yost. "News," he wrote, "deals fundamentally with events, with things that have happened or are happening, that are susceptible to observation and that may be verified, as any other concrete fact, by the evidence of the senses."

The journalist, then, was to be a detached spectator, collecting and recording facts that were concrete and sensually verifiable. Passion and prejudice were to be left behind. One's own humanism was to be kept in control as much as possible.

No one necessarily thought total objectivity possible, but it was an ideal —something to be sought and a standard to be used in measuring near approaches. Progress was to be found in a line from opinion to fact, and the confidence that progress would continue was high. . . .

But from where did the journalists' definition of objectivity come? And why did it become an ideal instead of a description of a method? And why did the ideal eventually assert a kind of intellectual hegemony over the field of newspaper journalism?

For an indication, it is useful to look at the late nineteenth century climate of opinion in which the change began to occur. The issue of objectiveness was hardly unique to journalism at that point. And it was hardly new in other fields. Theories of knowledge and logical method had long grappled with the question of how man knows his surroundings and how he distinguishes between an "objective" and a "subjective" reality. Different theories had been popular at different times.

In the nineteenth century, the dominant influence in the intellectual world was that of natural science. Impressed with scientific advances, many believed that the way to truth and knowledge was to be found in an infusion of the scientific method into those realms of human affairs where only conflicting "opinions" and not facts—where only philosophy and not science—had long prevailed.

Seeking the prestige of science, those who dealt with human affairs, such as historians, began to talk more and more of increasing their "scientific objectivity" and eliminating the effects of personal bias from their work. Objectivity was thus lauded in academics even before it became popular in journalism. It cannot be assumed that one caused the other, but certainly neither should it be assumed that journalists were totally immune from the climate of opinion of the day. And the opinion was that everyone should be more "scientific" and more "objective." How those words were defined depended on the type of ideology one accepted. Since journalists like to consider themselves "historians in a hurry," and the problems the two fields have had with the concept of objectivity appear similar, it is appropriate to look at what happened in American historiography at the time.

Two major strands of thought were in the fore in Europe: one, an idealism that traced its way through the works of Johann von Herder and Leopold von Ranke; the other, a positivistic strain that took its cue from the French philosopher Auguste Comte and his various misinterpreters. The differences between the two schools were critical when it came to defining objectivity.

In the concept developed by Herder and Ranke, it was vital that the historian first evaluate very critically his sources of information and then immerse himself in what physical evidence he had—documents, letters, artifacts—in an attempt to move intuitively beyond simple description of the evidence to an understanding of the dynamics of history, the forms moving within. Personal biases were to be suppressed, but the historian's own humanness was not to be effaced. Rather, he was to use his own human abilities to try to understand why events had occurred as they had. As the poet Goethe said in praising Herder, what was important was to move beyond the mere husks and shells of historical events and penetrate to their very core.

In what came to be called positivism, the aim and the approach were different. Comte's goal had been to develop a "social physics" that would describe natural and unvarying laws governing human development, much as Newtonian physics was believed to have established the laws of the physical world. He believed that true knowledge, "positive knowledge," had to be based on the scientific techniques of experimentation and observation, and he would have nothing of an "internal" knowledge, gained by introspection. His followers eventually converted positivism into an almost naturalistic study of nothing but the concrete facts and their immediate causes. Taking a cue from natural scientists who saw the universe as a clock, they thought of fields like the study of history as a problem of mechanics and the social scientist as a detached spectator, watching the laws unfold, just as natural scientists supposedly did. One could work from immutable laws to necessary effects, or—as in Ridgeway's concept of editorials—from effects to laws.

In the United States, historians adopted a curious mixture of both strands; they swore allegiance to Ranke and tried to use his method of critical analysis of sources, but they insisted on eliminating all opinion and intuition and concentrating solely on the facts. Their objectivity was positivistic, arrived at, not through critical analysis and human intuition, but through supposed detachment. A historian was to be like a camera, as one of them said in 1890, recording everything, dispassionately, without emotion and without value judgments, like a photographic plate.

The result was not a purging of opinion or prejudice, of course. Rather, the uncritical acceptance of an objectivity rooted primarily in positivism meant the acceptance of certain theoretical assumptions: for example, that the universe was as Newtonian physics had described it—a mechanical clock that one could stand aside and observe—and that in the study of history, progress meant moving from opinion to fact, and progress would continue. Even if complete objectivity were not possible now, it would be in the future, and history would be told with ever-increasing scientific precision. Once complete description could be obtained, perhaps even prediction would be possible. Thus, objectivity became not just a method, but a standard and an ideal. And the tenets of positivism and progressivism became the foundation for the concept.

Much the same thing apparently happened in American journalism. Today, however, American historiography has had to rid itself of such simple ideas and simple ideals. The issue of a historian's objectivity has been through a debate that makes the journalistic argument look mild, and, for many historians at least, positivistic objectivity has proven superficial and has, appropriately, collapsed.

It had to. Even while the so-called scientific historians were trying to imitate what they took to be the methods of natural science, physics itself was renouncing some of its basic Newtonian assumptions. The machine-like universe, the great clock that could be dispassionately dismantled and accurately described, was falling apart.

One discovery followed another: Maxwell found that electricity could not be understood within Newtonian premises, and when he tried, he ended with conclusions that refuted those premises. Einstein published his theory of relativity, and suddenly all those physical laws and forces that had been thought to inhere in a reality "outside" man were really mathematical formulas—creations of the mind that resembled natural forms, perhaps, but were not necessarily exact replicas. Views of physical determinism were shattered by the quantum revolution when Neils Bohr demonstrated in 1913 that energy was not emitted in orderly, continuous streams, but in discontinuous packets. German physicist Werner Heisenberg formulated his uncertainty principle, saying that every attempt to describe nature contained some irremovable uncertainty because the observer and the observed inevitably interacted. Bohr developed the complementarity principle, stating that matter could be studied in more than one way, as either a wave or a particle, for it was multidimensional.

The philosophical and scientific foundations of positivistic objectivity were collapsing. If something as basic and "simple" as a particle could be approached in different ways, and knowledge could be gained about it through those different methods, clearly simple data collection or study of causes and effects was not enough to understand man or his culture or his history. Reasons and purposes had to be studied, certainly, as well as causes and effects. The internal world had to be considered.

Even while its philosophical foundations were crumbling, the positivistic concept of objectivity was also encountering criticism from those in journalism and history who found it obviously inadequate when they tried to put it to use. A positivistic stance was not flexible or realistic enough to allow adequate explanation of events: journalists and historians did not just collect facts—they selected facts; they did not just present data—or if they did it made little sense—they interpreted the data.

In historiography, the result was an acrimonious debate about theory. Scientific historians still subscribed to the old ideal; a school of New Historians demanded that laws of history be sought and facts be studied for their present-day relevance; relativistic historians urged that facts be recognized as symbols, open to interpretations that depended on present concerns and experiences; others called on historians to recognize their own biases and values, and through that recognition of subjectivity become more objective.

The concept of writing an objective account of history began to seem a bad joke. Rather than observing in a detached manner, the historian, it seemed, subordinated the past to the present in selecting and interpreting facts. He uncritically accepted positivistic and progressivistic presuppositions even as he was proclaiming his scientific objectivity. He based his interpretations and his selection of important historical facts on, as the historian Charles Beard wrote, an "act of faith" concerning the shape of the future. History, presumably, was supposed to tell some kind of truth about the past, but the only truth seemed to be one that depended on the historian's own biases. The attempt to imbue the study of history with scientific prestige had ended in theoretical confusion.

Only at that point could American historiography begin to break its attachment to positivistic theory. The objectivity versus subjectivity debate had to be seen in a new way. Not all philosophies equated the term *subjectivity* with "opinion" and "bias." Not all presented the pursuit of science as a battle to efface the scientist's own humanness. And not all tried to mold the study of human affairs into containers made for the study of physical affairs.

Subjectivity could be a method of understanding that allowed an empathetic identification between the observed and the observer. Subjective, human abilities could be an aid to understanding, not an obstacle.

Historians began to realize that while they were indeed subject to present concerns, they also could transcend the present because they had at their disposal an ever-increasing amount of data about the past, and by using their human abilities, they could seek a better understanding about what that data meant to the people who had been affected by it. What was important was the historian's ability to stand back from the rush of things and examine them from a position that, while not absolutely detached, was also not submerged in the rush. Historians, like physicists, began to rid themselves of the assumptions underlying positivistic objectivity: that the world could be dispassionately observed; that certain truth and certain knowledge could be had through complete description.

As historian John Higham has written, "Historians no longer considered their own subjectivity as exclusively a problem or barrier to struggle against. It was that, of course. The task of historiography would always require the utmost divestment of bias and the penetration of a realm beyond the immediate self and its immediate society. But historians now knew that this achievement is not simply an act of self-effacement, not an effort to register passively the harmonies of an evolutionary pattern. It calls for a creative outreach of imagination and draws upon all the resources of the historian's human condition."

Journalists, particularly those in newspaper journalism, have not progressed as far in their theoretical debate as historians. In practice, their stories reveal varying degrees of empathy and attempts to penetrate the husks and shells; in theoretical development, they are still at the stage of confusion.

In the 1930s and 1940s, the first major attempt to adjust the ideal of positivistic objectivity to the realities of a complex world was made. An "interpretative revolt" among leading reporters caused newspapers to accept the idea of a midpoint between the objective (read *factual*) news story and the subjective (read *opinionated*) editorial; the *news analysis* was developed to explain the significance of certain facts. The reform took place within the confines of the ideal of objectivity, however. The line between interpretation and editorial comment was, and is, measured in terms of the reporter's ability to eliminate his own personal prejudices from the analysis.

A second, more sweeping, revolt occurred in the 1960s. The ideal of positivistic objectivity that had guided American journalism was rejected outright, and other types of journalism began to proliferate: advocacy journalism, New Journalism, personal journalism, alternative journalism. Each proclaimed its search for truth, as did objective reporting. But where both the earlier objective and interpretative styles had aimed more or less at the same type of truth—a truth about events, issues, and people that was primarily an external truth—the new forms often aimed at different styles entirely: as one of the practitioners of New Journalism, Gay Talese, put it, a "larger truth" going beyond "mere compilation of verifiable facts." Often, as in Talese's writings, it was an "inner" sort of truth that did not seek conclusions or causes and effects, but rather an understanding or portrayal of the inner dynamics of an event or a person's life.

In a journalistic application of the complementarity theory, writers were realizing that different approaches to the same subject would produce different types of truths about that subject. As in historiography, the practical result has been an acrimonious debate about theory, and different schools of journalism have sprung up. A new theoretical guideline and ideal, such as that once provided by "objectivity," have yet to be formulated. Part of the problem is that American journalists still see the debate in black and white terms—objectivity means fact, subjectivity means the demon opinion. One is the way to truth; the other, the way to partisanship. Thus, a challenge to objectivity is automatically interpreted as a challenge to the search for truth, when in fact it may only be a challenge to the positivistic conception of objectivity.

The problem is one of narrowness, rooted partly in the failure to recognize what philosopher Charles Taylor has called "intersubjective meanings." Those are the meanings that different cultures give to different words and, in the process, create the bounds of their own definition of reality. Two different societies may take different views of "negotiations" or the meaning of "dancing" (some societies may have only one word for dancing and working, in which case the two activities are merged) or the meaning of "objectivity."

But the problem for journalists is more than just recognizing that there may be different definitions of objectivity that are more philosophically valid than positivistic objectivity. It is also recognizing that, as Taylor points out, within their heritage, the validity of any introspective study of inner meanings is rejected, except as they are manifested in external behavior or action. The approach to the subject and the perspective on meaning is an outer one. If one, for example, writes about the Mafia, he collects information on its background, gathers data from crime reports, interviews police and Mafia officials, and then writes a story about the current status of the group. He does not, if he considers himself a detached observer, put together a book like Talese's *Honor Thy Father,* for the kind of truth and information about the Mafia conveyed by that approach is beyond his frame of reference. It is an inner picture. (Thus, all the trouble that "Old Journalists" have had in attaching labels to "New Journalists" —they don't know whether to call them fictional nonfictionalists or nonfictional novelists.)

All interpretation of behavior in the positivistic approach is not from the participant's standpoint, but from the observer's. The participant is assumed to be biased; the observer, detached and more factual. The result is always an unrecognized and uncriticized subjectivity, which is hidden under the guise of objectivity. Thus, in American journalism, "objectivity" has implied acceptance of a white, middle-class definition of American life, acceptance of American political mythology, of American economic and social organization, and of American progressivism. Objectivity has not meant realizing that a black community might differ—greatly or ever so subtly—in the meanings it attached to certain words; it has not meant that there might be differing interpretations of the "American way" or of "success."

Clearly, whenever the problem of *meaning* arises—the meaning of an event, an action, or even a word—the so-called objective journalist is in trouble if his objectivity is a positivistic one. Even if he manages to exclude his own obvious biases, he has not avoided seeing the event through the eyes of his own community and culture.

In practice, many journalists realize this, whether or not they attempt to overcome it. No man on earth is a detached observer from Mars, and everyone is raised within a culture. The problem in American journalism is that the guiding theory has been utterly unrealistic for decades. Alienated from their humanity, journalists, like others, constructed a new, scientistic "reality." They built a false ideal simply as a way to escape from the truth of reality and from the difficulty of understanding different meanings, not as a means to measure practical performance.

Positivistic objectivity is unsound. A new theoretical guideline needs to be found, one that will not abstract words like *objectivity* and *subjectivity* from their cultural heritage and obscure intersubjective meanings by casting issues in black-white divisions when each term can have multiple meanings.

Such a new guideline will recognize that journalism deals in symbols as well as simple or concrete facts and that symbols, by their nature, require interpretation. Penetrating beyond the surface of events and gaining an inner perspective also requires more than just collection of externally verifiable sensory data.

Perhaps journalism will be thought of more as a hermeneutical field, with journalists trained to apply the interpretative methods most likely to give the most understanding about a subject. Like a physicist who might study matter first as a wave, then a particle, so the journalist would move from vantage point to vantage point, from outside to inside, from empathy to detachment, realizing all the while that the important thing is the search for more understanding and recognizing that the method he uses to approach reality will determine the type of truth he obtains. Each angle will provide a type of information, and readers will better understand the phenomenon for having seen it from different perspectives.

The journalist, after more than seven decades, will be accepting his own anthropomorphism as an aid to understanding, yet he will be creating a new style of objectivity that recognizes the necessity of understanding meaning, not through one's own subjective and intersubjective biases, but through the eyes and feelings of other persons. The journalist will be recognizing that true objectivity does not come by self-effacement, but by self-transcendence, and that it is not the objectivity of the detached observer he seeks, but the objectivity of the ever-questioning, ever-empathetic reporter.

---

to the student : a commentary

Gary Atkins, a young reporter for the *Riverside* (California) *Press and Enterprise,* has thought much more deeply about the problem of objectivity than has almost any other journalist.

One question comes to mind, though. How many journalists can comprehend *any* meaning of events? Those who have trouble writing objectively probably should not attempt Atkins's prescription. As Atkins has learned, there are various kinds of expertness, many of them impossible for all but a few journalists.

Here I'll sketch the various methods of reporting so that you can understand the argument. The objective story, which is also known as the *straight-news story,* is simple. For example:

CONCORD, N.H. (AP)—New Hampshire voters choose today between Ronald Reagan and President Ford on the Republican side and pick from a crowded field of Democrats in the nation's first presidential primary.

Voter turnout at midday was running light to moderate. Drivers for car shuttles in Nashua said they made few trips in the early morning but requests picked up considerably at midmorning.

By tradition, residents of the tiny mountain resort of Dixville Notch cast the first ballots seconds after midnight and gave the nod to President Ford and former Gov. Jimmy Carter.

Ford got 11 votes to Reagan's four. Among the Democrats, Carter got six and Indiana Sen. Birch Bayh, Arizona Rep. Morris K. Udall and write-in candidate Sen. Henry M. Jackson of Washington one each.

Cloudy skies covered most of the state although southwestern precincts near the Vermont border were reporting sunshine and warming temperatures.

As Atkins would agree, there's plenty of room for this kind of reporting of simple facts. Journalists who are writing hurriedly must have this form preserved so that they can report it rapidly. Morever, how many reporters can reach toward Atkins's ideal of penetrating the husks and shells of events, no matter how much time they have?

Interpretation of a special kind, which emerged in the 1930s and the 1940s, is more reachable than is Atkins's prescription. This is known as *interpretive reporting,* which is illustrated by this story:

MANCHESTER, N.H., Jan. 29—Door-to-door political organization in New Hampshire is a difficult, discouraging and freezing task. And in the opinion of most of those involved, it may no longer be as important as it once was.

But more of it is being done this year than ever before by the staffs of Democratic Presidential aspirants entered in the state's Feb. 24 primary election.

Moreover, drawing heavily on lessons learned and immutable principles revealed in past political battles, the candidates' political organizations seem to be doing the job with more finesse and precision than before. No obscure young genius is likely to come into New Hampshire this year and startle the experts with an organization blitz, because most candidates have their own obscure young geniuses to compete.

The major Democratic grassroots organizational efforts in New Hampshire this year are being conducted by the staffs of Representative Morris K. Udall of Arizona; Fred R. Harris, the former Oklahoma Senator; former Gov. Jimmy Carter of Georgia and Senator Birch Bayh of Indiana; other candidates declared and undeclared, will probably not have the manpower for full-scale organizational efforts. . . .

It's obvious that this writer is more sophisticated than most journalists. Instead of merely reporting an event rapidly, as did the writer of the first example, this writer is looking at the entire event, choosing from among those things his sources have given him. But most important, he understands voting and electioneering in New Hampshire and is able to analyze the processes he's describing. However, he scrupulously avoids venting his own opinion. This is a first-class story of its kind.

So far, no one is asking more than many journalists can provide—when they have the time to interpret. But what of Atkins's ideal? He is asking that the journalists probe deeply, moving from "vantage point to vantage point . . . realizing all the while that . . . each [different] angle will provide a type of information, and readers will better understand the phenomenon for having seen it from different perspectives."

How wonderful! But who can do it? We have seen many examples, most of them from the tight coterie of the new journalists. Here is a short excerpt from "Sinatra Has a Cold" by Gay Talese:

Sinatra had been working in a film that he now disliked, could not wait to finish; he was tired of all the publicity attached to his dating the twenty-year-old Mia Farrow, who was not in sight tonight; he was angry that a CBS television documentary of his life, to be shown in two weeks, was reportedly prying into his privacy, even speculating on his possible friendship with Mafia leaders; he was worried about his starring role in an hour-long NBC show entitled *Sinatra—A Man And His Music,* which would require that he sing eighteen songs with a voice that at this particular moment, just a few nights before the taping was to begin, was weak and sore and uncertain. Sinatra was ill. He was the victim of an ailment so common that most people would consider it trival. But when it gets to Sinatra it can plunge him into a state of anguish, deep depression, panic, even rage. Frank Sinatra had a cold.

The enjoyment of experiencing Sinatra's cold, vicariously, leads you to the final paragraph. But only one who has the time to look into a subject, and one who has talent, can do it. But it is open to many others, and worth pursuing.

WLR

study questions

1. Since you, too, are part of the American masses of whom Rosten writes—"mentally lazy with deplorable taste"—do you accept his notion that what you like is because you are not among those who "have reasonably good taste and care deeply about ideas"? Is the process by which one acquires a certain kind of taste made clear by Rosten? Is taste genetically coded and static? Or is it something one acquires, and continually develops, after birth?

2. Could you have grown to prefer "more news, better plays, more serious debate, deeper involvement in ideas" if, from childhood, mass media had made such articles and programs more frequent and accessible? Do you accept Rosten's judgment that you—and millions of others—would turn to "sports, parlor games, gambling," if prime-time television programs became more diverse, with greater emphasis on, for example, documentaries? If more documentaries were offered, would a large audience develop a taste for documentaries? What would prevent a network—say, CBS—from experimenting with its weekly prime-time programming in an effort to find out if documentaries could eventually pull a large audience? What would NBC and ABC be doing in the meantime?

3. The Flat Earth Society—a group in England dedicated to the destruction of the popular notion that the world is round—has had some trouble sustaining the faith of their members (to say nothing of recruiting new ones) ever since space shots provided us with photos of the earth's curvature. Their rebuttal to the widely disseminated photos and television coverage of the Apollo program is simple and direct: They insist the photos in the papers and the live action on television are fakes, an elaborate scheme designed to perpetrate the round-earth myth.

If you were to seek to prove to a Flat Earther the error of his ways, how would you do it?

4. You see an old man stumble as he stoops to pick up a discarded cigarette butt from the sidewalk. He staggers, falls. As you approach, he wipes his forehead with the back of a varicose veined hand. He sticks the half-smoked cigarette in his mouth, smiles, and asks you for a light. You give him some matches and, still sitting, he lights up. He laughs and chats with you a moment, but you notice what appear to be tears in his eyes. After refusing your offer to help him up, he struggles to his feet and shuffles off, head down, now and then stopping to kick at other cigarette butts.

In describing the encounter to a friend, are you justified in interpreting what you saw and reporting on the old man's state of mind—that is, happy, sad, trusting? If so, what limits would you set on the extent of your interpretations?

tele- 2
vision
& cable

The articles in the following section deal with a diverse range of issues in television. The problems are as numerous as the medium is ubiquitous. There are more television sets in the United States than there are bathtubs; ninety-seven percent of the homes in this country have one or more sets. The average American adult watches slightly more than four hours per day; for children the figure is higher. It has been estimated that by the time today's children reach the age of sixteen, they have spent more time in front of a television than in school.

Some of the articles on television, along with two that deal with what may be future forms of the medium, are grouped under the heading "Social Force." The common thread of these independent discussions is that they focus on—or simply assume—the power of television to influence society. It is an assumption that can be made about any medium, of course, but here the range of issues reflects the pervasiveness of television itself.

The second category, "Constraints," presents some of the current restrictions, or attempts at restrictions, on the medium. It is by no means complete, but it identifies those issues that are central to the structure and function of the industry.

television & cable

social force

Courtesy of the Chicago Tribune–New York News Syndicate.

"Gee, when Archie Bunker makes an ethnic slur, everybody laughs."

40

Michael Novak

Television Shapes the Soul

For twenty-five years we have been immersed in a medium never before experienced on this earth. We can be forgiven if we do not yet understand all the ways in which this medium has altered us, particularly our inner selves, the perceiving, mythic, symbolic—and the judging, critical—parts of ourselves.

Media, like instruments, work "from the outside in." If you practice the craft of writing sedulously, you begin to think and perceive differently. If you run for twenty minutes a day, your psyche is subtly transformed. If you work in an executive office, you begin to think like an executive. And if you watch six hours of television, on the average, every day . . . ?[1]

Innocent of psychological testing and sociological survey, I would like to present a humanist's analysis of what television seems to be doing to me, to my students, to my children, and, in general, to those I see around me (including those I see on television, in movies, in magazines, etc.). My method is beloved of philosophers, theologians, cultural critics: try to *perceive,* make *distinctions, coax into the light* elusive movements of consciousness. It goes without saying that others will have to verify the following observations; they are necessarily in the hypothetical mode, even if some of the hypotheses have a cogency that almost bites.

Two clusters of points may be made. The first, rather metaphysical, concerns the way television affects our way of perceiving and approaching reality. The second cluster concerns the way television inflicts a class bias on the world of our perceptions—the bias of a relatively small and special social class.

1. Television and reality

Television is a molder of the soul's geography. It builds up incrementally a psychic structure of expectations. It does so in much the same way that school lessons slowly, over the years, tutor the unformed mind and teach it "how to think." Television *might* tutor the mind, soul, and heart in other

Reprinted by permission of Michael Novak and Douglass Cater, The Aspen Institute.
[1]There is no discernible variation between the hours spent watching television by the college-educated, or by professors and journalists, and the public as a whole.

ways than the ways it does at present. But, to be concrete, we ought to keep in view the average night of programming on the major networks over the last decade or so—not so much the news or documentaries, not so much the discussions on public television or on Sundays, not so much the talk shows late at night, but rather the variety shows, comedies, and adventure shows that are the staples of prime-time viewing. From time to time we may allow our remarks to wander farther afield. But it is important to concentrate on the universe of prime-time major network programming; that is where the primary impact of television falls.

It is possible to isolate five or six ways in which television seems to affect those who watch it. Television series represent genres of artistic performance. They structure a viewer's way of perceiving, of making connections, and of following a story line. Try, for example, to bring to consciousness the difference between the experience of watching television and the experience of learning through reading, argument, the advice of elders, lectures in school, or other forms of structuring perception. The conventions of the various sorts of television series re-create different sorts of "worlds." These "worlds" raise questions—and, to some extent, illuminate certain features of experience that we notice in ourselves and around us as we watch.

(1) Suppose that you were a writer for a television show—an action-adventure, a situation comedy, even a variety show. You would want to be very careful to avoid "dead" spots, "wooden" lines, "excess" verbiage. Every line has a function, even a double or triple function. Characters move on camera briskly, every line counts, the scene shifts rapidly. In comedy, every other line should be a laugh-getter. Brevity is the soul of hits.

Television is a teacher of expectations; it speeds up the rhythm of attention. Any act in competition with television must approach the same pace; otherwise it will seem "slow." Even at an intellectual conference or seminar we now demand a swift rhythm of progressive movement; a leisurely, circular pace of rumination is perceived as less than a "good show."

(2) But not only the pace is fast. Change of scene and change of perspective are also fast. In a recent episode of *Kojak,* action in three or four parts of the city was kept moving along in alternating sequences of a minute or less. A "principle of association" was followed; some image in the last frames of one scene suggested a link to the first frames of the new scene. But one scene cut away from another very quickly.

The progression of a television show depends upon multiple logics—two or three different threads are followed simultaneously. The viewer must figure out the connections between people, between chains of action, and between scenes. Many clues are *shown,* not *said.* The viewer must detect them.

The logic of such shows is not sequential in a single chain. One subject is raised, then cut, and another subject is picked up, then cut. Verbal links —"Meanwhile, on the other side of the city . . ."—are not supplied.

In teaching and in writing I notice that for students one may swiftly change the subject, shift the scene, drop a line of argument in order to pick it up later—and not lose the logic of development. Students understand such a performance readily. They have been prepared for it. The systems of teaching which I learned in my student days—careful and exact exegesis proceeding serially from point to point, the careful definition and elucidation of terms in an argument and the careful scrutiny of chains of inference, and the like—now meet a new form of resistance. There has always been resistance to mental discipline; one has only to read the notebooks of students from medieval universities to recognize this well-established tradition of resistance. But today the minds and affections of the brighter students are teeming with images, vicarious experiences, and indeed of actual travel and accomplishments. Their minds race ahead and around the flanks of lines of argument. "Dialectics" rather than "logic" or "exegesis" is the habit of mind they are most ready for. I say this neither in praise nor in blame; pedagogy must deal with this new datum, if it is new. What are its limits and its possibilities? What correctives are needed among students—and among teachers?

(3) The periodization of attention is also influenced by the format of television. For reasons of synchronized programming the ordinary television show is neatly divided into segments of approximately equal length, and each of these segments normally has its own dramatic rhythm so as to build to dramatic climax or sub-climax, with the appropriate degree of suspense or resolution. Just as over a period of time a professor develops an instinct for how much can be accomplished in a fifty-minute lecture, or a minister of religion develops a temporal pattern for his sermons, so also the timing of television shows tutors their audience to expect a certain rhythm of development. The competitive pressures of television, moreover, encourage producers to "pack" as much action, intensity, or (to speak generally) entertainment into each segment as possible. Hence, for example, the short, snappy gags of *Laugh-In* and the rapid-fire developments of police shows or westerns.

Character is as important to successful shows as action; audiences need to "identify" with the heroes of the show, whether dramatic or comic. Thus in some ways the leisure necessary to develop character may provide a counter-tendency to the need for melodramatic rapidity. Still, "fast-paced" and "laugh-packed" and other such descriptions express the sensibility that television both serves and reinforces.

(4) Television tutors the sensibilities of its audience in another way: it can handle only a limited range of human emotions, perplexities, motivations, and situations. The structure of competitive television seems to

require this limitation; it springs from a practiced estimation of the capacity of the audience. Critics sometimes argue that American novelists have a long tradition of inadequacy with respect to the creation of strong, complicated women and, correspondingly, much too simple and superficial a grasp of the depths and complexities of human love. It is, it is said, the more direct "masculine" emotions, as well as the relations of comradeship between men, that American artists celebrate best. If such critical judgments may be true of our greatest artists working in their chosen media, then, a fortiori, it is not putting down television to note that the range of human relations treated by artists on television is less than complete. The constraints under which television artists work are acute: the time available to them, the segmentation of this time, and the competitive pressures they face for intense dramatic activity. To develop a fully complicated set of motivations, internal conflicts, and inner contradictions requires time and sensitivity to nuance. The present structure of television makes these requirements very difficult to meet.

This point acquires fuller significance if we note the extent to which Americans depend upon television for their public sense of how other human beings behave in diverse situations. The extent of this dependence should be investigated. In particular, we ought to examine the effects of the growing segregation of Americans by age. It does not happen frequently nowadays that children grow up in a household shared by three generations, in a neighborhood where activities involve members of all generations, or in a social framework where generation-mixing activities are fairly common. I have many times been told by students (from suburban environments, in particular) that they have hardly ever, or never, had a serious conversation with adults. The social world of their parents did not include children. They spent little time with relatives, and that time was largely formal and distant. The high schools were large, "consolidated," and relatively impersonal. Their significant human exchanges were mostly with their peers. Their images of what adults do and how adults think and act were mainly supplied by various media, notably television and the cinema. The issue such comments raise is significant. Where *could* most Americans go to find dramatic models of adult behavior? In the eyes of young people does the public weight of what is seen on television count for more than what they see in their private world as a model for "how things are done"? Indeed, do adults themselves gain a sense of what counts as acceptable adult behavior from the public media?

If it turns out to be true that television (along with other media like magazines and the cinema) now constitutes a major source of guidance for behavior, to be placed in balance with what one learns from one's parents, from the churches, from one's local communities, and the like, then the range of dramatic materials on television has very serious consequences for the American psyche. While human behavior is to a remarkable extent diverse and variable, it tends to be "formed" and given shape by the attraction or the power of available imaginative materials: stories, models, symbols, images-in-action. The storehouse of imaginative materials available to each person provides a sort of repertoire. The impact of new models can be a powerful one, leading to "conversions," "liberations," or "new directions." The reservoir of acquired models exerts a strong influence both upon perception and upon response to unfamiliar models. If family and community ties weaken and if psychic development becomes somewhat more nuclearized or even atomized, the influence of television and other distant sources may well become increasingly powerful, moving, as it were, into something like a vacuum. Between the individual and the national source of image-making there will be little or no local resistance. The middle ground of the psyche, until recently thick and rich and resistant, will have become attenuated.

The point is not that television has reached the limit of its capacities, nor is it to compare the possibilities of television unfavorably with those of other media. It is, rather, to draw attention to television as it has been used in recent years and to the structures of attention that, by its presentations, it helps to shape.

The competitive pressures of programming may have brought about these limits. But it is possible that the nature of the medium itself precludes entering certain sorts of depths. Television may be excellent in some dimensions and merely whet the appetite in others.

(5) Television also seems to conceive of itself as a national medium. It does not favor the varieties of accent, speech patterns, and other differences of the culture of the United States. It favors a language which might be called "televisionese"—a neutral accent, pronunciation, and diction perhaps most closely approximated in California.

Since television arises in the field of "news" and daily entertainment, television values highly a kind of topicality, instant reflection of trends, and an effort to be "with it" and even "swinging." It values the "front edge" of attention, and it dreads being outrun by events. Accordingly, its product is perishable. It functions, in a way, as a guide to the latest gadgets and to the wonders of new technologies, or, as a direct contrary, to a kind of nostalgia for simpler ways in simpler times. Fashions of dress, automobiles, and explicitness "date" a series of shows. (Even the techniques used in taping shows may date them.)

Thus television functions as an instrument of the national, mobile culture. It does not reinforce the concrete ways of life of individual neighborhoods, towns, or subcultures. It shows the way things are done (or fantasized as being done) in "the big world." It is an organ of Hollywood and New York, not of Macon, Peoria, Salinas, or Buffalo.

I once watched television in a large hut in Tuy Hoa, South Vietnam. A room full of Vietnamese, including children, watched Armed Forces Television, watched Batman, Matt Dillon, and other shows from a distant continent. Here was their glimpse of the world from which the Americans around them had come. I wanted to tell them that what they were watching on television represented *no place,* represented no neighborhoods from which the young Americans around them came. And I began to wonder, knowing that not even the makers of such shows lived in such worlds, whose real world does television represent?

There are traces of local authenticity and local variety on national television. *All in the Family* takes the cameras into a neighborhood in Queens. The accents, gestures, methods and perceptions of the leading actors in *Kojak* reflect in an interesting and accurate way the ethnic sensibilities of several neighborhoods in New York. The clipped speech of Jack Webb in *Dragnet* years ago was an earlier break from "televisionese." But, in general, television is an organ of nationalization, of homogenization—and, indeed, of a certain systematic inaccuracy about the actual, concrete texture of life in the United States.

This nationalizing effect also spills over into the news and the documentaries. The cultural factors which deeply affect the values and perceptions of various American communities are neglected; hence the treatment of problems affecting such communities is frequently oversimplified. This is especially true when matters of group conflict are involved. The tendency of newsmen is subtly to take sides and to regard some claims or behavior as due to "prejudice," others as rather more moral and commendable.

The mythic forms and story lines of the news and documentaries are not inconsonant with the mythic forms represented in the adventure stories and Westerns. "Good" and "evil" are rather clearly placed in conflict. "Hard-hitting" investigative reporting is mythically linked to classic American forms of moral heroism: the crimebuster, the incorruptible sheriff. The forces of law and progress ceaselessly cut into the jungle of corruption. There is continuity between the prime-time news and prime-time programming—much more continuity than is detected by the many cultivated Cyclopses who disdain "the wasteland" and praise the documentaries. The mythic structure of both is harmonious.

It should prove possible to mark out the habits of perception and mind encouraged by national television. If these categories are not decisive, better ones can surely be discerned. We might then design ways of instructing ourselves and our children in countervailing habits. It does not seem likely that the mind and heart tutored by many years of watching television (in doses of five or six hours a day) is in the same circumstance as the mind and heart never exposed to television. Education and criticism must, it seems, take this difference into account.

2. The class bias of television

Television has had two striking effects. On the one hand, as Norman Podhoretz has remarked, it has not seemed to prevent people from reading; more books are being published and mass marketed than ever before in American history. It is possible that television stimulates many to go beyond what television itself can offer.

Secondly, television works, or appears to work, as a homogenizing medium. It presents a fairly non-representative, non-concrete, imagined world to a national audience. In many respects, it could be shown, the overall ideological tendency of television productions—from the news, through the talk shows, to the comedy hours, variety shows, and adventure, crime, and family shows—is that of a vague and misty liberalism: belief in the efficacy of an ultimate optimism, "talking through one's problems," a questioning of institutional authorities, a triumph of good over evil. Even a show like *All in the Family*, beneath its bluster and its violation of verbal taboos, illustrates the unfailing victory of liberal points of view: Archie Bunker always loses. A truly mean and aggressive reactionary point of view is virtually non-existent. There is no equivalent on national television to *Human Events* and other right-wing publications, or to the network of right-wing radio shows around the nation. While many critics of right and left find prime-time television to be a "wasteland," few have accused it of being fascist, malicious, evil, or destructive of virtue, progress, and hope. Television's liberalism is calculated to please neither the new radicals nor the classic liberals of the left, nor the upbeat, salesmanlike exponents of the right. In harmony with the images of progress built into both liberalism and capitalism, television seems, however gently, to undercut traditional institutions and to promote a restless, questioning attitude. The main product—and attitude—it has to sell is the new.

This attachment to the new insures that television will be a vaguely leftist medium, no matter who its personnel might be. Insofar as it debunks traditions and institutions—and even the act of *representing* these in selective symbolic form is a kind of veiled threat to them—television serves the purposes of that larger movement within which left and right (in America, at least) are rather like the two legs of locomotion: the movement of modernization. It serves, in general, the two mammoth institutions of modern life: the state and the great corporations. It serves these institutions even when it exalts the individual at the expense of family, neighborhood, religious organizations, and cultural groups. These are the only intermediate institutions that stand between the isolated individual and the massive institutions.

Thus the homogenizing tendencies of television are ambivalent. Television can electrify and unite the whole nation, creating an instantaneous

network in which millions are simultaneous recipients of the same powerful images. But to what purpose, for whose use, and to what effect? Is it
an unqualified good that the national grid should become so pre-eminent,
superior to any and all local checks and balances? The relative national
power and influence of state governors seems to have been weakened, for
example; a state's two senators, by comparison, occupy a national stage
and can more easily become national figures.

But in at least five other ways national television projects a sense of
reality that is not identical to the sense of reality actual individuals in their
concrete environments share. Taken together, these five ways construct a
national social reality that is not free of a certain class and even ethnic bias.

(1) The television set becomes a new instrument of reality—of "what's
happening" in the larger, national world, of "where it's at." In some sense
what isn't on television isn't quite real, is not part of the nationally shared
world, will be nonexistent for millions of citizens. Three examples may
suggest the power of this new sense of reality.

Experiments suggest (so I am told) that audiences confronted with simultaneous projection on a large movie screen and on a television set
regularly and overwhelmingly end up preferring the image on the smaller
set. The attraction of reality is somehow there.

On a political campaign, or at a sports event, individuals seem to seek
to be on camera with celebrities, as if seeking to share in a precious and
significant verification of their existence. A young boy in Pittsburgh exults,
"I'm real!" as he interposes himself between the grinding cameras and a
presidential candidate in the crowd. Not to be on television is to lack
weight in national consciousness. Audience "participation" (the ancient
platonic word for being) fills a great psychic hunger: to be human in the
world that really counts.

Finally, anyone who has participated in a large-scale event comes to
recognize vividly how strait and narrow is the gate between what has
actually happened and what gets on television. For the millions who see
the television story, of course, the story is the reality. For those who lived
through a strenuous sixteen-hour day on the campaign trail, for example,
it is always something of a surprise to see what "made" the television
screen—or, more accurately, what the television screen made real. That
artificial reality turns out to have far more substance for the world at large
than the lived sixteen hours. According to the ancient *maya,* the world of
flesh and blood is an illusion. And so it is.

(2) Television is a new technology and depends upon sophisticated
crafts. It is a world of high profit. Its inside world is populated by persons
in a high income bracket. Moreover, television is a world that requires a
great deal of travel, expense-account living, a virtual shuttle between Los
Angeles and New York, a taste for excellent service and high prestige.
These economic factors seriously color television's image of the world.

The glitter of show business quickly spread to television. In the blossomy days when thinkers dreamed of an affluent society and praised the throwaway society, the shifting and glittering sets of television make-believe seemed like a metaphor for modern society. Actually, a visit to a television studio is extraordinarily disappointing, far more so, even, than a visit to an empty circus tent after the crowd has gone. Cheaply painted pastel panels, fingerprints sometimes visible upon them, are wheeled away and stacked. The cozy intimacy one shares from one's set at home is rendered false by the cavernous lofts of the studio, the tangle of wires, the old clothing and cynical buzzing of the bored technicians, crews, and hangers-on. Dust and empty plastic coffee cups are visible in corners where chairs compete for space. There is a tawdriness behind the scenes.

In a word, the world of television is a radically duplicitous world. Its illusions pervade every aspect of the industry. The salaries paid to those who greet the public remove them from the public. The settings in which they work are those of show business. Slick illusion is the constant temptation and establishes the rules of the game.

Moreover, the selling of products requires images of upward mobility. The sets, designs, and fluid metaphors of the shows themselves must suggest a certain richness, smoothness, and adequacy. It is not only that writers and producers understand that what audiences desire is escape. (One can imagine a poor society in which television would focus on limited aspiration and the dramas of reality.) It is also the case, apparently, that an inner imperative drives writers, producers, and sponsors to project their *own* fantasies. Not all Americans, by far, pursue upward mobility as a way of life. A great many teach their children to have modest expectations and turn down opportunities for advancement and mobility that would take them away from their familiar worlds.

The myths of the upwardly mobile and the tastes of the very affluent govern the visual symbols, the flow, and the chatter of television.

(3) The class bias of television reality proceeds not only from the relative economic affluence of the industry and its personnel. It springs as well from the educational level. "Televisionese" sends a clear and distinct message to the people, a message of exclusion and superiority. (George Wallace sends the message *back;* he is not its originator, only its echo.) It is common for a great many of the personnel connected with television to imagine themselves as anti-establishment and also perhaps as iconoclastic. Surely they must know that to men who work in breweries or sheet metal plants, to women who clean tables in cafeterias or splice wires in electronic assembly plants, they must seem to be at the very height of the Establishment. Their criticisms of American society—reflected in *Laugh-In*, in the nightclub entertainers, and even in the dialogue of virtually every crime or adventure show—are perceived to be something like the complaints of spoiled children. There seems to be a self-hatred in the medium, a certain

shame about American society, of which Lawrence Welk's old-fashioned, honeyed complacency and the militant righteousness of Bob Hope, John Wayne, and *Up With America!* are the confirming opposites. To confuse the hucksterism of television with the real America is, of course, a grievous error.

Television is a parade of experts instructing the unenlightened about the weather, aspirins, toothpastes, the latest books or proposals for social reform, and the correct attitudes to have with respect to race, poverty, social conflict, and new moralities. Television is preeminently a world of intellectuals. Academic persons may be astonished to learn of it and serious writers and artists may hear the theme with withering scorn, but for most people in the United States television is the medium through which they meet an almost solid phalanx of college-educated persons, professionals, experts, thinkers, authorities, and "with it," "swinging" celebrities: i.e., people unlike themselves who are drawn from the top ten percent of the nation in terms of educational attainment.

It is fashionable for intellectuals to disdain the world of television (although some, when asked, are known to agree to appear on it without hesitation). Yet when they appear on television they do not seem to be notably superior to the announcers, interviewers, and performers who precede them on camera or share the camera with them. (Incidentally, although many sports journalists write or speak condescendingly of "the jocks," when athletes appear as television announcers—Joe Garagiola, Sandy Koufax, Frank Gifford, Alex Karras, and others—the athletes seem not one whit inferior in intelligence or in sensitivity to the journalists.) Television is the greatest instrument the educated class has ever had to parade its wares before the people. On television that class has no rival. Fewer than ten percent of the American population has completed four years of college. That ten percent totally dominates television.

It is important to understand that the disdain for "popular culture" often heard in intellectual circles is seriously misplaced. Television, at least, more nearly represents the world of the educated ten percent than it reflects the world of the other ninety percent. At most, one might say in defense, the world of television represents the educated class's fantasies about the fantasies of the population. To say that *kitsch* has always required technicians to create it is not a sufficient route of escape. Do really serious intellectuals (i.e., not those "mere" technicians) have better understandings of where the people truly are? What, then, are those better understandings?

The interviews recorded by Robert Coles, for example, tend to show that persons of the social class represented by Archie Bunker are at least as complicated, many-sided, aware of moral ambiguities, troubled and sensitive, as the intellectuals who appear on television, in novels, or in the cinema. Artists who might use the materials of ordinary life for their creations are systematically separated from ordinary people by the economic conditions of creativity in the United States.

(4) The writers, producers, actors, and journalists of television are separated from most of the American population not only by economic standing, and not only by education, but also by the culture in which their actual lives are lived out. By "culture" I mean those implicit, lived criteria that suggest to each of us what is real, relevant, significant, meaningful in the buzzing confusion of our experience: how we select out and give shape to our world. The culture of prime-time television is, it appears, a serious dissolvant of the cultures of other Americans. The culture of television celebrates to an extraordinary degree two mythic strains in the American character: the lawless and the irreverent. On the first count, stories of cowboys, gangsters, and spies still preoccupy the American imagination. On the second, the myth of "enlightenment" from local standards and prejudices still dominates our images of self-liberation and sophistication. No doubt the stronghold of a kind of priggish righteousness in several layers of American history leads those who rebel to find their rebellion all too easy. It is as though the educated admonish one another that they "can't go home again" and that the culture against which they rebel is solid and unyielding.

But what if it isn't? What if the perception of culture on the part of millions is, rather, that chaos and the jungle are constantly encroaching and that the rule of good order is threatened in a dozen transactions every day—by products that don't work, by experts and officials who take advantage of lay ignorance, by muggings and robberies, by jobs and pensions that disappear, by schools that do not work in concert with the moral vision of the home?

Television keeps pressing on the barriers of cultural resistance to obscenities, to some forms of sexual behavior, and to various social understandings concerning work and neighborhood and family relationships. A reporter from the *New York Times* reports with scarcely veiled satisfaction that *Deep Throat* is being shown in a former church in a Pennsylvania mining town, as though this were a measure of spreading enlightenment. It might be. But what if our understanding of how cultural, social, and moral strands are actually interwoven in the consciousness of peoples is inadequate? What if the collapse of moral inhibition in one area, for a significant number of persons, encourages a collapse at other places? What if moral values cannot be too quickly changed without great destructiveness? The celebration of "new moralities" may not lead to the kind of "humanization" cultural optimists anticipate.

Television, and the mass media generally, have vested interests in new moralities. The excitement of transgressing inhibitions is gripping entertainment. There are, however, few vested interests wishing to strengthen the inhibitions which make such transgressions good entertainment. Television is only twenty-five years old. We have very little experience or understanding proportionate to the enormous moral stakes involved. It is folly to believe that *laissez-faire* works better in moral matters than in economic matters or that enormous decisions in these matters are not already being made in the absence of democratic consent. When one kind of show goes on the air others are excluded during that time. The present system is effectively a form of social control.

I do not advocate any particular solution to this far-ranging moral dilemma; I do not know what to recommend. But the issue is a novel one for a free society, and we do not even have a well-thought-out body of options from which to choose. In that vacuum a rather-too-narrow social class is making the decisions. The pressures of the free market (so they say) now guide them. Is that so? Should it be so?

(5) Because of the structure and history of the social class that produces prime-time television, group conflict in the United States is also portrayed in a simplistic and biased way. The real diversity of American cultures and regions is shrouded in public ignorance. Occasional disruptions, like the rebellion of West Virginia miners against certain textbooks and the rebellion of parents in South Boston against what they perceived as downward mobility for their children and themselves, are as quickly as possible brushed from consciousness. America is pictured as though it were divided between one vast homogeneous "middle America," to be enlightened, and the enlighteners. In fact, there are several "middle Americas."

There is more than one important Protestant culture in our midst. The Puritan inheritance is commonly exaggerated and the evangelical, fundamentalist inheritance is vastly underestimated (and under-studied). Hubert Humphrey is from a cultural stream different from that of George Wallace or of John Lindsay. There are also several quite significant cultural streams among Catholics; the Irish of the Middle West (Eugene McCarthy, Michael Harrington) often have a quite different cultural tradition from the Irish of Philadelphia, Boston, or New York. Construction workers on Long Island are not offended by "pornography" in the same way as druggists in small midwestern towns; look inside their cabs and helmets, listen to their conversations, if you seek evidence. There is also more than one cultural stream among American Jews; the influence of the Jews of New York has probably misled us in our understanding of the Jewish experience in America.

It seems, moreover, that the social class guiding the destiny of television idealizes certain ethnic groups—the legitimate minorities—even while this class offers in its practices no greater evidence of genuine egalitarianism than other social classes. At the same time this class seems extremely slow to comprehend the experiences of other American cultures. One of the great traumas of human history was the massive migration to America during the last 100 years. It ought to be one of the great themes of high culture, and popular culture as well. Our dramatists neglect it.

Group conflict has, moreover, been the rule in every aspect of American life, from labor to corporate offices to neighborhoods to inter-ethnic marriages. Here, too, the drama is perhaps too real and vivid to be touched: *these* are inhibitions the liberal culture of television truly respects. Three years ago one could write that white ethnics, like some others, virtually never saw themselves on television; suddenly we have had *Banacek, Colombo, Petrocelli, Kojak, Kolchack, Rhoda, Sanford,* and *Chico.* Artists are still exploring the edges of how much reality can be given voice and how to voice it. These are difficult, even explosive matters. Integrity and care are required.

It must seem odd to writers and producers to be accused of having a "liberal" bias when they are so aware of the limitations they daily face and the grueling battles they daily undergo. But why do they have these battles except that they have a point of view and a moral passion? We are lucky that the social class responsible for the creative side of television is not a reactionary and frankly illiberal class. Still, that it is a special class is itself a problem for all of us, including those involved in it.

---

to the student: a commentary

Michael Novak has taught at Harvard, Stanford, and SUNY-Old Westbury, mainly in religious philosophy. But he is also an observer of the media, and has served as chairman of the Aspen Institute's Workshop on Television.

This article basically makes two points: that television affects our perception of, and approach to, reality; and that the effect springs from a "class bias" imposed by television.

Novak supports his first point by drawing on five different examples. First, he says, the pace of television has increased our demand for "pace" in our other activities. If the "rhythm of attention" doesn't match that of fast-moving TV programs we become unhappy. We can sense some truth in Novak's generalization. It is easy to buy the idea that most of us, victimized by the age of future shock, demand quick progress and resolution in all our activities. And there is some logic in pointing a finger at television as a source of such expectations. But a natural question must be raised: just how new is this demand for "pace"? Boredom is not unique to the television generation; exasperation is nothing new (Aristotelian logic may have begun as a direct attack on irrelevant information). And what audience, from those of Aristophanes to Shakespeare to Noel Coward, didn't envy the quick intelligence inherent in the actors' dialogue? The point is that the "rhythm of attention" may be an old demand, merely made more salient by television.

Novak's second point, one of his more chilling insights, is that television's use of "multiple logics"—the blending of simultaneous but not overtly connected action—has shifted a generation away from linear thinking. The old teaching system, "proceeding serially from point to point," is now under pressure from student minds that shift from subject to subject as quickly as scene cuts in *Kojak*. Again, one can feel quick agreement with this generalization. More than one media philosopher, Marshall McLuhan probably being the most notable, has seen a relationship between television and the cognitive ability of the young. But even with the assumption that the connection is valid, and that the relation is causal (that is, the television generation will perceive things differently *because* of television), we must ask about the extent or magnitude of change. It is true that we no longer need the disembodied voice to tell us "Meanwhile, back at the ranch," nor do we require visual flipping of calendar pages to signify the passing of time. Our experience with scene changes, through sheer repetition, now allows for a kind of visual shorthand. Yet we must be careful not to carry Novak's point too far. It might be a mistake to make a large leap from a mere visual shorthand to the assumption that the entire cognitive process is now being monitored by some form of miniature film editor.

Novak's third example is what he calls the "periodization of attention." Television, he says, teaches the audience to expect events to unfold—and, one might add, problems to be resolved—in discrete segments of time. Novak doesn't go as far, however, as semanticist S. I. Hayakawa, who claimed that one of the problems with the younger generation was that they expected a "sixty-minute solution" to all problems. But both proceed from the same assumption—that television has imposed its own structure of timing and development over that of the "real" or natural world. The thought may be valid, but once again, it shouldn't be carried too far. As an audience, most of us are generally aware that the structure of entertainment is stylized by the medium; who, for example, hasn't recognized the purpose of the cliff-hanging scene just before the commercial break? Do we truly expect all our days to be as "laugh-packed" and "fast-paced" as if they were some continous version of *Mary Tyler Moore?* We probably know better.

Novak also explores the possibility that television, by presenting role models with limited emotions and motivations, will weaken or thin out individual ability to deal with depth and complexity. He makes an interesting case, pointing out that most of our understanding of roles and behaviors, particularly in our mobile and "nuclearized" society, must necessarily come from the most pervasive teacher in existence. Does television rely on simple plots and shallow characters? Yes, most of the time it does. Does television use a limited range of stereotypes in its portrayal of people? Again, most of the time it certainly does. Does that mean future generations will grow up simple, shallow, and bound to stereotypic behavior? Well . . . wait a minute. First we have to consider the possibility that television presents us with a wider choice of characters, behaviors, and roles rather than a small number of aunts and uncles. If Novak's pre-television non-nuclear family served as socialization models, just how great a range could that have been? Certainly not as wide as that encountered in prime time. Secondly, we have to ask ourselves if the human psyche is so stiff and inanimate that it will only hold impressions etched from the outside. Isn't it more likely to be a dynamic, evolving entity that also creates from the inside out? In short, don't we recognize within ourselves a natural level of complexity—sufficient, at least, to know that neither you nor I can accurately be considered as stereotype?

Novak's fifth concern is that of television's "homogenization" of American culture. But he takes that concern a perceptive step further, pointing out that the standardized, nationalized portrayal of our society—even through such diverse forms as Batman and Matt Dillon—is not rooted in reality. It is not a reflection of Macon, Peoria, or Salinas. Or even New York or Hollywood. Television represents *no place,* he says, and is thus systematically inaccurate. It is an observation difficult to argue with. The only possible response is that these factors are *necessary.* Television, by its very structure as a mass medium, must be a homogenization of values, attitudes, and accents. How else can it bring together, and retain, an audience that is counted by the millions? Strong limitations, whether geographical or ideological, would be in direct contradiction to the goal of the largest possible national viewership. Though some may argue with the goal, given the current organizational structure of television, any other would be courting economic suicide.

The second part of Novak's essay deals with what he calls the "class bias of television." It should be noted that his basic premise is the opposite of the first article in this book ("The Intellectual and the Mass Media") in which Leo Rosten argues that television is the product of the masses—and thus the object of scorn by intellectuals. Novak, however, feels that the managers of television—the writers, producers, network executives—*are* the intellectuals. "Fewer than ten percent of the American population has completed four years of college. That ten percent totally dominates television."

That 10 percent, he says, rather than reflecting mass taste, are forcing their own taste and perceptions of reality—or what they would like it to be—on the masses. Novak equates, probably correctly, this educated, affluent group with a kind of liberalism. "Even a show like *All in the Family* . . . illustrates the unfailing victory of liberal points of view: Archie Bunker always loses." Here is where Novak's self-confessed innocence "of psychological testing and sociological survey" leaves an important point unconsidered. Not that he's necessarily wrong about the liberal tendencies of television productions —the producer, director, and stars of *All in the Family,* for example, would willingly put themselves in a liberal category. But Novak fails to recognize that he may be the victim of his own bias: what he sees on television is not what other people see. Novak—an educated liberal—does not account for the simple phenomenon of selective perception.

Research indicates, to use the show we've been citing, that *All in the Family* has two different audiences, and each sees a different program. In an article published in *Journal of Communication,* two researchers presented evidence that while liberal viewers saw the program as a satire on bigotry, with Archie Bunker losing the arguments and being the butt of most of the jokes, a second—and larger—audience saw something quite different. "Tells it like it is," was the most common phrase used by the second group, which saw Archie Bunker as the victor in most of the arguments. And only 15 percent of this group perceived Archie as the butt of the jokes.

Both audiences saw a funny program—which is why the ratings are so high —yet both also saw a program that supported their existing attitudes. "We found that many persons did not see the program as a satire on bigotry," the researchers wrote in their conclusion, "and that these persons were more likely to be viewers who scored high on measures of prejudice."

The factor of selective perception is a crucial element that must be considered when weighing Novak's concerns. If we are all capable of seeing different things in the same material, then the bias, if any, of the senders of mass communication will take a back seat to the bias of the receiver. It is something you might consider the next time you tune in your favorite show.

LLS

Alberta E. Siegel

Communicating with the Next Generation

. . . Psychological research on the impact of the new electronic media on children has been slow in coming of age. There are several reasons for this.

In the first place, with the advent of the movies in the late 1920s and early 1930s, there was a lot of discussion about their effects on children. With the primitive techniques of research then available, very little could be demonstrated about these effects. Psychologists remembered the non-results when the question of the effects of television was raised a generation later.

Second, the advent of TV came when child psychologists were thinking in terms of a stimulus-response model of behavior in which reward, reinforcement, and drive reduction figured prominently. We thought learning occurred when reinforcement was contingent on the learner's behavior. There is nothing which happens on radio, the movies, or TV which is contingent on the behavior of the listener, except turning on or off. When the viewer laughs, the TV comedian doesn't get funnier. When the viewer frowns or looks worried, the TV interviewer doesn't change the subject or interject a quip to change the pace. Since it was not clear how TV could enter into a chain of reinforcing or punishing sequences, psychologists found difficulty in conceptualizing how TV could be significant in modifying behavior.

An exception was the catharsis theory, which had been clearly and explicitly stated in testable form in 1939 in *Frustration and Aggression.* This book was one of our bibles in the postwar era in psychology, and much of the TV research in the 1950s and early 1960s centered on the catharsis notion. There was the additional fact that the catharsis notion had to do with aggression, and public concern about TV and children centered on the aggressive content of TV. Moreover, the catharsis theory held meaning for psychoanalysts as well as behavioral scientists, and the 1950s were a time of rapprochement between these two. We have a useful summary of the status of our knowledge about catharsis in Berkowitz's review chapter on aggression [in B. M. Caldwell and H. N. Ricciuti, *Review of Child Develop-*

Reprinted by permission of Alberta E. Siegel from *Journal of Communication,* Autumn 1975.

ment Research, vol. 3, 1973]. There is little or no evidence of catharsis of aggression through media experience; much of the evidence is inconclusive, and where positive findings do exist they are in the opposite direction. Experiencing aggression vicariously instigates or heightens aggressive motivation; it does not drain or purge it. Even the Surgeon General's Committee on TV, a super-cautious bunch, agreed with that conclusion.

Third, it is expensive to do research on TV, and where large amounts of money have been available for research, most psychologists have felt there were more urgent calls on it.

As we got more interested in the child's mind, its furnishings and functioning, our interest in TV grew.

Partly through the influence of Baldwin's ground-breaking textbook [*Behavior and Development in Childhood*], partly because more American psychologists were traveling to Geneva, and partly because Hunt [*Intelligence and Experience,* 1961] and Flavell [*The Developmental Psychology of Jean Piaget,* 1963] wrote interesting and persuasive books about Piaget's work, American psychologists began "rediscovering the mind of the child," as Martin phrased it. Having done that, they got interested in what was being beamed to that mind via its modern electronic appurtenances and extensions. American children spend more time watching TV than they spend in the classroom. We see few dropouts from the electronic school and very little TV truancy.

Perhaps even more significant than the rediscovery of the child's mind, in encouraging research on TV, were the pioneering investigations of Bandura in the early 1960s. His studies [published in *Journal of Abnormal and Social Psychology,* 1961, 1963] were within the context of behavior theory. Their results had the effect of stretching and augmenting that theory in useful ways. Bandura demonstrated that children can acquire new responses through observation and imitation, without external reinforcement and without extensive rehearsal or practice. This occurs when they are observing and imitating filmed or videotaped models, just as it occurs when they are observing and imitating live models in a face-to-face situation. The responses which Bandura studied initially were aggressive and antisocial responses, so his results raised a furor with those who felt that TV violence makes no difference in the lives of children. The ruckus about TV tended to obscure the significance of Bandura's findings for psychological theory. That has become clearer now, partly as he has written about his own explanation of his findings and partly as he has extended his research to other classes of responses, including prosocial behaviors [in *Aggression: A Social Learning Analysis,* 1973, and *Principles of Behavior Modification,* 1969].

A fourth consideration figures in our study of the effects of media on children. That is our commitment to the experiment. This commitment is at once our glory and our constraint. We know that experiments are more informative than correlational studies in identifying the sources of effects, in clarifying the direction of relations between events. Most of our recent progress seems to us to have come from the use of experiments, in which we isolate one variable from the others with which it is interwoven in ordinary life.

Experiments are well suited to the study of explosions, sudden and dramatic events with predictably sudden effects. But experiments are inefficient for the study of slow cultivation, erosion and corrosion. Bandura has shown us that experiments can isolate some effects of watching television. But we must suspect that some of the effects are slow and insidious rather than abrupt and dramatic.

We need to think about how to study insidious effects. If we knew how to do it, we might be farther along in the study of family interaction and family dynamics. We might be better able to specify just what the effects of schooling are on children. We might not face the appalling situation described by Herzog in her review chapter on fatherless families [in *Review of Child Development Research,* vol. 3, 1973]: despite many investigations, we can't cite evidence as to how and why fathers make a difference in the lives of their children. If we knew ways to design research to study long-term and chronic situations, we might be able to lend a hand to our medical colleagues as they attempt to study the effects of food additives, air pollution, cigarette smoking, high-cholesterol diets, excessive calorie intake, chronic dependence on alcohol or other drugs, habitual inactivity, and so on.

Our medical colleagues have an advantage over us, though, and this leads me to my fifth point about research on the effects of TV. We have no animal model. You can set a chimpanzee on a long-term course of imbibing alcohol or smoking cigarettes, and from subsequent observations you can learn something about man's long-term responses to those agents, for the chimpanzee is close to man in his blood composition, immune responses, and so forth. In urging the importance of an animal model for advances in our understanding of child development, I remind you of what happened to our understanding of dependency and attachment as a result of Harry and Margaret Harlow's work with rhesus macaques in the late 1950s and early 1960s.

Given a problem for which you have a history of research with frequently inconclusive results; a theory which cannot specify clearly what the observable effects ought to be; high expenses built into any reasonable effort at research, in a field with limited funding and many problems urgently needing investigation; a commitment to a research design, the experiment, which is limited in its relevance to the issues; and no animal model—you might very well decide that the best course of action is to turn your concern elsewhere, to invest your limited energies in more promising matters. C. P. Snow's remark is pertinent here: "Scientists regard it as a major intellectual virtue to know what not to think about."

The American public, and the Congressmen they elect, are not so fastidious. Senator Pastore, of the Subcommittee on Communications of the Senate Committee on Commerce, held hearings on TV violence in the spring of 1969. These were the latest in a series of hearings which had periodically enlivened the Washington scene since the early 1950s, with behavioral scientists reviewing the modest research knowledge currently available and with network spokesmen claiming that the research is inconclusive and that if TV violence has any effects, they are in the form of catharsis or draining of aggressive impulses. In an effort to move forward from that replay, the Senator asked the Surgeon General for a specific opinion, and the Surgeon General established a committee to advise him. Under the very able leadership of Dr. Eli Rubinstein, a psychologist with a long and distinguished history of public service in the NIMH, the committee used the funds available to it for new research by contracting with 23 different sets of investigators. The result was more than 40 technical papers published in five volumes early in 1972. These papers are still being read and digested, especially as many are just now reappearing in the standard journal series. Liebert and his colleagues at Stony Brook have written a popularization of the research entitled *The Early Window.* . . .

Only a few of the investigations can be said to have broken totally new ground. Others developed or extended approaches which were already on the scene, using larger samples, better stimulus materials, more sophisticated statistical analyses, etc. Committee members were disappointed that so few of the investigations concerned very young children, especially because Bandura's results had been with preschoolers, and because Harold Stevenson had prepared a review [in *Television and Social Behavior,* vol. 2, 1972] showing how little we know about media effects on this age group. Friedrich and Stein did study preschoolers, in a field study, and theirs is one of the most widely cited and influential experiments in the series [*Monographs of the Society for Research in Child Development,* 1973]. Perhaps the most significant long-term effect of the studies commissioned for the Surgeon General's Committee is that a new generation of researchers was launched; many of the young investigators who worked under these contracts are continuing research in the field.

The report of the Committee itself seems less satisfactory to me than the work done by the principal investigators. In part, this is (a) because of the time pressures under which we worked, all of us busy people with full-time responsibilities at our own institutions; (b) any committee effort is likely to resemble a camel more than a horse; and (c) we were at a disadvantage because of the method by which the members of the Committee were chosen. Forty names of possible members were listed by the NIMH and submitted to the Surgeon General, Dr. William Stewart, who would be leaving government service for a new assignment. These names were submitted to the presidents of the three TV networks and the president of the trade association. Seven of the 40 were then identified by these individuals as not being free of bias in the matter of television's effects. None of the seven was subsequently appointed to the Committee. The Surgeon General who was appointed to suceed Dr. Stewart, Dr. Jesse Steinfeld, subsequently stated that he felt this procedure was a mistake. So did the members of the Committee when they learned about it after they had been empaneled and set to work. But the damage had been done. We were denied the services and expertise of Drs. Albert Bandura, Leonard Berkowitz, and Leon Eisenberg as Committee members, and there was no member of the Committee from their fields, psychology and psychiatry, with the knowledge of the research and the issues that these men have. More important than that, perhaps, was the fact that there was no screening of the list of 40 names to identify individuals who might be biased in pro-industry directions, and in fact five of the 12 members of the Committee were individuals with long-standing links to the TV industry, two of them full-time employees in responsible positions. Suppose the professional associations had been given the same reviewing privilege that was given to the networks and the trade association. If the American Psychological Association, the American Sociological Association, the Society for Research in Child Development, and the American Psychiatric Association had been consulted at the same stage in the selection of Committee members, the Congress and the public might well have gotten a rather different report than the one written by the Committee empaneled by the method used by the former Surgeon General.

Given the way the Committee was composed, it is fortunate that all proposals for research were reviewed, not by the Committee, but by ad hoc panels set up by the NIMH from its usual set of consultants. It is fortunate also that the researchers published their own work in their own words, without any intervention or editorial control by the Committee. Most important, it is fortunate that after the Committee finished writing its report, Douglass Cater of the Aspen Institute, who is directing their program to study the media, convened several top social scientists to advise Surgeon General Steinfeld concerning the new report. They had copies of the summaries of each of the five volumes of research reports, written by the investigators, as well as copies of the report. One reason Dr. Steinfeld spoke so forcefully at Senator Pastore's hearings in March, 1972, is that these social scientists, including Albert Bandura, Orville Brim, Lloyd Morrisett, Ralph Tyler, James Short, and Meredith Wilson, had guided him through our jargon and elaborately careful phrasing.

Douglass Cater and Stephen Strickland have written a book about our effort, entitled *TV Violence and the Child.* It offers the judgment of two thoughtful and experienced observers as to where we made a contribution and where we erred. I am inclined to agree with their belief that the Committee could well have spent more time discussing and phrasing the best professional judgment of its members and less time fussing over the exact interpretation of a correlation of .30.

When we wrote our report to the Surgeon General, we knew it would be read also by Congressmen, their aides, and some members of the general public. We also knew these readers would need help in understanding our labored, cautious, and jargon-ridden prose. My own naïve notion, to the extent that I thought about the matter, was that a science writer would be writing the newspaper and magazine reports. In fact, news of our report appeared mostly on the TV and entertainment pages, written by reporters whose usual job is to relay puffery and PR from the industry admen. A show-biz atmosphere pervades American TV, and it clouds efforts at serious discussion. One member of the Surgeon General's Committee, a long-time employee of a major network, hardly ever spoke of "the audience" or "the viewer." His words were "the market." TV producers refer to children as "mice" or "kiddies," and TV for children is "kidvid." It appears on "the Saturday morning ghetto," also known as "Peewee TV."

In 1973, America's corporate tab for advertising to the "mice" approached $400 million, according to Melody [*Children's Television: The Economics of Exploitation,* 1973]. The advertisers may be responding to Lyle and Hoffman's study [in *Television and Social Behavior,* vol. IV, 1972] showing that the majority of the mothers they interviewed in Los Angeles reported their children were singing TV jingles by age two, and over 90 percent had joined this youthful chorus by age three. Many of the mothers were from poor and welfare families. They reported that 87 percent of their preschool children asked for food items they'd seen on TV, and 91 percent asked for toys seen on TV. The children themselves were interviewed as well. Almost 90 percent of the three-year-olds could identify Fred Flintstone from a photograph, and 70 percent could identify Big Bird. Among the four- and five-year-olds, recognition of various TV characters was higher.

By age 16 the average viewer will have spent 15,000 hours in front of a TV set. That adds up to 640,000 commercials. . . .

The Markle Foundation, under Lloyd Morrisett's leadership, is devoting its resources to TV. The Ford Foundation has been a major supporter of public television, and is now planning new initiatives concerning children and television. John D. Rockefeller has a small staff beginning to explore the possible functions television could play in the sex role learning of children and adolescents, and in their preparation for adult sexuality and parenting. At Harvard we have a center for the study of children's television. There has been some action on the proposal for a child advocate within the FCC. The National Foundation for the Humanities is growing rapidly, and is investing some of its increasing resources in healthful and constructive ways of communicating with the next generation via TV.

The NIMH is at work on the violence index which was proposed at the 1972 Pastore hearings. We shall have regular "smog bulletins" indicating how much violence is polluting the airwaves and enabling us to identify the industrial polluters. This should be helpful to groups wishing to bring social and commercial pressure to bear on business interests which have abused their access to the public airwaves, despoiling the social environment in which children grow up. Nicholas Johnson called them "child molesters."

We have Action for Children's Television, a public-spirited group of citizens which has been an effective spokesman for the needs of children. With its genius for demeaning individuals holding dissident views by labeling them pejoratively, the TV industry usually refers to ACT as "the ladies from Boston."

The most convincing research we have about TV's effects is the research showing that televised persons provide an example or a model for the viewer's behavior. Albert Bandura's research may be said to give empirical foundation to a remark by Albert Schweitzer: "Example is not the main thing in life—it is the only thing."

Capitalizing on that insight means recognizing that we need good television productions which others can imitate. That's why I've suggested that private foundations provide travel fellowships so that producers of American entertainment TV can go abroad to learn from those who do it better: the English, the Dutch, the French, the Swedish, the Canadians. In each of those countries, one sees television policies and programs which are more sensitive than ours to the needs of the next generation.

---

to the student: a commentary

Dr. Alberta Siegel, professor of psychology in the Department of Psychiatry and Behavioral Sciences at Stanford University, is a noted researcher. In her presidential address to the Division on Developmental Psychology, on which her article is based, she focused on the difficulties in, and importance of, research on how television affects children.

Siegel's up-to-date report is sobering, and so is the way in which the government attempts to conduct research. Here we'll explore the committee work on which Dr. Siegel served. She was, of course, critical of it.

Television and Growing Up: The Impact of Televised Violence, is the report of the Surgeon General's Scientific Advisory Committee on Television and Social Behavior. It began work in 1970 as a result of a letter to the Department of Health, Education, and Welfare from Senator John O. Pastore requesting an investigation directed by the Surgeon General "which would help resolve the question of whether there is a causal connection between televised crime and violence and anti-social behavior by individuals, especially children."

Senator Pastore seemed to expect the report on television and violence to be as unequivocal as the report of an earlier Surgeon General's Committee on Smoking and Health, whose consequences included banning cigarette commercials from television. Senator Pastore said, "I would hope that the Surgeon General in due time will come before this committee not with a lot of ifs and buts, but will tell us in simple language whether or not the broadcasters ought to be put on notice and be very, very careful in this area, because it might have an effect on certain people." Senator Pastore's disappointment was total. The report on television and violence carries many "ifs" and "buts," and more than its share of "howevers."

This was predictable. In an issue of *Science*, the official publication of the American Association for the Advancement of Science, Philip Boffey and John Walsh reported that broadcasters had been given veto power over the selection of the Scientific Advisory Committee and had blackballed the seven leading social scientists Dr. Siegel mentioned.

Robert Finch, then Secretary of Health, Education, and Welfare, explained, "It was probable in each case that the report of the advisory committee would contain substantial criticism of the industry, and it was felt that to *protect the Government* [his emphasis] from the charge of establishing a biased committee, whose recommendations would be suspect, the industry should be given the opportunity to identify any individuals whom it felt were not impartial." The bias, as it turned out, leaned the other way. When the seven had been eliminated from a pool of candidates, staff members at the National Institutes of Mental Health and HEW chose twelve to serve on the Scientific Advisory Committee.

Of these, five had links with the television industry, including two who are full-time executives of networks; two others served as industry consultants and another has done so.

The composition of the committee drew heavy fire. Possibly the sharpest criticism came from Representative John M. Murphy, New York Democrat, who spoke in the House of Representatives of "the shabby machinations of the television moguls on the latest study," and introduced legislation for a new study to be made by the Federal Communications Commission. An aide of Murphy's, Carl Perian, who was staff director of a 1964 Senate subcommittee that did a partial study of the same subject, looked at the documents in the new study and said that in view of "the involvement of the television industry" neither he nor Representative Murphy has any doubt "that the report is a fraud—purposeful fraud."

The report never seems to offer even a tentative conclusion in one sentence without withdrawing it in the next; it is not at all surprising that news stories on the report cover a wild range. The *New York Times* headed its story: TV Violence Held Unharmful to Youth. The *Washington Post* announced: Study Links TV, Child Aggression. The *Christian Science Monitor* came down in the middle: TV Violence Has Some Effect. *Newsweek* simply labeled its story: The However Report.

The report met such a barrage of criticism that Pastore, obviously frustrated by its ambiguous qualities, scheduled public hearings on the committee's controversial production. The Surgeon General's committee spent $1.8 million and more than two years to say "however."

It should also be said that a little study of television news by a senior lecturer and a doctoral candidate at the University of California at Berkeley needs attention. Andrew Stern, the lecturer, and Russ Neuman, the doctoral candidate, set out to determine what viewers remember from network television news reports. They made many telephone calls immediately after news programs broadcast by ABC, CBS, and NBC. Of those who watched all or part of a program, half did not recall a single broadcast story. Those who *did* remember usually recalled more than one story, but the average for all viewers was a recall of only one story per newscast (nineteen stories, on the average, were carried by each of the three network newscasts).

When the interviewers read off headlines, the average viewer recalled eight stories but could recall details about only four of them.

Senator Pastore may be interested to know that news stories picturing violence were well remembered. On one occasion, all three networks broadcast stories about troubles in East Pakistan. Only CBS showed brutality. When viewers were asked whether they remembered anything from the newscasts they had seen, not one of those who watched ABC and NBC recalled the East Pakistan story. Of those who watched CBS, 30 percent needed no reminding to recall the brutality.

It is obvious that research on the effects of television on children will go forward, as Siegel points out. It also seems that it is far better that government does not supervise it.

WLR

Meg Greenfield

Ethnic and Son

Chico, Rhoda, Florida, Horshack, Montefuscos and Jeffersons; this one's momma and that one's son—television . . . is an ethnic bath, an affirmative-action program gone mad. Who are all these Moldavians and Bengalis and Walloons? What are the networks trying to tell us?

I think the answer to the first question is that, give or take a little spaghetti sauce, they are all variations on the same family: a warmhearted momma, an irascible and comic papa, a couple of fractious adolescents and an elder female relative who is both a social drag and a religious nut. Color them any way you want, they are the Bumsteads in Bavarian national dress, Vic and Sade in blackface.

Exotic complexions

So the networks are telling us practically nothing—or nothing distinctive, anyway—about all these homey people with the exotic complexions and unpronounceable last names. They have merely grafted a few stereotyped ethnic and racial mannerisms onto the all-purpose American entertainment family, turning what once was a specialty—Molly Goldberg, Amos 'n' Andy—into a way of life. But they are telling us plenty, I think, about our current social and political condition. They are telling us that ethnic is beautiful, that ethnic is "in."

Consider the trends. Rhoda Morgenstern of "Rhoda" fame took on a surname that the fictional heroine of an earlier age had changed to "Morningstar." Old Man Sanford has many of the attributes that made Rochester and Amos 'n' Andy funny, but that also eventually made them objects of protest as racial stereotypes. Yet we seem to enjoy all that now. We are relaxed about it—sort of. The network entertainers, never known for wittingly giving offense to broad classes of people, understand. They are reflecting an important national change.

Part of that change strikes me as being healthy and overdue. Only a few years ago Richard Nixon could say that the nation should not discriminate against people "merely" because they were black. We have got rid of the put-down word "merely," the implication that people's racial or cultural

Reprinted by permission of Meg Greenfield from *Newsweek,* 29 September 1975.

make-up is some flaw they should be given a chance to "overcome." We are not, God knows, any longer a nation of closet ethnics; rather we all seem to be rummaging through the ancestral closet in search of the paraphernalia of some special ethnic identity. Two cheers—maybe only one. For the evidence of our eyes tells us that the trend is taking some highly dangerous turns and that it does not represent impulses in our political life that are wholly benign or reassuring.

The academic sociological literature on this subject is, if anything, even less entertaining than most of the ethnic TV shows. But it has a word—"retribalization"—for what is going on. And it offers a wide variety of analyses as to why. Some of these seem plausible to me:

• Class ties based on common economic interest have been weakened. So too have faith and pride in a national destiny. The sense of identity and common purpose each was once able to supply—being a worker, being an American—is now more readily supplied for many people by an ethnic or racial or cultural bond.

• The postwar assertion of rights by many previously left-out groups (blacks, chicanos) has spawned defensive counterclaims and countermobilization on the part of those ethnic groups that feel most directly threatened.

• The second and third generations of families that once felt that "losing" their ethnic identity was a condition of Americanization are seeking to make themselves historically whole by retrieving and acknowledging some part of that identity.

• Government—the newly and vastly enlarged welfare state—has become the cockpit of decisions concerning everything from housing to schooling to abortion that profoundly touches the interests of ethnic groups *as* ethnic groups. And government's newfound willingness to deal with groups of citizens on the basis of their ethnic background has strengthened people's impetus to organize politically along racial or cultural lines.

Mean skirmishes

Back in 1961, the Republican municipal ticket in New York came up with what will always be my favorite campaign song: "You'll be safe in the park/Every night after dark/With Lefkowitz, Gilhooley and Fino ..." Ethnic politics, obviously, is not something brand new, but I think that between the tube and the sociologists and our own everyday experience we can see what is becoming particularly worrisome about it. There is first the prospect of our politics breaking down (even further than it already has) into a series of mean skirmishes between racial, religious and national-origins groups. "Consciousness of kind," as it is known, produces the most visceral and intense kind of loyalties—and also the most visceral and intense kind of enmities.

Breaking down into our original ethnic parts would be a particularly weird way to celebrate the Bicentennial. I suppose that for many of those second- and third-generation Americans now organizing themselves into political blocs, and for many blacks and chicanos as well, all that fife-and-drum business seems like someone else's history. My own forebears, in fact, were still being chased around Europe a century later by a bunch of Cossacks—Kazak and son, as I have come to think of them. But it is worth remembering that what we are about to celebrate is not just an American historical moment, but rather the American idea.

Common bloodstream

That idea seems to me to be equally menaced by the increasing tendency of government, political parties and an array of private institutions to deal formally and officially with individuals on the basis of their ethnic background. In the first place, the precedents aren't very reassuring: blacks in the pre-1954 South, for example, Japanese-Americans on the West Coast. Again, there is a difference between preserving an ethnic heritage and encouraging the state and its far-flung semiofficial boards and bureaus to believe that a common bloodstream or a common accent or a common past creates common, even identical, interests among individuals. Do we really want government and the various institutions that have some power over our affairs to believe that we should be rewarded or penalized or otherwise dealt with on the basis of whether we were born Lassiters or Vitales or Jeffersons or Morgensterns?

It is one thing to come out of the closet, in other words, quite another to walk over the cliff. I get the idea that a lot of people are having trouble telling the difference. That is why, for all its blandness and fatuity, ethnic television makes me uneasy.

to the student : a commentary

Meg Greenfield is a columnist for *Newsweek* and a deputy editorial page editor for the *Washington Post*. As with most of her columns in *Newsweek*, she here provides a fresh and distinctive comment on an aspect of American society. Using the fairly recent flurry of ethnic television programs as a symptom of social change, Greenfield writes with some concern about the implications. She sees in the rash of ethnic shows—most of them situation comedies —signs of cultural fragmentation. The programs may tell us that "ethnic is in," she says, but in the process of producing cultural loyalties they may also have a hand in creating "the most visceral and intense kind of enmities."

Her concern is in direct contradiction to a standard generalization about the media: that they tend to homogenize the audience. The common worry is that television will eventually wipe out accents, regional perspectives, and cultural differences. Greenfield neglects—or rejects—the commonality generated by mass media. There is little doubt that prime time shows have replaced the weather as an easy topic of conversation; one can travel to any town in America and strike up a conversation about Archie Bunker or the Six Million Dollar Man. Television allows us to share, with a frightening and depressing universality, flash phrases like "Sorry about that" and "Sock it to me." As a society we share few things as much as we do television, and that includes whatever representations of ethnicity are packaged for entertainment.

Yet even if we share Greenfield's worry that television may serve to isolate subcultures, what is the alternative? For many years the only portrayal of ethnic minorities in the mass media was primarily rigid and pejorative— Stepin Fetchit, Poncho, and assorted sidekicks who were supposedly funny and consistently inept. At least now minorities are allowed equal characterization—bland and fatuous though it may be, it is a *shared* blandness and fatuity.

Minorities are still stereotyped by the media (stereotype: "something repeated or reproduced without variation . . . conforming to a fixed pattern . . . lacking individual marks or qualities"), but so is the mainstream culture. It has been said that the time constraints of television force the writers and directors into using readily identifiable and understood characters. With only forty-eight minutes (less the twelve minutes of commercials) in which to tell a story, it's argued that there is no time to create complex people. For example: the scene opens with a man standing in front of a blackboard. The man is wearing glasses, holding a pipe, and has leather patches on the sleeves of his tweed jacket. What is he? The writers haven't had to find the time to say "teacher," they used the stereotype. It may have little to do with what most teachers look like, but it allows them plenty of time for the mandatory automobile chase scene.

Minority stereotyping, however, has shifted somewhat in the last decade. According to one recent study of ethnic and sex representation in television dramas, a breakdown of 1,830 character portrayals revealed some interesting patterns.

First, the ethnic groupings (listed as white American, European, black, British, Chicano, and Oriental) did not match those in the national population.

White Americans were slightly overportrayed, and blacks were underrepresented. (Even British characters were portrayed more than black Americans.)

Secondly, there was a gross underrepresentation of females. Except for the Oriental category, where the number of male and female roles were nearly equal, females were portrayed less than 25 percent of the time. In the Chicano category, women were shown in only *two* roles—a nun and a maid!

Thirdly, there was an overrepresentation of all groups in professional and managerial roles, along with underrepresentation in occupations with little prestige. White American males were not shown in significantly higher roles than British, blacks, or Chicanos in major portrayals, but were in higher prestige categories generally. Minority women, however, were portrayed with higher prestige than white females.

Finally, ethnic groups with especially small numbers—American Indians, for example—tended to be portrayed homogeneously, and the greatest percent of minorities appeared in roles that lasted less than three minutes.

To this extent, television is presenting a distorted picture of society. In some areas it follows the expected pattern of stereotyping, yet in others, as with minority women, it seems to overcompensate. The format of ethnic programs undoubtedly falls prey to the same tendencies.

Yet with all the problems—and Greenfield's quite legitimate concerns—without ethnic programs minorities could be condemned, once again, to cultural anonymity. In many ways nonrepresentation in the media is nonexistence. In a rather hackneyed Zen question it's asked: if a tree falls in the forest and no one hears it, did it make a sound? In a similar manner one might ask: if a subculture is not portrayed in the media, does society see it?

Our vision now may not be clear, yet almost all of us have spent some time with the Jeffersons, Rhoda Morgenstern, and Chico and the Man. Whatever complaints we have about such shows—vacuous, silly, devoid of social reality—at least they are complaints that we can level at the medium in general. That, paradoxically, is a form of progress.

LLS

Gerhart Niemeyer

Sex and Violence

The "children's hour" on television has been purged of "sex and violence" by a form of internal censorship. Unorganized censorship, of course, goes on most of the time in most societies, as the words "seemly," "fitting," and "decent" in our language show. Every community of men has a need to protect its commitment to the good, however precarious it may be, by maintaining certain limits on all varieties of expression. All the more remarkable, then, that during the long centuries in which children have been reared on fairy tales and stories of brave men overcoming evil, stories replete with chopped-off heads and cruel punishments (just think of Hansel pushing the witch into the flames), nobody felt it necessary to keep fairy tales from children on account of such violent incidents.

So the problem of "sex and violence" we have today must be new and different, and one wonders whether censorship can solve it. Where standards are generally respected, occasional grossness or pornography may indeed be the suitable business of some watchdog. But the trouble today is that our literary and media production practically centers on "sex" and "violence" (both words in quotation marks because they have today a standing apparently independent of morality).

The phenomenon is recent. The word "sex," together with its repulsive companion "*making* love," has been in general use for about forty years. Today's screen stories, like operettas of old, have a message for which the plot is just a loose framework, and that message is the ever repeated and appallingly similar situations of sex and violence that form "the action." The settings change, patterns remain. Male comes into the presence of female; hungry eyes wander over bodies; nothing more is needed than an inner shrug—"Why not?"—and some small talk; shortly, we see the flesh in the motion of sexual excitement. Afterward, another few casual words, and each goes his way with no more ado than if they had taken a drink together. Violence is similar: a man carrying a gun finds another man thwarting his plans. A trigger is pulled, a body collapses, someone says, "He is dead," and everybody resumes what he has been doing as if nothing had happened.

But consider how stories of violence were told in the past. In *Macbeth*, a drama of dark bloody deeds, every one of the violent actions takes place

Reprinted by permission of Gerhart Niemeyer from *National Review,* 1 August 1975.

off-stage. What we hear and see is the rise of evil passions in the souls of two people, and their similar and yet different ways of deteriorating. Or *Hamlet,* where the violence occurs in plain view, but the drama is about pusillanimity, of which violence is a mere by-product. The way of telling about "sex" (how offensive the word becomes in this place!) is through the clearest of hints in the web of love, as in *Romeo and Juliet:*

Wilt thou be gone? It is not yet near day.
It was the nightingale, and not the lark,
That pierced the fearful hollow of thine ear.
Nightly she sings on yon pomegranate tree.

Or the story of Francesca da Rimini and Paola Malatesta in Dante's *Inferno:*

It was when we read about those longed-for lips now being kissed by such a famous lover, that this one (who shall never leave my side) then kissed my mouth and trembled as he did. . . . That day we read no further.

The subject here is the human soul, stretched between the passions of nature and its intuitions of goodness, so that violence and sex are incidental and derive their meaning from the struggles, strengths, and weaknesses of character.

Today's television has torn off this mantle of meaning. Sex and violence are presented, as it were, in moral nakedness. They are given the character of events in which somehow one hits the rock bottom of reality—they are treated as something ultimate. Ultimate they are, of course, only on the plane of nature separated from anything spiritual. However, sex and violence in the modern media play the role of *the absolute,* meaning the most fundamental, or the most final of realities. From seeing both sex and violence "in the raw," without any connection with good or evil, we are supposed to get a deep "experience" of amoral truth, TV style. In contrast with the fairy tales and Shakespearean dramas of old, today's sex and violence are treated as if by themselves they were fixities in the midst of fluidities, realities from which one could get orientation, the ultimate reasons for all other reasons.

Man, of course, must seek *the absolute* because he is a thinking being requiring meaning for both his actions and his existence. Insofar as we are physical strength, chemical excitement, material facticity, we need no meaning: animals prove the point. It is man's mind that craves to understand the world, the things in it, and himself; and he can understand only in terms of the absolute. We remember how Kant formulated the absolute: "Two things fill the mind with ever new and increasing admiration and awe: the starry heaven above me and the moral law within me." Kant's "starry heaven" stands for the divine creation, and his "moral law" for man's destiny above and beyond nature.

Not everybody agrees with Kant. All the same, he was looking for the absolute in the direction where men have always been looking. Voegelin has defined this direction in terms of "the Beginning" and "the Beyond." But the questions about the Beginning and the response to the Beyond have been systematically destroyed and suppressed, if not by aggressive relativism then by apathetic permissiveness. That does not mean that we have been excused from our quest for the absolute which is the quest for meaning. It means only that instead of rational answers we now get irrational ones, that instead of the divine absolute we now press toward the ridiculous counterfeit absolute of sex/violence. Our writers now feel constrained to wallow in both brutality and pornographic explicitness in order to deserve the label "realistic." And parents, unaware to what extent they are part of the problem, call for the censor.

---

to the student : a commentary

The column by Gerhart Niemeyer is a compact recital of a basic question of censorship: should sex and violence be purged? He plumbs the meaning of each word, pointing out that sex and violence form the action, and both go on as though little or nothing had occurred.

Man, as viewed by television, or popular art, is what we might call generalized man or common-denominator man. The major attention of the entertainment media must, naturally, be directed to the tastes and interests of the public. Is the concept of immature, susceptible man at too low a level? It is a very serious and fundamental question whether the concept of man as a rational being, able to distinguish between truth and error and make up his own mind, is compatible with the concept of entertainment-receiving man, unable to distinguish between truth and error, and dangerously susceptible to whatever doctrine appears in the popular art he experiences.

The television code, which is *supposed* to rule, is as heavily negative as the now outdated motion picture code, which indeed seems to have been a model for some sections of it. But not entirely. As propagator of public morals, the ethical telecaster has obligations similar to those of the movie maker. In his programs, he must respect law and order. Although the code recognizes that crime is a part of the world at large, the ethical telecaster, it says, will not lead the young to believe that crime plays a greater part in life than it actually does. He will portray criminality as "undesirable and unsympathetic." He will uphold law enforcement and the dignity of the law. He will not inspire his viewers to engage in crime, nor will he furnish them with information on criminal techniques.

The ethical telecaster will maintain respect, the code states, "for the sanctity of marriage and the value of the home." By implication, he will uphold what the movie code calls "pure love" and will not portray "impure love": he will not, for example, depict divorce with levity or as a "solution for marital problems." He will not portray illicit sex relations or sexual perversions.

The ethical telecaster will seek to hold in check the baser emotions of his viewers and to shield the viewers from temptation. "The presentation of cruelty, greed, and selfishness as worthy motivations," says the code, "is to be avoided." The ethical telecaster will transmit no scenes involving lascivious dances, indecorous costumes, excessive horror, cruelty to animals, and so forth. He will respect sobriety. "Drunkenness should never be presented as desirable," the code says. "Narcotic addiction shall not be presented except as a vicious habit." Another section forbids the advertising of hard liquor and requires that ads for beer and wine be "in the best of good taste." Gambling can be depicted only when essential to the plot and then only with discretion and moderation.

The ethical telecaster will respect religion. He will emphasize "broad religious truths" rather than "controversial or partisan views." He will respect national feelings by avoiding words, especially slang, derisive of any nationality or national derivation. He will not permit profanity of any sort.

Does television follow this code? Not at all. The spirit of the code is violated daily.

To illustrate the difference between the trivial and the significant in self-censorship, here are two cases quoted by the acceptance department of a broadcast network:

A character in a dramatic script said, "I followed the first commandment: 'Live it up.' "

Second, the network was considering a sponsored religion show to be called something like *Men in Black,* and to feature each week a different clergyman. The network liked the sample scripts and was given to understand that a sponsor was available. But the head of the network, after considerable thought and consultation, said no. He asked, "Where would you put the commercials?" He said that it would be improper and irreverent to sell goods when the audience is in the mood for looking at men of God.

Always, then, the center of a television production rests on a question: will it sell? Moreover, the question of whether a production is a work of art is seldom at issue. As Ernest van den Haag dismissed the audiences:

The circumstances which permit the experience of art are rare in our society anyway, and they cannot be experienced in the audience of the mass media. That audience is dispersed and heterogeneous, and though it listens often, it does so intermittently and is poised to leave if not immediately enthralled and kept amused. . . . And the conditions and conditioning of the audience demand a mad mixture of important and trivial matters, atom bombs, hit tunes, symphonies, sob stories, hotcha girls, round table, and jokes.

Did van den Haag write this contemptuously? Indeed he did. However, it is incorrect to say that all the mass audience is beneath him and other intellectuals. Quite often, after hours of work or simply thinking, some highbrows are exhausted; they are content with entertainment—even the kind that combines sex and violence.

What does the reality do to Niemeyer's argument? Does it mean that whoever prizes and looks for the kind of program that combines divine creation and man's destiny is to be disappointed? It does—because *nearly* every effort to achieve art is foredoomed. Those who can applaud Niemeyer's argument must at the same time recognize the basic questions. Writers for the mass audience do not have in mind the need for art. They have one idea: what will sell? Sex and violence is at the center. It will please many of those who watch.

WLR

Local Television News
in 31 Different Flavors

.

Early this year, a curious phenomenon made its way into the homes of television viewers in Columbus, Ohio. It had happened in New York, Chicago, San Francisco, Los Angeles—where strange things are supposed to happen. But now, it was in Middle America City, U.S.A.

WLWC decided to make a go of it with its own version of the misnomered "happy talk" news format. It was presenting The DeMoss Report with anchorman Hugh DeMoss, sportscaster Jimmy Crum, weatherman Jerry Rasor and his buddy, a bear.

It was Rasor's idea to get the bear. One evening, led by his trainer, the bear ambled up to the anchordesk, put his paws up and introduced himself to the startled DeMoss and Crum. They say Rasor's a pretty funny guy. But he didn't invite the bear back. Instead, on another night, a leprechaun followed Rasor around while he did the weather report. And not too long ago, the Golddiggers helped him give the highs and lows and predict the probability of precipitation.

Rasor and company were not the only ones getting into the act. The usually straight, no-nonsense DeMoss was no longer following the script. He was making conversation with Crum, Rasor and others on the set. The newscast was peppered with a few humorous and not so humorous remarks, some embarrassed and embarrassing pauses, and a few bad starts.

Was this the return of the "Amateur Hour"? The cards and letters were coming in. And the critics were aghast. No, it was just Avco Broadcasting's attempt to snatch some of the elusive, fickle Nielsen points. And executive news producer Scott Lynch was pleased because it was working.

Although the latest Nielsen ratings indicated WLWC was still No. 2, "we are now in an extremely competitive position with the No. 1 station," Lynch said.

This called for a toast. Nielsen ratings are the bread and butter of a television station. The higher a rating a station has, the more viewers it has, the more advertisers will want to advertise, the more a station can get for

Reprinted from THE QUILL, published by The Society of Professional Journalists, Sigma Delta Chi.

the advertisements, and hopefully, the more the station can pour back into its news operation.

Lynch was one of many television producers finding out what some of the larger markets had already known—the viewers were ready for a new television news format.

As Chicago *Tribune* television critic Gary Deeb wrote in a recent column: "TV was long overdue for a change from the tired local news format that found a somber, granite-faced anchorman delivering the news as if he were reading it off stone tablets. There was a godlike, Doomsday quality attached to many local anchormen that was patently ridiculous."

"Viewers are not going for the formality or staginess of the past," says Sam Zelman, CBS vice president for the network's owned-and-operated (O&O) stations. "They want people to level with them."

There are different ways a news team levels with the viewers, producers decided. One way was Eyewitness News.

"In New York, the Eyewitness News concept began in November 1968. Nobody came into the situation with a format in his back-pocket," says Al Primo, vice president of news for the ABC O&O stations and a pioneer in Eyewitness format when he was news director for WABC, New York.

"What we were trying to do was to allow these reporters to come in and tell their own stories, to appear live." Primo's idea is that "the best way to do a news program is to have the reporter who covers a story tell that story to an audience, eliminating all of the middle men in the process. What I knew we didn't want to have was reporters going out, preparing a story, sending the film in, turning it over to a writer who was never at the scene, who then re-edited it, rewrote it, and gave it to the anchorman who read it.

"What we in effect were doing was telling our audience that we had more than three people covering New York. The audience suddenly knew that we were going to send our people out to cover a story and come back and tell them that story directly," Primo says.

The idea caught on. Many ABC affiliates took up the format and got their reporters on the air. And they entitled their program "Eyewitness News." Viewers all over the country were seeing field reporters who were saying, "I was there and here's what happened."

Other stations took a different tack—the Walter-Cronkite-in-the-news-room-where-we-get-the-reports-on-what's-been-happening   approach. Some stations used an on-air set that resembled a newsroom. But the purists took the cameras directly into the clatter, clutter and chaos of the womb of journalists.

"It gives the viewer the feeling of being close, not to where the news is made but to where it is put together," Columbus' Lynch says.

It's all part of using television's many potentials. TV, after all, is a very personal medium. And now, the viewers not only could get the reports and hear the reporters themselves, they could see them and where they worked. And soon, they would be seeing *how* they worked together.

NBC Vice President Robert Mulholland says it stemmed from the Huntley-Brinkley Report—"two people who said 'good evening' to each other and said each other's names. Most of the viewing public think that those two guys ad-libbed to each other, talked back and forth. The fact of the matter is, Chet Huntley and David Brinkley never ad-libbed to each other. Yet, in the viewer's mind, the relationship of warmth, friendliness, interest in each other, grew."

It is difficult to say whether the network or local news stations had the first on-air interaction among on-air personalities. Credit or blame for the innovation has been placed randomly throughout the country. It may have sprung up simultaneously and accidentally at several television stations.

"The casual approach developed naturally," according to Primo. "If there are more than three people in the room, you tend to develop a sort of rapport or informality with those people after a certain period."

Joel Daly, who is with the No. 1 station in Chicago, says that's the way he fell into it. When he was with a station in northern Ohio, Daly says, he and another newsman developed a friendship outside the station and their rapport became evident on the air. They would exchange comments during the newscast, or Daly would poke fun at his partner. "It was natural," he says. And the idea went over well.

Later, he and his partner were asked to go to Chicago as a team. They would carry their informal, unusual format into a larger market, the station said. Daly went. But his friend did not. The station, which wanted co-anchormen, had a problem. Could WLS find a partner for Daly who could develop a natural rapport and informality? The station finally did. But it wasn't a simple task.

"The idea is that the interaction has to be 'real,' " said Clayton Vaughn, news director for KOTV, Tulsa, Okla. "The audience is going to know if you're putting them on. They're just not going to buy it."

He says they're not buying it at KABC in Los Angeles, where Vaughn was an on-air newsman.

But KABC will keep on bringing in various persons, plugging them into the co-anchor spots until something clicks. The station is lucky, he says, because it has the money to spend to find the right combination of person-alities. "If you don't have the budget . . . go with one anchor. You get rid of 80 per cent of your problems that way."

Some stations, Daly says, are going about the process of personalizing their news programs the wrong way. "They look at us and they think you have to have the fatherly figure, a younger guy, a nutty weatherman and an amiable sportscaster." But, there is no formula to the personalities, he says.

Others agree. What you should have, they say, are four persons who can relate to each other on the air. But it's not a bad idea to get some people the viewers can relate to—some age and experience, some youth and idealism, friendliness, and the ever-popular "fall guy."

Yukky weather

This is usually the weatherman. He's the one who usually takes the blame for the bad news, Daly says. Daly's news director John Mies says, "Weather is not hard news. And a weatherman is not a newscaster." So John Coleman can yuk it up, but only when the weather isn't serious, Daly says.

Since the weather in Chicago is seldom good, often bad, but not serious, Coleman's got a job on his hands. To make his presentation more palatable, he's been known to stand on his head during the weather. Or, just to break up the tension, he might whip wads of paper around the studio. He has a lot of fun.

And so do other weathermen. Vaughn's forecaster in Tulsa exchanges pleasantries with a puppet. Another Chicago weatherman plays the straight man to a videotape version of himself as a fall guy. And Rasor, in Columbus, has his guest assistants. A weatherman in Albuquerque is known there for his colorful barnyard set which at one time was complete with live chickens and pigs.

What Daly and Vaughn and many others using the informal approach are concerned about is that the "real," "personal" or "human" news show presentations will inadvertently be twisted into the so-called "happy talk," or worse yet, tabloid formats.

"Happy talk" is a difficult term to define. Morry Roth is said to have coined the term when he first made observations on the new television formats for *Variety*. Television newsland was not pleased.

"The man," says Primo of Roth, "is not to be criticized for inventing it, because that magazine uses that kind of jargon. It's a show business magazine. The unfortunate thing is that it has been picked up . . . and used unsparingly."

Critic Deeb writes that "happy talk" was designed "to appeal to viewers who'd rather see more good news than bad, with a vaudeville show on the side." And he accuses Daly's station of falling into the format with "slapstick boorishness" and "marshmallow commentaries."

News Director Mies replies, "We try to make the news understandable and appealing to the audience in terms of what it means to them. . . . The audience responds to our people because we talk *to* them rather than *down* to them."

Daly says it's the dilemma of hanging onto an audience while trying to present the news.

"Television is primarily an entertainment medium," Daly says. "The news portion is 10 per cent of local programming time. It exists in this environment of trivial entertainment—escape dramas, situation comedies, etc. We have to coexist in the milieu. We have to hold the viewer's attention."

Relating to the audience, he says, is a way to hold that attention. "If something human happens within the format, we should be able to react as humans—to smile, to use an aside."

"But," says Don Alloway, of the publicity department for ABC network news, "at certain times and at certain places you get out there and walk a very, very fine line between news and show biz. You've got to have a good news director and a good news team to keep the two separate."

Daly admits that sometimes the situation gets out of hand on the air. He says he didn't particularly care for the tuxedoed on-air celebration of a sixth anniversary. And there are jokes that might be unnecessary, he says. And sometimes the team has a bad night and the exchanges fall flat. But, "we try to act as we would when we are invited into someone's home —with responsibility," he says.

A public misunderstanding

ABC's Primo says some of the criticism of the informal format may lie with the audience. "The informality tends to come more with the sports person and the weatherman. That has been the damaging aspect. People don't distinguish this from the more serious part of (the) news program." Primo was referring to the audience, but Daly and Vaughn say there are local news producers who don't understand the purpose or design of the informal news broadcast. They are the "happy talk" stations which are giving the others a bad name, they say.

"They see us," says Daly, "and they think they've got the formula. They think they have to script it . . . that they *have* to do some jokes and gimmicks."

Lynch says when WLWC first began the new format, "we sort of overreacted." The on-air personalities felt they had to say something— make a comment, tell a joke or one-liner. It was an uncomfortable situation, he says. "We're doing less of that now."

WLWC and other stations like it are learning what the "informality" purists are screaming about. There apparently is hope for them. But Lee

Hanna, vice president of news for NBC O&O stations, is worried about something else.

"The thing that disturbs me is the headlong rush to emulate, duplicate," he says. NBC O&O's are the holdouts in the trend toward informality. They have retained the formal format.

"The thing that *really* disturbs me is the proliferation of stations who depend on style rather than substance. That goes directly to this business of consultants—to go into a market to say here's a formula designed by geniuses to be carried out by idiots. Because they can say: *you* do 60 stories in 30 minutes, and *you* do this little package of film clips to be glued together with a chuckle, and make sure the chit-chat between the anchorman and the weatherman lasts 15 seconds," Hanna says.

The two major consulting firms are Frank N. Magid Associates, Iowa, and McHugh and Hoffman, Inc., Washington. They are hired by local news stations to determine what sort of audience the station has, what sort of audience it would like to have and how it can get it. Their recommendations often are based on how other stations in similar circumstances succeeded in other cities.

The consultants contend they never make any recommendations on the content of the news program—merely the packaging.

ABC's O&O's use both consulting firms, Primo says. "On our five stations, no consultant gives journalistic advice—offers none, none is taken. The job of an outside consultant is to measure the impact of your news program on the audience it serves . . . to try to question a sample of people in your audience as to their impressions of what you're doing on the station. And to try to help determine for us what they consider to be the most important problems of the community."

Primo says he doesn't think a consultant should tell a station how to make its news more entertaining. "There are some charges, perhaps well-founded, by smaller stations that consultants do in fact get involved with journalistic judgment," Primo says. "If they do, I think that's a terrible mistake. There's a fine line, here. All of us here guard very jealously our dealings with them. We do not use consultants as news directors."

Getting to management

NBC's Hanna has no use for the consulting firms. "I have one of these monitoring reports from one of these so-called consultants, and you read that and I challenge you to find one reference to good journalism. No, it's simply the business of sort of slavishly following a formula."

Then Hanna recites a typical formula. "The opening story must run 45 seconds, and it must be followed by three stories that run 15 seconds each, followed by something in the fast film section, then there's got to be a laugh, then there's got to be . . . That's sickening. A client of one of these consultants will spend $40,000 or $50,000 for one of these reports. If they would spend that much on just their news operations, think about how much more they could accomplish. But this is a quick-buck sort of situation. These things don't last. I'd say it's like a Chinese meal, except I don't want to give Chinese food a bad name.

"The kind of thing Mike Wallace did on "60 Minutes," the kind of thing Rick Townley did in *TV Guide,* those are things that might come through to station management—that they are involved in a quick, slick, fast-buck type of situation. There is no way to build a valuable, interesting, vital news operation by cosmetic kinds of solutions. You do it with good reporters, smart news directors and with film. There is a lack of enterprise, and that is what is sad."

Station WBRZ in Baton Rouge, La., used the services of Magid not too long ago. Their complaint was not that the firm was involving itself with the news.

"We got away from the formula because we found we were getting more into the 'happy talk' than into the journalism aspect," says investigative reporter John Spain. "Magid says say it even if you don't have anything to say."

That attitude is disturbing to many on-air journalists. Pity the personality who finds he or she has read through the news too quickly and is left with 12 seconds to ad-lib and nothing to say.

"The occasion has happened, yes," says Roger Grimsby, co-anchorman for New York City's top-rated station, WABC. "I've made mistakes that could be criticized as far as taste or judgment are concerned. There has been something flipped through the back of my mind and I spit it out before realizing its full implication."

Grimsby feels there is an ever-present compulsion in TV newsrooms to play "can you top this." "A person should always remind himself that you don't have to be funny to do a good news program. If there is any humor in a program, it should be the frosting not the cake. And what was happening here (at WABC) for awhile was that even the assignment desk was trying to think funny. . . .

"However, unlike some of those who have emulated the Eyewitness News show in New York, the people on our program rarely talk to each other," Grimsby says. "It's very presumptuous, I think, that anybody at home would be interested in what your private life is like or whatever these other news people talk about. But occasionally I'll throw in a one-liner about what one of the other reporters may have reported or something my co-anchorman may have said. If the line doesn't work, it's still over in such a hurry that you don't dwell on it, and it doesn't seem contrived."

But "forget all that," Grimsby says. "We should cover the news better than anyone else—and then do it differently."

The combination of the two is going to grab the audience.

"We still look upon news as something a television station does as a public service," Primo says. "That's still the basic philosophy of why we do news programs. It has never changed. . . . The other thing that has not changed is that the basic principles of journalism applied then also apply now. What has changed, and I think changed for the good, is the method of presentation.

"What we try to do is never compromise our essential product," he says.

"The primary job is to give the news," says Daly. The ha-ha school of journalism is not going to make it. "If all you have are jokes, you won't last. To think you can do it with one-liners is demeaning to the audience."

At the top of the hill

Then station KGO in San Francisco must be the exception to the rule. It has the top-rated news program in the city. In fact, it has a higher rating than the other two stations put together. Saying KGO is doing it "differently" is an understatement.

Mike Wallace, on the CBS program "60 Minutes," recently sampled KGO's format and news content. These are excerpts: "And the latest on the little old lady who looked at the male nude foldouts of Jim Brown and John Davidson and said, . . . the congressman's bill, by the way, would not outlaw massaging arms, hands and legs, but would prohibit those ladies from tickling your fancy. . . ."

Wallace said, "On Thursday, January 24th, viewers who watched KGO didn't get much of what was happening in the world that day. KGO had only 58 seconds of national news, no foreign news. What they did have time for was the nude centerfold in *Cosmopolitan* magazine, the *Playgirl* mother of the month with another nude male, nudity on the beach, and the 'Nashville Stomper'—a man who had a fetish about stepping on women's insteps."

The station manager responded to Wallace's criticism of KGO's tabloid format. "The easiest thing to criticize is the news. We could sit around and do pontifical kinds of news day in and day out and we'd be back where we were in the old days when we were trying to be very clever and profound about news and died since nobody ever watched us."

The new format was killing the competition, and one of them, KPIX, turned with the tide, according to Wallace. News Director Jim VanMessel told him, "You don't save souls in an empty church."

But the city's cellar-dwelling station, KRON, retained its formal format. It was determined to resist the urge to compete. According to the news director, the station was "not going to bastardize our news for ratings."

San Francisco is an example of the extreme lengths a television station might go to grab an audience. The attitude is a throwback to the beginning of tabloid newspapers—screaming headlines, sex-sin-blood. Critics called it pandering to the baser instincts. The style sold newspapers and built empires. And it killed off some good, "straight" newspapers. But some of them survived. And NBC's Lee Hanna thinks some of the "straight" news broadcasts will survive, too.

Fifteen months ago, WNBC in New York was at the bottom of the charts, Hanna says. "We had an asterisk for a rating. Do you know what an asterisk means? No measurable audience. Our average rating was 2.3.

"Last week (late March) we had a share of about a 15. CBS had a share of 19, and ABC had a share of 23," Hanna says. "So you can see we're still far behind. But we have had a 300 per cent increase in our audience, and we haven't done it with laughter, jokes or gags or cosmetics. You don't have to be steamrolled into duplicating what the other guy is doing simply because he is doing it successfully."

But, he says, that doesn't mean the other formats shouldn't exist—even the tabloid format. "There's room for all—just as there's legitimate reason for the New York *Daily News* to sit side by side with the New York *Times*. There are different audiences. Why isn't there room for a tabloid-style newscast to go along with a more conservative newscast?"

Reasoner's reasoning

ABC's Harry Reasoner hopes television will continue to develop a style as newspapers did. "Occasionally, I see some revolting examples around the country of other stations doing the same kind of thing. I don't think it's the final corruption of journalism, nor do I think it's the final solution to journalism's problems.

"The New York *Times* has 500,000 circulation while the *Daily News* has 2 million. That, I suppose, is roughly the ratio of appeal of tabloid journalism to the more serious form. But what has happened over the years in newspapers, and what I hope would happen with television, is that eventually the tabloid form can also be serious. In other words, you can be bright, you can be brief, you can appeal to a mass audience, and at the same time gradually begin to uphold some principles."

Your guide to happy viewing

By now you've noticed that local television news programs aren't what they used to be—carbon copies (or videotape recordings, for that matter) of each other. Knowing you might like to discuss this phenomenon at future cocktail parties or other gatherings journalists attend, we give you this glossary of terms to facilitate discussion. It is by no means complete, since producers could come up with something revolutionary at any time. It also does not suggest that every news program will fall neatly into one category because 1) journalists hate labels, 2) some stations think a combination of previously successful formats have a synergetic effect, 3) some stations haven't decided they want to go with any of them, or 4) all of the above. If you find none of the terms suffice, make something up.

Formal format [*nearly obsolete*]—1. Godlike, Doomsday   2. Olympian 3. Format in which the anchorman sits in front of the camera and reads the news, the sportscaster and weatherman do same   4. No conversation between on-air personalities   5. No nonsense   6. No off-the-cuff or scripted remarks about recent haircuts, vacations, cute stories, etc.

Eyewitness news—1. Format in which station proves it had a reporter on the scene and the news did not come from wire services or the newspaper 2. Reporter has two minutes on camera to tell the story, preferably with appropriate background (on berm of highway for road construction story, knee-deep in water on floods, on street during lunch hour if interviewing the mayor, etc.); or reporter can be brought on newsroom set to tell anchorman the story (*see In-the-Newsroom Set*)

In-the-newsroom set—1. On-air personalities reporting from their natural working habitat—the busy newsroom (include cluttered desks, ringing phones and clacking wire machines)   2. Appears to the viewer to be actual newsroom, but can be staged.

Informal format—1. On-air personalities may show they have personality   2. On-air personalities permitted to look at each other and exchange comments   3. Weatherman may wear appropriate clothing to aid viewers in choosing proper garb should they wish to dash outdoors midway through the broadcast (discretion is urged when reporting on extremely warm weather)   4. Weatherman must also qualify as fall guy.

Happy talk [*derogatory*]—1. Of the ha-ha school of journalism   2. Jokes, slap-stick and other comedy spiced up with occasional news reports 3. More good news than bad with marshmallow commentaries and vaudeville atmosphere.

Tabloid news [*very derogatory*]—1. Story or film value based on sex, sin, blood, vulgarity or deviance   2. Variation of Happy Talk whereby jokes are written by former burlesque comedians   3. No news makes good news.

to the student: a commentary

Quill, the magazine for journalists published by Sigma Delta Chi, has published a wide-ranging report on broadcast journalism. Halina Czerniejewski and Charles Long, the associate editor and the editor of *Quill,* have sampled what is being broadcast almost everywhere.

Their report does not necessarily favor the trend in television, nor are we favorable. At its beginning we were disappointed because television news was so short. The local news and the network news programs were limited to fifteen minutes. A story would run one minute and fifty-eight seconds or even fifty-four seconds. On occasion, it went as far as two minutes, and very occasionally a story would run almost three minutes.

Then came the expansion of programs to thirty minutes, which seemed to give broadcasters plenty of time to devote more reporting to each story. Instead, the thirty-minute news program, which works out to about twenty-four minutes of news with six minutes given to commercials, continued to restrict their broadcast stories. They simply reported more stories. As a consequence, they are reporting so little about each subject that distortion is almost inevitable.

When, for example, Carl Stern of NBC was reporting the 1976 trial of Patty Hearst, there were days during which NBC would not allow him on the air. The NBC executives had decided that there was too much of Patty Hearst. When Stern was on the air one day, the executives gave him exactly one minute and thirteen seconds. In that time he could report in exactly *eight* sentences. How much could he say? What did he leave out?

Because they work in a medium devoted primarily to entertainment, and because ratings must be high, nearly all television journalists are resigned to presenting news as another kind of entertainment. They must be satisfied with the knowledge that more Americans rely on television for most of the news they receive than on any other medium—although, like David Brinkley of NBC, they may reflect that "When it comes to covering news in any thorough and detailed way, we are just not in the ball game, and we know it."

Even television stations that have expanded their news programs and have hired more reporters to cover additional stories tend to employ news generalists rather than specialists. Instead of employing, say, a political reporter, most stations prefer a generalist, someone who can report almost anything. Except for political journalists here and there and a few other specialists, not many broadcast journalists are equipped to interpret the news. None can report fully. Instead of covering regular beats or specialties—such as science, the environment, urban affairs—as most print journalists do, most broadcast reporters jump from subject to subject, seldom staying with one long enough to clarify events and trends.

The knowledge of the broadcast journalists would have increased substantially had they called on the same sources day by day. But because they are expected to check with everything from a visiting movie star to the local fire department, they cannot interpret political news—to explain and to clarify it —because they have neither the ability to concentrate on politics nor the time on the air to develop it. They are glib, and they *sound* fine, but they report more simply than the increasing complexity of the news warrants. Many of them are worlds away from the meaning of what they report. The viewers who do not read the metropolitan newspapers or the national magazines— and they are reading newspapers less and less—are actually becoming more confused because of the seeming simplicity of television.

Even when the importance of a political subject seems to warrant more time than television gives most stories, broadcasters fear that the attention of the audience will wander during long reports. As Walter Scott, chairman of the board of NBC, has observed, "Because television is a visual medium, it may scant the background and significance of events to focus on the outward appearance—the comings and goings of statesmen instead of the issue that confronts them."

When Serena Wade and Wilbur Schramm of Stanford studied the mass media, they came to this conclusion: "Television is more likely to be the major source of public affairs information for females, non-whites, and farm and blue-collar workers with little education than for others; whereas the print media are more likely to be the major source for the highly educated groups, white, male, professional, managerial and white-collar workers, and high-income groups than for others." It is understandable that we cringe at the thought: a preponderant majority depends on television.

Fortunately, one aspect of television news is encouraging. Although network news has much the same time limit that local stations have—almost as though the executives are saying, "You can't give it two minutes; the span of the audience attention is *short*"—there are excellent specialists in network news. Both Fred Graham of CBS and Carl Stern of NBC are reporter-lawyers, men who concentrate on trials and report on justice, and there are also many able political reporters. Such journalists have developed a range of expertise that enables them occasionally to report brilliantly in spite of the crushing time limit.

Moreover, while stations have been trying nearly every format imaginable, the three networks have stood fast. All the networks long ago adopted eyewitness news or something close to an in-the-newsroom set (see the section entitled "Your Guide to Happy Viewing"), but they broadcast nothing like the happy talk format. Will they continue to be journalists rather than quasi-comedians? We certainly hope so. We hope that, unlike the local newscasters, they will continue to deserve the name journalist.

WLR

William L. Rivers

Some Things You Should Know about Cable

Cable began by serving sparsely populated areas, especially where the terrain is uneven. Robert J. Tarlton, who owned a small radio sales and service shop in Lansford, Pennsylvania, began to sell TV sets when they became available in the late 1940s. (The same year, cable also started in Oregon.) Because the town is in the shadow of a mountain, and the nearest television stations were in Philadelphia, sixty-five miles away, the signals reaching Lansford were weak, and television reception was fuzzy. Tarlton had trouble selling television sets. He tried to solve the problem by setting up individual antennas on the mountain for some of his customers. Encouraged by a degree of success, he and several friends established the Panther Valley Television Company in 1949 and set up a master antenna atop the mountain. The weak signals from Philadelphia were picked up, fed into an amplifier to strengthen them, then fed into a cable. Lansford homes were hooked to the cable for an installation charge of $125 and a monthly service charge of $3. Tarlton's sales of television sets increased almost immediately. Panther Valley Television now provides twelve channels to about 3,000 homes in Lansford and a few other Pennsylvania hill towns. Tarlton is president of Panther Valley and another cable system.

Although the new technology that continues to grow up around cable is complex—especially the computer-based facilities that will enhance information flow for two-way communication—the cable systems themselves are much like Tarlton's original rig. A tower is erected in a place that promises good reception, an antenna system is installed on the tower, and a "headend" building is constructed at the base to amplify the signals and to rechannel UHF signals into VHF channels. Some operators import distant signals through a relay system of microwave transmitters, then place amplifiers along the trunkline that runs to residential areas to preserve the strength of the signals after they leave the headend. Those cable operators who charge installation fees usually charge less than Tarlton charged his first customers—an average of $20—and the monthly charge is usually more, an average of about $5.

Technology: a sketch

It is essential to describe the difference between over-the-air broadcasting and cable.

At the two ends of the broadcasting system, over-the-air television and cable television are the same. At one end a camera sees and hears a scene and encodes it in the form of an electric current. At the other end the current is decoded by the television set, the picture and sound becoming frame after frame of the scene on a cathode ray tube.

The difference between conventional television and cable television is the middle of the process, in which scene and sound are transmitted from the camera to the set. At the risk of oversimplifying, over-the-air television uses the airwaves for transmission; cable television uses a pair of wires or a coaxial cable.

In the over-the-air system, a transmitting antenna radiates an electro-magnetic wave. As a rule, any television set within about fifty miles that is tuned to the proper wavelength can intercept the wave and transform it into picture and sound. Because the wave spreads out and loses energy as it travels, the wave becomes weaker the farther the set is from the antenna. Hilly or mountainous terrain, or even tall buildings, can affect reception over sets that are much closer than fifty miles from the transmitter. This is transmission by radiation.

Pictures and sounds can also be transmitted over a pair of wires or cable. (Even the radiation system uses it in a limited way. The television signal goes from the camera to the transmitter by wire, then when it reaches the receiving antenna by radiation it travels by wire to the set.) The pure cable system uses wire transmission throughout, never relying on radiation.

Just as a radiated signal loses strength as it travels (eventually, the wave is also blocked from the antenna by the curvature of the earth), a television signal traveling along a cable loses strength, not because it spreads out (the cable keeps the wave the same size along its length), but because of losses in the cable conduction. Amplifiers must be inserted along a cable trunk line, others must be used to bridge the passage from the trunk line to the feeder lines that sprout into neighborhoods, and still others are often inserted where drop lines to individual homes come off the feeder lines.

Cable transmission is a much more versatile system than radiation. Filters can be used to block part of the band so that only certain households can have access to one or more channels. For example, if one channel were reserved for physicians, filters make it possible to present programs exclusively for them. Other electronic devices can be used to limit the user's access to certain channels that can be controlled from the headend.

The ability to remotely control access to channels is one of the most important qualities of cable. It allows pay-TV. Transmission of special programs to households that do not pay can be blocked.

The coming of the threat

In the days of Tarlton and other pioneers in small-town America, *no one* objected to their ventures or attempted to regulate them in any meaningful way. Certainly the over-the-air broadcasters did not object. Cable companies served out-of-the-mainstream areas that could not receive sharp pictures; their cables enlarged the audience for over-the-air broadcasters. As long as cable systems served small towns that had no stations, the growth of cable was valuable to broadcasters. Los Angeles broadcasters were quite happy, for example, that an entrepreneur in Palm Springs set up a cable operation that brought their seven VHF and three UHF channels to Palm Springs.

The value to the entrepreneurs and their freedom in those early days is illustrated by the career of Milton Shapp, who started his cable operations in 1950 with $500 and later sold his interest for a reported $10 million (and still later became governor of Pennsylvania).

When the cable began to move from the small town to the city, it became a threat to broadcasters in the city. Many cities began to franchise cable companies. A cable company began operations in San Diego, a city with a population of more than 600,000 already served by three television stations, and brought in all the Los Angeles stations. Residents of San Diego signed up for cable by the thousands, paying a $19.95 installation charge and $5.50 a month. The result, of course, was that much of the audience for the San Diego stations was drained off. Cable had proved that it could fragment audiences.

These and similar events in other large cities during the late 1950s and early 1960s caused broadcasters to appeal for protection to Congress and to the Federal Communications Commission (FCC). The FCC decided in 1959 that it had nothing to do with cable operations. But partly because of congressional pressure (a Senate bill to require the FCC to license cable operators failed narrowly), partly because of pressure from broadcasters, and partly because the importance of cable became more apparent, the FCC decided in 1966 that it did have jurisdiction over cable systems. Court decisions upheld the commission's authority.

But the movement of federal authority into the cable field by no means removed the burden from—and the potential for significant service of—the cities. Nearly all the decisions the FCC made in the 1960s had one purpose: to protect over-the-air broadcasters. Although the FCC first tightened restrictions, it is now loosening its hold somewhat.

The municipal record

The cities decide who provides cable service and what is required of the cable operator. What happened in many cities can be broadly illustrated by the differing approaches in two small suburban cities that are only a few miles from each other in the shadow of San Francisco.

In part because the city manager of that time was experienced in electronics and eager to bring cable to San Bruno, in 1966 city officials commissioned Stanford Research Institute to conduct a marketing survey to gauge citizen interest. The survey indicated that 60 to 65 percent of San Bruno residents would hook up to a cable system. Why could not the city itself provide cable service? The attitude of the officials was that the city should provide utilities as inexpensively as possible and that franchising a cable system to a company would result in higher costs to residents. (The only San Bruno service that is franchised is garbage collection.) Reasoning that even if too many troubles developed the investment would be safe because the city could sell out to a cable operator and thus recapture the original investment, the officials decided that San Bruno should establish its own operation.

Trouble came immediately. Engineering plans and specifications were drawn up by a company with headquarters in Philadelphia. The uneven terrain in and around San Bruno required stronger signals than the plans provided. The plans had to be drawn again.

Moreover, finding qualified cable workers and luring them into civil service jobs was difficult. The inexperience of nearly everyone involved created other problems. They were overoptimistic about timing. It took them eighteen months to prepare the poles for wiring. Even then they had not foreseen the problem of arranging for trimming trees to clear the way for the wires to homes. That cost $17,000. The telephone company underestimated by $23,000 the cost of clearing space on poles for wiring. Thus, the total additional cost was $40,000.

Nonetheless, the city retained ownership of the twenty-channel system at a cost of about $800,000, which came from Water Development loans and the General Fund. Officials believe that the investment will be repaid in ten years and that the city will make an annual profit of $180,000. It will be used to reduce taxes and cable subscription charges.

The monthly service charge is among the lowest in the San Francisco Bay Area, $4.75. A subscriber is charged $1 for each additional TV set that is hooked to the system, and $1 a month if he chooses to hook up to a radio outlet that will bring in twenty FM channels. Early subscribers were charged only $7.95 for hooking up. Later installations cost $15.

In September, 1971, San Bruno began operating twelve of its channels in one section of the city. It was believed to be the first municipally owned system operating in California, and one of the first in the country.

The more conventional cable system in Redwood City has had more conventional problems. It is instructive to consider those that came in view during several meetings of the city council.

The Redwood City Council first awarded the franchise to a company that accepted it, then withdrew. In August, 1967, the council voted to grant the franchise to Peninsula Cable TV. The report of the city manager favored the arrangement, which would bring in revenues for the company estimated at $30,000 a month, of which Redwood City would receive $1,330 a month. The company agreed to complete all installations, provide service, and "make service available to all developed parcels" by December 17, 1969.

By February, 1970, problems were piled atop one another. It was revealed that as a result of the city-company partnership that grew out of the franchise, the city had allowed Peninsula Cable to use municipal stationery to sell its services. It was also revealed that city council members in areas served by Peninsula Cable were receiving free service from the company—whereupon the Redwood City Council members announced that they expected to be billed.

At the meeting of February 23, 1970, Mayor Robert C. Bury said that he was disturbed by the operations of Peninsula Cable because many residents were complaining about poor service. Council member Mary Henderson said that the city should consider terminating the franchise. The deadline for completing installations and providing service had passed two months before, and yet it was obvious that the company had not met it. The relevant city ordinance required the company to meet the "highest standards" in the industry, she said, but it did not even have a high-quality master antenna. Some residents had been receiving such poor service, she added, that they had canceled their subscriptions. The general manager of Peninsula Cable said that an unusually heavy demand for the service had resulted in a backlog of 1,400 installation requests.

In April, 1970, Peninsula Cable TV requested from the Redwood City Council a $175,000 reduction in its performance bond. The city manager supported the company, saying that there had been "substantial" compliance with the terms of the agreement. The council voted to grant the request over the dissents of three members who said that there were serious questions about the performance of the company.

These experiences suggest some of the problems that grow out of cable franchising. There are, of course, many others. The city of Sunnyvale, which is about fifteen miles from Redwood City, reached a franchise agreement with a company that promised to run its cables underground. When the work was well under way, company executives said that underground installation was too expensive. Sunnyvale officials then allowed overhead installation in some parts of the city, much to the dismay of many residents—especially those who found workmen parking in their driveways, cutting limbs from trees, and trampling their gardens to set up the overhead system.

So many cable companies have trouble finding qualified workers that installations are much slower than anyone expected, and the service is often shoddy. The turnover in cable company personnel is so high that city officials may deal with two or three different general managers in a short period. In Redwood City, frequent and unannounced changes in the management personnel of Peninsula Cable TV, council member Henderson said, "made accountability a joke and buck-passing a regular event." Most of the city leaders of many municipalities who envisioned—and were promised—immense municipal revenues from franchise agreements have found that the money is slow in coming.

Action by the FCC

The Federal Communications Commission eventually took note of the growing number of scandals in cable franchising. TelePrompter, the largest cable operator in the United States, and its chief executive officer were convicted of bribery. The mayor and a city councilman in Johnstown, Pennsylvania, pleaded guilty to federal charges based on their receiving payment of $15,000 to get the cable franchise in Johnstown. (Although the cable operators admitted making the payment, they claimed the money was not a bribe but was extorted.) The award in 1968 of a cable franchise in Trenton, New Jersey, led to the indictment for extortion of four former city officials. Convictions, indictments, and conflicts of interest on the part of city officials involving franchise awards became almost commonplace.

Many other cases were less than criminal but surely slighted the public interest. Too many city officials ignored the potential for community service that cable represents and treated franchising as no more than a source of additional revenue. Few gave any attention to a critical concern: the number of channels provided by cable systems. Studying sixty-six franchises awarded in New Jersey, a group of Princeton investigators found that thirty-two did not specify a minimum number of channels, and nineteen others specified twelve channels or fewer. Forty-five of the sixty-six did not require that channel time be made available for public access. Judging by similar studies in other states, this is probably typical.

Too few city leaders guarded adequately against the "no show" franchise winner: the speculator who had no intention of building a system but aimed to sell his rights for a substantial profit. Nor did they protect the public interest by limiting franchises to reasonable periods. In New Jersey and New York, most of the franchises run for twenty years or more, some for fifty years.

This sad record pushed the FCC further into the cable field. In 1972, the commission issued a far-reaching set of rules that recognized the hapless record of the cities by setting minimum standards for franchising. In the top 100 markets, cable operators must provide at least twenty channels, and for every channel devoted to showing the programs of over-the-air broadcasters, another must be provided for other purposes. Each system in the top 100 markets must make a public access channel available without charge on a first-come, first-served basis (cable operators cannot censor the access channel or present advertising on it, and they must maintain production facilities for those using it).

Many groups had urged the commission to give special priority to education on cable. The National Education Association was especially vigorous, reminding the commissioners that in the 1940s public policy dictated that 20 percent of FM radio frequencies be set aside for educational and other noncommercial uses. When new broadcast television channels were established in the early 1950s, approximately 20 percent were reserved for education. NEA recommended that 20 percent of any cable system's capacity be reserved for "educational, instructional, civic and cultural applications." The commission refused to follow this recommendation, but did require that all cable systems carry the programming of all local educational stations, and allowed them to carry any number of foreign language stations. Perhaps more important, the commission required that cable operators reserve one channel for educational use and another for the use of local government.

In addition, all systems must be set up for return (or two-way) communications on "at least a non-voice basis." (This means that the least a cable operator can provide is a two-way system that enables the user to make digital responses so that he can answer a question Yes or No. More sophisticated systems allow voice conversations.)

The FCC ruled also that cable systems must begin construction within one year, and that facilities must be extended to at least 20 percent of the franchise area each succeeding year. It recommended that franchises run no more than fifteen years and required that franchising authorities demonstrate justification when the fees they collect from cable operators amount to more than 3 percent of gross receipts.

Significantly, the commission did *not* take from the cities their right to grant franchises. Acknowledging that federal licensing of cable systems (as broadcasters are licensed) would be an "unmanageable burden," the commission cited the value of local control and reserved for itself only the granting of certificates of compliance. These are to be issued after the franchise is granted and the cable operator has stated that he will comply with commission rules.

In effect, in addition to protecting the structure of over-the-air broadcasting, the FCC has set minimum standards for franchising and cable operation. These rules have established what the FCC has rightly described as a "deliberately structured dualism." The FCC itself is, of course, one pole of the dual authority. Almost everywhere, local government is the other.

Cable and the other media

How is cable television making a place for itself in the network of mass communication? It should be obvious from the defensive actions of over-the-air broadcasters and the protective reaction of the FCC that broadcast television is the medium that has the most to lose from the full development of cable. The FCC rules have so far prevented cable from developing fully as a commercial venture in the great urban centers, although the new rules are expected to permit this development to proceed. But to limit the discussion to development of cable as a commercial venture bypasses a more important analysis.

One of the most important distinguishing characteristics of mass communication is that it is mostly one-way. Seldom do the mass media provide quick and easy methods for the reader, viewer, or listener to talk back, to ask questions, or to obtain clarification. A newspaper or magazine reader can write a letter to the editor or to an advice columnist which *may* be printed and answered. A radio listener or television viewer *may* participate in a call-in program or respond to broadcast editorials. But anyone who tries to participate fully in public affairs knows that these are usually weak systems of response and involvement.

The second important characteristic of mass communication is that most of the media are addressed to some mythical modal point at which the largest number of people cluster. It is seldom the lowest common denominator, and thus it leaves out those at the lower end of the range. It does not approach the higher end, and thus leaves out a substantial number there. Because of their appeal to special interests, radio, magazines, and books are more likely than the other media to give their audiences a sense of participation. But no mass medium offers the intimacy of a message addressed to an *individual* who can respond. Cable TV provides that opportunity.

---

to the student: a commentary

William Rivers's article sketches some basic information about cable. The threat that cable may pose to the major networks is explored further in the following article on pay television. But the problems it might cause communities need further discussion. Rivers points out that FCC regulations require cable operation in the top 100 markets to make a public access channel available without charge. He also notes that cable operators are not supposed to censor the access channel.

That wide-open approach has already caused problems in New York. There the two cable systems, TelePrompTer and Sterling-Manhattan, have public access channels that are being used nearly two hundred hours per week. Some of the uses have caused cries of protest and complaints to the FCC. Videotaped broadcasts have included *The Bath,* in which a man smoking marijuana in a bathtub demonstrates the delights of bathing; *Body Movements,* in which a nude girl minutely examines herself; and *Transsexuals,* in which a woman shows the results of a sex-change operation.

Newsweek reported an example of public reaction:

One recent Sunday evening, the wife of a New York City lawyer heard giggles coming from the TV room of her Upper East Side duplex. Her curiosity aroused, she peeked into the room and saw her 11-year-old daughter huddled in front of the set. The screen showed a man massaging a naked girl with globs of spaghetti. Aghast, the woman flicked her gaze to the TV dial long enough to note that it was set to one of the city's cable channels. By now the scene had shifted to two partially clad couples frolicking on a large bed. The camera quickly panned over a pair of bare buttocks. There was a glimpse of a penis. A string of four-letter words filled the room. "I've got to call Kathy," squealed the daughter, but her mother had already commandeered the phone and was dialing the cable company. "Look," she shouted at the person who finally answered, "I'm a very liberal woman. My husband is a very liberal man. *But exactly what the hell is going on here?"*

The response of the cable companies to all such questions was fairly simple: the municipal board that set up the public access channels barred them from exercising any control over content. Their hands were tied.

If each community is to have control of the access channels, then each community must make determinations as to what will be allowed over those channels. While FCC rules do bar "obscene and indecent" material, it is not certain that those rules apply to access channels, and ultimate authority may rest with individual cities.

Although the movement for citizen access to broadcast channels was not truly strong until this decade, it is rooted in an FCC policy statement on the broadcasters' right to editorialize, issued in 1949. In that statement broadcasters were charged with being a "medium of freedom of speech and freedom of expression for the people of this nation as a whole. . . . We have recognized . . . the paramount right of the public to be informed and to have presented to it for acceptance or rejection the different attitudes and viewpoints concerning these vital and often controversial issues, which are held by the various groups which make up the community. . . . "

Lurking in that tangled maze of dependent clauses, to use the phrase of Tom Ballantyne, is the basis of the citizen access movement. Since the FCC is empowered to deny a license renewal to a broadcaster who does not meet the public interest, the first wedge was created. But community members who wanted to express dissatisfaction with a station's performance—or demand access—had no standing before the FCC until 1966. Until that time only persons with a direct economic interest in the license could appear before the commission or appeal its decisions.

The Rev. Dr. Everett C. Parker changed the situation in a landmark court case in 1966. Parker, director of the Office of Communications of the United Church of Christ, attempted to file a petition to deny the license renewal of WELT, a television station in Jackson, Mississippi. When the FCC told Parker that he had no standing to appear before it, he turned to the courts. The Court of Appeals for the District of Columbia ruled that community representatives who are victimized by a station's practices have standing before the FCC. Thus the groundwork was laid for citizen participation in the license renewal process. Community members now had a weapon—the petition to deny license renewal—to use to gain access to the airwaves. In the early parts of this decade there was a flurry of free speech messages, and guest editorials.

Cable systems, however, do not go through the same license renewal process as over-the-air broadcasters. The power to gain access by threatening to challenge a station's license stops where the cable begins. That was one of the factors the FCC considered when they mandated that cable systems provide each community with a public access channel.

As cable grows, so will the amount of access. And so will the problems. Until communities are able to devise acceptable guidelines for what should be allowed over these channels, they will be in the same situation as Jack

Banning, a vice president of the Sterling-Manhattan cable system, who said, "A guy just walked in and asked if we would run a tape of him and his wife dancing in the nude. And incredible as it sounds, I didn't know what to tell him."

LLS

James Nathan Miller

Pay-TV: Revolution or Rip-Off?

In August 1973, the Washington *Post* carried an ad whose clear intent was to throw a scare into the television-watching public. It showed a man holding a bill, on his face an expression that plainly said, "I've been had." The bill, from an imaginary outfit called Pay Television, Inc., was an accounting of what the man owed for watching television during a previous month: $6 for the Super Bowl, $3 for the movie *Patton,* and so forth. For the 16 shows on the list, the bill came to $41.47, or more than $2.50 a show.

The ad, run by the National Association of Broadcasters (NAB), which represents the networks and big television stations, implied that many of us would soon be getting such bills. "Pay-TV operators," it said, "are now planning to buy the exclusive rights to sports events, movies and popular entertainment shows—things that you get on free-TV right now—and convert your TV set to a box office for themselves. This process is called siphoning. When somebody siphons gas out of your car, *his* car runs fine. Yours is dead. We don't think you want this to happen to your television service."

It was an opening salvo in the battle between the backers of free- and pay-TV. Depending on which side you believe, pay-TV may either destroy the best of today's television, or elevate the medium to new levels of programming excellence. To understand what's involved, look at some recent television history.

Twin threat

First, a thumbnail history of pay-TV. Its concept is simple: the broadcaster sends out a scrambled signal, rents unscramblers to viewers, then charges the viewers according to how much unscrambling time they run up. During the 1950s and 1960s the scheme was tried in several cities (including New York, Chicago and Los Angeles), lost its backers millions of dollars, and by the early 1970s seemed about dead.

Why? Largely because pay-TV depended on movies and sports, which happen to be the stock-in-trade of two politically powerful industries: broadcasters and movie-theater owners. Whenever pay-TV popped up, these two industries tried to kill it. In 1968, they persuaded the Federal Communications Commission (FCC) to pass a series of tough "anti-siphoning" rules that declared out-of-bounds to pay-TV 99 percent of existing movies, plus most of the live sports events except boxing.

Another threat to free-TV was the industry called CATV, which stands for community-antenna television (or cable television). By the early 1970s, it too was in bad shape, and for the very same reason as pay-TV: a dose of regulatory poison. CATV is an industry that grew like a weed from a hole in the copyright laws. Unlike pay-TV, which attempts to broadcast and sell its *own* product, CATV is based on the idea of selling somebody *else's* product. The law says that it's legal to put up an antenna, grab whatever programs happen to be winging by, and sell them to viewers without paying royalties to anyone. So, during the 1950s and 60s, groups of smart operators zeroed in on communities too remote for regular TV reception, built supersensitive antennas on mountaintops and, for a monthly charge, sold residents the regular TV programs.

Owning the CATV antenna in a television-less town turned out to be like getting the oasis concession in the Sahara, and by the mid-1960s cable-TV was spreading so fast—even beginning to compete in cities that already had a TV station or two—that the big broadcasters asked their friends at the FCC to give it a dose of regulation. In 1966, therefore, the FCC declared that, while CATV could keep expanding into small towns, it was henceforth frozen out of the country's 100 biggest metropolitan areas, which contain 90 percent of the U.S. population.

Thus, by the early 1970s, the NAB seemed to have taken care of both its main competitors. Pay-TV was dead, and CATV confined to the sticks. But then something unexpected happened.

Surprise factor

As exiled CATV was stringing its cables through small-town America, the industry began to generate waves of excitement in a surprising quarter: the world of the big foundations and think tanks. The source of all the excitement was the coaxial cable carrying CATV signals, at once a humble object and an absolutely amazing instrument. Conceive of your telephone line—which can't carry more than a single conversation at one time—as a two-lane highway coming into your house. Now picture a 100,000-lane highway—that's coaxial cable. It can carry 50,000 telephone conversations—or 35 television programs—*simultaneously.* Or it can carry all the messages being sent out by the FM and TV stations in your area, plus short-wave and amateur radio broadcasts, as well as police broadcasts, transmissions to satellites, ships and planes—all of this simultaneously, through a single half-inch-diameter aluminum tube.

As the CATV people ran their lines along America's telephone poles, they were unwittingly installing the plumbing for a communications revolution. Indeed, as outside experts examined the number of simultaneous jobs the cable could perform, they saw a vision that boggled their minds. They called it the "Wired Nation"—computers wired to living rooms, living rooms to voting booths, classrooms, libraries, police stations, supermarkets, and on and on. You could have a newspaper printed in your living room in ten seconds, go credit-card video-shopping at home, have instant burglar- and fire-alarm service.

As enthusiasm for the wired-nation idea spread, CATV began to acquire very powerful new friends in Washington, people who saw in cable the opportunity for a great leap forward in any number of fields. These friends brought heavy pressure on the FCC to unfreeze CATV. Finally, on March 31, 1972, the FCC gave in and ruled that cable-TV could start wiring up the big markets.

Back in its coffin, the corpse of pay-TV lifted up its head, listened and winked. Here was its opportunity for a new life. All it needed to do was rent a movie film and an unused cable channel and, presto, it could be back in business again. Before the year was out, many cable-TV stocks had doubled and tripled, and the Stanford Research Institute was predicting that by 1985 there would be 25 million sets hooked into pay systems.

Battle lines

Three years later, however, there are only 130,000 pay-TV subscribers—one fifth of one percent of total set owners. Pay-TV has got virtually nowhere in the past three years. A major reason: the FCC's tough siphoning rules.

"The anti-siphoning rules were designed to protect the broadcasting monopoly," says David Foster, president of the National Cable Television

Association (NCTA). "Unless these rules are substantially relieved, pay-TV may never get out of the crib." Replies NAB president Vincent Wasilewski, "Relax the rules, and you'll put five percent of the people in a position to outbid the other 95 percent and deprive them of advertiser-supported television."

Thus the battle lines have been drawn. NCTA, with the backing of the movie *producers* (who see pay-TV as an enormous new customer for their product), has demanded a four-year moratorium on the siphoning rules. In response, the NAB, backed by the movie *exhibitors* (who are still convinced that pay-TV will close down their theaters), has raised over $500,000 for a public-relations campaign to "Keep Free-TV Free."

Here are the main questions affecting the battle's outcome:

How do present siphoning rules actually affect pay-TV? Under these rules, pay-TV can't run any sports event that's been on free-TV during the last two years. This means it can't attract subscribers by promising them the World Series or the Super Bowl. It has, however, been able to develop quite a number of other sports shows. For instance, Home Box Office, a New York outfit, offers weekday Yankee baseball games (which a local station dropped several years ago), plus home games of the basketball Knicks and hockey Rangers (never on free-TV), plus a fairly interesting odds-and-ends assortment of college sports, roller derbies and so forth.

As for movies, the FCC says basically that pay-TV can't put on anything that's over two years old. The free broadcasters say this should satisfy pay-TV operators; not only can they run almost all the new movies, but they can run them an average of four years before they appear on free-TV. Actually, there's an even more important advantage that pay-TV has: the amazing difference in enjoyment level between watching a movie on pay-TV—uncut, uncensored, uninterrupted—and watching it through the picket fence of commercials on regular television. But pay-TV chooses to ask why it must restrict itself to the roughly 300 films released during a two-year period. Why shouldn't it have access to the full list of 18,000 titles that are available to regular broadcasters?

Is the NAB right in claiming that pay-TV will merely charge us for what we're now getting free? This is the crucial question, and nobody knows the answer. The siphoning argument is about pay-TV not as it exists today, but as each side says it will exist in the future. The NAB sees disaster if the siphoning rules are relaxed, while the NCTA sees a garden of cultural delights—and each one makes a persuasive case. To understand how they do it, look ahead 10 or 20 years from now—when pay-TV may be in, say, half of the country's homes, or 33 million sets.

NAB scenario: Assume that 25 percent of the 33 million homes are willing to pay $5 each for *The Godfather*. That is 8 million sets times $5— or $40 million for a *single showing* of the film. Compare this with the $10 million that NBC is said to have paid for *The Godfather*—the largest payment ever made for a movie—and you'll see how much chance free-TV will have to compete with pay. "The chief victims of this," says the NAB, "will be low-income families and elderly viewers, who now depend almost exclusively on free-TV for entertainment."

NCTA scenario: Assume that only *two* percent of the 33 million homes are willing to pay $4 to watch a live, commercial-less, three-hour performance of *La Bohème* by the Metropolitan Opera. Though that's an audience of only 660,000 homes, it would produce $3 million in revenue for a single performance—which is more than free-TV gets for 99 percent of its prime-time shows, and 60 times what the Met grosses for a sellout performance. Not only that, but during *La Bohème* the same pay-TV broadcaster could be putting out five or ten other shows on unused cable channels: guitar lessons at 50 cents an hour, a Shakespeare performance for $1.50, a chess match, cooking lessons and so on.

Then why, you ask, is pay-TV putting on nothing but sports and movies? It's not yet big enough to do specialized shows. For instance, if two percent of *today's* audience paid $5 each to see *La Bohème,* the gross would be only $13,000 or a fourth of the Metropolitan's ticket-take from a single performance. Thus, says NCTA, pay-TV is in the position of having to put on mass-audience shows as sales promotions to build a large enough audience to pay for small-audience shows.

That's why NCTA believes the FCC should temporarily relax the siphoning rules. The industry is too small now to do any siphoning; and if siphoning does become a problem, the FCC can slap the rules back on. There's no such thing as a temporary relaxation, replies the NAB. If you loosen the rules, you attract investment and build pressures that will make it impossible to tighten up later.

What will the FCC do? Since the opposing forces are now pretty well balanced, the prospects are that the FCC will play it down the middle—allowing a few more minor sports events—to quiet pay-TV.

This may just turn out to be the policy that comes closest to serving the public interest. For if the FCC can keep both the free-TV and the pay-TV industries alive and kicking, with neither one getting so powerful that it can kill off the other, it's just possible that pay-TV can be forced to do what it says it wants to do—not steal away our present free shows, but give us a whole bunch of new ones that are worth paying for.

to the student: a commentary

The crux of the change is well presented by James Nathan Miller: is pay-TV a revolution or a rip-off? He answers by exploring the possibility, outlining the propaganda effort by those who oppose pay-TV: the networks and the big television stations.

Miller has done an excellent job of capsuling the argument, but he is so painfully careful not to overstep, so eager to make certain that both NAB and NCTA will approve, that he fails to go far enough. It seems to me doubtful that the NCTA will be happy. Instead, NAB will thank him, especially because Miller is writing for *Reader's Digest,* which has a circulation of nearly twenty million. In short, Miller's argument is much too cautious.

To get an appropriate view, it's worthwhile for us to look at the beginning of electronic media. It may be interesting to you that nearly *everyone* thought that there should be no place for advertising when broadcasting began. When radio sets began to make their entry into American homes, most people wanted to protect it from commercialization. Even David Sarnoff, who later became chairman of the Radio Corporation of America, saw broadcasting as a public institution free from commercial taint.

Printers' Ink, a voice of the advertising business, held in 1923:

Any attempt to make radio an advertising medium . . . would, we think, prove positively offensive to great numbers of people. . . . Imagine the effect, for example, of a piano sonata by Josef Hoffman followed by the audible assertion, "If you are under forty, four chances to one you will get pyorrhea." "Pickle Bros. are offering three-dollar silk hose for $1.98." Exaggerated, no doubt, yet the principle is there. To break in upon one's entertainment *in his own house* is quite likely intolerable, and advertising as a whole cannot be the gainer by anything of the sort.

The rise of radio as a big and costly purveyor of news and entertainment, and thus a full, fearsome competitor, began in 1920 with the broadcasting by station KDKA of the results of the presidential election. The economic objective of the industry during this period was not revenues from broadcasting but profits from the sale of receiving sets. Many groups pioneered in broadcasting but with no clear idea of how they were to cover costs. David Sarnoff has been quoted as arguing at the time that radio deserved endowment "similar to that enjoyed by libraries, museums, and educational institutions." He believed, according to Gleason Archer in his *Big Business and Radio,* that "Philanthropists would eventually come to the rescue of a hard-pressed industry."

Sponsored programs were first broadcast experimentally in 1922 on station WEAF. Thereafter they developed rapidly—though not without protests from government officials and the public. For example, at the First Annual Radio Conference in Washington, Herbert Hoover, who was then Secretary of Commerce, declared, "It is inconceivable that so great a possibility for service . . . be drowned in advertising chatter."

When Congress finally recognized the confusion and passed the Radio Act of 1927, the broadcasting industry began to develop its four main contemporary characteristics: submitting to legal and administrative control by a system of federal licensing, providing mass entertainment, acting as an adjunct of the marketing system, and concentrating its operational control in network organization.

As television stations began to take form after World War II, their owners scrambled to affiliate with the four national networks that dominated the industry. By the summer of 1955, there were 432 television stations, including 13 noncommercial educational stations. As the conquest by air of the nation's mass markets brought television programs into most American homes, the costs of broadcasting became enormous.

The smallest television station on the air requires an investment of $1 million in building and equipment. A medium-size station represents an investment of more than $2 million. The costs of programming are also impressive. When the astronauts on Apollo 11 landed on the moon in July, 1969, it cost the networks an estimated $11 million in expenditures and lost revenues to cover the spectacle. Production costs of a sixty-second black-and-white commercial were $12,595 in 1969, and that figure did not include talent, music, agency commission, or time charges.

If television sometimes appears to be "a collection of hollow men trying to fill a vacuum tube," in Leon Gerry's description, it is not just because it cannot afford to offend any substantial number of viewers, although that is a part of it. Since the networks are competing with one another and with magazines for advertising revenue, they also cannot afford to offend their advertisers. The very form of television drama is governed by advertising. Writers must fashion scenes not only to meet the needs of plot but also to provide breaks for commercials.

Substance, too, is governed by advertising considerations. The chairman of the Writers Guild of America, testifying at FCC hearings, said that "sponsors' fear of an unknown" contributed to the death of original TV drama. The late Rod Serling told how advertising considerations affected the entire treatment of his TV play based on the story of Emmett Till, a black boy from Chicago who was murdered in Mississippi. In Serling's version, the entire cast was white. At the insistence of the advertising agency, he had to move the locale from the South to New England, delete every suspected Southern colloquialism from the dialogue, and delete all references to Coca-Cola because it was "a Southern drink." Said Serling: "When the show finally hit the air, it had been so diluted and so changed . . . that the central theme I had my characters shouting about had become too vague to warrant any shouting.''

In a drama about the Nuremberg trials, the word *gas,* a cause of death in Hitler's concentration camps, was blipped because the sponsor was an association of gas interests. In a Chrysler program about the Civil War, all references to President Lincoln were deleted because he had the misfortune to bear the same name as a competing automobile. And in the Chevy Show no one could ever ford a stream.

These examples should make it clear that television is commercialized beyond recall. The basic question is not whether that will continue alone, but whether it should be protected. Nearly everyone has forgotten that radio and television might have grown up without advertising through some other support, such as taxes. We now need a greater variety of entertainment. It's not enough, as Miller says, that FCC will be ''allowing a few more minor sports events.'' Although it should not limit pay-TV so much, it needs greater elbow room to explore the possibility of pay-TV.

WLR

study questions

1. Examine yourself for media burn: How much time do you give to television each week? Which prime-time shows do you like? Which shows do you *watch?* Do you think of any TV characters as being similar to yourself? Why?

What kinds of information do you get from television that you don't get elsewhere? Do you notice styles of speech, behavior, and dress? Do you associate TV styles with people in your life? Do you expect people to act as TV characters do in similar situations? Do you draw from TV dramas any conclusions about law enforcement, crime, medical, and legal practice?

2. As a former TV child, what do you think the effect of television has been on your attitudes toward violence? Crime? Consumption of non-essential products? Do you regret the thousands of childhood hours you spent watching TV?

3. Meg Greenfield and Leonard Sellers both write about the effects of ''ethnic'' television programming *as if* TV has tremendous power to affect the nation's politics and create—or destroy—the credibility of ethnic identifications. Do you agree?

4. What is wrong with sex and violence on television? *Is* there sex on TV? Realistic violence? Do you agree that sex and violence on TV stand ''independent of morality''? Would ''anything goes so long as it sells'' suit you? Why or why not?

5. Suppose for a moment you are the producer of a local news show. Your show's format is ''formal''—that is, the anchor and co-anchor, sports, and weather persons read the news and narrate film clips. The format allows some flexibility, and some stories, if warranted, run longer than others. The show's ratings are down—lowest in the city.

Station executives hire a consulting firm that suggests changes to improve the ratings. They provide a formula for an "informal" presentation of an "eyewitness news" format that calls for scripted patter, uniform story length, and attempts at comedy. As producer you have the final say. (And in this case you won't be fired for making the wrong decision.) Would you accept the new formula or stick with what you have?

6. What do you see as the greatest potential of cable? Varied entertainment? Two-way communication?

7. Do you agree with the concept of uncensored community access channels? Should nudity or explicit sex be ruled out? What about nude ballets, paintings, sculptures, or musicals such as *Hair?* What is a "safe" censorship policy?

television & cable

constraints

©1976 Jules Feiffer.

Richard Jencks and Robert Lewis Shayon

Does the Fairness Doctrine
Violate the First Amendment ?

On its face, the issue of broadcasting's rights under the First Amendment is simplicity itself. Unfortunately, there are two quite different versions of what the "simple" answer is. According to one version broadcasting must share the same absolute freedom from government regulation that print media enjoy, simply because both are engaged in journalism. Another version is that broadcasters, as public trustees of scarce frequencies, have obligations to present all sides of significant, controversial issues. In a sense, their air time is the public's, not their own.

Take the debate a step further, and the illusion of "simplicity" vanishes altogether. The courts, journalists, scholars, lawyers—all have grappled with practical and theoretical aspects of the question. There is no consensus—but there *is* a legal requirement that sets broadcasters apart from others. That legal requirement, written into the Communications Act and enforced by the Federal Communications Commission, is the "fairness doctrine."

That the doctrine is binding upon broadcasters goes without saying. That it is truly in accordance with the First Amendment is open to question. The question was the subject of a debate conducted last month at the 50th annual convention of the NAEB [National Association of Educational Broadcasters].

Each participant is recognized as an articulate and effective representative of his own side of the question. In support of the proposition that the fairness doctrine violates the First Amendment was Richard W. Jencks, Washington vice president of CBS. In opposition was Robert Lewis Shayon, author, critic, and professor of communications at the Annenberg School of Communication, University of Pennsylvania. Their exchange, in edited form, appears below. . . .

Mr. Jencks: Does the fairness doctrine violate the First Amendment? Of course it does. And the Supreme Court will so decide when an appropriate case comes before it.

The argument made by the defenders of the doctrine is simple, and on the face of it, disarmingly appealing. It is that the fairness doctrine enhances the First Amendment by assuring the public's right to know.

Reprinted by permission of Richard Jencks and Robert Lewis Shayon from *Public Telecommunications Review,* December 1974.

If this argument is correct, a First Amendment applied to the nation's print media should be constitutional. Indeed, that very argument was forcefully made before the U.S. Supreme Court in the *Miami Herald* case in which a Florida statute providing a right of reply was at issue. The statute was analogous to the FCC's personal attack rules which form a part of the fairness doctrine. But the Court last June *rejected* the enhancement argument and unanimously held the Florida statute to be unconstitutional.

Speaking for a unanimous court, Chief Justice Burger declared: "The choice of material to go into a newspaper, and the decisions made as to limitations on the size of the newspaper and content and treatment of public issues and public officials, whether fair or unfair, constitutes the exercise of editorial control and judgment. It has yet to be demonstrated how government regulation of this crucial process can be exercised consistent with First Amendment guarantees of a free press as they have evolved to this time."

If, then, government-compelled "fairness" would not enhance the First Amendment as applied to the print media, how then can it enhance the First Amendment as applied to the broadcast media? The fact of the matter is that the case for a government guarantee of fairness is even poorer with respect to the broadcast press than with respect to the print press.

Item: The consequence of violating the right-of-reply statute held unconstitutional in the *Miami Herald* case was only to be convicted of a misdemeanor. It involves no government power to shut the newspaper down. In contrast, a broadcaster who flouted the FCC's doctrine could, and would, as in the case of station WXUR, lose its license and be utterly shut down.

Item: The opportunity of the *Miami Herald* to impede the free flow of information to the public through unfairness is far greater than that of any broadcaster. As Chief Justice Burger observed: "One-newspaper towns have become the rule, with effective competition working in only 4% of our large cities. By contrast, in 92 of the top 100 television markets, there are 3 or more television stations. Television and radio stations are nearly 5 times as numerous as daily newspapers."

Item: *Miami Herald* can comply with government-compelled fairness far more easily than could any broadcaster. The cost of preparing and inserting printed material into a newspaper is low, and a newspaper format is expandable. By contrast, the cost of producing visual material, as this audience well knows, is high, and a broadcast schedule cannot be expanded. Nothing can be added without something else being dropped.

In short, the burden on broadcasters of compelled fairness—and therefore its chilling effect on First Amendment rights—is not less, but is far greater than the burden of enforcing fairness upon newspapers.

Yet, television and radio are at present the American public's primary source of news and information. It is not merely *losing* a fairness doctrine case which demonstrates the crippling impact of the fairness doctrine. For a broadcaster to undertake the burden of *defending* against an FCC fairness complaint, even though he ultimately prevails, just as clearly kills First Amendment rights.

Two examples may suffice.

In June of 1970, following several presidential prime-time broadcasts, CBS initiated what it contemplated was to be a periodic series entitled *The Loyal Opposition,* featuring leaders of the party out of power. After the first broadcast, featuring Democratic National Committee Chairman Larry O'-Brien, the Republican National Committee filed a fairness complaint. The FCC upheld the complaint, and ordered us to provide free time to the Republicans. CBS appealed. Fourteen months and thousands of dollars of legal expenses later, the court of appeals reversed the FCC and vindicated CBS. But the FCC and court decisions so clouded the area in which our licensee discretion might be upheld, that the project was abandoned. Indeed, it might be asked what gain the Republican party would have achieved from the victory after 14 months had elapsed. The court, as editor-in-chief of a journalistic organization, is simply ineffectual.

Another landmark case—this time with a two-year delay between complaint and final judgment—involved NBC's 1972 pensions documentary, *Pensions: The Broken Promise.* The second-class citizenship of broadcasters also creates opportunities for burdensome harassment by the Congress, as well as by the FCC and the courts. Because of their FCC oversight responsibility, the Senate and House Commerce Committees often have conducted investigations and hearings on fairness charges, such as was done with the CBS News documentaries *The Selling of the Pentagon* and *Hunger in America* among others.

Newspaper executives do not troop resignedly up to Capitol Hill to explain and justify their stories and features. Can anyone think that it promotes fearless journalism for broadcasters to have to do so?

If the impact of the fairness doctrine on powerful and affluent organizations, like CBS, cannot be calculated, its impact on the small broadcaster cannot help but be shattering. Lawyers' fees for handling the smallest fairness complaint—and there were 2800 fairness complaints in 1972—are rarely less than 300 to 500 dollars.

Henry Geller, former general counsel for the commission, in his recent study of the fairness doctrine and broadcasting, reports that a fairness complaint over an editorial carried by a Spokane, Wash. station—a relatively innocuous editorial urging support of a bond issue to finance Expo '74—resulted in legal expenses alone of about $20,000, plus travel expenses and some 480 man-hours of executive and supervisory time. (This, mind you, was a complaint that didn't even reach the commission itself, let alone the courts.) After 21 months of proceedings, the FCC staff found that the station had offered a reasonable opportunity for reply to the editorial. But as Mr. Geller writes, because of editorials such as that on Expo '74, the renewal of a station's license can be put in question, and for a substantial period.

What effect, perhaps even unconscious, does this have on the manager or news director, the next time he is considering an editorial campaign on some contested local issue? What effect does it have on other stations? A short answer to Mr. Geller's rhetorical question is that the effect of such proceedings on the station involved, and on other stations, is to unconstitutionally inhibit freedom of expression and the dissemination of ideas.

Although Henry Geller is himself probably the most knowledgeable advocate of the fairness doctrine, his scholarly study indicates that he obviously reads the CBS vs. Democratic National Committee case as casting grave doubts on the constitutionality of the fairness doctrine as it has been administered since 1962. Mr. Geller points out that the court in that case rejected the idea of a constitutional right of access because that would have involved the FCC far too much in what the court referred to as "the day-to-day editorial decisions of broadcast licensees." Clearly, writes Mr. Geller, if that is true as to a right of access by persons to broadcast facilities for editorial advertisements, it is also true as to the application of the fairness doctrine. So, to save the fairness doctrine, Mr. Geller recommends that the FCC return to its pre-1962 fairness practice, but with the major difference that the Commission would make no attempt whatsoever to rule on individual complaints, but rather would determine at renewal time whether there had been such a pattern of conduct throughout the license period as to indicate malice or recklessness with regard to fairness obligations.

Now presumably, this debate concerns the fairness doctrine as the FCC now administers it. And even Henry Geller would not, if I read him correctly, support the argument that the doctrine as presently administered is constitutional. There are others, however, who do not believe that even the refinements suggested by Mr. Geller would save the doctrine from being struck down by the courts.

Senator William Proxmire (D-Wis.) was once so devoted to the fairness doctrine that it was at his suggestion in 1959 that it was elevated from mere FCC policy and made a part of the Communication Act. The Senator recently announced that he now plans the introduction of a bill to eliminate the doctrine from the statute books. "The heart of my position," Sen. Proxmire says, "is that the fairness doctrine is an appalling adman's name for justifying depriving radio and television of their First Amendment rights." Senator Ervin, often called the leading constitutionalist of the

Senate, has written of the fairness doctrine, "at its best it stifles controversy; at its worst, it silences it; in its present condition, it represents a fickle affront to the First Amendment."

They are not alone. Chief Judge David Bazelon of the U.S. Court of Appeals for the District of Columbia, a judge with a record of consistent support over the years for aggressive FCC regulation of the broadcast media, is also in that number. Characterizing the FCC's revocation of WXUR's license as a *prima facie* violation of the First Amendment, the judge said: "It is proper that this court urge the commission to draw back and consider whether time and technology have so eroded the necessity of governmental imposition of fairness obligations that the doctrine has come to defeat its purpose."

His language recalls a statement by the Supreme Court in its 1969 decision in the *Red Lion* case. That is the case—with its sweeping dicta about the "public's right to know"—on which the defenders of the doctrine must rely. The court said in *Red Lion:* "If experience with the administration of these doctrines indicates that they have the net effect of reducing rather than enhancing the quality of coverage, there will be time enough to reconsider the constitutional considerations."

That time has surely come. The nation's tragic experience with Watergate, if nothing else, must have the effect of forcing thoughtful people to re-examine the idea that we should entrust government with enforcing the flow of information under the First Amendment. What do the defenders of day-to-day government interference with the broadcast press have to say about all this? All they are left with is the iteration and reiteration of hackneyed slogans and outworn ideas.

One of those is that the airwaves belong to the people. That may be true enough as far as it goes. *But the whole lesson of American democracy is that we do not secure the rights of the people by vesting those rights in their government.* Isn't it clear that American newspapers and magazines belong to the people in a truer and more significant sense than the press of any country where it is subject to government control?

They also argue that there is a technical scarcity of broadcast frequencies, and in a highly technical sense, that's true enough. But that does not demand that we choose between applicants for such frequencies on the basis of their conformance with the government's ideas about how news and information should be reported.

I would remind you that those who call most persistently and eloquently for an ending of the fairness-doctrine experiment are not in the main broadcasters themselves. The exercise of unfettered First Amendment rights is not necessarily profitable. The unhappy fact of the matter is that most broadcasters have been content to be tame tabby cats on this issue, reasonably happy with their regulated status, relatively undisturbed by a regulatory regimen which encourages blandness and inhibits robust debate. When the FCC three years ago sent a questionnaire to broadcasters soliciting suggestions as to the "de-regulation" of radio, it obtained from 7000 radio broadcasters only 424 replies, and these mainly relating to trivia. Indeed, the passivity of most broadcasters on this issue is itself a damning indictment of the long-term effect of governmental regulation of the broadcast press.

I would close by reminding you of the words of Justice Douglas, no apologist for broadcasting, in his concurring opinion in CBS vs. Democratic National Committee. Said the Justice, "The fairness doctrine has no place in our First Amendment regime. It puts the head of the camel inside the tent, and enables administration after administration to toy with television or radio in order to serve its sordid or benevolent ends.

"What kind of First Amendment," he went on, "would best serve our needs as we approach the 21st century may be an open question. But the old-fashioned First Amendment that we have is the court's only guideline, and one hard and fast principle which it announces is that government shall keep its hands off the press. That means, as I view it, that television and radio, as well as the more conventional methods of disseminating news, are all included in the concept of the press as used in the First Amendment."

I trust and believe that when the issue framed by this debate squarely reaches the Supreme Court, Mr. Justice Douglas' brethren will agree with him.

Mr. Shayon: I want to make it clear at the start that I am not an unqualified defender of the fairness doctrine as it is. It has its faults. In fact, much of the public discussion about it has to do with suggestions for improving it, even for trading it for other measures that will protect fairness for the public. I'm prepared to talk about them—but I'm also saying 'No' to the clear proposal that the fairness doctrine *violates the Constitution.* That's the area we're constrained to discuss, and I'm sticking to it.

In a debate, when the pros and the cons don't know what each other will say, there's a lot of overlapping. Dick Jencks anticipated some of my comments, of course, and I anticipated some of his. But at the risk of redundancy, I'm going to formulate a line of reasoning which gives you a picture of the fairness doctrine as the negative sees it rather than the affirmative. Then we'll get into a trading of arguments later on.

The answer to the question before us, is of course, No—because the Supreme Court has *said* No. It said No, as Dick suggested, in *Red Lion,* the case which challenged the constitutional and statutory bases of the doctrine and its component rules. It even said No in CBS vs. DNC. (Indeed, it's curious to know that in that very case, CBS relied on the fairness doctrine to reject a right of paid access.) Again the U.S. Court of Appeals said No in the "Pensions" case which Dick mentioned. It said that the licensee did not make an unreasonable judgment in implementing the fairness doctrine, but had a wide degree of discretion in the handling of news documentaries. But the court in no way suggested abandoning the fairness doctrine. Whenever it has been at issue, the courts have by a majority sustained the fairness doctrine in broadcasting as a necessary control for the public interest. The broadcaster cannot assert a right to freedom of the press that transcends the public's right to know.

To be sure, there are dissenters. A good friend, the liberal Justice Douglas, is a First Amendment hardliner. Justice Stewart joined him in his dissent in CBS vs. DNC. And Judge Bazelon of the Court of Appeals has had doubts about the fairness doctrine. But, if you read a recent issue of the *New York Times,* you'd see that the good judge is wavering. He made a speech at the FCC Bar Association in which he expressed his doubts about the industry's performance in the public interest. In an outspoken attack on television not equaled since Newton Minow's "wasteland" speech, he said that the industry was making it difficult for judges and lawyers to ensure that traditional guarantees of freedom of the press continue to be applied to television. So you've got Bazelon wavering between the two extremes.

Nevertheless, as Chief Justice Hughes once said, we live under a Constitution, but the Constitution is what the judges say it is. As of now, the Supreme Court has said 8-to-0 in *Red Lion* that the fairness doctrine is constitutional, and they said it again in CBS vs. DNC, 7 to 2.

Of course, the Supreme Court has reversed itself in the past. Classic minority dissents have lived to see the day when they became majority opinions. Dick Jencks may be in the position of John Marshall Harlan, the great dissenter of the 19th century. He may be doing us a great public service by hammering away at the minority view.

I could stand on what the lawyers call *stare decisis* of the court and say "It is settled"—but that wouldn't be any fun. So let's go into the thicket of the constitutionality of the fairness doctrine and have another round.

I take it that Jencks, representing many broadcast licensees, wants to join the heavenly company of the print publishers, who are exempt from the regulatory powers of government, although of course, they are beneficiaries of salutary government intervention in their business, by virtue of enjoying favorable postal rates. (Publishers don't mind the camel's nose in the tent when it helps them to make a profit.) The broadcasters want the same First Amendment that the print media enjoy. Should they have it?

Justice Holmes once said, "The life of the law has not been logic; it has been experience." Nevertheless, let's try logic. Let's not have a debate; let's pursue truth. And again quoting Justice Holmes, "All I mean by truth is what I can't help thinking."

The purpose of the First Amendment was to keep government from prior censorship of the press so that ideas could flourish freely in the marketplace—robust, vigorous, clashing, antagonistic. Out of this would emerge the wisest decisions for a democracy. That was the faith. But in broadcasting, with the fairness doctrine, under the First Amendment, only political candidates and persons specifically attacked on the air have clear, unqualified rights to speak.

As for the rest of us: In determining whose rights are paramount under the First Amendment, the courts have said that it is the right of the people to be informed that is paramount.

Not the broadcasters' rights, not the viewers' and listeners,' not even the rights of those who want to speak their minds in public forums—but the right of all of us to have spread before us a diversity of opinion. On that, as Judge Learned Hand said, "We have staked our all."

Okay, "diversity of opinion" and "an informed electorate"—on those points the broadcaster and the regulator agree. The position of the regulators, however, is that it's not unconstitutional for the government to use the First Amendment affirmatively to ensure diversity of opinion. You know the arguments: scarcity of frequencies, the public-trustee concept, the idea that the recipient must give the people something in return when he gets a franchise. At the very least, he has an obligation to conduct informed public discussion on matters of concern, and when conducting them, to be fair to all shades of opinion. But the broadcaster is given the widest possible latitude in exercising this public trustee function. The broadcaster may even refrain from raising *any* controversial issues and still escape sanctions. This happens, as you know, in many years when stations fail to broadcast even the barest minimum of news and public affairs and get their licenses renewed.

The fairness doctrine, as I suggested, is hardly perfect in its implications and implementation. It has many derogators on right and left, but it is the bedrock of the public interest standard of the Communications Act. Take it away, and you *have* no Act.

The position of the broadcasters who urge the abandonment of the doctrine is that it invades the First Amendment rights of the broadcasters. Mr. Vincent Wasilewski, president of the NAB, argued in a fairness doctrine hearing in 1968 before a House Subcommittee that, even if the government grants the broadcaster a franchise with exclusive use of a frequency, the government may demand nothing in return without violating that broadcaster's First Amendment rights.

The argument further runs that most broadcasters will, by necessity and just plain natural virtue, be fair without regulation. "Go peddle your ideas to another station, to a newspaper, make a speech, write a book," they say.

"You ought not to have a direct legal remedy. There should be no way in which a broadcaster can be chastised for failure to give someone else the right of reply to anything the broadcaster says on the air."

This doesn't mean, say the broadcasters, that the listener is left with no remedy at all. There is a remedy. What is it? Listen to Mr. John J. Corporan, Vice President for news for Metromedia at the House Hearings in 1968: "There's a very orderly procedure for taking care of the bad broadcaster in the capitalistic system. That is, he will go broke, and be forced to sell. A bad broadcaster will not survive."

In short, the broadcaster should get his franchise and have no obligation to be fair other than his own sense of decency. That's how we get diversity of opinion, and serve the needs of a democratic society for informed discussion. To do otherwise, to insist that the broadcaster be legally required to be fair would be to "harass," to "inhibit" him, to "chill" him; rather than risk legal sanctions, he will engage in no controversy, and all his broadcasts will be bland, and there would be no diversity of public opinion.

What should one reply to this position? At the worst, it seems to me that it is unconscionable that one man should say to the people of the United States: "Give me a piece of everybody's electromagnetic spectrum and I will operate it for my own partisan purposes and profit and keep everyone I don't agree with off the air." But let's suspend judgment and try it out. Let's see how it would actually happen.

Many of you are familiar with the famous WLBT case in Jackson, Mississippi. The licensee was Lamar Life Insurance Co., and all through the late fifties and sixties it was asserted by citizens of Jackson that the station was guilty of racial and religious discrimination. It cut off network civil rights broadcasts with signs reading "Sorry, cable trouble."

Eventually, with no help from the FCC, the Office of Communication of the United Church of Christ persuaded the U.S. Court of Appeals to grant a hearing, and when the evidence was all in some five or six years later, the court itself vacated the license of Lamar Life. It said that the FCC's record in the case was irreparable, and it took the license revocation sanction into its own hands.

Now suppose we eliminate the fairness doctrine. A licensee operates one of two VHF stations in Jackson. It decides to put on racist editorials. You don't think that can still happen? Go down to Jackson. What's to stop him? Does a black citizen rush to the competitive station and beg time for a reply and possibly be refused? To the newspapers and get turned down? Perhaps they wouldn't turn him down, but they could, couldn't they? And he'd have no legal remedy, none at all.

I ask Dick Jencks: Do you really believe that such a system would serve our need for an informed public opinion, for fairness in the clash of ideas, presumably the lifeblood of our democracy? If you ever got the Congress to abandon the fairness doctrine, and broadcaster mavericks act up the way WLBT did, there would be such a public cry of outrage that the next fairness doctrine written into law would have the kind of teeth the present one lacks, and I don't think the broadcasters would care for that bite at all. They want the same First Amendment rights as the print media. What that means is that they want a monopoly based on scarcity of frequencies, and they want it free and clear of any legal obligation to be fair in public discussion. I'm not prepared to let them have it on those terms.

You wish to be free of obligations? Then I'll free you also of your monopoly position. No obligations, no monopoly. Turn pay cable loose. Let's have a real competitive market based on open entry, and we'll discuss it. But the broadcasters are trying to stop pay cable. They don't want an open entry. They want a protected market and on top of that they want no legal obligations for fairness. "Trust us," they say, "we'll be fair because we love fairness." And if there are a few bad apples, the system will take care of them. Now, *come on.*

There are other solutions: Let's rewrite the Act. Let's auction off the frequencies to the highest bidders. Give it to the winners, free and clear of any fairness doctrine restraints, but on condition that they set aside 10% of prime time for public access and that they give—you'll love this—10% of their gross revenues to public broadcasting. Then you can have your unharassed, uninhibited First Amendment.

Does CBS want that? If it has no fairness obligations, why should it be allowed, as CBS is, to own 5 VHF stations in the top markets? Why not just one? The so-called "chilling" effects of the fairness doctrine are legendary; despite the protestations of professional journalists, our scholarly expert Henry Geller says that these effects never even have been documented.

Everyone knows that the fairness doctrine is really a mild regulation. Broadcasters have lived with it and maintained their profits. What the broadcasters are really worried about is access. That's what they're concerned about. People are not content to let Cronkite, Reasoner and Chancellor speak for them and say every night, "that's the way the world is." Is it? People want counteradvertising. There will be more court challenges.

In 1969, at a panel of the American Bar Association, Dick Jencks accepted *Red Lion* as the farthest permissible reach of government. The figures show that the networks got hooked in only one case—the famous NBC–Chet Huntley case, where he broadcast an editorial favoring cattle raisers when he had conflict of interest. In the NBC case, the courts overturned the FCC.

In 1971, there were 2000 fairness doctrine complaints. In only 168 cases did the FCC send inquiries to the stations, an 8% ratio of inquiries to complaints. There were only 69 FCC rulings, and only five out of 2000 were adverse to licensees. Even in 1972, Dick, in Aspen, Colorado, you still found that the fairness doctrine had worked fairly well. You relied on it in CBS vs. DNC. Judge Tamm of the U.S. Court of Appeals, dissenting in the NBC "Pensions" case, said: "The fairness doctrine as it has been utilized here is the yeast of fairness in the dough of the telecaster's right to exercise his journalistic freedom."

Nobody asked the broadcaster to be a public trustee. He volunteered for the license. He volunteered for it, and he did it with his eyes wide open as to what the terms of the game were: a right to make a mint of money in return for fairness to the public in controversial issues, a balancing of his rights against the people's rights under the First Amendment. If CBS or any other licensee doesn't like the way the game is played, let them turn in their licenses and resign. There are plenty of others waiting on the sidelines, eager to get into the game under the exceptionally mild and generous conditions of the constitutional fairness doctrine.

Mr. Jencks: I'll try to deal with some of the matters that Bob Shayon raised. He says that the Supreme Court has firmly decided that the Fairness doctrine is constitutional, which I don't think is the case, and the real test will be when the Supreme Court gets a case in which a license hangs in balance, such as the Brandywine (WXUR) case, which did not go to the Supreme Court. Judge Bazelon was among others who do not think that *Red Lion* is dispositive as to the legality of the fairness doctrine.

And it's very curious indeed that last June in the *Miami Herald* case—while striking down a right of reply regulation it had upheld five years before—the Supreme Court of the United States did not even *mention the Red Lion case,* did not attempt to distinguish it, did not attempt to justify it.

Now, Bob says that I'm asking you to rely upon the decency of broadcasters. I'm not, any more than I ask you in the print field to rely on the decency of publishers. Rather, I'm asking you to rely upon their contentiousness and their desire to reach their readers, if they are running media for general circulation. He says the bedrock of the Communications Act is the fairness doctrine; "take it away and you have no Act." Well, you *had* no fairness doctrine from the inception of the Act in 1934 until 1949, and you had no fairness doctrine embodied in the statute until 1959. So, clearly you can have a Communications Act and proper regulation of broadcasters without a fairness doctrine.

He talks about commercial broadcasters desiring to strangle pay television; if that's the case, there are laws suitable to cope with that—the anti-trust laws, for example. Justice Douglas made clear in his opinion—from which I previously quoted, and I quote again: "The commission has a duty to encourage a multitude of voices but only in a limited way, viz.

by preventing monopolistic practices and by promoting technological developments that will open up new channels."

Bob got quite a laugh from the audience talking about the possibility that he would be willing to auction off our First Amendment rights if we would be willing to give 10% of our gross profits to public broadcasting. If he would really be willing to abandon his precepts for a price, then I think we have gauged his depth of feeling about the First Amendment.

He asks me a rhetorical question: Can I really believe, he says, can I really believe that the system of untrammeled freedom would serve our needs? And I ask back: Can *you* really believe that the press of this country, the print press, serves our needs? And if it doesn't, why not? Look about you, when you read your morning newspaper, whether it be the *Las Vegas Sun* or the *New York Times,* or the *Los Angeles Times,* or the *Washington Star-News,* or the *Washington Post,* when you read your news magazine, whether it be *U.S. News and World Report* or *Time* or *Newsweek.* Do you yearn to have a federal commission with the power to make that publication do its will? Do you yearn to have the licenses of those publications terminated? Do you yearn to have a federal court in Washington decide when their articles and features have been fair and unfair? And more to the point, do you yearn to have those decisions come one year, two years, three years after the controversy which precipitated them? Does that strike you as improving the press upon which you depend every day of your life?

If it does not, then the humorous solutions and the decency of broadcasters are really beside the point. Broadcasters are no more decent, nor any less, than newspaper publishers. The question is: What is the risk of allowing that freedom to prevail?

Mr. Shayon: As to the constitutionality of the fairness doctrine, I would welcome a test confronting the issue head on. Dick is right. The courts have hedged very often in confronting the issue squarely. Even in the WXUR decision, the argument was that the decision was based—the revocation of the license—on what the majority opinion called "a very narrow ledge." The judges are very, very sensitive to getting into a confrontation of the issue, and I for one would like to see a case come before the court where the issue was met head-on. As of the present moment, however, the best indication we have is that, whenever the Supreme Court has faced the issue in a tangential situation, they seem on the whole to have upheld the necessity for the fairness doctrine.

Now, Dick says that there was no fairness doctrine until 1949. I disagree with that. If you read the history of the Federal Radio Commission, you will see that in its initial rulings, it specifically and explicitly set forth the principle of fairness to all shades of opinion. Very quickly the politicians got into the act and got section 315 written. It took a little while longer for everybody else to get their bit into the act, but the concept of fairness was inherent in the regulatory scheme of this country's broadcasting licensing system from the very beginning on, and if Dick would like we could go to the records, we can check it out.

He talks about the press serving needs. I for one happen to believe that the press in many respects did not serve the need of the people. I happen to agree with Jerome Barron: I'd like to see an experiment made in the right of access for reply to newspaper space—it's much easier for the newspapers to add pages than it is for a broadcaster to add time, that's true. But I don't think that the present system adequately meets the demands of the 20th century for all the people to get into the act of diversity of opinion.

Barron is right. The romantic conception of the First Amendment that was in view when the founders of our republic framed the Constitution is no longer adequate to the needs of the 20th century. We have different means of communication, massive means of communication, which take a lot of money, as our moderator says, and the ordinary citizen just can't get into that game, so we have a realistic notion of the marketplace of ideas, and it presents new problems. I don't say that the fairness doctrine, as is, is the answer; but I say that it's the final bastion we have under the present system for the legal protection of the citizens' rights, and I'm not prepared to forego it and take the risk of trusting either the wisdom, or the decency, or the fairness of broadcasters to implement First Amendment rights.

Let's talk for a minute about this "chilling" of the press. It's argued that this arises as a result of the economic and procedural and time burden imposed upon broadcasters. I have a different theory about the chilling effect. It comes from the economic structure of the industry. The industry is foremost committed to entertainment, so it says to its people in news and public affairs, "Here's a little corner of the total spectrum. You operate that little corner, and don't you dare get out of it." So the Cronkites and the Reasoners, naturally they're human like all of us, they say, "That's my little corner. That's my territory. I'm in charge of it, so I'm going to be the judge of what goes in and what goes out, and I'm going to be the public voice, and I'm going to be the trustee." But they resist attempts of anybody else to take a little piece of their precious corner and play with it, and I say that's not adequate to represent the rights of all citizens today.

There's a clamoring, a hunger for public discussion by spokesmen who want to initiate controversies that the public media do not even recognize as controversy. How are we to deal with that problem? There are suggestions for improving the fairness doctrine. I would be in favor of an experimental situation to see whether any of these suggestions would really provide a solution to the fairness doctrine's defects, but I'm not prepared to scrap the fairness doctrine until I see whether or not this system proves out. What I'm arguing is that broadcasting is still not the print media; the public still needs protection in the area of limited frequencies; and that the fairness doctrine line should be held until something better can be demonstrated.

to the student : a commentary

The articulate spokesmen Richard Jencks, a vice president of CBS, and Professor Robert Lewis Shayon of the University of Pennsylvania argue whether the fairness doctrine violates the First Amendment. Some authorities consider the doctrine to be vital; Fred Friendly, the former president of CBS News, carries a small card in his wallet that spells out the necessity. It reads: "The Fairness Doctrine: One, to devote a reasonable time to the coverage of controversial issues of public importance. Two, to do so fairly, to accord a reasonable opportunity to the contrasting points." But if this doctrine were applied to the newspapers, it would be unconstitutional. Is it constitutional in broadcasting? Shayon supports the doctrine.

In support of Shayon, let's consider the case of *Pensions: The Broken Promise,* an hour-long documentary broadcast by NBC in 1972. This case is important because it goes to the heart of the fairness doctrine, which requires that broadcasters who present one side of a controversial issue afford reasonable opportunity for response by those who represent the other. The case is important to us for another reason: it emphasizes the danger of failing to present counterarguments.

Early in the program, the narrator stated that "the pension system is essentially a consumer fraud, a shell game, a hoax." These were keynote words; most of the rest of the narrator's statements and all of the scenes were in tune with them. This harsh judgment surprised—and perhaps outraged— millions of Americans: those who benefit from good pension plans, not to mention those who administer good pension plans. Worse, the harsh judgment misled many viewers who had not known whether pension plans in general were good or bad. Perhaps some viewers who were counting on pensions to support them in later years began to fear that they were being defrauded. After sharply criticizing several specific pension plans, the program concluded that "it is almost inconceivable that this enormous thing [a system of pensions] has been allowed to grow up with so little understanding of it and so little protection and such uneven results for those involved."

The narrator, Edwin Newman, did say near the end: "This has been a depressing program to work on. But we don't want to give the impression that there are no good pension plans. And there are many people for whom the promise has become a reality."

But by the time the narrator made *that* statement, it was too late. It was also too little. Everything else that had been stated and shown argued strongly that the synonyms for "pension system" are "fraud," "shell game," and "hoax." No doubt this emphasis altered some viewers to analyze their own pension plans. If they found flaws that led to changes for the better, the program served a good purpose. But the cost in misinformation, and perhaps outrage and fright as well, was especially high for this small return because it was unnecessary. Had the positive information at the end of the program been presented earlier and more fully, the broadcast might have served the same good purpose without the cost.

Note the italicized word: "is *essentially* a consumer fraud. . . ." The writer did not write that it *is;* he wrote that it is *essentially,* which means in essence, but not entirely. He tried (perhaps unconsciously) to reduce the strength of his statement, to qualify it. The effort was worthwhile, but the word is too weak. In a sentence with words such as *fraud, shell game,* and *hoax, essentially* has no force. Did anyone who watched that program even hear "essentially" as a qualification of the strong words that follow?

Many individual viewers, groups, and corporations protested that the program was distorted; it had failed to emphasize that most pension plans worked well. An NBC executive responded that the program was accurate in making the point that "not all pensions meet the expectations of employees or serve all persons with equity."

This did not satisfy the protesters, of course. An organization called Accuracy in Media complained to the Federal Communications Commission (FCC) that NBC should be required to show more positive aspects of the pension system as well. The FCC agreed. NBC took the case to court.

My review of the case seems to be fully supportive of Shayon. To allow a network to broadcast a one-sided argument may seem criminal. But is it? Remember that there were no broadcasts, not even radio, fifty years ago. We then had only the newspapers and the magazines. The First Amendment was in force; there was no fairness doctrine. If the system worked then, why should we bind the broadcasters?

The chief reason, lamentably, is that few of the broadcasters care. Most broadcasters are in the business for profit, period. It is entertainment. How many of them care about news and public affairs at all? As Jencks has reported, when the FCC three years ago sent a questionnaire to 7,000 broadcasters soliciting suggestions as to the de-regulation of radio, only 424 replies were returned, most them trivial.

Inasmuch as government is engaged in the licensing of broadcasters, the electronic media are not quite in the same status as newspapers and magazines. Yet there are at least a few broadcasters who care passionately about free speech. The very best of the halfway measures has been set forth by Henry Geller, the knowledgeable former FCC counsel. He suggested that the

FCC should make no attempt to rule on the individual complaints according to the fairness doctrine, but would determine at renewal time (every three years) whether there has been a pattern of conduct throughout the license period as to indicate malice or recklessness with regard to fairness obligations. At least in regard to what should be done now, Henry Geller has outlined a reasonable method.

WLR

Rawleigh Warner, Jr.

Energy Resources— and the Public

It became clear to us in Mobil three or four years ago . . . that our country was heading for a severe energy crunch.

Here was the greatest industrial power in the world, with its entire economy built on an abundance of low-cost energy, about to enter an era of unnecessarily heavy reliance on other countries—mainly because, for one reason or another, industry was not being allowed to develop our very strong domestic energy resource base adequately.

There seemed to be very little understanding of this situation or of the economics of business in the press, in the Congress, or among the general public. We in Mobil felt there was an urgent need to try to inform people.

That, in brief, was the setting in which we initiated our communications program. What are we doing in it, what results have we had, and what problems have we encountered?

To some extent, we do pretty much the same sort of nuts-and-bolts things many large companies do. Probably our most effective tool, however—and, I suppose, the one that sets us apart—is our use of paid advertising in newspapers. We have found it ineffective to rely on letters to the editor to rebut even the most misinformed reporting. Retractions by the press are rare, and seldom catch up with the original charge. News releases are of limited usefulness.

We elected initially to rely mainly on newspaper advertising because we felt we had to address ourselves primarily to opinion leaders as the group best able to grasp complex issues.

We publish a quarter-page advertisement virtually every Thursday, year-round, on the page opposite the editorial page of *The New York Times* —called, as you might deduce, the op-ed page. This is the only space the *Times* will sell on those two facing pages. It therefore has pretty high visibility, which we try to enhance with an off-beat approach. The space gives us enough room for essay-type ads similar in tone to other material appearing on those two pages.

We try to surprise readers of the *Times* with our selection of subject matter, our headlines, and our brisk and often irreverent text. We try to

Reprinted by permission of Rawleigh Warner, Jr., from *Vital Speeches,* 15 July 1974.

be urbane but not pompous. We try not to talk to ourselves and we accept that we can never tell the whole story in any one ad.

Our ads have ranged over a wide gamut—the energy crisis in its many ramifications, the role of profits, earnings as expressed in rate of return, capital requirements and capital formation, the need for national energy policies . . . why we support the New York Public Library, public television, the United Negro College Fund, the Better Business Bureau . . . the need for economic growth . . . the dangers of simplistic knee-jerk reactions . . . the need to conserve energy, and ways to use less gasoline. The list is a long one.

We try to help people understand what options are open to them and what sort of costs are involved in the various trade-offs. The response has been strong and generally favorable, though in addressing ourselves to opinion leaders, we deliberately opted for a rather thin cut of the total public. We believe we have had some impact and that we have been reaching people other than just those already wedded to the free market, but we realize we have not yet done enough to reach the public at large. In sum, we think the exercise has been useful, albeit somewhat expensive *in toto,* and sufficiently productive to continue.

One reason we think our advertisements, along with those of other oil companies, may be having some effect is that several Congressmen and Senators have recently tried to inhibit us. We believe *The Wall Street Journal* was close to the target when it said, "Indeed, the reason their critics are rushing to have them gagged is that the oil companies have been making legitimate arguments worthy of being heard."

We have recently been publishing these institutional ads regularly in 15 to 20 papers in addition to the *Times,* and are . . . enlarging the program to around 100 papers. . . .

We have our differences of opinion with various of the newspapers in which we are buying space. But what we are trying to do in the mass media is to broaden the spectrum of information and viewpoints available to the American people, to help them reach the conclusions necessary to sound public policy in a democratic society. We believe the continued viability of our open society depends heavily on robust debate and controversy in the marketplace of ideas. We are in no sense eager to stifle those who oppose us. On the contrary. We just want to be heard, too.

That brings me to the biggest roadblock we have encountered—the refusal of national television networks to sell us time in which to state our viewpoints on matters of great public import.

When the energy crisis hit full-blown, there were very few reporters in any media anywhere in the country, outside of oil-producing areas and the oil trade press, who knew much about oil. This was particularly true of commercial television, and seems still to be true. As a result, we have a very difficult communications problem, and we recognize that. The energy crisis is complex, both in its origins and in its manifestations. The TV networks, by their very nature, seldom seem able to do justice to such a complex issue.

There appear to be at least five major elements that account for the structural deficiency of network television news programs.

The first is time limitations. A 30-minute news program, such as the Cronkite show, shrinks after commercials to around 23 to 24 minutes. An essay by a Sevareid or a Brinkley will consume about three minutes, leaving only 20 to 21 minutes for news. During this tightly limited time the show will often try to cover as many as 15 or more items, which would average out to a little over a minute for each item. But the biggest stories may consume close to two minutes each. So you end up with a good many stories being handled in well *under* a minute each.

Also, if the newsrooms are to have time to develop and edit film and to add the requisite dramatic elements, topical stories for the evening news show usually have to be filmed in the morning or at the latest in the very early afternoon. Otherwise, they may get short shrift.

Second, there are the economic limitations. Camera crews and transmission by satellite, for instance, are expensive. The cost to a network of keeping camera crews in many different locations could be prohibitive. Even when willing to spend the money, a network cannot always fly a crew to the scene of a news development in time to obtain the film that is TV's lifeblood. Also, most national TV news personalities earn far more than newspaper reporters.

The third limitation has to do with the networks' tendency to personalize the news. By this I mean their ever-present need for the highest ratings. We have the Cronkites, the Chancellors, the Reasoners, the Howard K. Smiths. As these people fight for the highest ratings, they sometimes tend more toward showmanship than toward balanced presentation of the news. As a former executive director of the ABC Evening News put it, "The evening news is not the highest form of journalism. It is partly an illustrated headline service and partly a magazine. And, yes, it is part show business, using visual enticement and a star system to attract viewers."

The fourth of the elements that tend to emasculate network news is personal limitations. There seems to be little room for specialists. Indeed, the only ones I can think of are the sports announcers and the weather forecasters. Understandably, most of the rest of TV's news correspondents are generalists, competent to cover hard-news stories and features of several kinds, but limited in the spheres of economics, finance, and technology.

Finally, the fifth element of weakness: TV is by its very nature an entertainment medium, and a highly visual one at that. The problem was summed up this way by a former president of NBC News: "Every news story should, without any sacrifice of probity or responsibility, display the attributes of fiction, of drama. It should have structure and conflict, problem and denouement, rising action and falling action, a beginning, a middle, and an end."

While we are not accusing the networks of bias in their reporting, we nevertheless feel that their structural deficiencies have combined to make much of their coverage of oil news inaccurate and misleading.

By way of characterizing our problem, it seems to us almost as simple as having to try to talk about elementary economics to people who are essentially illiterate in that field. As you can appreciate, . . . we try to relate our earnings to our invested capital. This is one of the few ways we can satisfy ourselves that our rate of return is adequate to attract or amass additional capital to continue to do what is expected of us.

But this is a very difficult concept to get across to the consuming public, which sees only two things: the price of the product, which has risen dramatically; and the size of our earnings, which in absolute terms are large. All too few people in public office or in the media are adequately equipped or motivated to help people understand that it is primarily the oil-exporting countries that have increased the price and that, in Mobil's case, our 1973 earnings of almost $850 million have to be viewed in light of the more than $10.5 *billion* of assets required to generate those earnings.

We therefore start out with an almost insurmountable problem, which is bad enough in and of itself. But when we then have to cope with television reporters and commentators who usually know next to nothing about the business and seldom seem to have the time or the desire to learn, and when we have to try to impart some understanding in the very limited time allotted—that really is impossible.

Let me illustrate this for you with a personal experience. . . . When I was chairman of the American Petroleum Institute, two other oilmen and I went up to CBS, at its request, and had lunch with Walter Cronkite. Mr. Cronkite told us that CBS was planning to broadcast a series designed to give the viewing public some insight into the energy crisis that was shaping up, and he assured us of CBS's determination to be fair.

We therefore agreed to cooperate. I personally spent more than three hours with CBS reporters and camera crews trying to answer their questions and to impart information on the energy situation in our country. The fellow in charge of those interviews assured me CBS was going to do the "most thorough study they'd ever done on any subject for the Cronkite show," and I think those are very close to his exact words. The problem was that the reporter was simply rounding up the raw material. That raw material was cut and edited by a group of people we never saw; who, as far as we could tell, had not been exposed to any first-hand discussion of what was involved; and to whom, I can only surmise, fairness did not seem an overriding preoccupation.

Our reaction to what CBS finally broadcast, in January and February of 1973, was one of utter dismay. What we saw and heard struck us as being one-sided and unfair to the industry. For all my own pains, I believe I got about a minute and a half on the air and was identified as "chairman of the industry lobby," which by implication would make me the chief lobbyist for the oil industry. The basic points I had tried to make died on the cutting-room floor.

I would be less than honest and less than fair myself, however, if I failed to point out that NBC has done special energy broadcasts that were quite well-balanced. The producers of those programs kept their promise to us —that we would have our day in court, along with those holding opposite views. We got a fair shake.

Incidentally, those NBC producers showed their understanding of the complexity of this subject by allotting three consecutive hours of prime time to it . . . in the first of their special broadcasts on energy. When they followed that up, . . . they devoted an hour of prime time to the subject on each of two evenings a week apart.

Mobil has sought to buy air time for commercials that would convey our point of view—commercials that would deal in ideas rather than in products. But networks have refused to sell us time for many of the commercials we have submitted. Their position was pretty well summed up in a letter . . . from the law department of the Columbia Broadcasting System to a vice president of Mobil, from which I quote: " . . . it is the general policy of CBS to sell time only for the promotion of goods and services, not for the presentation of points of view on controversial issues of public importance. CBS has adopted this policy because it believes that the public will best be served if important public issues are presented in formats determined by broadcast journalists."

In simple terms, that means that what the people of this country are to see and hear on commercial television is to be decided largely by two or three people at each of two or three TV networks—an extraordinary concentration of decision-making.

Interestingly enough, that letter from CBS was written right around the time the Cronkite evening news show presented—in a format determined solely by broadcast journalists—that one-sided material I mentioned earlier.

It occurred to us that the networks might be afraid they would have to give free time to opponents of our points of view. We therefore offered to pay twice the going rate to have our commercials telecast, which would have covered the cost of any free time given to someone holding different views to reply to us—Ralph Nader, the Sierra Club, or anyone else selected by the network. We felt this underscored our basic posture: that we are not trying to alter what the TV networks broadcast as news. We just want to offer a broader spectrum of information and viewpoints to the American people and are perfectly willing to take our chances in the marketplace of ideas. If our ideas are no good, the public most assuredly will shoot them down, and deservedly.

The networks have refused to sell us time even on this basis, yet have permitted our critics—principally politicians—to keep up a stream of unsubstantiated charges against us and to get their views televised almost at will.

I should like to describe one of our rejected commercials. You be the judge. We see nothing wrong with it, but two networks won't carry it. This commercial opens, without narration, on a shot of beach and ocean. Then, as the camera moves out to show only the sea, the narrator comes in, and here I quote verbatim his entire script:

According to the U.S. Geological Survey, there may be more oil beneath our continental shelf than this country has consumed in its entire history.

Some people say we should be drilling for that oil and gas. Others say we shouldn't because of the possible environmental risks. We'd like to know what you think.

Write Mobil Poll, Room 647, 150 East 42nd Street, New York 10017.

We'd like to hear from you.

NBC accepted this commercial.

ABC rejected it, saying it had reviewed the commercial and was "unable to grant an approval for use over our facilities."

CBS also rejected it, saying, "We regret that this message addresses a controversial issue of public importance and as such cannot be considered under our corporate policies."

I have these comments to make on that.

First, this country was founded in controversy—hard, openly expressed controversy—and it has remained free and democratic through the continuing clash of opinion and of value patterns.

Second, if the networks dedicate themselves almost exclusively to merchandising products, via the entertainment route, they may raise serious questions as to whether what they merchandise as news is actually just entertainment.

Third, today's energy crisis is controversial largely because the media have helped make it controversial by printing and broadcasting material so inaccurate that anyone with any knowledge of our industry would have to disagree with it.

When as powerful and pervasive a medium as television will not sell time for controversial issues, it seems to me our country has reached a rather critical juncture. How can a democracy operate effectively without broad public access to clashing points of view?

It is worth recalling what the U.S. Supreme Court said in 1969, in what is known as the Red Lion case: "It is the right of viewers and listeners, not the right of the broadcasters, which is paramount. It is the purpose of the First Amendment to preserve an uninhibited marketplace of ideas in which truth will ultimately prevail, rather than to countenance the monopoliza- tion of that market, whether it be by the Government itself or by a private licensee. It is the right of the public to receive suitable access to social, political, esthetic, moral, and other ideas and experiences which is crucial here."

The real issue seems to be whether the commercial networks should have total control over what is broadcast to the American people. Since network broadcasting is among the most concentrated of U.S. profit-mak- ing industries, it would appear that our country may be facing a danger of monopoly censorship.

I hope you realize how reluctant we in Mobil are to adopt any posture that would appear to place us in an adversary position. We would much rather just live and let live. But we have concluded that we have no alternative to standing up for what we believe to be right. It is a dreadful set of circumstances at which we have arrived. What we're battling for is something at least approaching fair treatment in a medium that seems to be the main source of news for the vast majority of the public, yet one that seemingly has decided that in order to be successful, it must concentrate more heavily on showmanship than on presenting news in any depth.

It might interest you to know that in our industry no one company has as much as 8.5% of the U.S. gasoline market, as much as 9% of the domestic refining capacity, or as much as 10% of U.S. crude oil production. The three largest oil companies in each of the following categories together have less than 22.5% of the gasoline market in our country, less than a quarter of the refining capacity, and only a quarter of the crude oil produc- tion.

In national commercial television, three major networks dominate the scene. They particularly dominate the scene with respect to national and international news, since the news programs prepared by the local stations tend to present mostly local news. The three commercial networks com- bined have an audience estimated at more than 50 million people for the evening news programs broadcast at 7:00 p.m. Eastern Time. It is my understanding that no newspaper in this country has a circulation larger than about 2 million daily and 3 million on Sunday.

Among the newspapers there are some such as *The New York Times,* which not only dominates certain parts of its market—including, I believe, the New York market for help-wanted ads—but is also vertically integrated to the extent of owning substantial equity interests in three Canadian companies that make newsprint.

The *Times* is quite critical of oil company earnings. It called Occidental Petroleum's 718% increase in the first quarter of [1974] "a mirror image of what consumers are paying." Well, I doubt that anyone in this country is paying seven times as much for gasoline now as a year ago, but the *Times* neglected to mention that Occidental does not market in the United States. Nor did the *Times* tell its readers that Occidental's earnings in the first quarter of 1973—the benchmark period in this comparison—had dropped to a meager 6 cents a share, down more than 80% from eleven years earlier.

The Washington Post said recently that the government had an "urgent" duty to correct what that paper called the "vast enrichment" of the oil companies. This offers the opportunity for an instructive comparison. The net earnings of Texaco, one of the more profitable oil companies, increased 57% between 1970 and 1973. During this same period, the net income of the Washington Post Company increased about 160%.

True, 1970 was a bad year for the Washington Post Company but, taking the media as our models, we would have to conclude that benchmark years are not very relevant in such comparisons, because few of the media seem to have mentioned how bad 1972 and the first quarter of 1973 were for a lot of oil companies.

[In 1973] Mobil's worldwide earnings were up 48% over 1972. Those of the New York Times Company were up 58%; of the Washington Post Company, 37%. The networks also apparently had a good year in 1973. According to a news release from the Federal Communications Commission, the pre-tax profits of the three television networks combined—excluding earnings of the stations they own—were up 66.7% over 1972. The FCC doesn't seem to report profits *after* taxes, and the networks don't seem to report them very widely on either basis.

It seems to me we might witness a most interesting development if reporters and editors in electronic and print media were suddenly to develop an interest in the business side of their businesses and start poring over the income statements and balance sheets of their employers and their competitors. Once they learned how to pick their way through the figures to which few of them seem ever to have paid much attention . . . once they learned how to calculate rate of return, and grasped its importance as an index of profitability . . . and once they developed enough skepticism and reportorial curiosity to do some research on their own employers' price increases . . . once some of this transpired, they might well feel they had discovered a new and different world.

The more perceptive and open-minded among them would probably be shocked to discover that in some instances their own employer—whether a newspaper holding company or a network or whatever—was more profitable than many of the industries it was criticizing daily. With respect to concentration, they might learn that the overwhelming majority of the approximately 1,500 cities in which daily newspapers are published can be considered newspaper monopoly areas and that, as I mentioned earlier, national commercial network television is possibly the most concentrated U.S. industry. They might, in fact, in the process of overcoming deep-rooted preconceptions, develop additional insights and learn things that would make them better informed and more competent.

I hope nothing I have said . . . will be construed as ignorance or insensitivity on my part toward the contributions a free press has made throughout our country's history. Quite the contrary. We could not have remained a free people without it. Freedom of the press is clearly an essential ingredient of a democratic society—essential not only to the press itself, but to all of us. I submit, however, that it is inseparably linked to freedom of speech, and that both are in turn linked to a free economy.

Unlike some politicians, I am urging not less but more free speech, and for everyone—including most importantly those whose views some of us may find totally abhorrent. I would hope that those who write and speak the most about freedom of the press will come to comprehend that if they help to destroy our free economy, no matter how unwittingly, it could be only a matter of time before they lost their own freedom. I do not know which of our freedoms might be the first to go, but I do know that once we lose any one of them—whether free speech, free press, or our free economy—the others are apt soon to follow.

---

to the student : a commentary

Rawleigh Warner, as chairman of the Mobil Oil Corporation, one of the largest oil companies in America, might seem an odd person to be making public complaints. Yet his personal concern about the media coverage of the energy crisis, and what he sees as a distorted and one-sided view of the role of oil companies, leads him to air grievances about media treatment of an important national issue.

Warner is not alone. A growing number of people are dissatisfied with the news coverage of the business community, but Mobil Oil is one of the first to be willing to go on the offensive. Warner identifies what he sees as structural weaknesses in broadcast news and tells how Mobil, in an attempt to offset these deficiencies, asked to buy air time to present their side of the story. The networks turned them down. Mobil offered to pay for air time for those who wanted to rebut their version. The networks again refused.

It is here that Warner begins to touch on the crucial media issue. Should anyone be allowed to buy time on the public airwaves to present points of view on public issues?

The networks have said no, citing their rules—upheld in a 1973 Supreme Court decision—against paid time on controversial subjects. Part of the reasoning behind the logic is that the wealthy—either companies or individuals —would be able to dominate the air waves with self-interested messages. Mobil, however, tried to resolve that problem by paying for the opposition's message too, and it didn't do any good.

The disadvantage of being unable to enter, via broadcast, the "marketplace of ideas," was highlighted in 1976 by Mobil's confrontation with WNBC-TV in New York. The network's flagship station had run a five-part series in its local newscast on the price of gasoline. Mobil objected to what they considered inaccuracies (and there was no question that the station had some of the facts wrong—even neutral bystanders pointed out basic errors) and to deliberate distortions, such as the use of old film clips that were presented out of context. The oil company asked to buy time to reply, and the station turned them down, citing network policy. WNBC did offer, free, several minutes of air time for a response. Mobil said no, because they needed more time. "These are complex issues," one company spokesman said. "We're not talking about selling dog food."

Mobil turned to the print medium, where they could buy access, to do a point-by-point rebuttal of the broadcast. Taking out a full-page ad in the *New York Times,* the *New York Daily News,* and the Eastern edition of the *Wall Street Journal,* at a cost of nearly $36,000, Mobil asked in large type: "Whatever happened to fair play?" They then listed seventeen "warmed-over distortions, half-truths and downright untruths," beginning each one with the words "hatchet job" and the sketch of a hand-axe.

WNBC stood by its series, pointing out that it had assigned three staffers for six full weeks to research and write the story. The station did not, however, answer Mobil's specific complaints.

It might be helpful to provide some background explanation as to *why* the networks have a strong rule against controversial "commercials." As is often the case with issues in the media, the problem boils down to economics.

Warner's complaint is based on the fairness doctrine. In 1967 the FCC ruled that the fairness doctrine applied to commercials. Under siege at the moment were cigarette commercials, and because of the FCC ruling local stations were forced to provide free time for "counter-commercials." The networks had to distribute to their affiliates, free, a growing number of anti-smoking ads. Giving away free time didn't sit well with the networks, and in this case it wasn't making the tobacco companies happy either.

At the same time there was a court challenge of the fairness doctrine, and many broadcasters hung their hopes on the *Red Lion* case. On November 25, 1964, radio station WGCB in Red Lion, Pennsylvania, aired a program by the Rev. Billy James Hargis of the Christian Crusade. In that program Hargis attacked writer Fred J. Cook, who some months before had written an article entitled "Radio Right—Hate Clubs of the Air." In that article Cook had called Hargis a bigot. Hargis responded in the broadcast by calling Cook a mudslinger and accusing him of dishonesty and of falsifying stories.

Cook, citing the fairness doctrine, demanded time of WGCB to reply to the attack. When it was refused, he sued. The case began to slowly make its way through the courts.

In 1969 the U.S. Supreme Court handed down a decision on the *Red Lion* case, unanimously upholding the fairness doctrine. Shortly after the decision the networks and the tobacco companies stopped fighting the counter-commercial ruling of the FCC and let it be known that they would rather have no cigarette advertising at all. Congress obligingly passed a law banning cigarette commercials from the air. Broadcasters lost revenue that amounted to more than $200 million a year.

There was an increasing demand by consumer groups for counter-commercial time to rebut such products as automobiles and drugs. The broadcast industry, obviously worried, turned to the FCC. In 1974 Chairman Richard Wiley announced that the fairness doctrine should not apply to product commercials.

What the FCC did not deal with, however, was "issue" advertising. While commercials selling *things* were free of the fairness doctrine, nothing was said of commercials selling *ideas.* Since the energy crisis began, the oil companies have wanted to buy time to tell their side of the story (separate from merely selling their products), and opponents would naturally want time to reply.

Broadcasters, still feeling the sting of the cigarette controversy and not willing to get caught in the same position, found a simple solution: they refused time to both sides.

That, for the networks, may be a good economic decision. But what does it mean for the public? If a free and robust debate is necessary for there to be a "marketplace of ideas," what is the effect when someone, citing "fairness," closes the gates to the marketplace?

LLS

Paul Laskin

Shadowboxing
with the Networks

In December 1974 the Department of Justice for the second time filed suit
in the federal district court, Los Angeles, against NBC, CBS and ABC,
charging them with violating the antitrust laws in the operation of their
television networks. The gist of the suit is that the three companies have
abused their power to decide who shall have access to network air time in
order to concentrate in themselves "ownership and control of television
entertainment programs broadcast during prime evening hours." The government alleges that the three networks have forced outside producers to
give them a financial interest in evening programs; that they have refused
to show programs in which they have no financial interest, or to sell air
time to advertisers and outside suppliers for the screening of independent
programs; and that they are trying to control the prices of movies made
for television, either by going into the business of movie production (in
the case of CBS and ABC) or by contracting with a single large supplier
(in the case of NBC). The overall effect, according to the government, has
been to restrain competition in the production, distribution and sale of
entertainment programs, and to deprive the public of the benefits of free
and open competition.

The first suit against NBC, CBS and ABC, filed in April 1972, was
couched in substantially the same terms as the current one. Antitrust suits
can be Dickensian in their protraction, and the next two and a half years
were spent on skirmishes over the networks' preliminary legal defenses
and in "discovery" (a pretrial mechanism that enables each side to examine
the other side's documentary evidence). Then in November 1974, the court
dismissed the suit, "without prejudice," which meant that the government
could begin again if it wished. And that is what it has done.

Why the dismissal? It was the court's way of untying a difficult knot.
The networks argued that the original suit was invalid because improperly
motivated. It was not brought to enforce the antitrust laws, they said, but
to punish them for criticizing the Nixon administration and to intimidate

Reprinted with permission from "Shadowboxing with the Networks," by Paul Laskin,
The Nation, 14 June 1975.

them into something approaching silence. As the network saw it, the White House was consciously trying to curb their free speech, in violation of the First Amendment. They also argued that the government was applying the antitrust laws in a discriminatory manner, in violation of the due process clause of the Fifth Amendment, and that it had breached its constitutional duty to execute the laws "faithfully."

In their supporting briefs, the networks stressed the Nixon administration's hatred and fear of them. They cited a number of speeches and public comments by former Vice President Agnew and other administration officials. The networks also pointed out that the Nixon administration was quite willing (as the Watergate affair has proved) to use the regular processes of government to harass those whom it perceived as "enemies." And White House officials were well aware that the antitrust laws might be an effective tool to use against the networks. In October 1969, Magruder wrote Haldeman: "The real problem that faces this Administration is to get to this unfair coverage in such a way that we make major impact on a basis which the networks-newspapers and Congress will react to and begin to look at things somewhat differently." Then Magruder suggested: "Utilize the antitrust division to investigate various media relating to antitrust violations. Even the possible threat of antitrust action I think would be effective in changing their views in the above matter."

The networks also made much of the staleness of the complaints (a separate one for each network) and of the haste with which they were filed once the Department of Justice decided to act. Their lawyers said that the complaints dealt with matters that were known well before Nixon took office. This staleness, alleged the networks, indicated that the complaints were dredged up simply to harass them. As for the haste, the networks said that only a week before the event were they formally told that the complaints would be filed. Lawyers for the networks were summoned to the Department of Justice on very short notice ("a few hours," according to one lawyer) and informed that suit would be filed unless the networks agreed in principle within seven days to the government's demands for relief. All this was unseemly, said the networks, suspiciously so.

To this mixture of things, the networks added a recital of various threats made from time to time by White House officials. In February 1971, Ronald Ziegler told Dan Rather, the White House correspondent for CBS News, that the networks were "anti-Nixon" and that "they are going to have to pay for that, sooner or later, one way or another." On one or two occasions in 1970 or 1971, Ehrlichman apparently told Rather that "the networks will get theirs, of that you can be sure." And seven months after the antitrust suit was filed, Charles Colson, then Special Counsel to President Nixon, said to Frank Stanton, then vice chairman of CBS: "We'll bring you to your knees in Wall Street and on Madison Avenue."

In September 1971, Atty. Gen. John Mitchell approved the complaints against the networks on the recommendation of Asst. Atty. Gen. Richard McLaren, then head of the Antitrust Division. After signing them, however, Mitchell ordered that the filing of the suit be delayed so that Herbert Klein, White House director of communications, might have a chance to inform the networks of what was about to happen—and, in particular, to say to them that the suit was not politically motivated. (As things turned out, Klein never spoke of motivation to the networks—apparently because Ehrlichman instructed him not to.) When Mitchell resigned to become director of President Nixon's 1972 re-election campaign, the suit still had not been filed, and the complaints had to be freshly approved by his successor—Richard Kleindienst. When Kleindienst signed the complaints, he was still Acting Attorney General. He relied upon the recommendation of Acting Asst. Atty. Gen. Walker Comegys, then in charge of the Antitrust Division. The suit was thereupon formally instituted.

After Watergate, one's instinct is to side with the networks on the defense of improper motive, but they had constructed no more than a web of inferences. They had offered no hard evidence that either Mitchell or Kleindienst had approved the suit in order to retaliate against or to intimidate the networks—either at the express direction of the White House or out of a shared hatred of the networks. It was clear that the networks had to go beyond the inferential evidence if they were to carry their point. Therefore, they asked the court to let them take the depositions of Mitchell and Kleindienst and of most of the White House officials involved in the Watergate affair. (Nixon was still President, and his name was not on the list.) The networks also asked for access to whatever government records might be pertinent.

The government's immediate response was to deny that there had been any improper motive behind the filing of the suit. (This response later received support from the Special Prosecutor's office, which reported that its investigation of the Nixon White House had uncovered no evidence of improper motive.) The government also argued that the question of motive was irrelevant. It had charged the networks with violation of the antitrust laws, and the only question was the validity of that charge. But the court was not persuaded by this last argument. It felt, quite rightly, that motive was relevant and that the networks should have an opportunity to prove their point, if it could be proven.

On July 17, 1974 the court entered an order authorizing the networks to take the depositions of Mitchell and Kleindienst and to examine the government's records bearing on motive. The order covered the Nixon tapes as well as more conventional materials. Less than a month later, President Nixon resigned, and the networks immediately began to worry about the continuing availability of his papers and tapes. On August 16, a week after the resignation, a court hearing was held to find out where matters stood. The government's lawyer assured the court that the government understood quite well its duty to retain custody and control of whatever records were subject to the court's July 17th order. Everything seemed satisfactory—and then came the agreement on the Nixon papers and tapes between President Ford and his predecessor. The White House now said that, while it still had physical possession of the Nixon materials, it no longer had control over access to them.

There was another hearing; and then in mid-November the court decided to dismiss the suit "without prejudice." That was clearly the court's way of getting rid of a thorny issue that had nothing to do with the kinds of economic issues that lie at the heart of a major antitrust suit. A fresh suit, freshly approved by another attorney general, would presumably be free of any Nixon taint, and the case could then be decided on its own merits.

I say "presumably" because the networks are not letting go. They contended that the failure of the government, despite its promises, to comply with the court's July 17th order called for a dismissal "with prejudice." They also said that the issue of improper motive could not be so easily sanitized—that a fresh suit would be "the fruit of a poisonous tree." The networks appealed the "without prejudice" feature of the dismissal directly to the Supreme Court and when the government refiled its antitrust suit Justice Douglas granted the networks' request for a stay. Then . . . the Supreme Court dismissed the appeal "for want of jurisdiction."

The antitrust suit will now resume its course. If the past is prologue to the future, it will be a slow and tortuous one. And at some point, the court will hear from the networks about "the fruit of the poisonous tree." Meanwhile, it is worth asking what the government hopes to accomplish by its antitrust suit—and whether it is enough.

First one must look briefly at the institutional structure of television. At its core are CBS, NBC and ABC, which together spend more than $1 billion a year for programs. The networks perform two vital roles. The first is to provide the stations they own (each owns five) and the stations affiliated with them (CBS and NBC each has about 200 affiliates, ABC somewhat fewer) with a steady stream of programs of high technical quality, often with star performers. No individual station can afford to do that for itself. The cement between the networks and their affiliates is money. The networks pay their affiliated stations approximately 30 per cent of their revenues from sales to advertisers. In addition, each affiliate receives an allocation of advertising time that it can sell directly to local advertisers (and the affiliate pockets the proceeds). The fifteen network-owned stations are, by and large, in the most populous markets, and through them each network can reach about 25 per cent of the nation's viewers. In the case of these stations, the networks simply transfer money from one pocket to the other.

The network-station relationship is in turn the basis for the networks' second role: they can provide advertisers with a national audience for their commercial messages. That is the real business of a network, programs being the means to that end.

In the late 1950s, about a third of network programs had as sponsors a single advertiser or two advertisers acting cooperatively. A network sold a sponsor air time for an entire program, not just the time for his commercial message. But that changed in the 1960s. As program costs spiraled, advertisers were no longer willing to bet all their advertising dollars on a single program. They now preferred to spread their risk by allocating their advertising budgets among a number of programs. And so a program today may have as many as five or six sponsors; some, as many as a dozen. All the advertiser buys is a spot—usually thirty seconds—for his commercial.

By 1960, control over most of the nation's television programming had come to the networks. The individual stations had handed over their program responsibilities to the networks for money, and advertisers had backed away from program control because they did not want the financial responsibility that went with it. Program control, of course, means control over content. In general, the networks have always produced their own news and public-affairs programs; in the field of entertainment they have not, but their control is equally pervasive. They select the programs, usually on the basis of a script and pilot film, watch over them while they are being made, and review them before they are aired.

The networks welcomed this shift for a variety of reasons. One was the quiz show scandal of 1959. The prominent quiz shows had been provided by outside producers working with advertisers and their agencies; the networks said they had had little or no control over these programs. The obvious remedy seemed to be a greater assumption of responsibility by the networks. Another reason was the problem of "audience flow." The networks found that a television audience is inert. If a program is popular and attracts a large audience, much of that audience will stay with the channel into the next program. Thus, an evening's schedule is not a series of programs; it is a discrete unit, and the networks wanted the power to deal with it as such.

But the most compelling reason was money. Popular programs were extremely profitable, earning money from reruns in the United States and from sales to foreign television organizations. When a network selected a program series and watched over its development and preparation, it was in a position to demand a share in the program's ownership. And so it was not surprising that network participation in ownership became the prevailing pattern. The networks said that it was only fair because they bore an element of the risk of failure. To some, however, the pattern seemed an abuse of economic power. In either event, network profits went up and up.

The Communications Act of 1934 places upon the Federal Communications Commission the duty of regulating television broadcasting in "the public interest." During the early 1960s, the commission watched the growth of network control with considerable anxiety. In 1965, after more than five years of study, it concluded that the networks had "achieved virtual domination of television program markets" and that "it is not desirable for so few entities to have such a degree of power with respect to what the American public may see and hear over so many television stations." It was also disturbed because "this intense concentration of power decreases the competitive opportunity for independent program producers."

After another five years, the FCC promulgated a set of rules designed, so it said, to make it economically more attractive for existing producers to increase their program offerings and for new producers to come into the field. The expressed hope was that the new rules would promote greater diversity in television programming—by which the commission meant more programs for minority tastes and interests, more children's programs and more local programs.

The 1970 rules had two objectives. One was to make it possible for independent producers to earn more money. Because a network usually took a heavy share of the profits from a program accepted for national exhibition, the production company rarely recovered its costs from a first network run. It took subsequent runs within the United States and sales abroad to do that and to bring the company a profit. The FCC felt that the economic risk for an independent producer was too large—that it was deterring many who might otherwise come into the program production market. It said, therefore, that henceforth a network could not, except when it was the sole producer, engage in syndication (the sale and distribution of programs to non-network stations); could not distribute programs abroad nor share in the profits from foreign sales; and could not acquire any financial interest whatsoever (other than the right of network exhibition) in a program produced in whole or in part by an outside company.

The second objective was to make evening air time on the networks more accessible to independent producers. This was to be achieved by what has come to be called the prime-time access rule. Before 1970, when the rule was adopted, the common practice of the networks had been to furnish three and a half hours of programming to their affiliates in the four-hour period from 7 to 11 P.M. The FCC said that in the top fifty television markets, the networks could henceforth furnish only three hours of programming in this period. The rule would insure that an hour of evening time would be available for independent producers.

Five years later, it is clear that the 1970 rules have failed to diminish the networks' control over what is broadcast during the evening hours. The 1970 rules did not stimulate the entry of new producers into the field of television production. And paradoxically, the networks have become stronger and richer. There are several reasons for the continued growth of network power. While it is true that the prime-time access rule deprived the networks of the right to program one hour of evening time, it seems to have made their affiliated stations more dependent on them than ever for the remaining three hours. Moreover, since the rule made network programs somewhat scarcer, the fees for advertising on the remaining programs went up. And finally, the networks, this time acting through the stations they themselves owned and operated, naturally had the largest hand in determining the fate of independent syndicators who sought to produce programs for the new access hour.

While the FCC may and does take economic considerations into account in regulating the television industry, the primary responsibility for enforcing the antitrust laws rests with the Department of Justice. Like the FCC, the department's Antitrust Division has long been casting an anxious eye on the three networks, but throughout the 1960s it made no direct move against them. In 1969, when the new commission rules were being considered, the division commented approvingly on them; it thought they would have a beneficial effect on economic competition in the field. It was not until three years later that the Department of Justice took action itself by filing an antitrust suit.

When the government's first suit was announced, it was spoken of in the press as a fundamental attack on network control over television broadcasting. This view may have reflected the networks' immediate reaction: that the government was out to "get" them. Or it may have been the result of too hasty a reading of the formal complaints filed by the government. In any event, the suit was something less than an attempt to bring the networks to their knees. And so, too, is the second suit.

Perhaps the most significant feature of the [second] suit is what it does not do. The fundamental institutional structure of network TV broadcasting is to remain intact. The suit accepts and does not challenge the relationship that has grown up over the years between the networks and their affiliates, although that relationship lies at the heart of the networks' control of TV broadcasting. It also accepts and does not challenge network ownership of five TV stations. The government seems to feel that the networks should continue to be not only the conduit for programs aimed at a national audience but also the final arbiter of what is shown nationally.

The Justice Department, saying that it wants to bring the benefits of free and open competition to the public, asks for three specific remedies. One, that each network be prohibited from obtaining any interest in television entertainment programs produced by others (including movies), except for the right of first-run exhibition. Two, that each network be barred from the syndication business. And three, that each network be forbidden to transmit whatever entertainment programs (including movies) it produces itself or that are produced by the other commercial networks.

What does the government hope to achieve with these remedies? First, that the networks will choose among the programs offered for network exhibition in an open manner, that is, free from the bias of financial self-interest. Second, that the networks will not use their control over access to their air time to overreach, that is, to enrich themselves unfairly and to preclude competition in areas that are normally competitive (like movie production). These are certainly desirable objectives—and traditional ones under the antitrust laws. But in the context of the pervasive network control that exists today, it must be said that they are limited goals.

Two of the specific remedies proposed by the government—that the networks be prohibited from acquiring any financial interest in programs produced by others and from engaging in the business of syndication—are already contained in the rules issued by the FCC in 1970. The only new remedy that the government is asking for is an order prohibiting the networks from showing any entertainment programs they produce themselves. The networks point out that they produce very few of the entertainment programs they exhibit, probably less than 10 per cent. And while it is true that CBS and ABC have moved into the production of feature films for television, they say that they did so for quite legitimate motives —to assure fair prices and a sufficient and steady supply.

The networks also object to the new remedy on constitutional grounds. They say that it is tantamount to prohibiting them from producing any entertainment programs on their own, and that for this reason it will violate their right of free speech. The networks are not arguing that because they are engaged in the business of communicating, they are not subject to the antitrust laws. But they say that if they have violated the antitrust laws, the remedies must take into consideration and must respect their freedom to communicate. And they add that entertainment programs are as much entitled to the protection of the First Amendment as are news and public-affairs programs (which are untouched by the government's suit).

But the real question is: whose First Amendment are we talking about? In the *Red Lion Broadcasting Company* case, the Supreme Court considered the Fairness Doctrine, which requires broadcasters to "afford reasonable opportunity for the discussion of conflicting views on issues of public importance." The Court ruled that it "is the right of the viewers and listeners, not the right of the broadcasters, which is paramount. . . ." With the new remedy proposed by the government in the antitrust suit, one may argue that the networks' right to transmit their own entertainment programs must give way to the public's right to reap the benefits of free and open competition in TV entertainment. The Fairness Doctrine is not a perfect analogy, of course. The doctrine does not say that a broadcaster may not present his own views on a controversial issue; it says only that when he presents one side, he must present other sides. In the antitrust suit the government is asking for silence: that the networks be flatly prohibited from presenting their own entertainment programs. The prohibition adds weight to the networks' claim that the First Amendment will be violated. Still, the application of the First Amendment is not as simple as the networks would have it appear, and it is hard to predict where the Supreme Court (if it is called upon to decide the issue) will find the balance lies as between the networks' claim of protection and the government's assertion that the public is entitled to all the benefits of competition.

But if we put the constitutional question aside and assume that the Court grants the government the specific remedies it is requesting, what is likely to happen? Probably very little. There will be greater purity in the economic relationships between the networks and outside program producers, but network control will be as strong as ever. The 1970 rules of the FCC made little difference, and the situation is not apt to be changed by the new remedy that would bar the networks from transmitting network-produced entertainment programs. The sad conclusion is that, even if the government gets all the remedies it is specifically asking for, the power to decide what the American public sees and hears on the air will remain with the networks.

The FCC is disappointed by the effects of its 1970 rules. It is not yet ready to abandon the prime-time access rule, but it is pruning it—basically, by reducing the access period from one hour to thirty minutes (which is what it was originally as a matter of practice). But the failure of the 1970 rules to diminish network control does not necessarily mean that the concept of access is wrong. It may also be taken to prove that if a sound concept is applied in a half-hearted way, nothing will happen.

What the FCC should now do (and should have done in the first place) is prescribe a longer access period—say half of the evening hours. If the commission were to do that, it would open up a large enough block of time on every television station to provide a strong incentive for the development of new companies to serve these stations on a national basis. Such companies might be entirely new, or new outgrowths of established companies. They might be constructed along network lines (in which case we might have six networks instead of three) or on different economic principles. We need not foresee the precise line of development. My point is only that if we wish to encourage the entry of new suppliers into the field of TV programming and reduce the dependence of the individual stations on the existing networks, there must be a sufficiently long access period.

As a corollary of a rule of expanded access, the commission would also have to limit network ownership of television stations. As matters stand, the networks, acting as program purchasers for their owned stations, can decide the fate of any new production company and thus subvert the rule. Each network should be forbidden to own more than one station and should be required (over a reasonable period of time) to divest itself of ownership of the remaining four.

In the current antitrust suit, the government makes the allegation that "the networks ... generally will not offer to sell air time to advertisers except for their commercial messages which are broadcast in conjunction with television entertainment programs already selected and placed in schedules by the networks." The allegation suggests a remedy that is even more drastic than a rule of expanded access: that the networks be confined to the role of selling air time to others for entertainment programs. There is no doubt that the remedy would end network control over entertainment programming once and for all. But there are two objections to so sweeping a remedy—one practical, the other conceptual. The practical objection is that there would probably not be enough buyers of air time for individual programs. There will always be the need for an economic institution—a network if you will—that brings together stations, program producers and advertisers. The conceptual difficulty is that if the networks are confined to the sale of air time for programs procured by others, they would in effect become common carriers. And this would run counter to the intent of the Communications Act. In defining a common carrier, the Act states that "a person engaged in radio broadcasting [and by extension, television broadcasting] shall not, insofar as such person is so engaged, be deemed a common carrier."

In proposing a rule of expanded access, I have no illusion that the FCC will prescribe one. It is too timid, too dilatory and too muddy in its thinking. But the government can and should seek the same result in its antitrust suit. As we have seen, all the government is now asking from the court are remedies designed to insure that the networks do not enrich themselves unfairly and have no conflict of economic interest when they make up their entertainment schedules. None of these remedies will diminish the concentration of control over television programming that is now lodged in the three networks. And yet only if that is broken, can we have the economic and social benefits, whatever they might be, of free and open competition.

to the student : a commentary

Paul Laskin is a lawyer who has studied national television broadcasting policy, often with backing from large foundations. He draws upon his expertise here to put an antitrust suit, filed by the Department of Justice against the three major networks, into a meaningful perspective. The first suit by Justice, filed in 1972, was dismissed by the court. The new suit is expected to be drawn out by legal skirmishing for some years. In his brief sketch of the first antitrust suit, Laskin explains that it was dismissed because the networks had claimed the suit was politically motivated, a part of the Nixon administration's attempt to hurt the national media. This is worth exploring a bit further.

In May of 1973 ex–White House Counsel John Dean testified before a Senate committee that the Nixon administration kept a list of "enemies," and that government agencies, such as the FBI and Internal Revenue Service, were used to collect embarrassing information on them. When copies of the enemy list were released, the names of fifty working journalists, as well as other media people, were included.

The White House tactics against those on the list ranged from childish to illegal. The *Washington Post* society reporter covering the White House, for example, was kept from reporting tea parties in the Rose Garden. On a slightly higher plane, the president and his aides granted interviews to *Washington Star* reporters, in the admitted hope of denting the Post's circulation. But the battle became serious when two *Post*-owned television stations in Florida had their license renewal applications challenged—and the leaders of each challenging group turned out to be high-ranking Republican party officials.

Additional tactics against the media were revealed when the Senate Watergate committee made public a White House memo written by Jeb Stuart Magruder to H. R. Haldeman, outlining several ways to "get the media." Among the methods listed in the memo were: having the Federal Communications Commission begin "an official monitoring system" to prove bias on the part of the networks; threatening IRS investigations of "the various organizations that we are most concerned about"; and—as Laskin points out—threatening antitrust action against various media organizations.

While threatening to use a federal agency for political reasons may belong in the fuzzy area of ethics, actually *using* an agency is flat-out illegal. And it happened.

Daniel Schorr, a CBS Washington correspondent, found himself the subject of an FBI investigation. Friends, colleagues, and his employers were questioned by FBI agents, and many were told it was because Schorr was being considered for a government job. It was news to Schorr, who had not been—and never was—approached about a position. The investigation was soon suspected of being, as Schorr wrote, "a new wrinkle in the war on the media."

If so, why me? I was, after all, a relatively small reportorial planet in a galaxy of anchormen and commentators. Some in CBS theorized that some specific piece of reporting had created some specific antagonist. They suggested that investigative reporting, undermining studied public relations postures, could have raised more hidden hackles than critical commentary, which could be refuted or simply dismissed.

Schorr was right. The investigation, John Dean later testified, was ordered by top presidential aide H. R. Haldeman. Schorr's name was on the list, and next to it was a written notation: "A real media enemy."

The weight of such evidence, gathered and packaged by network lawyers, is what moved the court to dismiss the first suit. But since the dismissal was "without prejudice," the Justice Department was free to begin again, this time without the dark entanglements of the Nixon administration.

If the new suit, free of political taint, is ultimately successful, the networks will be cut out of the production end of the business, and in theory, independent producers would have a chance to compete in a newly attractive economic marketplace. But how realistic is this "Adam Smith" view of television economics? Would many new and hopeful producers be able to compete with those few large and already established companies, such as the Norman Lear and Mary Tyler Moore organizations, outside of the networks?

Jeff Greenfield, a writer and political media consultant, has investigated the extent to which networks must invest money to find successful television shows. Some of his findings:

- A single half-hour pilot can cost a network at least $275,000.
- A one-hour pilot means a commitment of about $600,000.
- The thirty-four pilots NBC funded for the 1974–75 season cost that network about $15 million.
- An unsuccessful one-hour series could cost a network $5 million just to wipe the show off the air, and the loss in reduced advertising costs could amount to another $5 million.

A hard look at those figures makes one thing obvious: without the networks, production of television entertainment programs is going to be limited to people with very big checkbooks. The "free and open competition" Laskin talks about, and which the Justice Department says it seeks, would be a long way from free, and open mainly to those who have the ability to pick up the tab.

The fight for television audiences is really more like a war, with elaborate research armies, scheduling battle plans, and programming directors who marshal their forces much as if they were field generals. It's a war the networks take with deadly seriousness. The "concentration of control" over programming that they have is in part a result of their control over production, which may be a crucial factor in the desperate battle for ratings. For example, in the 1974–75 season, CBS came out ahead of NBC by nine-tenths of a rating point. It wasn't much of an advantage—the difference, perhaps, of one successful half-hour show—because one Nielsen point roughly represents only two million viewers (a single hit show, like *Sanford and Son,* draws as many as 40 million viewers a week). But for CBS that one rating point meant an *additional* $17.5 million in advertising revenues.

When the competition is that close (and it should be pointed out that ABC, for years a distant third place, has been quickly closing the gap), and yet the outcome of the difference so great, it is easy to understand why the networks intend to contest the Justice Department every step of the way.

Laskin feels that even if the networks are eventually forced out of production it will make little difference, since local television stations are not themselves forced to fill larger blocks of time. They would still take whatever the networks buy from others and send out, rather than contracting independently with producers. If this would be the case, it's far from certain that forcing the networks out of business is automatically positive. The 1970 FCC decision to force an hour of access (non-network) time on local stations—7 to 8 P.M. in most places—didn't result in what one could call social benefits. A look at any television log shows what most of the time has been filled with: *Truth or Consequences, Concentration, The Price is Right, $25,000 Pyramid, Hollywood Squares,* and on and on.

Obviously, the issue of network control is not a simple one, and there are no easy answers in the complex tangle of laws, economics, politics, and audience desires. But since it affects what you will—and will not—see whenever you turn on your set, it is an issue worthy of your continuing attention.

LLS

---

study questions

1. In the *Red Lion* decision the Court ruled that "it is the purpose of the First Amendment to preserve an uninhibited marketplace of ideas in which truth will ultimately prevail." In other words, its purpose is to ensure the people's "right to know." Do you think that the fairness doctrine accomplishes this purpose, as its defenders say, by forcing broadcasters to present all sides of a controversial issue or topic, or do you think it impedes this purpose by making broadcasters hesitant about programming any sort of controversy at all?

2. Richard Jencks argues that the First Amendment's protection of the print media from government interference should be extended equally to the broadcast media. Considering both the differences and the similarities in the nature and function of these two types of media, is there any justification for this demand?

3. Does television need to be constrained?

4. Rawleigh Warner, Jr., complains that Mobil Oil Company has been denied access by ABC and CBS, in the form of political advertisements, to explain its policies to the public. Should television stations be obligated to allow access to anyone claiming to speak to the public interest? If they were so obligated, what would be the implications of this in terms of First Amendment rights and the economic realities of television as a business?

5. The crux of the argument about the fairness doctrine is First Amendment rights. Which is predominant: the people's right to know, or the broadcasters' right to free speech and freedom of the press? Explore the arguments for both sides.

6. Richard Jencks states that "the whole lesson of American democracy is that we do not secure the rights of the people by vesting those rights in the government." How then are these rights to be upheld in television broadcasting, especially in regard to fairness and access? Is there any evidence that television can regulate itself?

7. The basis of a democratic society is the delicate and precarious balance between freedom and responsibility. What are the television medium's freedoms, and what are its responsibilities? How can the balance between them best be maintained?

8. The Nixon administration has shown that the government can exploit its powers of regulation over the TV industry and use them as a weapon against the medium, especially in terms of its journalistic adversarial position. How does this affect the debate over the government's right to regulate broadcasting?

3 ra-dio

Radio is a personalized medium, with each local station attempting to slice off a specific and identifiable piece of the listening market. From country and western to all-news, rock and roll to classical, radio is programmed for distinct audiences, whose similarity in taste often arises from similarities in age, education, cultural background, buying habits. It is also a mobile medium, traveling freeways and country roads, appearing at beaches, parks, and in the pockets of millions of people.

But "radio" involves more than the radio industry. It is also the principal salesman for the huge record industry, which in turn spins off live concerts, television shows, and even books. The following section thus includes articles that move beyond radio into such areas as song lyrics and the record business.

The articles on all-news stations and "topless" radio make clear that radio can be other than music. More important, these same articles serve as samples of radio economics and regulatory problems. With the growth in FM stations, foreign language broadcasting, and all-news formats, along with a variety of other attempts to capture special-interest audiences, the radio industry has become an increasingly complex aspect of the mass media.

151

radio

social force

Drawing by Weber; © 1962 The New Yorker Magazine, Inc.

"I'm sick of playing Twenty Questions. Turn on the radio."

John P. Robinson and Paul Hirsch

It's the Sound that Does It

In 1967 the owner of a large chain of radio stations launched a campaign against "filth" in the record industry. With the support of the Georgia State Legislature, several rural broadcasters' associations, the Executive Council of the Episcopal Church, and numerous citizens' groups, he organized a panel of prostitutes and drug addicts to advise him in weeding out suggestive records. "We've had all we can stand of the record industry's glorifying marijuana, LSD and sexual activity," he fumed.

The crusade was not particularly successful. Today you don't have to hire a prostitute or addict to translate lyrics for you; mass magazines freely supply the supposed hidden messages (such as the Beatles' "*L*ucy in the *S*ky with *D*iamonds"). Still the furor continues in energetic spurts. Parents become incensed. Radio programmers reply that pop songs have always been opposed to traditional morality ("Teach Me Tonight"). Recently some teen-agers organized a Rally for Decency in Miami, protesting "immoral" rock music and an "obscene" stage performance by the Doors.

This controversy is part of what has been called the *revolution in rock*. Early rock 'n' roll in the 1950s was essentially a lower-class phenomenon, expressing attitudes, concerns and habits common to this stratum (boredom with school, drag-racing, dating). It was performed by young working-class people who rehearsed on brownstone stoops and street corners. Contemporary rock . . . is electronic. It requires expensive equipment and, since the advent of the Beatles, often more serious musicianship. Its performers are from predominately middle-class backgrounds and have attended some of the best colleges. The new rock, like its predecessor, reflects the concerns of its creators. Some songs express antiwar feeling (as in "The Eve of Destruction" or "2 + 2"); a large number refer to drug usage ("Step Out of Your Mind," "Strawberry Fields Forever"). Songs with sexual themes have been around since man discovered music—at roughly the same time that he discovered sex—but these days they are often blatantly orgasmic ("Heavy Music"). Since in all of these cases an important feature of the song is its message, we can characterize such new rock music as social *protest.*

Teen-agers, of course, are the major consumers of rock-'n'-roll music. They listen to the Top 40 (the best-selling current hits) an average of two hours a day, often devouring hit records as soon as they are released. Teen-agers buy 60 percent of all 45-rpm singles; the under-25 set buys 80 percent. Many of these hits become popular with the majority of Americans shortly afterward. Rock artists play in top night clubs to enthusiastic adult audiences; softened versions of hard rock hits are piped into supermarkets; even Lawrence Welk gets around to recording the Top 10.

Given the influence that this adolescent minority has on the musical tastes of America, it is surprising that we don't know much more about it than the number of records they buy. Adults tend to view teen-agers as an undifferentiated horde, ears glued to transistors, chuckling gleefully at obscene lyrics designed to put one over on the Establishment. Adults reasonably assume that the teen-agers who like rock songs also understand them. They assume that records with protest messages are bought because of those messages. Finally, the record industry believes that it provides what its listeners want. "The kids are no longer interested in ditties," said a record-company magazine.

To what extent are these assumptions true? To what extent has the record industry created the demand for . . . rock?

To answer these questions, we surveyed 430 high-school students in metropolitan Detroit (population 4 million), and 340 in the smaller Michigan community of Grand Rapids (population 500,000), located about 160 miles west of Detroit. We chose eighth-and 11th-grade classrooms, as these had varied widely in social class, race and religion. The questionnaires were administered by public-school teachers taking a course in mass communications.

Our first finding will come as no surprise to anyone who is or knows a teen-ager: the popularity of the Top 40 among high schoolers is nearly total. Given three choices—"like a lot," "O.K." and "don't like"—over 75 percent said they liked current popular hits A LOT. Fewer than one percent of all our students said that they disliked current hits. These were mostly upper-middle-class youngsters in Detroit, or religious fundamentalists from rural areas around Grand Rapids.

Our respondents rated (in descending order of preference) modern jazz, folk songs, show tunes, and classical music as generally O.K. But country-and-western was least popular among all students in both cities—with well over two-thirds saying they DON'T LIKE this type of music. The few who really liked it live in rural areas or have migrated from the South. . . .

Having determined that almost everyone liked current hits in general, we set out to find what particular style of rock they preferred. We asked

DETROIT	
Rhythm and blues	36%
Protest	13%
Other hits	45%
Square	6%
	100%

GRAND RAPIDS	
Rhythm and blues	15%
Protest	14%
Other hits	63%
Square	8%
	100%

the students to list their favorite songs, their favorite artist, and the names of three records they had recently bought. These favorites fell into four broad categories: rhythm and blues ("soul"); social protest (contemporary or psychedelic rock with a message); other current hits; and square (anything not on the Top 40, such as "The Old Rugged Cross"). The distribution of favorites [is shown in the table above].

We found that teen-agers tend to cluster predictably, according to which type of rock they prefer and buy. Far from liking all the top hits indiscriminately, they carefully select the ones they like, and they may not even be aware of the others—though all hits on Top 40 radio stations are given the same exposure.

For instance, let's look at soul music. This sound was far more popular in Detroit, largely because there are many more blacks in Detroit than in the smaller city, and this is reflected in our sample. We had expected that the black students would prefer rhythm and blues, particularly since Detroit is the home of many famous black singers. But even so the correlation between race and musical preference was enormously high (.87). This means that knowledge of a student's race enables us to predict with 75 percent accuracy whether he likes and will probably buy rhythm-and-blues records. (Most correlations obtained from survey research seldom exceed .50 or a 25 percent accuracy in prediction.) In Grand Rapids also, blacks knew the latest blues releases but were largely unaware of other hits. Their aversion to the rest of the Top 40 was strong; many said that they tuned in at night to a soul station broadcasting from Tennessee.

On the other hand, many white working-class teen-agers were oblivious of the soul music so popular with their black classmates. A considerable number said that they had not even heard the current blues hits. Instead, they like what we have lumped together under the heading OTHER

HITS. This category included rock songs with conventional themes ("The Last Train to Clarksville," by the Monkees); or traditional love songs ("Cherish," by the Association); or movie hits ("To Sir With Love").

Who preferred the protest songs? A relatively small group of white middle- and upper-class teen-agers. By and large, they were above-average students with fathers in white-collar and professional occupations. In other words, the contemporary rock that is composed and sung by middle-class rebels appeals primarily to middle-class listeners. Traditional rock (our OTHER HITS) still has more appeal among working-class teen-agers.

Far from being universally liked, then, the psychedelic sound was least popular of all the records on the Top 40. Do teen-agers understand those controversial lyrics? The answer seems to be: sort of, more or less, sometimes.

We asked our students to tell us the meanings of several popular records. These songs and their general themes, were "Ode to Billy Joe" (indifference to tragedy); "Incense and Peppermints," "Lucy in the Sky with Diamonds" and "The Condition My Condition Was In" (drugs); "Heavy Music" and "Gimme the Green Light" (sex); and "Skip-a-Rope" (parental hypocrisy).

Again we found consistent class differences. Upper-middle-class teen-agers were more likely to understand the meaning of the songs, just as they were more likely to prefer them. The higher percentage of middle-and-upper-class people in Grand Rapids helps account for the differences between our two cities. For example, in Detroit 20 percent of the students who had heard the song made explicit reference to drugs in describing the drug songs, but 31 percent in Grand Rapids understood the theme.

Even so, the large majority of the students did not get the message of these hits. Only a third of them could write a half-way reasonable description. "Ode to Billy Joe" was most widely recognized among the teen-agers. But descriptions were either very literal ("Billy Joe jumps off a cliff"); or very vague ("What one says he knows is not always true; life is a mystery"); or a little muddled ("It's about a girl who falls off a bridge"). Occasionally they got the idea ("It's about life and how people are indifferent to a tragedy not concerning them"). Our favorite was, "It's about a boy who just couldn't take this thing we call life."

In short, most of the teen-agers did not understand the lyrics or were indifferent ("No real meaning, just a good sound"). They were much more interested in *sound* than in *meaning* anyway: when they were asked to make a choice, 70 percent of all our students said that they liked a record more for its beat than for its message.

Finally, we asked the students whether they would like more, fewer, or the same number of songs on several themes: drugs, school is dull, parents' lack of understanding, social problems, love affairs, freedom for teen-

	DETROIT			
	Ode to Billy Joe	*Incense and Peppermints*	*Heavy Music*	*Lucy in the Sky*
No meaning given	15	48	41	46
Inadequate description	63	32	39	27
Understood theme	22	20	20	27
	100%	100%	100%	100%

	GRAND RAPIDS			
	Ode to Billy Joe	*My Condition*	*Green Light*	*Skip-a-Rope*
No meaning given	16	34	26	32
Inadequate description	67	35	32	25
Understood theme	17	31	42	43
	100%	100%	100%	100%

(Table includes only those teen-agers who had heard song in question.)

agers, love and understanding. Most students wanted fewer songs about drugs and more about love and understanding. On the others, they indicated that they would like just about what they had been getting.

How much does it matter what the teen-agers want? We described earlier the indirect influence that adolescents have as a result of their consumption of hit singles. Does the music business manipulate its audience or is it really responsive to their wishes?

The answer, unsurprisingly, is both. The record industry is a mixture of cautious conservatism and competitive innovation. Low costs and the promise of huge profits sustain many small recording companies that are willing to experiment with musical styles. They serve as try-outs for the major companies, whose young A&R (artists and repertory) men keep ears to the ground for promising new sounds. A&R men, composers and performers all provide creative input for the industry. The older, more conservative policy-makers decide which performing groups they think will be successful and then promote them extensively. For example, both early rock 'n' roll and rhythm-and-blues began on small labels. RCA Victor bought out Sun Records in order to get Elvis Presley, and we know what happened to *him*.

As part of their effort to expose their new acquisitions to wider audiences, record companies release their singles to the Top 40 radio stations. The programmers filter out a relatively small number of "pick hits" from all the possibilities. As we've seen, their selections tend to form an eclectic bag of songs, beamed at a diverse group of listeners.

From here the teen-agers take over. Whether a new record receives continued exposure depends on the strength of its sales during its first few days on the air. If the record sells noticeably, it is added to the station's play-list; otherwise it is dropped from the competition. The best seller, of course, becomes No. 1; the others are ranked accordingly.

Thus the record business serves its audience much as a political primary serves voters: individuals are given an opportunity to provide feedback about candidates preselected for them. To the extent that teen-agers keep buying (and thereby ranking) hits on Top 40 radio, they do influence the kind of music that stations will continue to play. But to the extent that their choice has been limited—by record companies that choose to promote only some groups and by radio stations that choose to broadcast only some releases—the music industry determines the sounds that their listeners will hear and come to like.

The evolution of contemporary rock illustrates this system. Drug, sex and antiwar songs . . . were first broadcast on underground FM stations in large cities. Middle-class teen-agers and college students involved in various protest movements bought the records in huge numbers. Several groups became very popular on small labels; a spate of imitators followed. The race was on. With one sniff of the sweet smell of success, every major record company began to acquire groups with the new psychedelic sound. Once they took this risk, they set about protecting their investments. So the Jefferson Airplane appear[ed] on Perry Como. Ed Sullivan tolerate[d] at least one rock group a week (although the Rolling Stones had to change "Let's Spend the Night Together" to "Let's Spend Some Time Together"). And Leonard Bernstein embraced the new rock in a TV special, the highest accolade of all ("Inside Pop: The Rock Revolution").

So . . . rock music is well on its way to a respectable place in the Establishment. Its protest has been co-opted. As long as the . . . sound is a commercial success, we can be sure there will be more of it—along with the controversy over its message. However, since most teen-agers buy records for sound and not for meaning, the furor over "filth" is probably unnecessary. In the words of one student. "The song's a whole lot of words mixed up, and it comes out nice."

---

to the student: a commentary

Sociologists John Robinson and Paul Hirsch present one of the few empirical studies about teenagers as record consumers. Although their research is several years old, it provides an unusual look into one part of a multi-million dollar industry.

There is a bit of irony in the fact that teenagers decide "not to hear" some of the records being aired, considering how statistically unlikely it was for those records to get played to begin with. It has been estimated that the Top Forty AM stations receive from the record companies more than 7,000 singles each year, along with 4,000 albums. With approximately twelve songs per album, the radio station has, in theory, some 55,000 songs a year to pick from. Only a small percentage, of course, are actually aired.

But as anyone who has listened to Top Forty radio has realized, those songs that do get aired are played again and again. Who decides which song to play? One West Coast station may serve as a typical example. The disc jockeys are given seven different categories of songs to pick from, ranging from "old gold" to the current top hits. The categories are color-coded, and the DJs follow a clock on the wall that signals which category to pick from. The DJ pulls a card from the proper file which has the title of the record and other information. He calls off the card number to the engineer, who in turn puts in the proper cartridge. (A decreasing number of radio stations are actually using records. Tape cartridges simplify the operation.)

When choosing a card from the "top ten" file, the DJ has to make sure not to pick one that has been played in the last two hours; the time limit for the rest of the "top 40" is three hours. The pace picks up at night, when there is greater call-in demand for songs. The hottest hits are played every other hour.

Different shifts are formulated according to the audience at that time of day, and the color-categories are expanded and contracted. There is more "gold" in midday, for example, because of the housewife audience. (The total number of "golden oldies" played during a day averages out to four an hour.)

The repetition, according to the program director of the station, is based on demand, and the telephone calls show that most young people don't listen for a great length of time. "We'll play, say 'December '63' by the Four Seasons and the minute it gets off the air someone will call and request it. You are going to hear about nine songs in a 30-minute period and chances are someone will call up and ask for one of those nine again. These requests help us get an idea of what is currently popular in our area. Most people only listen to the radio about 25 minutes at a time, and that's why they keep calling."

Does calling the station with a request do much besides create a tally-sheet for what is popular? It doesn't make much difference, according to the program director, "because they call for songs that are coming up anyway."

If repetition doesn't bother the average listener because he isn't tuned in that long, what does it do to the disc jockey stuck in the studio for four hours a day? "Repetition does bother us," the program director said. "And it shows up on some jocks. They get depressed because they have to play the same songs over and over again. But it's a cancer you have to control, because when you consider that this is what you do for a living, that this is what they are paying you for . . ."

On most Top Forty stations the disc jockey is strictly limited as a "personality." Given the highly structured and predictable music format, the average twelve minutes per hour of commercials, the station identification jingle, the required public service announcements, and the quick incursions of "20–20 News," disc jockeys, as music writer Serge Denisoff has pointed out, often seem little more than an appendage to a Top Forty chart. "Brian Wilson has just spent nine months of his life wrestling with this thing that takes two minutes and forty seconds," jocks were told at one station. "So unless you got something really terrific to say, for your eight seconds, shut up." It has even been rumored that some Top Forty stations have buzzers that go off after eight seconds of disc jockey air time.

There is something odd, and a trifle sad, in the fact that rock and roll radio stations show so much concern with their "sound," creating rigid programming formats, while the audience is made up of inconsistent listeners. The audience doesn't stay tuned in for very long, they can't remember—and therefore "don't hear"—those songs they don't care for, and according to Robinson and Hirsch, they don't even pay much attention to the words of even those songs they do like.

What does it all mean? Maybe not much more than a familiar line from the old American Bandstand: "It's got a good beat. You can dance to it. I give it maybe a 75."

LLS

David Shaw

All-News Radio:
Talk that Rates

It's seven in the morning, and all over Los Angeles, people are awakening to the sounds of their clock radios—tens of thousands of them tuned to the fanfare of trumpets and xylophones that herald the beginning of each newscast on KFWB.

The KFWB theme lasts only 12 seconds, but it is clearly designed to give the impression that something V-E-R-Y B-I-G is about to happen; nothing in the announcer's stentorian tones is likely to contradict that impression:

"This is KFWB Los Angeles . . . Group W . . . Westinghouse Broadcasting . . . serving Southern California . . . All news, all the time . . . You give us 22 minutes: we'll give you the world . . ."

All news? All the time?

Eleven years ago, when KFWB's sister station, WINS, introduced the all-news concept in New York, most people in radio thought the station's executives were certifiably crazy.

"There was no way they could find enough news or enough audience to make it work," says Reg Laite, then a reporter for WINS' major competitor, WCBS. "They were out of their minds, all of them."

That was Reg Laite in 1964. But in 1967, Laite's own station went all-news, and now both WINS and WCBS are still all-news and Laite himself is the news director of all-news KFWB.

All-news radio is the broadcasting phenomenon of the last decade. In almost every major city where there is an all-news station, that station ranks at or near the top of the market in the two critical measures of radio success—audience size and advertising revenue.

WINS and WCBS rank in the top five among New York's 64 radio stations. Los Angeles' two all-news stations, KFWB and KNX, hold similar rankings in the area's highly fragmented, 73-station market.

In Philadelphia, an all-news station is the No. 1 rated station in town. In San Francisco and Miami, the all-news stations are No. 2, in Chicago and Boston, they're No. 3.

Reprinted by permission of David Shaw from the *Los Angeles Times,* 2 September 1975.

There are now 50 all-news stations in 44 different American cities and the numbers are growing almost daily. . . .

But why is all-news suddenly so popular? Haven't people been complaining that they're tired of news, tired of reading and hearing about crises and shortages and riots and trials and wars and violence and . . .

"That," says George Nicholaw, general manager of KNX, "is precisely the point. Look at the news we've had in the last eight or 10 years—Watergate, Vietnam, a man on the moon, the '68 Democratic convention in Chicago, women's liberation, the assassinations of Martin Luther King and Robert Kennedy. . . .

"There's a growing awareness that what's happening in the world affects everyone directly today. Thanks to modern communications and transportation, the world is smaller today. Things happen faster. People want to know about them. They need to know about them."

Robert Mounty, general manager of the NBC all-news network, puts it this way:

"If I'd walked outside my office 10 years ago and asked people what Saudi Arabia was, most of them would have thought it was some new kind of imported sportscar.

"But when King Faisal was assassinated a few months ago, people immediately wondered what that would do to the price of gas for their cars."

Most journalists, sociologists and psychologists who have studied the all-news concept tend to agree with Nicholaw and Mounty. To them, the success of all-news is born of insecurity and curiosity.

"It's part of a general social-psychological phenomenon," says Harold Mendelsohn of the University of Denver School of Communications. "Americans are now very anxious about knowing what happens the instant it happens. Deep in the recesses of their consciousness is the damn thermonuclear thing and the related fear that we must all be ready at an instant's notice for some tragic catastrophe.

"People constantly feel in imminent danger. Subconsciously, they're terrified that if they don't keep up, they'll be caught short."

To some in radio, that kind of theorizing is just so much psychological gobbledygook. They see all-news radio as simply the most convenient, most accessible form of news available to people who wish to remain informed.

"When you want water, you turn on the faucet," says Art Schreiber, general manager of KFWB. "When you want news, you turn on us."

The ratings, however, would seem to lend some credence to the theories of men like Mendelsohn, Mounty and Nicholaw.

All-news radio attracts its largest audience, for example, during what the industry calls "morning drive time"—from 5 or 6 A.M. to 9 or 10 A.M., when most people are waking up, dressing, eating breakfast and driving to work or school. The demand for news is so great during those hours that many stations with formats other than all-news shift to a three- or four-hour all-news block during that time.

KABC does that in Los Angeles. So do KIRO in Seattle, WBZ in Boston and KRMC in Oklahoma City, among more than a dozen others.

It is not unusual, in fact, for the three largest audiences in Los Angeles radio during morning drive time to be KNX, KFWB and KABC—all of them then broadcasting news exclusively.

All-news formats are similarly successful in morning drive time in other markets. In Miami, for example, WINZ vaulted from the No. 22 station in the rankings during that time-period to No. 2 in less than a month after switching to all-news.

"Ours has become a rather frantic society," says Ken Draper, program director at KFWB. "There's something comforting about waking up each morning, turning to an all-news station and learning right away that everything's still OK, that we haven't been invaded by either the Russians or the Martians while you were asleep."

George Mair, director of community service for KNX, thinks many listeners take an almost perverse delight in listening to all-news radio each morning.

"They're the same kind of people who go to the circus for the high-wire act or go to Ontario Speedway hoping to see a big crash," Mair says.

"They get a psychic pleasure out of a sense of impending disaster, an anticipation of tragedy, and they want to be in on it, part of it, the first to know about it."

Draper doesn't fully accept that explanation, but he does think people listen to all-news because they want to be the first to know something.

"It's socially advantageous," he says, "to walk into your office or meet some people for lunch and be able to say, 'Hey, did you hear Joe Busch just died?' or 'Hey, the Dodgers just blew another one' or 'Hey, I just heard that Cher is getting a divorce; she only got married nine days ago.'"

Psychologist Chaytor Mason thinks the ability to share that kind of "impersonal gossip" is especially appealing to those who feel "inadequate and overpowered in contemporary society.

"They're afraid to reveal themselves in conversation," Mason says. "They don't know what to say. So they chatter about news stories—the newer, the better. It makes them feel like they're on top of things, in control, one-up on their otherwise intimidating peers."

There are, of course, almost as many theories about why people listen to an all-news station as there are listeners to all-news stations—if only because there are so many all-news listeners, cutting across so many demographic lines, that it is difficult to generalize. (Both KNX and KFWB, for example, consistently reach more than one million *different* listeners every week—a spectacular performance in a radio market as fragmented as Los Angeles.)

There are, however, a few common denominators in even the most diverse of audiences.

People tend to listen to all-news, it is generally agreed, because—as our existence becomes more specialized and compartmentalized—we seek at least the superficial knowledge in other areas that a brief but regular exposure to all-news radio can provide.

All-news radio also seems to offer listeners a sense of community in an otherwise amorphous and impersonal urban society—"almost like gathering around the old village well to exchange gossip," says Miriam Bjerre of KNX.

At its most basic level, all-news radio can be seen as simply providing company in an empty house or car—"the security or sexual attraction of one voice, talking directly to you, when you're alone" as one radio news executive sees it.

Trying to identify the precise appeal of all-news radio is almost as difficult as trying to pinpoint its origins.

The format seems to have had its tentative beginnings in Portland and San Francisco in the mid- to late-1950s. But it wasn't until Gordon McLendon brought all-news to XTRA in Tijuana that network executives began to see its potential.

XTRA was a renegade station of sorts, audible in Los Angeles and throughout parts of the Southwest, but Jim Simon—now the director of news and programming for KABC—can barely stifle his laughter when he recalls his early days with XTRA.

"We had two men to read the news," he says. "One guy looked exclusively at the AP tickertape; the other guy looked exclusively at the UPI tickertape. We took turns on the air, 15 minutes at a time. It was strictly rip-and-read—no rewriting, no checking, no individual enterprise."

The modern all-news stations are far more sophisticated—and far more expensive—than XTRA. KNX and KFWB each has a staff of more than 100, about half of them reporters, writers, editors and announcers.

Each station also has an annual budget of more than $4 million—more than almost any other station in town. (The combined budget of background music stations KBIG-AM and KBIG-FM, for example, is slightly more than $1.6 million.)

The new NBC all-news network is also an expensive operation—a staff of 160, $10 million for start-up and first-year costs and an anticipated budget of $11.6 million annually thereafter.

Because a good all-news format requires so many people, NBC is hoping to convince many stations that might otherwise go all-news on their own to subscribe to the NBC service instead.

Rates for the NBC News and Information Service vary with market size, but even in a city as large as Los Angeles, . . . the annual charge would be only $180,000—far less than the cost of running an independent all-news station, even including the station's additional costs for developing its own local news.

NBC provides up to 47 minutes of national and international news per hour, and local stations subscribing to the service must fill in the balance with local news. Stations may, however, take as little as 28 minutes per hour if they prefer to use more local news—as many do during morning drive time, so they can repeatedly give the time, weather forecast and traffic conditions.

The NBC format is especially appealing to stations in small and medium-sized cities that neither produce enough local news nor generate enough advertising revenue to support an independent all-news station. Thus, NBC all-news subscribers include stations in such cities as Sarasota, Fla., Bangor, Maine, Columbia, S.C., and Edinburg, Tex.—some of them paying NBC as little as $9,000 per year.

The NBC all-news service was slow in attracting stations at first, primarily because of the success of CBS and Westinghouse in most major markets. Other stations were simply unwilling to change formats and compete with such entrenched giants as KNX and KFWB in Los Angeles, WCBS and WINS in New York, WBBM in Chicago, KYW in Philadelphia and KCBS in San Francisco.

With no AM outlets in these key markets, NBC executives had considerable trouble convincing stations in other markets that their all-news service would be good enough—or last long enough—to warrant the expensive and risky commitment to a new format.

Even the AM stations owned and operated by NBC were reluctant to make the switch—only WRC in Washington, D.C., did so—and when NIS went into effect, . . . NBC had signed up only 27 stations—far fewer than they had expected.

What NBC executives finally have done in the critical larger cities—and in some smaller cities, as well—is sell their service to FM, rather than to AM stations.

NBC executives now claim they prefer FM stations in many markets because of the changing listening habits of many urban audiences, but most people in radio tend to scoff at that as ex post facto rationalization.

"Given the nature of an FM signal," says one East Coast radio man, "even the most powerful FM stations fade in and out in certain cities. That's not generally conducive to building a regular audience with a new format."

Nevertheless, necessity may well turn out to be the mother of success at NBC, for adult listening habits are, indeed, changing. FM listenership has increased dramatically in the last six or eight years, and in [one] rating period, an FM station (WJIB-FM) placed No. 1 in Boston, another (KBIG-FM) placed No. 2 in Los Angeles and a third (WRFM) placed No. 3 in New York . . . an unheard-of phenomenon just a few scant years ago, when FM audiences were so small, they almost thought of themselves as a cult.

What is happening, it seems, is a polarization of the listening audience. Just as many listeners want more news, many others want more music—and FM, with a far cleaner sound (in those areas where it is audible) and far fewer commercials, can provide that.

"The success of FM has fractionalized the music-listening audience," says Jack Adamson, general manager of KIRO-AM in Seattle. "An AM station just can't out-music an FM station. We need other attractions. That's why we went to all-news in drive-time."

The dual evolutions toward FM and toward all-news are really the almost inevitable by-products of a shift from general-interest to special-interest radio programming that began with the rise of television.

"Too many people found they could get radio's brand of variety entertainment on TV," says Stanley Spero, general manager of KMPC. "Radio programming had to become more specialized—jazz music, country music, personalities, talk and, now, all-news."

Many listeners perceive today's all-news stations as being almost identical from city to city, and it is true that there is a strong similarity among many stations; most, generally, are at their best in swarming over a big, breaking news story—a riot or an earthquake or a fire—when they can reach their audiences more quickly than either newspapers or television. But there are some clear differences among the various stations in their daily programming philosophy and performance.

KYW-Philadelphia, for example—a Westinghouse station—is generally conceded to have some of the best local news coverage of any all-news station, providing responsible, thorough reportage that often includes major interpretive and investigative efforts.

In contrast, WBBM-Chicago—a CBS station—fills the airways with four hours of often-corny domestic banter surrounding the news each day during the time slot filled by Bob and Betty ("Mr. and Mrs. News") Sanders.

CBS and Westinghouse now compete head-to-head in three cities. In one—Philadelphia—the CBS all-news operation is too new for any qualitative or quantitative comparisons to be meaningful. But in New York and Los Angeles, the CBS stations are generally thought to be more successful on both counts.

Los Angeles, because of its temperate climate and its reliance on the automobile, is a unique case. People drive farther to work—and to play— [there], so they listen to the radio longer and more frequently. They also spend more time outdoors—working or relaxing in the yard or playing on the beach or in a park—where radios are the most convenient source of companionship and/or entertainment.

KFWB's Ken Draper, who devised the "You give us 22 minutes; we'll give you the world" format, calls radio in Los Angeles "a subliminal medium.

"Even driving 45 minutes on the freeway, from Woodland Hills to downtown, you'll be distracted by traffic or by your own thoughts. The same news story may come on the radio two or three times. but you'll really only hear it once," he says.

That, according to Draper, is the theory behind the 22-minute format on KFWB. Most stories are repeated at least twice an hour, and major stories are mentioned six times—once in the "headlines" that begin each 22-minute newscast, again into the body of each newscast.

For a major, breaking story, the KFWB format is designed to provide 12 mentions an hour—in effect, one every five minutes.

KNX also repeats some stories within any given hour, but their repetition is less frequent—partially because of a difference in programming philosophy, partially because of the KNX commitment to use CBS network material at specific times every hour.

It is generally agreed that people seldom listen to any all-news station for more than 15 to 25 minutes at any one time, and the KFWB 22-minute format would seem to cater to that habit—and to give listeners the feeling that, at any time of the day, they're never more than a few minutes away from the day's big stories.

But the 22-minute format also would seem to discourage a longer listening span, and that may help explain why listeners tend to stay tuned to KNX about 25% longer than to KFWB each day.

KFWB did defeat KNX in the ratings early this year. But since then, KNX has reclaimed the lead it has generally held in recent years.

KFWB's sister station in New York, WINS, switched to the 22-minute format in January, but the CBS station there, WCBS, also has continued to win the ratings war.

The differences between the CBS and Westinghouse stations in New York and—especially—in Los Angeles have become more discernible under the new Westinghouse format.

KFWB is clearly more entertainment (rather than information) oriented than KNX, for example—seemingly aiming for a less-sophisticated, less demanding audience.

KFWB officials tacitly acknowledge this.

"When I joined KFWB," says Ken Draper, "I didn't think we were doing news for the people who pumped gas, only for the people who had white-collar jobs and made a lot of money. I think the entertainment value of news is the most critical. I think news can be exciting. In any survey I've ever seen, people put the desire to be educated at the bottom of the list of their priorities in deciding what radio station to listen to."

KFWB covers local news well and also provides listeners with generally sound national and international news and commentary from Westinghouse reporters around the world. Nevertheless, there is a certain tone, a certain feeling, about the overall programming that clearly reflects Draper's philosophy.

Sandwiched around the news are light features, whimsical essays and pun-filled weather reports. Even the news stories themselves are sometimes more frivolous than those on KNX. . . . One . . . morning, a story about the development of pre-deodorized underwear was a major news story on KFWB—repeated six times every hour, all morning.

"KFWB is the top 40 of all-news radio," says one radio executive.

"It's the three Rs of all-news radio—rapes, robberies and wrecks," says Dick Casper, general manager of WINZ-Miami.

Perhaps that explains why, when the 1971 earthquake struck Los Angeles, listeners turned to KFWB by the hundreds of thousands. Their ratings almost tripled that day and the next day; KNX ratings increased only 25%.

"KFWB is like a tabloid newspaper, like the New York Daily News," says Jim Simon of KABC. "KNX is more like the New York Times. It's a news machine. It just keeps pumping out the news, more news than you could ever want to hear in your whole life."

KNX has tried to brighten its format in the last two or three years, but it is still a sober and more sophisticated—at times, even stodgy—dispenser of news. KNX blends network celebrities like Walter Cronkite, Dan Rather and Daniel Schorr into local programming that is generally serious-minded, seldom lighthearted, often featuring documentaries on such subjects as illegal aliens, women in prison, homosexuality, alcoholism, rapid transit and the energy crisis.

Not surprisingly, KNX generally scores heaviest with the better-educated, higher-income listeners; KFWB generally scores heavier with blue-collar listeners and minorities.

KFWB also is beginning to draw more successfully from younger listeners.

Some students of all-news radio contend that all-news is the ideal medium for young audiences—"the broadcast generation," one radio executive calls them, "the kids raised on radio and television, rather than newspapers, books and magazines."

But that is demonstrably untrue. The all-news stations in almost every city do less well among the young than among any other single age group —and they do the best among the older listeners.

In Los Angeles, KNX and KFWB rank one-two among listeners in their fifties and older—listeners who generally have a greater interest and a greater stake in (and, concomitantly, a greater anxiety about) the day's events. But KNX and KFWB rank 13th and 14th among listeners 18 to 24 —and they rank 16th and 22nd among teen-agers.

Clearly, if young people aren't reading newspapers as previous generations did, neither are they listening to all-news. If they are exposed to news with any regularity at all, it is in the three-to-five minute hourly headlines screamed out on the rock stations.

KFWB hopes to change that with its brighter, lighter, tighter format.

But even with these differences between the two stations, the lines of demarcation still aren't completely clear, and both stations overlap considerably in all demographic areas.

Listener loyalty is, however, remarkably consistent. Few people who listen to KNX also listen to KFWB—and vice versa. There is less duplication between these two stations than between any other two stations in [Los Angeles] with similar formats.

---

to the student: a commentary

David Shaw, a superb journalist who reports on the media for the *Los Angeles Times,* here surveys the fast-increasing all-news radio stations; the total is certain to become many more than one hundred stations.

Shaw's news story is scrupulously objective; it is impossible to tell whether he is praising or criticizing the all-news stations. For the most part, we are critical. As far as we can determine, the all-news stations serve their constituencies admirably—provided radio news is the *beginning* of the listener's information. Unfortunately, listening to the radio is becoming a habit. People listen to the all-news radio and perhaps also watch television news; that gives the headlines and a little more. But they are barely looking at newspapers. Newspaper circulation fails to keep pace with the growing United States population.

We were interested when KCBS, the first of the San Francisco stations, announced nearly ten years ago that the station was becoming an all-news operation. At a meeting of Sigma Delta Chi, the general manager of KCBS announced half-jokingly to the newspaper journalists, "We are going to bury you." It sounded like a real challenge. When they heard the news on KCBS, however, the newspapers relaxed. KCBS was nothing more than a headline service, with its little stories repeated again and again. But many of the listeners seem satisfied with their radio and television sets. How can they understand the news when it is treated so superficially?

For example, consider the way in which a radio journalist reports the day's news:

Here's a collection of stories on Washington.

The Labor Secretary and most of the president's Labor-Management Advisory Committee have gone on record in favor of a 10-billion-dollar tax cut.

A presidential committee on equal-employment-opportunity says Negroes are winning a bigger share of federal government jobs. In the last fiscal year one out of every six new federal jobs was filled by a Negro.

The Commerce Department reports that personal income has climbed more than two million dollars in October. That's the largest gain since April and represents a 5 percent hike over last year.

In another report on the aerospace industry, 14 million dollars has been allocated to the National Space Agency's Research Center at Moffett Field. The money is to construct four new research facilities there, including one facility that will simulate space flight to the moon and the planets.

If the radio listener watches television news the same evening, perhaps he or she will see again one or two of these four radio reports. In any case, television adds only a visual representation; the newscaster will say much the same thing that the radio reporter said. Lost to an increasing number of American citizens who are no longer interested in reading is the ability to understand the news.

Although the number of radio stations is increasing yearly, we have yet to hear the kind of all-news radio station that gives sufficient time and talent to the news. Note especially that time is not crucial; when a radio station has twenty-four hours a day, the journalists can report at length. What if the station loses many listeners to the all-news station that reports superficially? It is our contention that a station will lose many, but it is likely that in a city that has, for example, three all-news stations, repeating what is reported is foolish. If a station can report at length on the major stories of the day, it can become almost a *New York Times*. Just as the circulation of the *Times* is compared embarrassingly to the circulation of the *New York Daily News*—the *Times* has 800,000 subscribers, the *News* has two million—the *Times* is nonetheless a great newspaper, and profitable.

We certainly hope that such a revolution is coming. Radio has already shown its adaptability. It seemed to disappear with the first growth of glamorous television. In 1955, radio revenues dropped to $554 million, and only 2,669 radio stations were broadcasting. But radio recovered so thoroughly that Richard Tobin of the *Saturday Review* observed in 1962 that "old-fashioned radio is making a fantastic comeback."

The renewed strength of the radio stations came at least partly because of a turn from national to community programs. Radio stations that had once attempted to bridge many different levels of listener interest began to focus on a special audience: teenagers, sports enthusiasts, lovers of the latest in popular music, or those who would listen only to serious music.

In the past fifteen years, the turn toward all-news has just begun. There are nearly 7,000 radio stations, and only a handful have started the all-news format. Some day, though, hundreds of radio stations will be broadcasting news hour after hour after hour. Perhaps one radio station in a large city will recognize that the time has come to test whether it can chisel out a share of the market by becoming the *New York Times* of radio.

WLR

study questions

1. The Robinson and Hirsch article states that teenagers don't hear, much less understand, the lyrics of songs on Top 40 stations. If this is true, is it likely to be true of other formats and other audiences? If so, what does this imply as far as radio's effectiveness as a means of communication?

2. Why do people listen to all-news radio stations?

3. All-news and Top 40 stations both operate with highly repetitive schedules. Do you think that listeners of all-news stations suffer from the same problem as those of Top 40: namely, they don't really hear or remember what is being broadcast? If so, what kind of news service is being rendered? What kind of information is communicated? And are listeners any more informed than they would otherwise be?

4. Do you think that all-news radio stations are damaging newspapers by taking away their readership? Are they damaging the public by offering headline stories as an alternative to in-depth reporting?

5. What are the implications of having the news at our fingertips twenty-four hours a day?

radio

constraints

"They're playing our song."

John C. Carlin

The Rise and Fall
of Topless Radio

Is "electronic voyeurism" in the public interest?
Precedents establish FCC authority to rule on the issue.

It is quite possible that the name "Sonderling" will take a place in the history of broadcasting similar to that held by "Roth," "Memoirs," and "Miller" for the other media. For it was the Sonderling Broadcasting Corporation which ran afoul of the Federal Communications Commission's drive against obscenity in broadcasting.

The drive came to light at the National Association of Broadcasters banquet held on March 28, 1973. Guest speaker and the FCC Chairman Dean Burch threw down the gauntlet against what he called "the prurient trash that is the stock-in-trade of the sex-oriented radio talk show." Referring to the then current rash of "topless radio" shows, i.e., talk shows where listeners are invited to call in and discuss matters oriented to sex and sexual activity, Burch called them "garbage" and said they feature "the suggestive, coaxing, pear-shaped tones of the smut-hustling host" who conducts conversations "on such elevating topics of urgent public concern as the number and frequency of orgasms . . . or the endless varieties of oral sex . . . or a baker's dozen of other turn-ons, turn-offs, and turn-downs." In sum, he called topless radio "electronic voyeurism." Burch urged the broadcast industry to voluntarily clean up the airways, leaving the impression without explicitly saying so that if the industry did not do the requisite house cleaning, the FCC might intervene. Within a few days Burch, in moving against Sonderling Broadcasting Corporation, backed his words with action.

On April 13, 1973, the FCC announced its intention to fine Sonderling's station WGLD-FM, Oak Park, Illinois, $2,000 for obscene programming. The Commission made no attempt to hide the fact it was seeking a "test case." In its notice of intent, the Commission included an invitation to Sonderling to seek judicial review, noting that the courts are "the final arbiters in this sensitive First Amendment field."

Reprinted by permission of John C. Carlin from *Journal of Communication,* Winter 1976.

173

But the FCC was to be disappointed. Sonderling agreed to pay the fine, thus denying the Commission the test case to prove its authority to move against alleged obscenity or indecency.

Although the Commission did not get its court case, it remains worthwhile to look at the "test case" against topless radio.

Topless radio programs developed, innocently enough, from the all-talk and telephone-talk formats which were established features in larger markets throughout the United States by the mid-1960s. In the original telephone-talk format, listeners were invited to call in and give their opinions on controversial subjects normally selected from either the political or social spectrum. But as these programs gained popularity, more universal topics were sought which would hold existing listenerships and yet have the necessary appeal to acquire new ones.

In early 1971, station manager Ray Stanfield of Station KGBS-AM/FM, Los Angeles, selected Bill Ballance, one of his all night jockeys, to moderate a new concept: a live, midday, female-only, two-way talk show. The show was titled "Feminine Forum" and its success was meteoric. Within twenty months, it was the top-rated program in the nation's largest radio market, with an estimated 400,000 listeners daily.

Imitators began springing up in New York, Miami, Cleveland, Toledo, Kansas City, and Chicago. By early 1973, there were between 50 and 60 programming daily shows in the "topless" format. The common denominator among these programs was that only women were allowed to talk on a pre-determined topic-of-the-day. The degree of explicitness in the exchange between female caller and talk jockey depended to a great extent on the seductiveness of the latter. And, as more and more shows attempted to mimic the success of Bill Ballance's "Feminine Forum," a seeming race for "one upmanship" in explicitness developed.

In March 1973, the Federal Communications Commission sat down to listen to a composite tape recording of the various topless programs then being aired around the country. Two segments apparently stood out, both of them aired over WGLD-FM on "Feminine Forum." These two broadcasts, on February 21 and 23, 1973, carried oral sex as the topic of the day and on the programs, the several woman callers discussed quite openly the problems they had, and overcame, while engaging in it.

For the cited broadcasts, the FCC fined the licensee, Sonderling Broadcasting Corporation, $1,000 per program, the maximum fine the Commission could levy under ... the Communications Act of 1934. The FCC struck for two obvious reasons. First, based on the expressed desire of its chairman, the FCC hoped to stamp out "topless radio." Second, by fining WGLD-FM the maximum, the Commission hoped to induce the licensee to take the matter into federal court where it believed its authority to control "obscenity and indecency" in broadcast content would be upheld.

In rendering its decision, the Commission declared it had analyzed the two broadcasts in light of past and present Supreme Court decisions on obscenity, and had found the material to be obscene within those guidelines. It then went on to compare the broadcast medium to other means of disseminating information, placing the broadcast industry in a special category. The Commission noted that broadcasting is designed to be received by millions in their homes, cars, on outings, or "even when they walk the streets with a transistor radio to the ear, without regard to age, background, or degree of sophistication." As in past decisions, the FCC cited the inherent "obtrusiveness" of radio and noted that unlike other media "broadcasting is disseminated to the public under circumstances where it comes directly into the home, frequently without any advance warning of its content."

Opponents to the FCC decision cried "censorship." Four major legal arguments were cited to denounce the Commission's action.

1. The FCC exceeded its legal authority in attempting both to investigate and enforce violations of criminal law, i.e., Section 1464 of the United States Criminal Code which bans broadcast of obscene, indecent, or profane material.

2. The Statute, i.e., Section 1464, is itself unconstitutional, both on its face— too broad and vague in its language—and as applied by the Commission in the Sonderling case.

3. The Commission actions being challenged "were both in intent and effect censorship" of the kind prohibited by Section 326, Communications Act of 1934.

4. The Commission's action violates public interest standards governing the Commission's regulation of broadcasting and underlying First Amendment values.

The above claims question the very nature of the FCC and the charter upon which it is based. Viewed in one light, the arguments have validity inasmuch as the FCC has never been able to establish firmly through the courts its right to monitor and "judge" broadcasts. But if it lacks legal judgments, it at least has administrative precedent.

There is no court precedent establishing the authority of the FCC to punish a broadcaster for obscene, indecent, or profane programming based solely on the "Commission's analysis of the content of that programming."

There have been several cases, however, in which the FCC, through administrative authority, has refused to renew licenses or levied fines based upon a determination that programming standards were not "in the public interest."

In 1962, the FCC refused to renew the license of Station WDKD in Kingtree, South Carolina, on the grounds that material aired on the Charlie Walker Show was "coarse, vulgar, obscene, suggestive, and of indecent double meaning." Although agreeing with the station's counterarguments that the material was not by definition obscene, the commission held the "obscene, indecent, or profane" test of the United States Code, Section 1464, does not then require the FCC to find that which is only coarse, vulgar, and suggestive to be in the public interest. And, even though obscenity was not an issue in this case, the FCC declared in its "unchallenged" findings that it has the authority to find material broadcast over a radio station to be "obscene, indecent, or profane and in violation of the criminal code."

The term "unchallenged" does not mean WDKD accepted the FCC's ruling. It did not. The station appealed and the case was heard in a federal court of appeals. However, the presiding judge refused to rule on the indecency and public interest issues. Rather, he reaffirmed the FCC decision on the grounds the license had misrepresented the facts during the hearing. But in his deliberations, the judge, Judge Wilber Miller, although not ruling directly on the obscenity and the public interest issue, did touch on obscenity versus censorship. Judge Miller espoused that "denying renewal of a license because of the station's broadcast of obscene, indecent, or profane language—a serious criminal offense—can properly be called program censorship. But if it can be so denominated, then censorship to that extent is not only permissible but required in the public interest. Freedom of speech does not legalize using the public airways to peddle filth."

A second case involved the use of profanity during an interview. On January 4, 1970, WUHY-FM (Eastern Education Radio) aired an edited, pre-taped interview in which the interviewee's comment's were frequently interspersed with four-letter expletives. Following the taped interview, a live interview with a local entertainer was conducted and again, expletives were in frequent use.

The FCC reviewed the show and slapped WUHY-FM with a $100 fine. The Commission reasoned that the speech "had no redeeming social values and was patently offensive by contemporary community standards with very serious consequences to the 'public interest' in the larger and more effective use of radio." The Commission went on to say that however much a person may like to talk that way, "he has no right to do so in public arenas, and broadcasters can clearly insist that in talk shows, persons observe the requirement of eschewing the language." According to the Commission, such language can be avoided on radio "without stifling in the slightest any thought a person wishes to convey."

Since the incident was a one-time occasion, loss of license was not deemed appropriate. Hoping to establish a test case in court, the FCC levied the minimal but precedent-setting fine of $100. But, as Sonderling later was to do, Eastern Education Radio refused to accept the challenge and, without dissent, paid the fine.

Without specific court rulings, it would appear the FCC has no legal platform upon which to rest its authority to judge the decency of program content. On the other hand, past uncontested FCC decisions such as WDKD and WUHY-FM have established, at least in principle, that authority. In its case against WDKD, the Commission established its authority to determine whether or not broadcast material meets the criteria of obscenity, and its power to deny license renewal based on that determination. A federal judge, although deliberating on another question in the case, issued his opinion that such a denial could not properly be called program censorship in that freedom of speech does not legalize using obscenities on the public airways.

An assessment of the Commission's action must take into account the nature of American society of the 1970s.

The number of published books containing explicit references to sex and sex-related activities has steadily increased. The motion picture industry, taking its cue—and often its plots—from the literary field, has experienced a similar trend toward explicitness. Television's films and weekly drama shows contain numerous implicit, and often explicit, references to sex.

Because of this "exposure," it would be fair to surmise that the average adult American is no longer shocked by the description or visualization of the nude human body. Nor is he or she necessarily offended by the verbalization or visualization of intimate sexual acts. Such a proposal is reinforced by the President's Commission on Obscenity and Pornography's finding that the majority of Americans now accept the right of the adult to gain access to the most explicit of materials. But . . . there is a limit.

The Commission's report noted the reservation by the public that such accessibility should not be so universal that non-consenting individuals would be unwillingly or unwittingly exposed. This proviso indicates that, although society does not mind reading about or viewing contrived sexual activities, it considers personal relations sacred, i.e., it recognizes an element of privacy surrounding individual experiences and exposure. So, on the one hand, society is more amenable today to the mass media presenting sexual activities and, on the other, it demands protection from being exposed to such material without consent.

It is this dichotomy which made the FCC's action against Sonderling so momentous for the broadcast industry. Certainly, based on the popularity of "Femme Forum" and similar shows, a significant portion of society was not offended by the new morality in radio. But the FCC obviously did not believe this acceptance to be universal. Its action was a rejection of the notion that a program's popularity is synonymous with public interest.

It can easily be shown Congress and the courts have given the FCC the "burden of determining the composition of broadcast traffic."

It is in the execution of this responsibility that the Commission walks the thin line of administrative review vis-a-vis censorship. Congress, very much aware of this latter censorship potential of certain provisions within the Communications Act, included in Section 326 the specific caution that "nothing" in the Act should be construed to give the Commission censorship authority. Yet, there is little question that censorship was the central issue in the Sonderling case. Sonderling, two protesting civic groups, and the lone dissenting FCC Commissioner, Commissioner Nicholas Johnson, all accused the FCC of violating Section 326. But their arguments fly in the face of court precedent. In a case involving two licensees whose licenses had been terminated, the Court of Appeals for the District of Columbia provided the following distinction between prior restraint, i.e., censorship, and punishment after an offense had been committed:

This contention [of censorship] is without merit. There has been no attempt on the part of the commission to subject any part of appellant's broadcasting matter to scrutiny prior to its release. In considering the question whether the public interest, convenience, or necessity will be

served by renewal of appellant's license, the commission has merely
exercised its undoubted right to take note of appellant's past conduct, which
is not censorship.

This ruling established that any effort on the part of the Commission
to require advance governmental approval prior to airing would constitute
censorship. But review of material subsequent to airing would not, and is,
in fact within the legitimate powers of that body.

By exercising its punitive powers to the fullest, the FCC ended the
female-only, two-way sex talk shows. WGLD-FM and other stations
dropped the topless format. They did so not only because they feared
possible future fines, but also because they feared loss of their license at
renewal time. The FCC action gave clear warning that Sonderling Broadcasting Corporation, and its subsidiary, WGLD-FM, overstepped the
bounds of propriety in airing, with little regard for the public interest,
matters which might have a place in private communication but not on the
public airways.

to the student : a commentary

John Carlin, who researched his article as part of his Master's thesis at the
University of Florida, provides a comprehensive summary of the growth and
quick decline of "topless radio." Giving a brief background of the origins of
such shows, Carlin focuses on the FCC drive to rid the airwaves of "electronic
voyeurism."

The airwaves are considered public property, and the FCC assigns individual broadcasters certain frequencies and power levels to keep stations from
overlapping and drowning each other out. Because the air belongs to the
people, and no two stations can occupy the same frequency within a given
area, each broadcaster, in effect, is being granted a monopoly on public
property. But broadcasters, most of whom make a profit with their monopo-
lies, are given permission—in the form of a license—on the condition that
they operate "in the public interest, convenience, and necessity."

The FCC, funded by Congress, is made up of seven presidentially appointed commissioners and has a sizable administrative staff. It grants licenses
—or more commonly, license renewals, since each station must reapply
every three years—and has the responsibility of regulating the use of the
airwaves. All this is fairly straightforward, but it quickly becomes complicated
when the seemingly simple responsibility of operating "in the public interest"

begins to conflict with First Amendment rights. Freedom of speech is guaranteed by the Constitution, and any form of regulation that restricts speech automatically has, as the U.S. Supreme Court has said, "a presumption against Constitutional validity." In short, almost any effort to restrict speech is likely to be found illegal. This puts the FCC in the obviously awkward position of trying to balance two major, and sometimes conflicting, obligations. On one hand, they have the mandate to ensure that the airwaves are used "in the public interest"—a phrase sufficiently vague to keep broadcasters nervous—and on the other, they must respect nearly any form of speech not specifically disallowed by the courts.

Since the major part of the untested WGLD-FM issue was the FCC's ability to control the airwaves for "obscenity and indecency," it may be valuable to discuss just what the courts do consider obscene. In general, as the constitutional scholar C. Herman Pritchett has pointed out in *The American Constitution*, there seem to be two classes of concerns. First, obscenity has been regarded as bad in and of itself. It is indecent. It is a violation of good moral standards. In the words of the federal postal law, the obscene is the "lewd," the "lascivious," the "filthy."

Second, according to Pritchett, obscenity may be regarded as criminally punishable because of its evil effects on individuals and society. "Obscene material, it is alleged, will have a tendency to deprave the minds or characters of persons exposed to it. It will corrupt the public morals. It will lead to immoral or antisocial sexual conduct. It will result in the advocacy of improper sexual values."

Obscenity *per se* has never been given the protection of the First Amendment. As Justice Brennan wrote in the Supreme Court decision in *Roth* v. *United States,* obscenity was "not within the area of constitutionally protected speech." The First Amendment, he said, protects "all ideas having even the slightest redeeming social importance—unorthodox ideas, controversial ideas, even ideas hateful to the prevailing climate of opinion. . . . But implicit in the history of the First Amendment is the rejection of obscenity as utterly without redeeming social importance."

But if obscenity is not constitutionally protected—in which case the FCC would have no problem with the courts—just what is obscene and indecent? That's a question the courts have never been able to resolve. Even attempts to define the seemingly obvious area of hard-core pornography have proven frustrating; Justice Stewart threw up his hands with the statement: "I shall not attempt to define [it]. . . . But I know it when I see it. . . ."

In 1973 the Supreme Court made its latest attempt to define obscenity in *Miller* v. *California.* The new standards for determining obscene material are: first, it appeals to pruriency; secondly, it contains patently offensive descriptions or depictions of sexual conduct specifically defined by state law; and third, taken as a whole it lacks serious literary, artistic, political, or scientific value. The court admits that the material being proscribed is that which is "hard-core."

The definition, as it stands, does not greatly restrict broadcasters. Consider, for example, a television show that is prurient (appeals to lust) and presents "hard-core" sexual conduct. Could it be argued that the performance has literary or artistic value? If so, it would not be legally obscene. As lawyer Paul McGeady pointed out, "Most Americans obviously would not tolerate this. While they might tolerate these distinctions in books, magazines, or even motion pictures, they would not tolerate the concept that they must switch the dial to avoid such performances on TV or radio or that they must be concerned that their minor children may be exposed to the same."

McGeady argues that where "intrusiveness" is present, obscenity need not be proved.

Just as a citizen is entitled to walk down the public street without the necessity of having to avert his eyes to avoid a public nude performance, so too he is entitled to "flip the dial" without [encountering] intrusive nudity or explicit hard-core sex. Is he supposed to review the program for 30 minutes or one hour to determine if the work "taken as a whole" has artistic, literary, political, or scientific value? Most probably the Supreme Court did not intend this result and is awaiting the opportunity to correct this deficiency as soon as a proper case in this area presents itself for adjudication. In the meantime, we are left with the anomaly.

Both the Supreme Court and McGeady may have to wait a long time. If the Sonderling case is any example, broadcasters have no intention of testing the legal limits of "obscene and indecent." The reason is not a moral one; when topless radio was a rating success, one station after another jumped onto the bandwagon. The reason was summed up by Commissioner Nicholas Johnson in his dissent from the Sonderling notice: ". . . any FCC pronouncement against a particular kind of programming will cast a pall over the broadcasting industry—not so much because these broadcasters fear the imposition of fines, but, rather, because they fear the potential loss of their highly profitable broadcast licenses."

LLS

Paul M. Hirsch

The Economics of Rock

Rock and roll radio emerged in the fifties as part of the radio industry's confused response to the onslaught of television. As soon as television began cutting into network radio's "lowest common denominator" audience, it became clear that the older medium could not compete as an equal. Radio was forced to find, or create, new audience markets. American youth was thus given a medium "all its own" as the accidental by-product of a revolution in communications technology and its economic consequences.

Stunned parents and veteran radio men considered screaming Top 40 radio a vulgar intrusion into their personal and professional lives. Not fully comprehending that old-time radio was very dead, they expected that the broadcasting of this raucous music was a passing fad, but radio's early, reluctant experiment with the Top 40 rock format was only the beginning. It initiated a much broader trend toward specialty programming of all types—each directed at a limited audience. This new subcultural programming slices the total audience into homogeneous marketable parts. Thus *all*-news, *all*-country, *all*-Top 40, *all*-soul, and *all*-"underground" stations are each broadcasting the same news, *or* views, *or* music, repetitively, twenty-four hours a day.

Almost every cultural group in major metropolitan areas has its very own radio station. The older "something for everyone" formula has been replaced by what W. H. Honan calls "broadcast parochialism." Paradoxically, this encourages cultural pluralism and cultural isolation simultaneously. If the generation gap in musical taste is wider today than ever before, it is due in large part to the near total segregation of one age group's media listening patterns from the other's. Studies have shown that most people isolate themselves from alternative viewpoints and cultures as a matter of course. While cultural pluralism is enhanced at the aggregate level by special formats, it is more likely to be retarded at the individual level.

The rock music explosion, however, can be attributed only in part to the impact of television on the radio industry. While the air play of rock and roll records has stimulated the present situation, it is hardly in itself the sufficient cause. It has provided young people an unprecedented opportu-

Reprinted by permission of Paul M. Hirsch from *The Nation,* 9 March 1970.

nity to learn of new and unusual records, but it did not create their eagerness to seize the opportunity once it was made available to them.

The "youth market" was there long before radio stations began catering to specialty audiences. It was smaller a generation or two ago, and relatively poorer, but young people lined up for hours in advance to hear Benny Goodman and Frank Sinatra, to mob them on stage, and to be with other young people in an *ad hoc* counter culture. They, too, purchased tremendous quantities of their idols' records, ignoring their elders' distaste for such "uncouth" music.

Three notable changes characterize today's youth from those of earlier periods. First, there are now about 10 million more Americans between the ages of 15 and 26 than there were twenty years ago. In the 1960s, the postwar baby boom yielded a 43 per cent increase in the 18-to-25 age group. Second, they are wealthier than any previous generation of American youth. Expenditures of teen-agers alone have more than doubled since 1959, from $10 billion to more than $20 billion. And third, they take for granted much of the technology which still impresses their parents and teachers. Each of these changes has tremendously affected the record industry, its consumers and young professional musicians.

Until the middle fifties, 75 per cent of all domestic hit records were produced and distributed by four record companies. Among them, they controlled the recorded output of America. Their access to the public, however, was through network radio, directed at the lowest common denominator, and not surprisingly the big four tended to gear their products to what the networks selected for that radio audience. They produced few rhythm-and-blues records, little progressive jazz or rock and roll. "Specialty" labels like Atlantic, King and Blue Note won these subcultural markets by default. For network radio to have played some of Billie Holiday's best records available (on specialty labels), or to have interviewed Cisco Houston coast to coast, would have been commercially equivalent to having Lenny Bruce on *The Ed Sullivan Show*. Under these circumstances, subcultural markets remained underdeveloped, with information passed largely by word of mouth. The media presented the dominant culture.

America's youth became numerous and prosperous at just about the time when radio was forced into those subcultural markets. Top 40 programming took the four major record companies by surprise. Long used to producing for the mainstream, they were unable and, at first, unwilling to plunge into subcultural marketing. The vacuum was filled by numerous small entrepreneurs, eager to enter the hit-record sweepstakes. A 45 rpm single costs only several hundred dollars to record *and* manufacture, and the prospect of huge returns on such small investment was irresistible.

Once the sales of rock records began to cut into the previously stable markets of the big four, remedial action was begun. The big companies simply bought up the enterprising little ones (which is how, for example, Elvis Presley became associated with RCA records). But the major labels were clearly on the run, and mainly reacting. The steady increase in the recording freedom allowed musicians in their dealings with record companies can be traced back to pressures upon the big four to maintain sales leadership and to strengthen their competitive position in the rock and roll field. Singers and musicians were for the first time allowed a major say as to which songs should be recorded.

Many analysts attribute the sometimes daring and radical lyrics of rock and roll songs to the desire of record companies to please (or to convert) their consumers. They argue that today's controversial lyrics reflect a radical shift in the attitudes of young people (or record company magnates). More attention should be given to the companies' loss of control over the musicians, and to the gradual intrusion of the musicians' own values into the songs they record. These values are by no means clearly perceived or shared by the mass of young record buyers. . . .

In spite of its apparent turmoil, including the payola scandals of 1958, the record industry experienced no major crises after the advent of rock. Volume sales have increased for most major firms at such a phenomenal rate that it has been possible for a company's profits to rise at the same time that its share of the market decreased. Gross sales . . . climbed from $99 million in 1945 to more than $1 billion in 1968.

Subcultural radio programming has spurred sales by providing needed exposure for more and more records to more and more kids with more and more money. "Underground" radio stations are the latest example of this trend. The now conservative Top 40 station does not distinguish among styles *within* rock and roll (of which there are many, as "rock" has now absorbed elements of all other types of music); its appeal is directed primarily to all sectors of the teen-age population. The newer FM "underground" stations are heavily weighted with rock styles which appeal most strongly to older, more well-to-do students, and to recent college graduates. This group, increasingly dissatisfied with "bubble gum rock," provides the main audience for the controversial songs that are being written today. The material which knocked the Smothers Brothers off network television would sound tame enough on most underground stations.

Many of the early "specialty" firms have prospered. The Atlantic, King and Blue Note labels, for example, have been added to the growing roster of record companies now functioning as independent subdivisions of large conglomerates. Although recording costs have risen in the last few years, the initial investment is still quite low. Record companies "lend" musicians the money to cover studio costs when the records are cut, and deduct it "off the top" if the record is successful. Increasingly massive promotion funds are required to convert records by new groups into hits, but the prospect of huge returns on this investment is a steady lure. By 1967, it is reliably estimated, more than 300 record companies were each releasing an average of one 45 rpm single per week. The competition for radio time among the estimated annual total of more than 15,000 singles is convulsive. Many say the race track offers a better deal.

Finally, the contribution of modern technology is important. All phases of rock music have become increasingly tied to technology, from concert staging and recording techniques to record retailing and audience management. Musicians and their audiences regard better amplifiers, microphones, tape recorders, film techniques, record packaging, outdoor festivals and speaker systems as a natural and desirable part of their environment. They assume, with accustomed indifference, that the gadgets they've grown up with are to be used when needed, and simply ignored when irrelevant. Most young people, including "dropouts" and "dissenters," are neither alienated, as some have argued, by such signs of the age as television, moon shots and atomic weapons, nor are they particularly impressed. They seem only "natural" to a generation which has always known them. While this attitude is now starting to be challenged by a growing concern for our environment, it is still too early to pronounce today's vanguard youth seriously hostile to modern gadgetry. Persuasive evidence that we are still far from a wholesale "back to nature" movement is the overwhelming popularity of rock and roll, and all the technology it encompasses.

---

to the student: a commentary

Paul Hirsch, coauthor of another article in this book, is one of a handful of sociologists who have investigated popular music in this country. He has analyzed the record industry carefully and provided insights into the related business of radio. In "The Economics of Rock," Hirsch takes us on a quick tour of the technological connections of radio's rock and roll.

But it is the shift in the record industry that may be the most interesting aspect of Hirsch's article. *Industry* is not too strong a term for a business that grosses more than $1 billion a year in domestic sales alone. The market, according to one study, is divided up this way: rock and "underground" account for 29 percent of the record sales; country and western 16 percent; middle-of-the-road or "easy listening" gets 15 percent; pop instrumentals account for 14 percent; classical, jazz, rhythm and blues, folk, Broadway

Production	
Artist's fee	$2,000
Studio for recording	500
Tape for recording	100
Mastering seven dubdowns	300
Tape for mastering	30
Master acetate disk	80
Metal parts	60
Cover art	200
Type	100
Negatives	100
Total	$3,470

Cost per 1,000	
Labels	$ 20
Printing of covers	50
Printing backs	10
Assemble jackets	70
1,000 LP disks	350
Total	$ 500

shows and movie soundtracks take 14 percent; and everything else accounts for the remaining 12 percent. The clear fact arising from all the figures is that rock and roll—which covers a wide range of "youth-oriented" styles—has nearly double the market of the next largest category.

With a large market, and a chance of tapping into its pocketbook, what kind of investment does a record company have to make? Although costs vary widely, depending on the record company, the performers, and production requirements, the set of figures above was obtained by sociologist Serge Denisoff.

The president of Arhoolie Records provided a breakdown, shown in the table, of the minimum cost of a record.

For small companies the cost of producing an album can run from 80 cents to $1. For the larger companies the cost of an album is between 30 and 40 cents. Considering the record store price of most albums, it would seem that high profits would be easy. But other costs have to be paid. Denisoff estimates that retailers take 30 cents, wholesalers take 60 to 70 cents, publishing royalties average 24 cents, the American Federation of Musicians gets about 7 cents, and the performing artist makes from 30 to 50 cents. The average record company profit is about $1 per album.

Given the total investment into a record album, and the large number being produced, it is estimated that seven out of every ten new albums lose money. That rate of success would seem to be courting bankruptcy. But one executive explained how it can work:

Our industry is a classic example of crap shooting. When you win, you win big. You can afford to take a 70 percent stiff [loss] ratio. On the three that make it you more than make up your cost and profit on the entire 10. And if you spend on 10 records, say a million dollars, and 7 of these records earn back $50,000 but on the other 3 you earn back one million dollars, you still have a $100,000 profit over the million. That's still a 10 percent profit.

In one recent year the American record industry sold 183,000,000 singles and 196,000,000 albums. From those gross figures one can begin to understand the economics of rock.

LLS

study questions

1. Are all attempts to control what is broadcast over the radio instances of attempted censorship?

2. Is the fact that some people find certain things objectionable, such as drug-oriented song lyrics, enough to label such things as being against "the public interest"? In other words, how is it to be determined whether something is or is not in the public interest?

3. If one begins making exceptions to anyone's freedom of speech, where is it to stop? Is it necessary to prohibit any censorship of this freedom in order to safeguard it as a general right? Or are there standards by which to judge and control abuses that will not threaten the basic concept of free speech itself?

4. A Supreme Court justice once said that the freedom of speech did not give one the right to yell "fire" in a crowded theater; in other words, that we be responsible in the exercise of our freedoms. In the area of radio broadcasting, what constitutes yelling "fire" in the crowded theater? On what do you base your judgment?

5. The television industry has had a powerful effect on the nature of radio broadcasting. How has radio been forced to change in order to adapt to the new realities of the television age? Has it changed for the better or worse? What further changes may lie ahead?

6. Do our tastes and desires determine what is broadcast on the radio, or do we adapt our tastes and desires *according to* what is presented?

7. Our institutions are shaped in part by their relationships with other institutions and their reactions to social forces. What institutions and what social forces have helped to shape the radio industry as it is today?

news-papers 4

For centuries the newspaper was the preeminent news medium, but since 1950, people have begun to rely increasingly on television even though it provides little more than the headlines. In recent years, 65 percent have said that they rely much more on television for news than on any other medium. For newspapers, that's bad news.

How can newspapers compete with television? They can't. No matter how many pictures the newspapers publish, and no matter how many great reporters the papers have, they can't vie with television for the sheer impact of displaying the world's news at a glance.

What can newspapers do? First, they can emulate the *New York Times,* our leading newspaper, by employing the most capable reporters available. Second, they can modernize their format and approach to the news. Even the stodgy, crowded pages of the *Times* are changing—to a more open, six-column layout. The *Times* has also unwrapped a new Friday Weekend Edition that is adapting to the lifestyle of the community. At last it has awakened.

The following two sections examine other leading problems that confront the newspapers, including the continuing wars between newspapers and government officials and the slow march to respectability of the campus press. In the constraints chapter, we present first the everlasting issue, the business of newspapers. In this section, we realize that the chief work of journalism has broadened. Journalists, who used to be called "newspaper reporters," are now often referred to as the "press" because some are also journalists for television, radio, and magazines. This is a tribute to the kind of reporting that newspapers have always done; but they need to do it better.

newspapers

social force

"Finished with the papers, honey-bun?"

Ithiel de Sola Pool

Newsmen and Statesmen: Adversaries or Cronies?

An image housed in the psyche of many journalists is that of themselves as St. George and the government as the dragon. In current jargon that is called the adversary relationship of government and the media. Most Washington reporters believe in it. They see themselves embattled in defense of the people against self-serving politicians.

As an empirical description of how the media behave, the adversary view is one-sided and inaccurate. As a norm for how they should behave, it is destructive. As either a description of what is or a guide to what ought to be, it is a deficient stereotype.

As with stereotypes generally, this notion is more often vaguely felt than stated baldly. It is usually implicit, for it need only be stated for any informed mind to see its incompleteness. And yet it is there. It is there in the sense that, more than its opposite or its qualifications, it has a powerful pull on the journalist's imagination. One can find innumerable quotations from journalists in which the implicit assumption is that the politician is normally engaged in trying to do things adverse to the people's interest and that the journalist's normal job is to discover and expose these malfeasances.

Here is one journalist's description of the gladiatorial combat:

The politician seeks to lull the people with pleasantries of government. The journalist seeks the cold, hard facts of government. Sometimes these don't jibe, whereupon the politican reaches for the nearest microphone and assures the people that the journalist is the worst sort of skunk.

The quotation is not about Spiro Agnew. It is from a speech delivered by V. M. Newton, Jr., of the *Tampa Morning Tribune,* at the University of Florida School of Journalism and Communication in 1954. The next sentence reads, "Need I remind you that President Truman once called Drew Pearson ... an S.O.B. in a public statement?" So the adversary notion is not a new one, but perhaps it is an increasingly accepted one. . . .

Reprinted by permission of Ithiel de Sola Pool and The Aspen Institute.

Journalists have often exposed malfeasance in office, and more power to them! But that is, at best, a partial image of the complex liaison between government and the media. There is also a relation between cronies.

The Washington journalist is a symbiont on the body politic. The politician is the newsman's *raison d'être.* His daily work and nightly gossip concern the foibles, fights, and policies of politicians. His gratifications include both secret knowledge of the frailties of the mighty and opportunities to cavort in their penumbra.

A bright young journalist who is sent to Washington by his medium can hardly not be titillated when a senator hops to his table, slaps him on the back, and calls him by first name. He can hardly not be excited if a presidential aide confides to him the calculations behind moves of some historic import. In the Washington complex reporters are persons whom high officeholders treat with deference and attention.

In this process friendships develop over the years and, more importantly, so do working relationships. Ever since Lincoln Steffens's *Autobiography* it has been a truism in the literature on journalism that reporters are engaged in tacit bargaining with the "pols" they cover. By holding back some of the more embarrassing things they know, they keep their contacts in debt. It is a gentle and often unconscious blackmail that keeps the reporters' channels open for more information to come and, at the same time, tames the reporter from going the last mile in his exposés. It may tame him to the good by making him think twice before playing to the gallery with every ounce of sensationalism he can muster. It may tame him to the bad as he becomes part of the system and comes to feel more stake in supporting that system than in exposing abuses.

If journalists and politicians become cronies in practice, then what becomes of the adversary notion? Is it not false to describe the journalists who are part of this symbiotic system as also holding to an adversary stereotype? In fact, there is no contradiction. Ironically, the very seduction of which the journalist is conscious may strengthen his adversary view; for the danger of co-optation is clear. Every honest journalist—and most are honest—is aware and troubled by the seductions that politics provides. He cannot help but be disturbed by the triangles into which his job places him. To do his job he must grow close to politicians and win their trust, but his job is also to publicly expose them. To do his job he must develop confidential relations with sources and protect those sources, but his job is also to strip the veil of privacy from everyone else's business. . . .

The whole relationship of reporter and politician resembles a bad marriage. They cannot live without each other, nor can they live without hostility. It is also like the relationship of competing athletic teams that are part of the same league. It is conflict within a shared system.

The adversary theory holds that the element of hostility in this system is a good thing; it is a defense against an alliance that would leave the public unprotected. If the government were the public's enemy, that would be a valid thesis, as to some extent it is. But to some extent a democratic government is also the expression of the people. And if that is so, then it is equally true, though equally partial, that the media are not the government's adversary but rather its ally in the struggle for national goals. . . .

Those who feel alarm at the notion of the media helping the government will probably have some controversial issue, most often the Vietnam war, in the back of their minds. But for every divisive issue like Vietnam there are dozens of less controversial ones about which the government needs to talk to its people. To control inflation the government pleads with people not to hoard, to look at posted prices, and to moderate their demands for wage increases. To reduce traffic fatalities the government urges people to fasten their seat belts and observe speed limits. To protect the environment the government urges people to recycle cans and paper, to reduce use of DDT, to close their taps tight. In general, the media promote such old-fashioned pieties, Smokey the Bear gets free publicity, as do bond drives and public health information. Yet even such noncontroversial governmental uses of the media are subject to challenge by those who hold to the newer adversary notion of the media's role. Even Smokey the Bear can be seen as a menace.

Indeed, it can be argued that, taking the media as a whole, the problem is not an inadequate willingness of the media to perform the function of helping the government, but an uncritical overeagerness. In this regard one must make the crucial distinction between national and local government, for the alarm that is here raised about the adversary notion has to do with national policies. Most local media are anything but critical of the local establishment; their pages are filled with civic-minded stories on behalf of every church, fraternal group, charity, or improvement association. The paper becomes a willing bulletin board. Rarely will the mayor have reason to complain that a local medium will not carry his message, for most local media recognize that helping the community to operate is a large part of their mission.

Can it be that a well-ordered national community does not need some of what a local community so clearly requires? The national needs for cohesion and organization are equally great, yet media practitioners are decreasingly inclined to accept a positive civic role when it is more needed than ever.

Historically, mass media have been one of the major forces for nation building. They have helped produce civic consciousness and a sense of identity. It is happening now in the developing world. Daniel Lerner describes in *The Passing of Traditional Society* (1958) how the emergence of mass media is a prerequisite for the development of a sense of nationhood.

Based upon observation in the Middle East, his thesis has stood up in about a dozen more test studies in different parts of the world. The same sort of nationalistic thing happens in modern states as well. In an Israeli survey 68 percent of the respondents said that newspapers were very helpful in feeling "pride that we have a State."

In this country the creation of a sense of identity has always been one of the main functions of the mass media. Stations sign off the air with the national anthem. The press defines anything the President does as important to the whole country. International news (whether politics or sports) is reported in a "we-they" framework. . . .

. . . Whether the alienated critics like it or not, the government in this country is what the majority have opted for, and the majority have the right to expect that such a major social institution as the media will not systematically undercut their democratic choices and values. A society in which most journalists, or the leading journalists, do not share the presuppositions and values of the mass of the people is a sick society. Is ours a sick society? Is that, perhaps, the explanation for the prevalence of the adversary notion?

Even if a chasm exists between government and the media—and we are far from conceding that it has become a chasm—that does not constitute an explanation. To offer it as an explanation is begging the question. The sickness of our society, if it is sick, is precisely the alienation of the intelligentsia from the government. Their adversary attitude toward those public officials who command the support of the majority of the people is the sickness, not an explanation of the sickness. The sickness is the difference in perception between an American government with its supporting majority on the one hand and the most voluble stratum of the population on the other. The government and public sincerely believe that their efforts around the world are in support of peace, decency, and freedom. Much of the intelligentsia with equal sincerity perceive it differently.

Vietnam is, of course, the star example. On tactics there were differences even within the consensual majority; but, setting details aside, the basic issue in the American debate is clear. Three Presidents in a row, virtually all their top foreign policy advisers, and the public majority had no doubt that our aims were proper and legitimate. Not so the vocal intelligentsia, for whom this was not just an unwise or badly conducted war but an immoral one in which we were on the wrong side. The trauma for American society has been that such polarized and sincere conflicts of perception could exist between the government on the one hand and the vocal intelligentsia on the other.

As far as the media are concerned, all that one should ask is that they reflect this genuine division—and they have. We should not overstate the problem. The media are not in rebellion against national policy. They do

their part on the Smokey-the-Bear issues, the President still has his decla-
rations reported straight, and both versions of the war are given a voice.
The consistent expositors of the philosophy of adversary journalism have
not yet won the day. There is a trend in their direction, however, and it
is that trend which is cause for concern. The prophets of the adversary
notion, who tend also to accept dogmatically the intelligentsia's version of
Vietnam, would have us believe that the proper role of the media is to
challenge the government and show it to be in error. But a press so parti-
sanly aligned on one side of the issue would indeed be symptomatic of a
sick society. It is unhealthy enough that the literary and academic intelligentsia are solidly convinced of one set of perceptions and the government
of another. Fortunately, such solidity has not been the case in the mass
media, too, or there might have been a genuine revolutionary situation.

There are subtle reasons why the press tends often to be more critical
than constructive. It is a cliché but a fact of life that tragedies, crimes, and
scandals are news while progress and good deeds are not. Readership
figures support that bias, as does the psychology of some newsmen. . . .

There are other reasons for the acceptance of the adversary theory.
Critics of the press such as Agnew or Moynihan argue that at least the
leading east coast organs of opinion, notably the *New York Times* and the
Washington Post, are unduly loaded with journalists who identify with the
intelligentsia in its present confrontation of opinion with the government.
To a degree they are certainly right. The particular cream of journalism that
reaches the *Times* and *Post* does come from and associate with the literary
and academic intelligentsia. It is hard for them not to share whatever is
current dogma in those circles.

This constitutes a genuine problem, which becomes acute at moments
like the present, when the government and the intelligentsia are polarized.
Fortunately the elite media that are produced and read in a more liberal
milieu than the national average are not the whole press,* nor have those
media succumbed in practice to the adversary notion of their relation with
government, though many of their journalists may give it at least lip
service.

When Moynihan accused the press of reflecting the adversary culture
of the intellectuals, Max Frankel of the Washington Bureau of the *New
York Times* replied. [See the summary of that exchange on pp. 197–98.] He
conceded a growing unwillingness of the leading papers to accept what
they are told by the Administration. "If this shift from simple credulity to
informed skepticism is the change of balance you deplore, then once again

---

*As of the end of September 1972 the *Times* was one of 38 papers that had endorsed
George McGovern, as against 668 backing Richard Nixon. The *Washington Post* does not
indulge in endorsements.

I plead guilty." And he conceded that "it is also true ... that there are among some of the newest recruits to our business young men and women who are impatient with the objective, or, more accurately, 'neutral' standards of journalism to which their elders aspired. ... A few of them are impatient with *any* standard that would prevent them from placing their own views before the public. It is an important subject and an interesting debate." But Frankel's main point is that it is not snippishness by the press that accounts for any growing distrust of what the government may tell it but rather the conduct of the government itself. He says of "the President's near limitless capacity to make news, to dominate events of public concern":

He can exhort, rally and inspire. He can ruin and degrade. He can breathe life into American attitudes and, often, institutions. Or he can distort and discard them. ...

If you find the underlying truths obscured, you must begin by noting not the power for occasional deception in the White House, but the *habit* of *regular* deception in our politics and administration. By and large, it is the President and the Federal Government who establish the agenda of public discussion, and they must choose whether their purpose shall be uplifting and educational or merely manipulative. It is the damnable tendency toward manipulation that forces us so often into the posture of apparent adversaries. ... A President or government dedicated to truthtelling and eager to inform the public could very rapidly turn the wolves of the press into lambs.

To calculate a score for the Moynihan-Frankel exchange would be naive. When men of such quality debate, each clarifies important truths, though these truths often flow past one another unacknowledged. Insofar as fault must be found for the decline of comity between the President and the press, Frankel is clearly right. However, to a considerable degree the trend is not anyone's fault but merely the reflection of structural problems that are causing rebellion in all institutions in our society. Still, the President is the man we have appointed to embody in his person the moral values and aspirations of our society. If he fails to engender trust, he can blame no one else. The buck stops with him. ...

... The American press operates on the principle that what the President does and says is news and what the reporters believe is not news. ...

After he left his Cabinet-rank position as assistant to President Nixon in 1970, Daniel Moynihan wrote a widely debated article, "The Presidency and the Press," for the February 1971 issue of *Commentary*. It is summarized here.

1. What Lionel Trilling has called the "adversary culture" in journalistic practice is likely to have even more serious consequences than the now well-established muckraking tradition. Large numbers of journalists are shaped by the attitudes of this adversary culture because the profession has tried to improve itself by recruiting reporters of middle- and upper-class backgrounds who were trained at the universities that are associated with the adversary position. The result is that the press grows more and more influenced by attitudes genuinely hostile to American society and American government.

2. The distrust of government implicit in the muckraking tradition is curiously validated by the overly trusting tradition of a "textbook presidency," which recurrently sets up situations in which the President will be judged as having somehow broken faith. Papers like the *New York Times* and the *Washington Post* are reinforced in their attachment to the "textbook presidency" by the leanings of readers whose character they inevitably reflect. Thus the newspapers help to set a tone of pervasive dissatisfaction, whoever the presidential incumbent may be and whatever the substance of his policies.

3. Washington reporters depend heavily on clandestine information from federal bureaucracies that are frequently and, in some cases, routinely antagonistic to presidential interests. This disloyalty to the presidency springs from the self-regard of lower-echelon bureaucrats who either want to let the reporter know how much *they* know or are just trying to look after their agency. Such disclosures mean, among other things, that the press is fairly continuously involved in an activity that is something less than honorable, benefiting from the self-serving acts of government officials who are essentially hostile to the presidency.

4. The fact that news will be reported whether or not the reporter or his publisher likes it is a proud tradition. However, a decision must be made as to whether an event really *is* news or whether it is a nonevent staged for the purpose of getting into the papers or onto the screen. The accusations that filled the American air during the period of Vietnam have been no more credible or responsible than those of McCarthy during the Korean period. Yet the national press, and especially television, has assumed a neutral and even sympathetic posture, enabling the neofascists of the left to occupy center stage throughout the latter half of the Sixties, with consequences to American politics that have by no means yet worked themselves out.

5. The most important circumstance of American journalism relevant to this discussion is the absence of a professional tradition of self-correction. In this respect Irving Kristol is right in calling journalism "the underdeveloped profession."

Max Frankel, who headed the Washington Bureau of the *New York Times* when Moynihan's article appeared in *Commentary*, responded in a letter that is summarized below.

1. The news media have had to develop a more educated corps of reporters to keep up with the credentials and footwork of the holders of public office. But reporters are not nearly smart enough yet to cope with the scientific, technological, pseudosociological expertise that is peddled to the public by both government and its critics.

2. Americans do have an exaggerated expectation of our Presidents, few of whom ever fulfill their own promises and boasts, even in hindsight. The press reflects public expectations and records the efforts of our Presidents and presidential candidates to nurture them. In trying to match promise against performance the press draws a pretty good portrait of the strengths and weaknesses of the presidency and our President. But if the underlying truths are obscured, one must begin by noting not the power for occasional deception in the White House but the *habit of regular* deception. A President who told the truth could "very rapidly turn the wolves of the press into lambs."

3. Deliberately disclosing information to injure the President is relatively rare. Even more rarely is such information printed without the other side being questioned and given a chance to discuss the deeper issues and even the motives of those who may have done the leaking. Most leaks result from a diligent study of public papers and diligent inquiry among dozens of officials, with reporters carefully playing one set of clues against another. Most officials who help do so because, *over time,* they have found their accessibility to be desirable for *loyal* purposes. It is true that in this process, when reporters have some interesting facts—but by no means all—and find themselves shut out by government, they publish what they know to light a fire that will smoke out much more.

4. Thoughtful journalists are aware that they can never be sure about motivation and cannot know consequences. These are horrendous problems, but they are not solved by the automatic assumption in the editorial suites of the absolute power to decide that one person deserves to be heard and another does not. Consider the agitator who may be encouraged in his extremism because he finds it to be newsworthy. What would he do to project his cause and gain attention for himself if he were shut out of the news? Burn, perhaps, instead of only shouting "burn"? Journalists are sometimes taken in, and readers are sometimes taken for a ride. But the culprit, far more often, is the government—the President—than the random extremist.

5. Those who figure in news coverage do occasionally need more space to explain their points of view or actions than is provided in existing columns for guestwriters and letters to the editor. But such an opportunity for correction is rarely denied to the White House. Men of power are able to make their views known, almost by definition. It is the ordinary citizens, sometimes including the editors of the eastern press, who require an outlet.

This is as it should be, but it is not enough. The press still exercises a great deal of judgment on what is an "important" statement. . . . Should the press have that much power to decide what is important news?

To function well, the government must have ways to get out information that journalists do not regard as meeting their private criterion of important news. And it does. It has the Government Printing Office, which produces mountains of reports and pamphlets. It has farm agents and other bureaucrats who meet the public directly. Most important, the government has a special relation with the electronic media.

On the electronic media candidates and public officials talk directly to the public without the interpretive intervention of reporters and editors. The amount of such communication is limited, but it is very important. During campaigns candidates can buy spot messages (and, indeed, ads in the print media) in which they present themselves as they wish. There is also live coverage of the conventions and of occasional campaign speeches. And even on such journalistic interview programs as "Meet the Press" or in the presidential press conference the politician has a substantial opportunity to answer as he wants in the words that he chooses.

The most important opportunity for direct communication is the President's power to preempt time on all three networks at once. Since President Roosevelt invented the radio fireside chat, Presidents have recognized that the electronic media enable them to circumvent the prejudices and opposition of the press and establish direct and personal communication with the people. . . .

Among journalists and other groups there are many who begrudge the President the power to preempt prime time on all three networks at once. The networks do not like it (they lose revenue); the political opposition does not like it (they would like equal time to reply); the fans of a preempted "Marcus Welby" don't like it. There have been suggestions that the President be allowed to preempt only one network at a time, rotating the assignment among networks. It has also been suggested that the networks be more selective about allowing the President on the air, exercising their legal right to determine whether what he wants to say is newsworthy.

These suggestions go in exactly the wrong direction. We are fortunate indeed that there is one medium that is available as a unified national forum for our national leaders. If we have a complaint, it should be that the forum is not used regularly enough. The President is afraid of overexposure, and from his point of view, well he should be. But from the citizen's point of view there is considerable justification in the complaint that the President can choose to talk to us only when he finds it advantageous. The cry of manipulation is legitimate, and it might be more desirable to schedule a regular half-hour of presidential broadcast time every week. Some popular politicians have used such time effectively. Mayor La

Guardia had his regular Sunday morning hour, reading the funnies and establishing his liaison with the people of his city. Similar exposure should be demanded by the public for every mayor, governor, and President. But for the moment let us certainly not move away from whatever little direct leadership the President exerts when he talks to the people on TV.

Unfortunately, technology is likely to undercut the present unifying role of television, as it earlier did with radio. If cable TV gives us 20 or 40 channels to choose among, the unified network audience will be fractioned. Today, when the President speaks on all three networks much of the public hears him; when he talks on only one network he gets substantially less than one-third of the same audience. There is no easy answer to the problem that cable poses, but let us not overlook the blessing we now have in possessing one medium of national unity, and let us insist that the President continue to use it as long as it is there. When we lose that mobilizing medium the country will be harder than ever to unify and govern.

The dilemma of national consensus and free discussion, as well as its resolution, should be clear enough by now. A free society cannot demand of any medium that it support public policies of which it is critical. But a free society certainly can demand that the total media system be such as to give to the government abundant opportunity to talk to its people. The government has a real problem of media access, just as opposition groups do. There are many devices to provide this access, some through existing media and some through new channels that could be invented.

The existing media can serve their own self-interest by offering to provide much of the communication for the civic cohesion that society needs; for to the extent that the need is met by the established media, the demand for competing new channels is reduced. One way or another, access by the government to its people must be provided. Let us enumerate possible channels:

1. The press now generally accepts the convention that what the President and other top officials say is news, to be reported straight in the news columns without editorial evaluation or denigration, regardless of the medium's own editorial point of view. The press could, in addition, provide a separate section (comparable to the editorial column or the letters to the editor column) called something like "The Government Explains." The televised presidential press conference is essentially that, but there is rarely anything like it in the print media.

2. Reporters could from time to time write stories explicitly headlined "The Administration's View of X . . ."

3. Regular programs could be provided on TV at the local, state, and national levels for the mayor, the governor, and the President to talk to their constituencies.

4. The presidential press conference should be regularized and revitalized. A President who lets a month pass without a press conference should be subjected to criticism. To make the conference more meaningful, perhaps some conferences should have a single preannounced main subject to be explored in depth. And perhaps specialists not part of the normal White House press corps should be present to ask questions on particular subjects.

5. On cable television there should be a federal channel, just as special channels are made available by present FCC regulations to local governments and to the schools. It could carry Congressional hearings, farm programs, health programs, and, sometimes, statements by the President and Cabinet members.

6. There could be a federal journal to provide that minority of highly politicized, public-minded citizens with source documents and public records of the kind that even the *New York Times* decreasingly carries. Or perhaps there should be a series of specialized journals such as the *Survey of Current Business*. In any case, the government should be encouraged to publish its conclusions and justifications in a readable, economical form addressed to the citizen body.

All these suggestions, and indeed all of the comments so far, have dealt with the incumbent government's need for access to the media. But in a democracy the official opposition must be a part of the state system just as much as is the party that won the last election. Certainly the government and the opposition are not on a par; the government needs large channels for administrative communication. Smokey the Bear needs to be heard, not necessarily answered. Yet in the total system substantial time needs to be given to the opposition. Indeed, everything we have said in this essay applies *mutatis mutandis* to the established opposition as well. Both the opposition and the administration should be heard in their own voices on the issues they feel are important, not just via the interpretations of journalists who see their job as keeping the klieg lights on the rascals.

Insofar as the opposition does not get a fair hearing, the reason is not, as the opposition often argues, primarily because the administration swamps it in the press. Rather, it and the administration together, as part of the state establishment, suffer from inadequacies of the media. Both suffer from the propensity of the media to report the sporting contest between administration and opposition rather than the substance of the issues with which they are both grappling. Both suffer from the media's penchant for viewing politicians as scoundrels to be exposed rather than as leaders with a message to be explained. Both suffer because they are seeking access to media that belong to private owners who have their own criteria for allowing space and time. As joint parts of a single establishment, both suffer from being interpreted through the jaundiced eyes of an alienated intelligentsia. And both have the same needs for better media access if the country is to be governed well.

No easy solution follows from all of this. Other than the proposal that there be a federal cable channel when CATV becomes our nation's TV system, none of the administrative suggestions we have mentioned seem likely to do very much to change the relations of newsmen and statesmen. The problems we have been addressing are essentially psychological and attitudinal. If improvement comes, it will be by the slow processes of education and understanding. It will come from subjecting such simplistic notions as "the adversary relationship" to the harsh analysis they deserve.

Certainly I am not recommending that journalists become uncritical agents of government, parroting the line handed to them. If I am arguing against the biased view that journalists should be critics, I would equally deplore the biased view that they should be promoters. Their view of themselves should be that they are telling it as it is, however the chips may fall.

This is an old-fashioned notion. It once was axiomatic that journalists should be objective reporters trying to help build a healthy polity by getting the facts straight. They often fell far short, but they seldom doubted that this was the norm. Today the practice of reporting is probably as good as ever, but the norm is under attack by the newer breed of advocacy journalists. It is their ideas that erode the prospect of tomorrow's press doing its proper job of social integration. It is their challenge to the linked norms of objectivity and national service that may sharpen social schisms, leaving the press as one of the first victims of a disintegrative struggle.

The alternatives are not adversary journalism or pro-government propaganda. Just as the opposition is part of the establishment, committed to the long-term goal of the state but exposing current failings, so too a national media system in a healthy society is also part of the establishment. With the exception of a minority of organs of total dissent, which have the right to their views, the general press can and should see itself as sharing national goals and striving to help explain and clarify these goals, as well as being responsible for an absolute and ruthless objectivity in factual reporting.

---

to the student : a commentary

Ithiel de Sola Pool, professor of political science at the Massachusetts Institute of Technology, states that the growing adversary relationship between the journalist and the government official has gone too far. As a consequence of the timing of Pool's writing, his provocative article, written in 1972, has been all but ignored. At that time, the clouds had gathered around President Nixon and were slowly breaking. Eventually the Watergate affair doomed the president; in 1974 Nixon resigned in disgrace.

Pool's article is, I believe, the strongest argument presented so far for a sharing of goals between journalists and public officials. Although my own view is that there is not enough adversary reporting, his argument certainly should be considered carefully.

In debating this issue, one should examine the status of adversary reporting. When the Watergate affair began in 1972, of all the two thousand correspondents in Washington, there were exactly *fourteen* reporters giving it their full time. Moreover, getting the information was so difficult that the leading reporters, Carl Bernstein and Robert Woodward of the *Washington Post,* worked for months before they cracked the case.

Bernstein and Woodward were extremely persistent during nearly two years of investigation. They were the first reporters of the Watergate case to make a connection between the burglary and the White House; the first to describe the "laundering" of campaign money in Mexico; the first to involve Attorney General John Mitchell; the first to involve Presidential Appointments Secretary Dwight Chapin; the first to explain that political espionage was an intrinsic part of the Nixon campaign; the first to trace the Watergate affair to Nixon's White House Chief of Staff H. R. Haldeman. Ultimately, the *Washington Post* reporting led to a chain of investigations that forced President Nixon to resign.

More and more Washington correspondents are diligently pursuing investigative reporting—or how they think it's done. Many of them have learned two of the three requisite qualities: an almost endless patience and a mental toughness that few possess. The third quality, though, is indefinable. When Robert Donovan, who was then the bureau chief of the now-dead *New York Herald Tribune* and who is now an associate editor of the *Los Angeles Times,* struggled to define an investigative reporter, he said, "I'm not an investigator. People with a flair for investigation are hard to find. Sure, there are so many notes and documents lying around on the surface, but the incentive for digging. . . ." He threw up his hands. "Somehow it's the basic makeup of the reporter. No one can *really* define it."

But a large portion of the two thousand correspondents in Washington will not turn to investigative reporting. Indeed, many who want to investigate will not have time. Something is happening every day in Washington, and it must be reported.

The adversary relationship is not, of course, dependent on investigative reporting. Any reporter who asks embarrassing questions is almost surely an adversary reporter. For example, President Gerald Ford was asked to comment before a national audience on a televised press conference on the fact that he was too dumb to be president. He answered that his school grades had been so good that he recalled that he was in the upper third of the law class at Yale. The next day, reporters demanded that the White House produce his grades.

Surprisingly, not many of the correspondents are adversary reporters. After the Watergate affair, I questioned fifty of the Washington correspondents, asking them what common practice among the correspondents is most damaging. Almost all of them answered in tones like those of James McCartney, the national correspondent of the Knight Newspapers: "the conventional wire-service-style hard-news story that frequently misleads as to the real truth or probable truth. To be satisfied today with old-fashioned hard-news reporting is to mislead the public by blandly reporting what are often lies." This was, of course, an objection to the so-called objectivity approach. Fred Graham of CBS added that reporting official statements uncritically is the major mistake. "Government has become skillful about using 'objective' statements to propagandize the public. Too many reporters play it safe by accurately reporting what the official *said,* which may often be thoroughly misleading."

Thus most correspondence carries little adversary reporting. If writing according to the objective formula prevents the correspondent from editorializing, it plays into the government official's hands. Moreover, the "objective" story, many correspondents argue, is a straitjacket that prevents the correspondent from reporting more than a small slice of life at a particular time; it also prevents reporting any of the surrounding events that might provide meaning and allow the full truth to emerge. One correspondent wryly commented that he could not precede the senator's latest lie with a note that said, "For the truth about what you read below, see tomorrow's editorial page."

For example, the late Senator Everett Dirksen of Illinois benefited enormously from the "objective" story. Puzzled by his seeming contradiction of earlier statements, the *Chicago Sun-Times* made a study of his seventeen years in the House of Representatives before he became a senator. Dirksen changed his mind sixty-two times on foreign policy matters, thirty-one times on military affairs, and seventy times on agriculture. No one had reported that until the *Sun-Times* discovered it.

In addition, when he was in the Senate, a group of Americans who objected to the United Nations' declaration of war against Katanga formed a committee and invited many luminaries to join, including Dirksen. He sent a telegram consenting to the use of his name. That evening when he was questioned by several reporters about his support of the Katanga Committee, he replied that he had never authorized the use of his name. One of the reporters then sent him a Xerox copy of his telegram. He replied in his lofty tone, "As Lincoln said, the dogmas of the quiet past are inadequate to the stormy present."

The tones of the senator, incidentally, often mesmerized the reporters. One of the reporters for the *National Review* made what he called an "intellectual schematic," a sentence by sentence paraphrase, of one of Dirksen's speeches. "I am telling you," the correspondent said, "that speech was utterly meaningless—empty of content—lacking in any development. He received a standing ovation. The audience had come to him on his own terms. They desired the resonant tones, the patriotic attitudinizations, the diapasonal rhetoric. I should add that, notwithstanding, I was enraptured."

Although it seems to me that there is far too little adversary reporting, I pause over Pool's persuasive argument. It is necessary to weigh his argument, and to consider the ill effects of both adversary *and* overly friendly "objective" reporting.

WLR

J. William Fulbright

On the Press

Heresy though it may be, I do not subscribe unquestioningly to the Biblical aphorism that "the truth shall make you free." A number of crucial distinctions are swept aside by an indiscriminate commitment to the truth—the distinction, for instance, between factual and philosophical truth, or between truth in the sense of disclosure and truth in the sense of insight. There are also certain useful fictions—or "myths"—which we invest with a kind of metaphorical truth. One of these is the fiction that "the king can do no wrong." He can, of course, and he does, and everybody knows it. But in the course of political history it became apparent that it was useful to the cohesion and morale of society to attribute certain civic virtues to the chief of state, even when he patently lacked them. A certain dexterity is required to sustain the fiction, but it rests on a kind of social contract —an implicit agreement among Congress, the press, and the people that some matters are better left undiscussed, not out of a desire to suppress information, but in recognition, as the French writer Jean Giraudoux put it, that "there are truths which can kill a nation." What he meant, it seems, was that there are gradations of truth in a society, and that there are some truths which are more significant than others but which are also destructible. The self-confidence and cohesion of a society may be a fact, but it can be diluted or destroyed by other facts such as the corruption or criminality of the society's leaders. Something like that may have been what Voltaire had in mind when he wrote, "There are truths which are not for all men, nor for all times." Or as Mark Twain put it, even more cogently, "Truth is the most valuable thing we have. Let us economize it."

In the last decade—this Vietnam and Watergate decade—we have lost our ability to "economize" the truth. That Puritan self-righteousness which is never far below the surface of American life has broken through the frail barriers of civility and restraint, and the press has been in the vanguard of the new aggressiveness. This is not to suggest in any way that the press ought to pull its punches, much less be required to do so, on matters of political substance. I myself have not been particularly backward about criticizing presidents and their policies, and I am hardly likely at this late date to commend such inhibitions to others. I do nonetheless

Reprinted by permission of J. William Fulbright from *Columbia Journalism Review,* November–December 1975.

deplore the shifting of the criticism from policies to personalities, from matters of tangible consequence to the nation as a whole to matters of personal morality of uncertain relevance to the national interest.

By and large, we used to make these distinctions, while also perpetuating the useful myth that "the king can do no wrong." One method frequently employed when things went wrong was simply to blame someone else—in a ceremonial way. When I began publicly to criticize the Johnson Administration, first over the Dominican intervention in 1965, then over the escalating Vietnam war, I was at some pains to attribute the errors of judgment involved to the "president's advisers" and not to the president himself—although I admit today that I was not wholly free of doubts about the judgment of the top man.

Our focus was different in those days from that of more recent investigations, especially Watergate, but also the current inquiries concerning the CIA and the multinational corporations. It was sometimes evident in hearings before the Foreign Relations Committee on Vietnam and other matters that facts were being withheld or misrepresented, but our primary concern was with the events and policies involved rather than with the individual officials who chose—or more often were sent—to misrepresent the administration's position. Our concern was with correcting mistakes rather than exposing, embarrassing, or punishing those who made them.

In contrast, a new inquisitorial style has evolved, which is primarily the legacy of Watergate, although perhaps it began with the Vietnam war. That protracted conflict gave rise to well-justified opposition based on what seemed to me—and still does—a rational appreciation of the national interest. But it also set loose an emotional mistrust—even hostility—to government in general. Somehow the policy mistakes of certain leaders became distorted in the minds of many Americans, especially young ones, as if they had been acts of premeditated malevolence rather than failures of judgment. The leaders who took us into Vietnam and kept us there bear primary responsibility for the loss of confidence in government which their policies provoked. I am as certain today as I ever was that opposition to the Vietnam war—including my own and that of the Senate Foreign Relations Committee—was justified and necessary. Nonetheless, I feel bound to recognize that those of us who criticized the war as mistaken in terms of the national interest may unwittingly have contributed to that surge of vindictive emotionalism which now seems to have taken on a virulent life of its own.

The emotionalism has not survived without cause, to be sure. The Watergate scandals provoked a justified wave of public indignation, and a wholly necessary drive to prevent such abuses in the future. Moral indignation, however—even *justified* moral indignation—creates certain problems of its own, notably the tendency of indignation, unrestrained, to

become self-righteous and vindictive. Whatever the cause and anteced-
ents, whatever too the current provocation, the fact remains that the anti-
Watergate movement generated a kind of inquisition psychology both on
the part of the press and in the Congress.

If once the press was excessively orthodox and unquestioning of government policy, it has now become almost sweepingly iconoclastic. If once
the press showed excessive deference to government and its leaders, it has
now become excessively mistrustful and even hostile. The problem is not
so much the specific justification of specific investigations and exposures
—any or all may have merit—but whether it is desirable at this stage of
our affairs—after Vietnam and Watergate—to sustain the barrage of scan-
dalous revelations. Their ostensible purpose is to bring reforms, but thus
far they have brought little but cynicism and disillusion. Everything revealed about the CIA or dubious campaign practices may be wholly or
largely true, but I have come to feel of late that these are not the kind of
truths we most need now; these are truths which must injure if not kill the
nation.

Consider the example of the CIA. It has been obvious for years that
Congress was neglecting its responsibility in failing to exercise meaningful
legislative oversight of the nation's intelligence activities. A few of us tried
on several occasions to persuade the Senate to establish effective oversight
procedures, but we were never able to muster more than a handful of votes.
Now, encouraged by an enthusiastic press, the Senate—or at least its
special investigating committee—has swung from apathy to crusading
zeal, offering up one instance after another of improper CIA activities with
the apparent intent of eliciting all possible public shock and outrage. It
seems to me unnecessary at this late date to dredge up every last gruesome
detail of the CIA's designs against the late President Allende of Chile.
Perhaps it would be worth doing—to shake people up—if Watergate were
not so recently behind us. But the American people are all too shaken up
by that epic scandal, and their need and desire now are for restored stabil-
ity and confidence. The Senate knows very well what is needed with
respect to the CIA—an effective oversight committee to monitor the agency's activities in a careful, responsible way on a continuing basis. No
further revelations are required to bring this about; all that is needed is an
act of Congress to create the new unit. Prodding by the press to this end
would be constructive, but the new investigative journalism seems preoc-
cupied instead with the tracking down and punishment of wrongdoers,
with giving them their just deserts.

My own view is that no one should get everything he deserves—the
world would become a charnel house. Looking back on the Vietnam war,
it never occurred to me that President Johnson was guilty of anything
worse than bad judgment. He misled the Congress on certain matters, and

he misled me personally with respect to the Gulf of Tonkin episode in 1964. I resented that, and I am glad the deceit was exposed. But I never wished to carry the matter beyond exposure, and that only for purposes of hastening the end of the war. President Johnson and his advisers were tragically mistaken about the Vietnam war, but by no standard of equity or accuracy did they qualify as "war criminals." Indeed, had Mr. Johnson ended the war by 1968, I would readily have supported him as my party's candidate for reelection.

Watergate, one hopes, has been consigned to the history books, but the fame and success won by the reporters who uncovered the scandals of the Nixon administration seem to have inspired legions of envious colleagues to seek their own fame and fortune by dredging up new scandals for the delectation of an increasingly cynical and disillusioned public. The media have thus acquired an unwholesome fascination with the singer to the neglect of the song. The result is not only an excess of emphasis on personalities but short shrift for significant policy questions. It is far from obvious, for example, that Watergate will prove to have been as significant for the national interest as President Nixon's extraordinary innovations in foreign policy. The Nixon détente policy was by no means neglected, but it certainly took second place in the news to Watergate.

Similarly—to take a more recent topic of interest to Congress and the press—it strikes me as a matter of less than cosmic consequence that certain companies have paid what in some cases may be commissions, and in others more accurately bribes, to foreign officials to advance their business interests. Such laws as may have been violated were not our own but those of foreign countries, and thus far the countries involved have exhibited far less indignation over these payments than over their exposure by a United States Senate subcommittee. I should not have to add, I trust, that I do not advocate corporate bribery either abroad or at home; nor would I object to legislation prohibiting the practice. At the same time the subject does not strike me as deserving of a harvest of publicity. It disrupts our relations with the countries concerned, and what is worse, it smacks of that same moral prissiness and meddlesome impulse which helped impel us into Vietnam. Furthermore, "commission" payments are not unknown in government business in the United States, and hypocrisy is not an attractive trait. Even in our business dealings with Italy or Saudi Arabia, there is relevance in the lesson of Vietnam: whatever the failings of others, we are simply not authorized—or qualified—to serve as the self-appointed keepers of the conscience of all mankind.

A recent instance of misplaced journalistic priority, which came within my own domain, was the media's neglect of the extensive hearings on East-West détente held by the Foreign Relations Committee during the summer and fall of 1974. The issues involved—the nuclear arms race and the SALT talks, economic and political relations between the United States and the Soviet Union and China—were central to our foreign policy and even to our national survival. At the same time that the media were ignoring the détente hearings, they gave generous coverage to the nomination of a former Nixon aide as ambassador to Spain, a matter of transient interest and limited consequence.

To cite another example: the press and television gave something like saturation coverage in 1974 to Congressman Wilbur Mills's personal misfortunes; by contrast I do not recall reading anything in the press about the highly informative hearings on the Middle East, and another set on international terrorism, held in the spring of that year by Congressman Lee Hamilton's House Foreign Affairs Subcommittee on the Near East and South Asia. The crucial ingredient, it seems, is scandal—corporate, political, or personal. Where it is present, there is news, although the event may otherwise be inconsequential. Where it is lacking, the event may or not be news, depending in part, to be sure, on its intrinsic importance, but hardly less on competing events, the degree of controversy involved, and whether it involves something "new"—new, that is, in the way of disclosure as distinguished from insight or perspective.

The national press would do well to reconsider its priorities. It has excelled in exposing wrongdoers, in alerting the public to the high crimes and peccadilloes of persons in high places. But it has fallen short—far short —in its higher responsibility of public education. With an exception or two, such as the National Public Radio, the media convey only fragments of those public proceedings which are designed to inform the general public. A superstar can always command the attention of the press, even with a banality. An obscure professor can scarcely hope to, even with a striking idea, a new insight, or a lucid simplification of a complex issue. A bombastic accusation, a groundless, irresponsible prediction, or, best of all, a "leak," will usually gain a congressman or senator his heart's content of publicity; a reasoned discourse, more often than not, is destined for entombment in the *Congressional Record*. A member of the Foreign Relations Committee staff suggested that the committee had made a mistake in holding the 1974 détente hearings in public; if they had been held in closed session and the transcripts then leaked, the press would have covered them generously.

We really must try to stop conducting our affairs like a morality play. In a democracy we ought to try to think of our public servants not as objects of adulation or of revilement, but as *servants* in the literal sense, to be lauded or censured, retained or dispensed with, according to the competence with which they do the job for which they were hired. Bitter disillusionment with our leaders is the other side of the coin of worshipping them. If we did not expect our leaders to be demigods, we would not be nearly as shocked by their failures and transgressions.

The press has always played up to our national tendency to view public figures as either saints or sinners, but the practice has been intensified since Watergate. President Ford was hailed as a prince of virtue and probity when he came to office. Then he pardoned President Nixon and was instantly cast into the void, while the media resounded with heartrending cries of betrayal and disillusion. Many theories, often conspiratorial, were put forth in explanation of the Nixon pardon—all except the most likely: that the president acted impulsively and somewhat prematurely out of simple human feeling.

Secretary Kissinger, for his part, has been alternately hailed as a miracle worker and excoriated as a Machiavellian schemer, if not indeed a Watergate coconspirator. I myself was criticized by some of the Kissinger-hating commentators for "selling out" by cooperating with the secretary on East-West détente and the Middle East. Until that time it had never occurred to me that opposition itself constituted a principle, and one which required me to alter my own long-held views on Soviet-American relations and the need for a compromise peace in the Middle East.

My point is not that the character of our statesmen is irrelevant but that their personal qualities are relevant only as they pertain to policy, to their accomplishments or lack of them in their capacity as public servants. Lincoln, it is said, responded to charges of alcoholism against the victorious General Grant by offering to send him a case of his favorite whiskey. Something of that spirit would be refreshing and constructive in our attitude toward our own contemporary leaders. None of them, I strongly suspect—including Dr. Kissinger, President Ford, and former President Nixon—is either a saint or a devil, but a human like the rest of us, whose proper moral slot is to be found somewhere in that vast space between hellfire and the gates of heaven.

A free society can remain free only as long as its citizens exercise restraint in the practice of their freedom. This principle applies with special force to the press, because of its power and because of its necessary immunity from virtually every form of restraint except self-restraint. The media have become a fourth branch of government in every respect except for their immunity from checks and balances. This is as it should be—there are no conceivable restraints to be placed on the press which would not be worse than its excesses. But because the press cannot and should not be restrained from outside, it bears a special responsibility for restraining itself, and for helping to restore civility in our public affairs.

For a start, journalists might try to be less thin-skinned. Every criticism of the press is not a fascist assault upon the First Amendment. One recalls, for example, that when former Vice-President Agnew criticized members of Congress and others, the press quite properly reported his remarks, taking the matter more or less in their stride. But when he criticized the media, the columnists and editorialists went into transports of outraged excitement, bleeding like hemophiliacs from the vice-president's pinpricks.

More recently, since Watergate, the press has celebrated its prowess with a festival of self-congratulation, and politicians have joined with paeans of praise. The politicians' tributes should be taken with a grain of salt in any case—they have seen the media's power and few are disposed to trifle with it. The real need of the press is self-examination, and a degree of open-mindedness to the criticisms which are leveled against it. Journalists bear an exceedingly important responsibility for keeping office holders honest; they have an equally important responsibility for keeping themselves honest, and fair. . . .

---

to the student: a commentary

Former Senator James William Fulbright, who lost his seat in the Senate in 1974 after twenty-nine years of service, is a modest but powerful man. In submitting the record of his career to *Who's Who in America,* he gave the editors enough information for only thirteen lines. In the Senate, he balanced the interests of his state Arkansas with his own passionate interest in foreign policy. During his career, he marked out foreign policy so emphatically that he was the foremost senator of his time. He was also the best writer, always thoughtful.

When I attempt to challenge Fulbright's article, I find myself pausing over his charge that the media have turned to personality. If this is so—and it seems true—where did it begin? Indeed, it may well have begun with President Kennedy, who was killed in 1963. How he maintained a personality cult with the correspondents is worth exploring.

When Kennedy came to the White House in 1961, no president had ever granted an interview to correspondents, with two exceptions: Franklin Roosevelt had given Arthur Krock of the *New York Times* an exclusive interview, and Harry Truman had also granted Krock a single exclusive interview. In both cases, the other correspondents had brewed up such a violent storm that neither Roosevelt nor Truman ever tried again. Before President Kennedy came to the White House, he was warned by the many correspondents about the venom of *other* correspondents. He nodded. But a few hours after the Inaugural Ball, President Kennedy showed up at the home of columnist

Joseph Alsop. A few days later, the president drove to the home of Walter Lippmann, then went to dinner at the home of Rowland Evans, Jr. When President Kennedy went to Hyannis Port he invited a newspaper columnist named Charles Bartlett, an old friend.

All this made it quite clear that the presidency had changed dramatically. Kennedy was amazingly accessible, not only to his friends but also to the deep conservatives, such as columnist George Sokolsky, who then became a warm supporter. The correspondents went to the White House for exclusive interviews, ecstatic; they attended the White House press conferences in hundreds, during which they were filmed while the president answered them. He won them with an appealing style. For example:

Q. Mr. President, have you given any thought to some of the proposals advanced from time to time for improving the Presidential press conference, such as having the conference devoted all to one subject or to having written questions at a certain point?

The President. Well, I have heard of that, and I have seen criticism of the proposal. The difficulty is—as Mr. Frost said about not taking down a fence until you find out why it was put up—I think all the proposals made to improve it will really not improve it.

I think we do have the problem of moving very quickly from subject to subject, and therefore I am sure many of you feel that we are not going into any depth. So I would try to recognize perhaps the correspondent on an issue two or three times in a row, and we could perhaps meet that problem. Otherwise it seems to me it serves its purpose, which is to have the President in the bull's-eye, and I suppose that is in some ways revealing.

The president spoke brightly, toughly. But the correspondents did not seem to know the real Kennedy—a complex man, humorous, hard, tough on his friends. He said to Benjamin Bradlee, then the bureau chief of *Newsweek:* "When I was elected, you all said that my old man would run the country in consultation with the pope. Now here's the only thing he's ever asked me to do for him [appoint an incompetent judge], and you guys piss all over me."

The most important thing about Kennedy, however, is the style of life that became known only in 1975. Consider first what Walter Lippmann wrote in 1913 in his first book, *A Preface to Politics:*

For one item suppressed out of respect for a railroad or a bank, nine are rejected because of the prejudices of the public. This will anger the farmers, that will arouse the Catholics, another will shock the summer girl. Anybody can take a fling at poor old Mr. Rockefeller, but the great mass of average citizens must be left in the undisturbed possession of its prejudices. In that subservience, and not in the meddling of Mr. Morgan, is the reason why American journalism is so flaccid, so repetitious, and so dull.

In contrast today, almost anything that becomes known can be considered worth print. *Time* has reported that a young woman who was in love with Kennedy was with him and they were interrupted "by a knock on the Lincoln bedroom door. Angered, Kennedy threw the door wide open. There stood two top foreign affairs advisers with a batch of secret cables and a clear view of the woman in bed. Never bothering to close the door, Kennedy cooled down, read the dispatches and made his decisions before he returned to his friend."

At the extreme, author Richard Condon has said that he has done fifteen years researching the late Kennedy's life. He said Kennedy had "scored" with 470 girls by the time he was elected to Congress. "When he entered the Senate only five years later his total, by his own records, was up to 903," according to Condon. "By the time he was President his score had soared to nearly 1600." Although many of those who read those figures are certain that it is a fabrication, is it realistic? If, for example, 1600 seems mind-boggling, consider first that it covers at least twenty years. Thus the number of women comes to 80 a year, or about 1.5 women a week. Realistic? Probably.

It seems only in recent years that the correspondents have begun to print the whole truth about Kennedy. Moreover, they have to come to know—and to tell about—the worst traits of all the succeeding presidents. Johnson: a vulgar man. Nixon: a liar. Ford: a stupid man.

Are these pictures too limited? Indeed they are, but certainly they point to the extremity that Fulbright focused on. This new emphasis on personality is sobering; as Fulbright suggests, it may be unfair to the all-too-human public official. On the other hand, our officials, it can be argued, should be able to withstand this close scrutiny.

WLR

Wesley Gallagher

Accountability Reporting

It is obvious that all our societies are undergoing fundamental changes which can be peaceful or violent. As predicted in Toffler's *Future Shock,* our computer societies are also becoming more irrational in their behavior.

Public servants strike; firemen even start fires apparently; bombs are exploded indiscriminately in major cities by radical revolutionaries who do not even seem to know what their programs are.

It is little wonder that the general public feels fundamentally threatened and uneasy and reacts more with emotion than logic.

The press is an institution, whether you like the term or not, and is under challenge today as are all institutions.

I am not talking here of the special interest critics—liberal or conservative, union or employer, oil interest or farm interest, generals or civilians —all of whom speak with axes to grind. Far more serious is the attitude of the public at large because without their support a free press cannot exist.

Nor am I talking about being popular, because the press has never been popular. But I am talking about the press being believed and respected.

The American public is under an information barrage, unprecedented in human history. It goes on ceaselessly, 24 hours a day—newspapers, radio and television, magazines, CATV, special journals, and professional special interest letters.

American citizens either are going to be the best informed elite in the world or the most confused and disillusioned.

It is the press—print and broadcast—which will decide. The responsibility is enormous.

If the public is left confused, cynical and disillusioned, you can rest assured of one thing. A free press will disappear. But the responsibility is far greater than this. If a free press disappears, so will our other democratic institutions.

Reprinted by permission of Wesley Gallagher from *AP Log,* 3 November 1975.

Lack of faith in our democratic institutions comes when we have more and better technical tools with which to communicate and a thousand new things to write about.

It therefore follows there is something wrong and we must do our job better.

We can make our time a golden age of public service or a dark age for all of journalism.

With the great opportunities we have today, go great responsibilities and dangers.

I would like to talk about some changes I think we must make.

Our news priorities are becoming twisted with what could be fatal results. It is ironic this is happening in the aftermath of two of the American press' greatest triumphs—getting the truth out of Vietnam and exposing the truths of Watergate. In part, it is because of these that there is a lack of faith today.

Many sectors of the press are developing a Cassandra tone. We pose many problems, but suggest few solutions. We expose the petty machinations of politicians but virtually ignore some of the massive public problems of the day.

Watergate touched off an investigative reporting binge. But after all, what do you do for encores after a president is exposed and forced out of office?

My answer is "yes," we need investigative reporting but we need different priorities, a better job and a less strident tone, and perhaps a different name for it—one more to the point.

It is titillating to read or hear long speculative articles about whether Presidents Eisenhower or Kennedy, or both, knew of plots to kill Castro; or that the CIA infiltrated the Catholic missionaries in Vietnam and had a bishop on the payroll.

But does this advance us very far in determining what kind of a CIA we should have for protection and at the same time not infringe on our civil liberties?

Which is more important? To learn that an American submarine bumped into a Soviet submarine on a spy mission off Russia some years ago or to learn why New York City is broke and could it happen to Los Angeles, San Francisco or your home town?

In this investigative binge many stories are written in an accusatory tone.

Watching for scandal in public office, of course, remains one of the press' duties, but in the wake of Watergate let's not blow minor points into major disclosures.

The basic economic theory of American industry is that free enterprise will automatically adjust inequities in the economy—the law of supply and demand. If there are high unemployment, excess goods and low demand, prices and wages will go down.

Well, it isn't happening. Someone seems to have repealed that law when we weren't looking.

Auto makers can't sell their automobiles but raise prices anyway. Steel makers are at reduced capacity but raising prices. There are millions of unemployed but wage settlements continue to rise.

What is happening? We haven't answered. Probably because politicians haven't, can't or won't.

But why should the press wait? Why don't we devote the reportorial manpower to explain what is happening, explore alternatives and let the people see a little light?

The intensive New York investigations now under way disclose no glamorous villains to intrigue the reader. Just dismal political ineptness, greedy contractors, equally greedy unions, welfare corruption and economic lamebrains in public office.

Glamor, the story does not have, but importance it surely does. It is estimated 100,000 to one million small investors in New York City bonds may lose their savings, certainly their income. Unmet police payrolls can mean chaos in the streets. And the repercussions of a New York credit failure of $3 billion could affect the bonds of every city in the country.

Furthermore, we allow, even abet, the technical gift of instant communication world wide to be misused by politicians, political and economic ax grinders, extremists of the left and right, and some plain nuts.

How many times have we allowed ourselves to be misled on the national and local level by the quick announcements of politicians—either promising glory round the corner or exaggerating some incident—or how long has it taken, if we did it at all, to straighten out such statements?

It is this type of turmoil that I think has turned the public against journalism. It is not unreasonable for the public to expect journalists to evaluate the real significance of a statement or a speech or an event and put it in perspective before it goes to the public, and not in an exaggerated form. They do not understand some of the technical problems and we do not enlighten them.

One of our problems has been that the revelations about the Vietnam war and Watergate have been so bizarre and illogical that we have come to believe anything is possibly true, no matter how far out, so we publish reports that a few years ago we would have questioned.

Our judgments have become distorted by the bizarre events of the past few years. We need to restore our sense of balance and be more questioning.

What we and the country need today might better be called "accountability reporting" instead of investigative. We have an accountability responsibility to the citizenry on how the nation's institutions are functioning. Politicians are accountable to their constituents for their actions. It is our job to make certain the constituents get accurate and timely reports.

Much of this accountability reporting must be explanatory instead of accusatory. Many times there are no fancy villains, just incompetents and publicity seekers. We must clearly explain the problems of a complex civilization. Accountability reporting is an extremely difficult type of reporting and editing, requiring expertise in many areas. It requires hard, grinding work. Some reporters do not have the patience for it.

It is not enough to do this months or years after the fact, as has happened in New York.

It must be done faster and better or all our institutions are in desperate trouble.

An example of accountability reporting done in a timely fashion is a story we [Associated Press] sent [not long] ago. You . . . heard George Meany and others complaining that the grain we sell to Russia will create scarcities and force up the price in the United States. We . . . found undisputed facts that the current sales will make only a small dent in the U.S. stockpiles after U.S. consumption and non-Russian sales. So it's simply not true that the Russian sales alone threaten a scarcity which would boost U.S. prices. Prices may go up but not for reasons of scarcity.

Perhaps all of the hullabaloo and talk of imagined shortages will force up the price. If so, the press has contributed to it.

But daily we accept without challenge such political statements as Meany's.

Such reporting is more difficult than investigations of the CIA or Pentagon. But also more important to the public at large.

Accountability reporting must be done with accuracy, not innuendo, and be in an objective, impartial tone—explanatory, not strident or accusatory.

The public is tired of accusations—it seeks solutions.

There are many other areas beside the economy demanding public enlightenment: rising crime in every community, overcrowded courts that threaten the judicial system, the decline of railroads and airlines—most running deficits, the growth of public service unions whose strikes leave the public helpless and in danger when it's the police or firemen, the lack of energy policies months after an oil boycott brought high prices and triggered a recession. The list is endless.

Another legacy of Vietnam and Watergate has been that the press, instead of being an observer and reporter, more and more has become a part of the action.

The press was pushed more and more into the public's eye by the Vietnam war. The government, seeking support for an unpopular war, attacked the press and reporters in Vietnam, charging their personal involvement and involving them in the debate about the war itself. The fact that press reports proved far more accurate than the government's only made these attacks more fierce.

Our priorities must be re-ordered to cover the truly important problems of our society, and the lower personal profile we have, the better.

In closing, we must not confuse press popularity with respect. The American press has never been popular even in Revolutionary times, certainly not in the Civil War and never in troubled eras like this one.

But we can be respected and supported if we do our job right, just as we have been supported by the public in the past.

And it will be up to us to decide whether we have the most elite, informed nation in the world or the most cynical and disillusioned.

---

to the student : a commentary

Wes Gallagher, once president and general manager of the Associated Press, is a rare kind of media executive—one who sometimes drops small bombs into the journalism community. He is quite willing to criticize the performance of news organizations, his own and others, if he thinks it will serve to improve the quality of the press. Here he calls for accountability reporting, which is not so much a request for a new kind of in-depth journalism as it is a warning against the abuse of an old kind.

Because he lays the burden of his charges on investigative reporting, it might be worth exploring what this form of journalism is, and what is expected of it.

Investigation, simply defined by *Webster's,* is "a careful search; a systematic inquiry." That general tag can be applied to many, if not most, forms of journalism. But what is usually meant by the term *investigative reporting* is the general definition provided by the *Dupont-Columbia Survey of Broadcast Journalism:*

... Investigative reporting would be regarded as digging beneath the surface of the news in an effort to expose or call attention to acts or conditions which should give the public cause for concern. Investigative journalism is not limited to exposés of crime or corruption; it may also include programs calling attention to slum conditions in a community or inadequate hospital facilities, or dealing with such broad social issues as hunger, environmental pollution, poverty and racial tension.

Some reporters, however, see the field in more narrow terms. A pure investigative effort is then defined as that which seeks information that is *deliberately* hidden because it involves a legal or ethical wrong.

Involved in either definition are elements of what Gallagher might call an "accusatory tone," because that is the *realm* of the investigative reporter. The stories such reporters produce are identifiable in content and purpose: the content reveals some form of wrongdoing, and the purpose is to bring it to public attention in the hope of correction.

Some editors and reporters, however, don't care for the label at all. Any good reporter, they say, is automatically an investigative reporter, and the term is therefore redundant. Harry Rosenfeld, assistant managing editor of the *Washington Post,* has said, "After all, all reporters should be investigative reporters. That is what the job is all about."

Sometimes such objections are based on an unwillingness to acknowledge any difference between types of journalism. But more often the objection is based on the assumption that all good reporters can handle all different types of news stories as the need arises. There is no investigative reporting, the argument goes, merely a difference between good and bad work.

Yet there are different kinds of reporting—a train wreck is not a political trial, a supermarket opening is not a gold crisis—and some stories may require particular kinds of experience and expertise not demanded by others. In addition, not all reporters, even the best of them, have both the required talents and the drive to put together a solid investigative piece. When Mary McGrory of the *Washington Star* was asked if all reporters should be doing investigations, she replied, "Yes, except that some of us can't do it. It's a gift, investigative reporting, and a lot of people don't have it. They don't have the stomach for it; they don't have the will for it; they don't have the brass that it takes to go up to a total stranger and take him by the lapels and say, 'Now, you tell me!' It's not everybody that can do it. I can't, for instance."

Some journalists persist, however, in thinking that any working reporter can be an investigative reporter—which makes the double error of both underestimating the difficulties involved, and overestimating the average reporter. "Bob Woodward and Carl Bernstein were police reporters," according to Martin Nolan of the *Boston Globe.* "And the story we're talking about [Watergate] was a burglary, and it is that simple. It was a local metropolitan desk story at the *Washington Post.* And they did the very best job they could do on it, and they followed it right through."

It's true that the Watergate story started out as a burglary (a "third-rate" one at that) and that it was assigned to two city-side reporters. But when one considers the talent and tenacity necessary for good investigative reporting, it is quite possible that the *Post* got lucky. Had the "burglary" been assigned to just any "good" reporter, Watergate might mean nothing more than the name of an apartment complex in Washington.

The investigative process is often nerve-racking, tedious, and frustrating, and frequently without success. It's sometimes expensive, often demoralizing, and occasionally dangerous. But it's also an important part of American journalism, particularly because of the crucial role it plays in a democratic society. The often-stated purpose of the press is to provide citizens with information on which to base social decisions; only an intelligent people can make a democracy work. As James Madison once wrote, "A popular government without popular information is but a prologue to a tragedy or a farce, and perhaps both."

Few kinds of information can be as important as those which tell the people that their system is malfunctioning. It is not an oversimplification to say that legal and ethical wrongs, uncorrected, will in time weaken the fabric of a society. Corruption breeds and feeds the feeling of social hypocrisy. It strengthens the impression, the grassroots intuition, that the difference between law and enforcement of the law, between civic ideals and social reality, between the stated and the accepted morality, is so wide that only fools would believe in an honest and honorable society. When social wrongs are made fully public, society has a chance to respond. It is often the press that brings individuals and institutions into the spotlight so that corrections can be made, and so that the real and ideal in society can be brought more closely together.

Supreme Court Justice Potter Stewart, referring to the press and Watergate, said, "Perhaps our liberties might survive without an independent, established press. But the founders doubted it, and I think we can be thankful for their doubts. It is my thesis that the established American press . . . particularly in the last two years, has performed precisely the function it was intended to perform by those who wrote the First Amendment. . . ."

"Too many of our critics," said CBS News President Richard Salant, "believe that there is something sinister and improper about what almost all observers of the American press since the beginning have accepted as a proper role of adversary and watchdog."

Gallagher charges that much of the investigative reporting being done today is accusatory in tone. There is undoubtedly some truth in what he says. But before one wholeheartedly accepts the complaint, it would do to remember the response of a turn-of-the-century journalist, Ray Stannard Baker: "We 'muckraked' not because we hated our world, but because we loved it."

LLS

David Rubin

The Campus Press: Slouching Toward Respectability

A clear sign that a decade of knee-jerk, barricade journalism on the nation's campuses has finally run its course appeared during a strike at the University of Pennsylvania. A leader of the striking employees accused the *Daily Pennsylvanian,* a paper with a radical political tradition dating from the Vietnam protest years, of being anti-labor in its coverage. Five years ago such a strike against a major university would have occasioned editorial cries from the student press for solidarity with the workers and perhaps "trashing" of campus buildings to pressure administrators into a settlement. The union leader may have been expecting the same help. But it didn't get it. *DP* editor Laurence Field credits the paper's objective news coverage and editorial neutrality with "calming campus tensions" and keeping violence to a minimum. The strikers eventually settled for the university's first offer.

Like a fast-forward film of a flower in bloom, the campus has passed rapidly through an anti-war phase, a drug phase, antipathetic phase, a lingering sex and pornography phase, and a few other phases. Along the way it has managed to alienate the faculty, the administration, and occasionally even the student body, which has rarely been as freaky as the editors.

Exhausted from all this, the campus press has at last shaken its radical image and returned to respectability. This is particularly true on Ivy League campuses and at the large state institutions where most of the 110 college dailies and the "prestige" papers can be found. Their behavior is likely to set the pace for smaller colleagues. Editors are more mature, more savvy to problems of financial survival, more knowledgeable about First Amendment rights, and less willing to hop on any ideological bandwagon.

The pied piper of campus radicalism, the *Daily Cardinal* at the University of Wisconsin (Madison), is still spreading "Tania" Hearst on its Hearstian/tabloid front page and printing dispatches from the Liberation News Service, now purchased by only a handful of college newspapers and radio

Reprinted by permission of David M. Rubin from *Change,* April 1976.

223

stations. But most of the others have turned inward, like the student populations they serve, to worry less about the CIA and Chile and more about tuition, curriculum, and jobs. "We are," says *Columbia Daily Spectator* editor David Raas, "disgustingly responsible."

It is admittedly dangerous to generalize about more than 2500 college papers serving 9.1 million students, ranging from 30,000-circulation mammoths like the *Minnesota Daily, Ohio State Lantern,* and the *Daily Texan,* to weeklies and semi-weeklies like *Student Printz* (University of Southern Mississippi) or *Good 5 Cent Cigar* (University of Rhode Island). Some are adjuncts of the journalism department, some are house organs for the administration, some are funded by student government, and others are independent corporations which own their own buildings and equipment. But ten years of turmoil seem to have produced *news*papers once again, papers which share three traits in short supply in the last decade: a preprofessional attitude by the staff, an interest in investigative reporting, and a concern for the source of the next dollar to run the paper.

The pre-professional attitude is due to the glamourization of journalism as a career in the wake of Woodward and Bernstein and the resultant tight job market for journalists. Editors at many schools, including Harvard and Columbia, report that more and more staffers plan to pursue journalism careers, with campus newspaper experience the diamond in the résumé designed to dazzle the recruiter. "We seem to have fewer of the brilliant eccentrics turning up at the *Crimson,*" says Harvard editor Nicholas Lemann. The *Crimson* and other college papers have long been a home to talented dilettantes who leave journalism to clerk at the Supreme Court or join the underground or perform brain surgery. As they are edged out by eager pre-professionals, college papers are likely to become more responsible and acquire the look and feel of the "establishment" papers to which the students aspire.

Woodward and Bernstein also demonstrated that there is more power in a well-researched news story than in the sort of editorial harangues and expletives which used to mark the campus press (and still do on occasion). Investigative reporting now seems to be the goal of every college reporter. The *Daily Princetonian,* for example, has uncovered problems in the Princeton food services operation. The University of Florida *Alligator* has revealed a major cheating scandal in which students were bribing janitors to rummage through trash cans in search of old exams. The university has so far not permitted the paper to attend proceedings of the student honor court which is hearing the evidence. In response the *Alligator* has filed suit against the university under Florida's open meeting law to gain access to the sessions.

The *Daily Texan,* which serves the main Austin campus of the university, continues to prove that despite close supervision by an editorial board and the presence of a faculty member who must pass on each piece of copy, it is still possible to print embarrassing stories about important state and university officials (the two often being the same). Recently the paper has investigated construction of a $1 million home for the chancellor of the UT system; the controversial appointment of Lorene Rogers as president of the university, over the unanimous opposition of students and faculty; and possible corruption in the construction of a new branch of the university system in west Texas, presented under the catchy headline, "What If They Built A University And Nobody Came?" A recent sports editor even had the temerity to question the social value of football as coached by Darrell Royal.

Many papers are taking a close look at the equity of the tenure system on their campuses and reviewing the cases of specific professors. Others are focusing on progress in minority hiring and promotion. The most important beat has become the central administration, as student reporters struggle to chart budget cuts and analyze policy decisions designed to reduce expenses and raise income.

The intensity of the fiscal crisis in higher education is accompanied by concern for the precarious financing of many of the papers. Throughout the last decade the tension between administration and student paper, and the availability of national and local advertising revenues, made the possibility of independence an attractive one for many editors. A widely circulated, controversial report titled *The Campus Press: Freedom and Responsibility,* sponsored by the John and Mary Markle Foundation, recommended that independence was the *best* course. In recent years the *Stanford Daily, Florida Alligator, Daily Californian* (UC Berkeley), *Diamondback* (University of Maryland), and *Daily Emerald* (University of Oregon), among others, have made the break. They joined such long-time independents as the *Harvard Crimson, Cornell Daily Sun,* and *Yale Daily News.*

However, according to Professor Leonard Sellers, a close observer of the college press and adviser to the paper at San Francisco State, the move to independence is "dead—the cost is prohibitive." He notes that both the Stanford and Oregon papers have had financial difficulties and that the "off-campus movement has gotten very quiet."

Part of the financial problem is that the campus daily is no longer the only advertising vehicle to reach the college audience. More than thirty campuses have at least two papers going head-to-head. Many of the competitors were founded in the last decade as conservative political alternatives to the established paper, which had swerved uncontrollably left. That accounts for the birth of the *Badger Herald* at Wisconsin, the *Harvard Independent, Phoenix* at San Francisco State, and others. Boston University, Arkansas, Alabama, Georgetown, and City College of New York all have two or more papers in competition.

Even papers without competition on campus are fighting for readers with a youth-oriented breed of metropolitan tabloids distributed free on all college campuses throughout a city or region. Such papers as *The Press* (New York City), *The Drummer/Planet* (Philadelphia), *Fresh Fruit* (Rhode Island), and *City Lights of Indianapolis* provide articles on rock music, film, and local leisure activities. They have cut significantly into the already soft advertising market. (Peter Hanson, President of National Educational Advertising Services, the national advertising representative for 1200 college papers, recorded his worst year in 1974–75, primarily because of the drop in job recruitment advertising. Business is improving this year, but it is not at the booming 1968 level, when the company grossed $3.8 million.)

Gone are the days when the chairman of the *Yale Daily News* could take home $5000 (1963), or the editors of the *Harvard Crimson* could split $28,000 (1968). Yale expects no profits this year and is without the reserves to purchase needed equipment. The editors are considering an appeal to old "Newsies." The *Crimson* lost $26,000 in 1973 and 1974 and will earn only a small profit in 1975, thanks largely to a new job-lot printing operation.

In 1974, its second year of independence, the University of Florida *Alligator* needed an emergency transfusion of $12,000 from student government to pay its bills. The *Columbia Daily Spectator* cannot repay an emergency $25,000 loan made more than three years ago by the university for typesetting equipment. *Spec* is generally one step ahead of either the Internal Revenue Service (for payroll taxes), the telephone company, or the printer, who once threatened to stop the presses when the outstanding bill reached $18,000. *Spectator*'s editors are also mounting a canvass of alumni. The *Wisconsin Daily Cardinal* lost $12,000 during the 1974–75 academic year, although editor Alan Higbie says most of that has been made up this year. Among non-independents, the *Daily Pennsylvanian* is trying to increase its $15,000 subsidy from the university, and many papers, including *The Campus* (City College of New York) and *The Oracle* (University of South Florida) are just trying to hold onto their shares of the student-fee pie.

In addition to money the campus press faces two additional problems: continued harassment from administrators, and an inability to bring minorities into the largely white newsrooms.

Harassment in the form of confiscating issues, demanding sources, cutting off funds, killing stories, and toning down language continues despite court decisions which make clear that college papers (at least at state institutions) have the same First Amendment rights as the established press. (Many experts think it is only a matter of time before this is extended to private schools as well, given the heavy state and federal presence in these schools.) The Center for the Rights of Campus Journalists in

Denver has been monitoring such harassment for the past couple of years and providing legal assistance to beleaguered editors. Legal Services Director Pat Stanford estimates they receive from five to ten calls a week, and that number is increasing as word of the Denver center spreads. He says that the most serious trouble spots are church-related schools in the south and southwest, where stories on abortion or drugs can still outrage alumni and bring the wrath of the administration down on the paper.

Censorship problems come most frequently, says Stanford, from situations in which a paper is funded by student fees and saddled with an advisor from the journalism department. "Anything that offends either group," he says, "can get the paper into trouble. The student pols and the faculty have such totally different views of a university that when you put the paper in between them, there is a real crunch."

The racial problem is highlighted in results of a 1973 mail survey by sociologist Troy A. Zimmer, reported in the *Journal of Higher Education.* Zimmer found that a scant 1.6% of a sample of 246 college editors were non-white. (By contrast, nearly one-third were women.) Recent interviews with editors around the country confirmed that sad statistic.

Harvard's Lemann says there are so few blacks on the *Crimson* (5) that "we don't know what the black student body is thinking or feeling, simply because we have less contact with them." The paper has made a special effort to recruit blacks, but without notable success. Field "cannot remember the last time a black was on the managing board" of the *Daily Pennsylvanian.* The only two blacks on the news side now are not active. Each of the last two years minorities have occupied the office of the *Yale Daily News.* The first time was in reaction to coverage of the controversial race theorist William Shockley, who was speaking on campus. The second was to protest publication of an Oliphant political cartoon caricaturing third-world figures as cannibals munching on the bones of Israel outside the United Nations. The managing board at Yale is all-white and mostly male.

Some colleges have funded weekly or monthly papers run by blacks, such as Maryland's *Black Explosion,* but few schools have yet been able to bring racial minorities into the mainstream of campus journalism.

Despite the chaotic pace of the last decade and the problems that remain, alumni will be cheered to know that undergraduates of both sexes are still "comping" at the *Crimson,* "heeling" at the *Yale Daily News,* or otherwise learning the journalistic ropes in one-on-one tutorials from juniors and seniors. The campus paper is still the repository of campus tradition, and its process of socialization breeds perhaps the strongest esprit found in any student activity. At the height of the campus turmoil in 1969, the editor of the student paper at the University of California, Santa Barbara, wrote affectionately that *El Gaucho* had been "our education in the realities of sociology, politics and psychology. We wouldn't trade it for the world." The current return to responsibility in the campus press is not likely to change that.

---

to the student : a commentary

David Rubin, a professor of journalism at New York University, presents a clear and concise summation of the current state of the college press. He points to the shift in campus concerns over the last decade and the new emphasis on "professional" coverage of news. He also notes the increase in financial worries, and its effect on editorial priorities.

Because most campus newspapers cannot support themselves on advertising revenue, they are often the awkward stepchild in the educational house. The majority of papers are supported either by the college directly or through a percentage of student body fees, and they are often expected to return this generosity by adopting the proper attitude. When the president of Johns Hopkins University was asked whether his suspension of two student editors violated freedom of the press, he replied, "Don't ask a stupid question like that. That newspaper is subsidized by the university. It is paid for by us. It is a house organ."

This stance has long been considered appropriate for college administrations. In the eighteenth century, for example, Oxford expelled two student editors for reporting that the easiest way to pass exams was to go out drinking with one's masters the night before. In more recent years, events were similar: The University of Florida *Alligator* editor and his staff were fired by the publication board for editorials critical of local and state governments; editors of the Monmouth College paper were expelled for calling a trustee a "political hack"; and the publication board at the University of Michigan refused to allow a new editor to take office because he had accused a trustee of conflict of interest. (The state attorney general agreed with the student journalist, and the trustee resigned, but it still took a threatened student strike to reinstate the editor.)

Those newspapers funded by the student government, rather than the administration, often find that the relationship isn't much better. At Alabama, the Student Government Association denied funds to both student magazines and cut the budget of the newspaper. At the Colorado School of Mines, the student council fired the editor of the newspaper for printing an obscenity even though the school president said he was willing to give the editor another chance. And the student government at Edinboro State College cut off newspaper funds in retaliation for an unfavorable editorial policy.

In an effort to solve the seemingly inevitable conflict between student papers and their funding agencies, many schools have tried to shift the weight of responsibility onto the shoulders of a professional adviser. But this is still a method of student press control. The adviser is often trapped between the distrust of the students and the demands of the administration. And even though the adviser may belong to the train-'em and trust-'em school, he is not likely to be able to forget that each issue of the paper may jeopardize his job. One survey of small-college papers, for instance, showed that 94 percent had faculty advisers, and more than half of those advisers read material prior to publication. Twenty-eight percent of the papers reported that during the preceding two years someone other than a staff member had barred publication of at least one item or forced significant changes.

The adviser should not be stereotyped as the sole villain, however. The late Hodding Carter, liberal publisher of the *Mississippi Delta Democrat-Times,* once angrily resigned as adviser to the *Hullabaloo,* the paper at Tulane University, calling the staff "dishonest little jerks." They were, he said, "in a very cold and calculated manner, testing just how far they can push administrators."

The awkwardness of dealing with campus newspapers, particularly for college administrators, is increased by the strong legal rights granted to the papers in the last decade. In 1967 an appellate court, in *Dickey* v. *State Board of Education,* ruled that Troy State College in Alabama did not have the right to expel a student editor for criticizing the state legislature. The college president, the court noted in its decision, had testified that the policy of prohibiting criticism of the governor and state legislature was applied "regardless of how reasonable or justified the criticism might be." The court continued:

On this point [the college president] testified that the reason for the rule was that a newspaper could not criticize its owners, and in the case of a state institution the owners were considered as the Governor and the members of the State Legislature. . . . The imposition of such a restraint . . . violates the basic principles of academic and political expression.

In other words, the court made it clear that a quasi-government publisher could not exercise the same controls over its editors as a private publisher could—at least not in an academic setting.

In *Antonelli* v. *Hammond,* a federal district court again ruled on the student press in 1970. John Antonelli was a student editor who sued for an injunction and a declaratory judgment that the announced plan of Fitchburg State College President James Hammond to censor materials for publication was unconstitutional.

While the court granted no injunction, the declaratory judgment read:

We are well beyond the belief that any manner of state regulation is permissible simply because it involves an activity which is a part of the university structure and is financed with funds controlled by the administration. The state is not necessarily the unrestrained master of what it creates and fosters. . . .

It may be lawful in the interest of providing students with opportunity to develop their own writing and journalistic skills, to restrict publication in a campus newspaper to articles written by students. Such a restriction might be reasonably related to the educational process. But to tell a student what thoughts he may communicate is another matter. Having fostered a campus newspaper, the state may not impose arbitrary restrictions on the matter to be communicated.

More recent court cases, dealing with both college and high school newspapers, have strengthened First Amendment protections for student journalists.

Although the rights of student reporters *should* be protected, it must be remembered that the student newspaper will always create problems. First, a student staff is composed of amateurs. Even though Rubin points to an increasing concern with professionalism, and student journalists have the positive qualities of youthful energy and iconoclasm, they can also tend to be foolish, self-righteous, and libelous. More than one intransigent student editor has jeopardized the job of a good administrator. Second, a student staff is part-time. Although many willingly sacrifice class grades upon the altar of the deadline, staff members are still students first and journalists second. To remain a student requires at least a minimum commitment to classes, term papers, and exams. Third, a student staff has high turnover. The historical memory of a staff seldom extends beyond four years.

But whatever the problems, today's student reporters are tomorrow's journalists. They have to learn to deal with academic community and the rest of the world in a responsible and realistic manner. As an editor of the *Daily Princetonian* once said, "If you write releases you get a pat on the back. If you do a good job, you get a nervous handshake. We prefer the nervous handshake."

LLS

study questions

1. What is the purpose of a free press?

2. The authors of the Constitution included in their document no requirements that the press be responsible, that it practice self-restraint, or that it serve the public. What are the justifications for the current demand that it do these things?

3. Fulbright objects to new trends in journalism that stray from the traditional concept of "objectivity." Is objectivity still a workable ethic for the press? Does it truly inform the public, or does it present an incomplete picture of events?

4. The public no longer has much faith in its social institutions. Is this the fault of the press? Can the press be expected to do anything about it?

5. Wes Gallagher claims that most investigative reporting is accusatory in tone and as such tends to undermine our public institutions. Professor Pool says the same about the adversarial relationship of the press with government on the national level. Do you think that investigative reporting and adversarity are valid functions of the press, or are they examples of press excess?

6. The purpose of investigative reporting is to bring to public attention instances of legal or moral wrongdoing in the hope of seeing them corrected. But if Gallagher is right in claiming that the results are more often increased cynicism and disillusionment, rather than constructive efforts to correct the situation, can investigative reporting be justified as a valid function of the press? Why?

7. How does one reconcile the function and responsibilities of the press with the business aspects of running a newspaper? Is it possible to serve and uplift the public and sell newspapers at the same time?

8. To whom is a free press accountable? Is it reasonable to allow an institution wielding such power to go unchecked?

9. Fulbright says that "because the press cannot and should not be restrained from the outside, it bears the special responsibility for restraining itself." What forms could this self-restraint take? What methods are there for implementing internal restraint?

10. Are the critics of the press confusing the bearer of ill tidings with the ill tidings themselves? In other words, is it really the press that is undermining public confidence in our institutions, or is it simply the conduct of those within the institutions, brought to light by the press, that is the real undermining force?

newspapers

constraints

From *Herblock's State Of The Union* (Simon & Schuster, 1972)

New hand in the newsroom

Ben H. Bagdikian

The Bu$ine$$
of New$paper$

I once worked for a newspaper whose business manager liked to return from lunch with reporters so that he could say to them as they passed the door to the business offices, "Every time you people pass these doors you should get down on your knees, because if it weren't for us you wouldn't get your paychecks every week."

It was necessary to wait for this otherwise kindly and intelligent man to come to the newsroom gate to say to him, "Every time you go by this door you should get down on your knees, because if it weren't for us you would be trying to sell ads in the biggest shopping news in the city."

Newspaper economics has always been a contentious subject within the trade. In the business office they do nothing but make money. In the newsroom all they do with money is spend it. It is one of the many contradictions that make journalism a unique enterprise.

The tension between business office and newsroom has its roots in the strange nature of the American newspaper.

On the one hand, the daily paper in the United States is a product of professionals whose reporting is supposed to be the result of disciplined intelligence gathering and analysis in order to present an honest and understandable picture of the social and political world. If this reportage is in any way influenced by concern for moneymaking it is regarded as corrupt journalism.

On the other hand, the American daily newspaper, like any other business enterprise, has to remain solvent and has to make a profit or else it will not survive. If it doesn't make money there will be no reporting of any kind, ethical or unethical. If the corporate end of the enterprise does not have an effective concern for making money it will be regarded by everyone, including journalists, as incompetent, negligent and a disservice to its community. . . .

This split personality of the American journalism corporation is further complicated by an old question: does the quality of the professional news

Reprinted by permission of Ben H. Bagdikian from *feed/back*, Winter 1976.

operation make any difference to the profits made in the business office? There are some newspaper operators who believe it does not. These are the owners who boast that they can buy a monopoly paper, cut its journalistic staff to the bone and make a healthier profit with a minimal news product. One of our largest chain operators has insisted on this through the years. There are other owners and operators who insist the opposite, that most papers that are sick or have died suffered the original disease of bad journalism. Most professional newspeople hope that there is a positive relationship between journalistic quality and business survival, but if there is such a relationship it is not a simple one, it does not show itself in any quick and direct way, and no one has proven it yet in a scientific study.

So the relationship of business office to newsroom remains tense, uncertain and intriguing.

The alternative to this kind of juxtaposition of money-making and professional journalism is not attractive. We could have a government press, thus solving the money-making problem. This would mean that the President of the United States would be editor-in-chief of the country's newspapers and the 535 members of Congress the managing editors, a thought that has not escaped the attention of the White House and the Congress. But if that happened we would not only lose a free and independent press, we would raise the political leaders of the country to an even higher position of power and manipulation than they already have. It would totally ruin both politicians and the press.

Or we could depend solely on partisan and special interest papers, run not for the general public's information, but as a propaganda for the particular individual or party or ideology being promoted. This can be useful and we have many such papers, usually small and recognized as special. In our earlier history this was, in fact, the nature of most newspapers. The notion was that if you have a multiplicity of these voices, each a special pleader, but in opposition to other special pleaders, then the collective efforts of all these papers would produce a complete spectrum of leaders, ideas and programs from which the public would choose. It works in some cases and we need such efforts to introduce and promote partisan ideas, but as a systematic way of informing the public daily this did not work in the past and it certainly does not work today.

So though we have each daily paper in America divided against itself, one turning its back on money-making and the other part totally devoted to it, no one has yet come up with a better substitute.

There seems little doubt that economics—the money-making and money-spending part of newspapering—is going to be of concern to us for a long time to come.

Given that, there is some strange behavior in the economic side of our institution. It keeps most of its vital economic information secret. Newspaper economics constitute the most badly analyzed of all major industries and this is so primarily because the trade insists on it. This is ironic in an industry that enjoys local monopoly in almost every place it operates. We have over 1500 cities with daily newspapers but in only 45 are there local daily competition. So one would think that there is no overwhelming competitive problem in disclosing finances. But in some cases, the more secure a paper the more paranoid it is about its finances.

What is more ironic is that genuine modern economic analysis of newspapers is unknown to most owners themselves. Some general industry data exist but these are not as reliable nor as complete as exist in other major industries of comparative size and importance. Each paper tends to use its own bookkeeping methods and is loathe to tell anyone else how it counts its money. The result is that each proprietor lacks the accumulated knowledge and insight that might be available from others, and has no way to make valid comparisons among new methods. . . .

. . . Why the obsession with secrecy about finances in newspapers?

The answer lies partly in history. In the 18th century most newspapers were individualist efforts. Proprietors were selling a cause or a candidate or a product or an idea; they did it as small enterprises in which they presided as publisher, editor, printer and distributor. Individual privacy was the standard of the time when it came to untaxed finances, and there were strong feelings about taxes applied to newspapers. Furthermore, this proprietor was often fighting political enemies with his paper, usually with the financial support of an unannounced group of backers who, if publicized, could be hurt by the authorities or simply remove the image of the lonely editor fighting a cause out of the pocketbook and courage of his convictions. If the paper was against the authorities, as they often were, then the financial backers could be coerced or punished if their identities were known. So the tradition grew that the finances of a paper was nobody's damn business. . . .

. . . Papers were [however] often corrupt, accepting money for changing their political line, or being secretly owned to push private or commercial interests in columns that masqueraded as news. Furthermore, circulation figures were commonly false. At first it was done to exaggerate the political importance and boost the ego of the publisher. Later it was done to give artificial increases in advertising rates. Papers escalated in the lies about circulation, lies that would be revealed if true finances became known.

After the turn of the century, lies about circulation became so bad that advertisers began to doubt the reliability of all newspapers as a medium of commerce. So in 1914, newspapers formed the Audit Bureau of Circulation which, by mutual agreement, goes meticulously into circulation figures and publishes precise and reliable figures on how many daily papers are sold. The integrity of this audit has seldom been challenged but it has survived partly by keeping its background data from each paper secret, and issuing only the final numbers on categories of circulation.

Secret ownership and financing of papers became so bad that the United States Post office moved in. . . . The post office historically has granted special mailing privileges to newspapers as educational publications. . . . The idea was to provide tax-paid service only for non-commercial content. But business enterprises, notably public utilities after World War I, but also powerful political and industrial interests, began buying secret interests in daily newspapers and planting propaganda as news stories. As a result, the post office now requires each publication granted second class mailing privileges to publish once each year a statement of ownership. It is an ineffective requirement since it requires only the listing of all owners of 1 per cent or more, without differentiation between a 1 per cent and a 90 per cent owner, and does not require the listing of the real beneficiary of the ownership but permits banks, trustees and other agents for ultimate parties to be listed.

So there is a long and complicated history of secrecy in American newspaper economics, adding mystery and suspicion to the subject. Mystery and suspicion are, of course, the best ingredients for paranoia. . . .

. . . And as in a nice genuine paranoia, it's all self-worsening. The more the outsider tries to get behind the bookkeeper's curtain, the more certain the publisher that he is surrounded by malicious enemies who want to destroy his institution, and so he tightens secrecy. This newly tightened secrecy convinces the outsider that the publisher has something to hide and this increases the pressure and accusations about concealed malfeasance. . . .

[But] why should professional journalists, whose job it is to report the news regardless of money matters, pay attention to the economics of the newspapers they work for, or the economics of their trade in general?

Publishers are often found urging journalists to pay more attention to the economics of newspapers so that journalists will understand better the terrible problems of publishers. The idea seems to be that if the reporter and editor appreciates the fact that the publisher has serious problems there will be fewer demands for higher pay, more fringe benefits, bigger newsroom budgets, and larger newsholes.

I think this is the primary goal of owners talking about newspaper finances to reporters and editors.

But I also think that there is something strange in the way most publishers handle this: the information they give to the reporters and editors is minimal; it usually consists of vague generalizations and alarming predictions and is almost totally devoid of hard, documentable numbers. You can't educate an intelligent journalist by cliches and rhetoric, you can only produce greater cynicism. A publisher may repeat that the paper will go bankrupt if it accedes to the demands of its journalists for money. Reporters and their unions respond with demands of proof. The demand is usually met with the statement that finances are managerial prerogatives and nobody else's business. If the reporter accepted that kind of an answer from a news source who had made an assertion without a show of evidence, the reporter should be fired for incompetence or idiocy. He or she should not be expected to take at face value anything like that from any source, including business managements being covered for news. So why accept it in the reporter's own business? . . .

In the newspaper business if there are union negotiations imminent, or if there is an announcement of an increase in advertising and subscription rates, then we hear from the front office a stream of alarming statements about rising costs, of crippling inefficiencies, and of danger of either suspension of the business or such drastic surgery that many jobs will be lost. It is usually equated to a generalized disease in the entire newspaper industry, a disease of spiraling costs and decreasing revenues, of plummeting productivity and gouging labor, bringing this historic institution to the brink of disaster. Then the contract is signed, or the new rates go into effect, and a new set of statements emerge.

These new statements may be provoked by a new campaign by a major advertiser on television, and a claim by the broadcasting industry that only the vivid, personal communication of broadcasting is an efficient carrier of commercial messages, and that this is drawing even larger amounts of revenues to this new industry to the detriment and obsolescence of print. Behind the scenes the ad managers are sabotaging confidence in the opposing industry in a ferocious battle, mean and dirty, and seldom seen by the public.

On those occasions we are then told by the same front office leaders that the newspaper industry was never more strong, that it has increased its revenues and profits steadily, that it is beating all the competition in getting most of the ad revenues. *Editor & Publisher's* [recent] figures for a smaller paper, a 36,000-circulation daily, shows 26 per cent return on sales.

This later, more euphoric statement of newspaper prosperity seems closer to the truth. In 1950, before television really took off, newspapers received $2 billion of advertising, or 36 per cent of all money spent on advertising in the United States. That year, radio and television combined got only $775 million, or 14 per cent of all advertising money spent. In 1972, the newspaper share of all advertising had risen from $2 billion to $7 billion, and was 30 per cent of all ad money spent. Combined radio and television got $5½ billion, or 25 per cent.

There are some newspapers in financial trouble, in a number of cases tragically so. [But, on the whole,] the American daily newspaper industry is remarkably stable and remarkably profitable.

There are more daily papers today than there were ten years ago. In December of 1973 there were 1,774 dailies, in 1963 there were 1,754. Total circulation in 1973 was 63 million daily, the figure for 1963 was 59 million. During that period the average circulation of a daily paper, despite the increase in the number of papers, rose from 33,600 to 35,500. . . .

During the ten-year study period [between 1961 and 1970] about 76 dailies died, 33 merged and dropped their identity, and 51 reverted to less than daily publication, for a total disappearance of dailies of 160. But during the same period 170 new dailies started.

Thus, in a ten-year period only 1 per cent of American dailies suffered failure, a very low rate indeed.

And most of the papers that died were, contrary to popular impression, new enterprises. . . .

This is a contrast to the general feeling inside and outside the industry that we are seeing an industry decimated of its major units.

This impression is understandable. When the average daily paper dies in the United States it is a local phenomenon with no impact on the national scene. It is usually a major event in its own community, but it almost never is noted by the outside papers or the national magazines and networks. What does crash into the national consciousness is the dramatic death of large, old metropolitan papers. And this is significant despite the small average age and size of papers that die, there are some that are very old and very large. The average age of death of the younger half of all failed papers is 7 years. But of the older half is 81 years. The oldest paper in the study that died during this period had been a daily since 1813.

Neither is there any doubt that the average circulation of failed papers is larger than the average of new ones. We don't know what is going to happen to the new papers in the years to come. But there is no doubt that in general a few very large metropolitan papers died, while there are no new ones of like size to take their place right away.

Neither can we ignore the fact that a disproportionate number of competitive papers have died so that today face-to-face competition among daily newspapers is a rarity.

Nevertheless, it is safe to say that we are not talking about a fatal disease epidemic in American newspapering. . . .

You could make a case for professional news people ignoring the economics of their business. First, the main body of business is healthy and thriving. Second, the part that directly affects them, the editorial budget, is a small part of the total, generally running to about 10 per cent on a daily paper. So if you raise or lower it 30 per cent, you're only talking about 3 per cent of the paper's budget, less than 1 per cent after taxes. So except for papers that are hemorrhaging fatally, changes in the editorial budget seldom are economically crucial.

One might also argue that reporters and editors should ignore their company's economics because of the peculiar schizophrenia in journalism companies. They are supposed to inform the citizens of the community what the reporter and editor believe in all professional judgment the citizens need to know in order to understand their environment. That should have nothing to do with money.

But whether we like it or not that does have something to do with money. For one thing, to inform the community adequately takes a certain minimum of space, and in a newspaper space is money. It also means applying reportorial and editorial resources at a certain minimum to certain stories and that means money: if you are short handed you simply can't develop important stories in depth and with proper care. But having enough hands and minds also means money. Crucial information is not always readily available and often requires extensive research, travel and documentation, and that also means money. And lastly, to do this consistently and well, you need a highly skilled and stable staff, and that means money.

So money turns out to be essential to good journalism and therefore of legitimate concern to the journalist.

It is not an easy process to resolve. Most serious journalists want to do more elaborate and deep things than they presently do. For this they need longer stories with good graphics, which means more space. If they have a compulsion for comprehensiveness and for tracking information down to the source, as they should have, then they want to travel. Editors who are good want to do this and they also want to cover their communities like a blanket so they inevitably want larger staffs and they want larger newsholes. In addition, they want to be able to move fast and have deadlines near time of publication, which means equipment, which means money.

Someone has to resolve these demands. I believe that daily papers, given their profits, do not spend enough on their news product, do not have adequate staffs, do not have a large enough newshole, and do not pay sufficient attention when designing and buying to the impact on the speed and quality of the news handling process.

But I also believe what is obvious, that none of these desires can be fulfilled ideally, if each editor and reporter had everything he or she wanted. I don't doubt that a good metropolitan staff could produce 600 columns a day of news, but I doubt that the front office could pay for it under the best of conditions and if they did I doubt that a sane reader would accept it.

So someone has to make difficult decisions about money that directly affect the quality and quantity of news. It is almost never the professional journalist. It is almost always a business office decision, often implemented by an elderly and obscure employee operating off an ancient formula and rewarded when the newshole can be kept at a minimum or staff costs cut to a level just above wholesale rebellion.

This does not square with the idea of the professional journalist deciding the quantity and quality of news printed every day.

What does the ad manager or the business manager or the invisible dispatcher know about the daily flow of news and the genuine informational needs of the community on any particular day? Some are remarkably good at this but not often—that is not their business.

The alternative is to let the journalist do the calculations needed to see what is practical in meeting the needs of high quality and adequate quantity of news, which is really the journalist's function. To do this the journalist, the reporter and the editor, has to be concerned with economics, not just with a formula for dividing news and advertising space, issued as a sacred number beyond question, but a decision based on the realities of the institution's economic resources, which means its basic finances.

And there's the rub. Reporters and editors are seldom given access to the basic finances of their papers. So it is impossible for them to make intelligent and responsible decisions about the limits to place on news operations. Even when an executive editor is privy to some of these figures, he is usually under severe sanctions not to reveal the basic figures but merely to announce the conclusions based on undisclosed figures.

So the study of newspaper economics has importance on both institutional and journalistic grounds. In order for there to be a truly intelligent and responsible decision made on the economic limits of news operations the traditional secrecy about American newspaper finances must end.

---

to the student: a commentary

Ben Bagdikian, probably the most powerful critic of the news media, has produced the best contemporary criticism of the financial structure of the newspaper. He is primarily a critic only of the editorial function, but in all the many studies of the economics of newspapers, this speech is one of the clearest and most emphatic.

One of the most paradoxical aspects of most newspapers is their dedication to disclosing the secrets of everyone else and their passion for hiding their own. We can recognize, of course, that newspapers are a business and thus have a certain stake in preserving some trade secrets. But it is ironic that newspapers denounce special interests, then seek special protections for their own interests, as in their successful quest for an exemption to the anti-trust laws.

After finding that meaningful research into the economics of the press was almost nonexistent, I tried to interest the American Newspaper Publishers Association in cooperating with me in a study designed to analyze cost factors and to recommend adjustments to help failing newspapers. The response was a firm, curt no. At about the same time, mathematical economist Dr. James Rosse was making a similar effort. Rosse, now at Stanford University, was superbly equipped to analyze one of the central problems of newspapers: economies of scale. He was turned down as emphatically as I was. He did a complete study by laboriously approaching individual newspapers, but it was much more limited than could have been accomplished with ANPA cooperation. Others have been similarly rebuffed over the years.

Secrecy in the newspaper business reaches high official levels as well. The Securities and Exchange Commission, which reports on the profits of manufacturing companies, carefully excludes newspapers. Here, surely, is a subject rich in the ingredients of exposé. Information is being withheld. The people's right to know is being subverted. Can an investigative reporter detect the fingerprints of some powerful pressure group at work here?

Newspapers, of course, cannot compete with television as an entertainment medium, and they are well aware of it. They seem equally aware that their strength is in the breadth and depth of the information and opinion they bring. David Brinkley has pointed out that as a news medium television is not even in the game with newspapers. Walter Cronkite made the point clear by pasting the words he spoke on one of his programs against the front page of the *New York Times*. The program covered less than one page.

It is instructive to consider which papers have died. The forces that are reshaping American living patterns have worked inexorably against many metropolitan papers. The movements from the metropolis to the suburbs, many of which are far distant from the central cities, have created a different kind of citizen relationship to the community. In many metropolitan areas, families that can afford more than one newspaper subscribe to a metropolitan daily for international, national, and state news, and to a suburban paper for local news and features. The result is the growth of a new, suburban-centered journalism existing side by side with a few giant metropolitan dailies.

One of the mainstays of the metropolitan paper is the syndicated feature. An editor in Stockton, California, far from the San Francisco Bay Area, said that some of the syndicated features he wanted were unavailable because of the *San Francisco Chronicle* exclusives. The *Chronicle* pays heavily for such wide-ranging rights and says that it needs its joint contract with the *San Francisco Examiner* for both to survive.

What are the costs of syndicated material? Syndicates too seem to consider their operations top secret, but some of it leaks out, thanks in a measure to prying reporters. Syndicated features gross about $150 million a year. Although there are between 200 and 300 syndicates, 2 percent of the syndicates have 40 percent of the income. Thanks to those who pry into the financial structure of the newspapers and the syndicates, we are slowly learning the basic economics.

WLR

Jesse Helms

The Question of Federal "Newsmen's Shield" Legislation

Foreword

In June 1972 the U.S. Supreme Court issued decisions in several cases pending before it which involved questions of so-called "newsman's privilege." In the *Branzburg, Pappas,* and *Caldwell* decisions the Court held that requiring newsmen to appear and testify before State or Federal grand juries did not abridge the freedom of speech and press guaranteed by the First Amendment.

At principal issue in the cases was the refusal of the newsmen involved to disclose to grand juries sources of information obtained in the course of their work.

With growing frequency in recent years grand juries and trial courts have sought the testimony of newsmen whose activities have resulted in information—both published and unpublished—deemed relevant to pending proceedings. The refusal of some such newsmen to breach the confidentiality of the source of such information, based on the claim of a privilege conveyed by the First Amendment, has resulted in contempt citations and subsequent appeals in a number of cases, including those on which the Supreme Court ruled in mid-1972.

In the aftermath of the Court's decisions several widely-publicized instances have occurred of the jailing of newsmen who, under subpoena, have refused to disclose sources of information. Courts in some jurisdictions, citing the Supreme Court's rulings as authority, have taken more stringent actions than previously to compel testimony from newsmen claiming a privilege of confidentiality of source.

I reject the notion that a so-called "shield law" for newsmen is either needed or desirable.

Reprinted by permission of Jesse Helms from *Congressional Digest,* May 1973.

243

In fact, the news people who are now crying for such special treatment would do well to ponder whether they are not asking for the handcuffs at some point down the road.

I cannot buy the assumption that such a protective umbrella is necessary to continued press freedom.

Before becoming a Senator in January, I spent most of my life in the field of journalism. I worked as a reporter, a city editor and a TV editorialist. Now this doesn't qualify me as any sort of expert in the field, but I do have a personal knowledge of the work-a-day world faced by today's reporters.

In all these years, I have done my share of investigative reporting. I have not, however, encountered the so-called dilemma of some newspapermen today who are asking for a special exemption. I never found a need for a shield to get the facts.

I have dealt with confidential sources all my working career and I have been subpoenaed before grand juries.

On one occasion, I declined to identify a source. The incident dealt with a story I had written disclosing malfeasance in public office. I explained to the grand jury that my source was completely innocent and that identification could endanger this person's well-being. Once explained, I had no trouble at all. I was not, in any manner, arrogant about it.

I have a hunch, really without knowing definitely, that some of these people in trouble with grand juries have been self-serving newsmen and it has gotten to be a personal thing. I believe the reporters recently jailed for contempt in the much-publicized cases could have avoided such trouble.

I would never make any commitment of secrecy to a criminal. I have had people, who were at least questionable in character, give me information, but rather than go around protecting them, I made an effort to learn whether they were telling me the truth.

In short, during my years as a newsman the crisis to press freedom some see today never materialized.

It is rare when responsible reporters, using sound judgment in dealing with secret sources, are faced with such a so-called crisis. In my view, skillful newsmen can oftentimes relate their story without indicating the source. It is the few irresponsible writers who act without corroborating evidence who leave the profession open to public criticism.

In a desire to gain a scoop, too many reporters and editors rush to the trough to feed without knowing the exact contents or the aftermath effects. Deadlines, far too often, are allowed to pull rank over cautiousness.

Before making a special social order of journalists, we need to rethink some fundamental questions. I simply cannot favor giving newsmen any right, protection, privilege, or immunity not enjoyed by all other citizens.

The few isolated arrests of reporters for refusing to divulge their confidential sources have brought on a falling-sky hysteria among some media people. The threat they see just doesn't exist. The danger lies in the singling out of any segment of our society for special treatment. Every citizen has a duty under our laws and the Constitution to give testimony in criminal and civil proceedings. Like butchers, bakers, and candlestick makers, the press should be no exception.

Promisingly, some media people are beginning to have second thoughts on this question of immunity. They realize there is an inherent danger in governmental intrusion. Past experiences show that with legislative goodies come regulatory strings.

While this reexamination by some newsmen offers some reassurances, it is currently overshadowed by a mass of shield law bills already introduced in the Congress. The threat of panic is obvious. Opposing a shield law is, in the minds of some, akin to being against motherhood and apple pie.

It must, nevertheless, be opposed. For 197 years, the First Amendment has been adequate in affording the free press guarantee. That seaworthy ship has carried us across much troubled water, and while at times it may appear to be imperfect, it is a far better vessel than the frail, plastic boat of legislative shield.

If we allow the law to decide who can write, how soon will come the day when the laws tells us what we can write? Under a shield law, someone must define a newsman and someone must legally describe the media. Do we want a committee of the Congress, the press, or the private sector to make such decisions?

What are the mechanics of such proposals? Would it be fair to grant the same canopy to a budding high school journalism student as given to a full-time major media editor? Would a mimeographed pamphlet demand the same treatment as a large metropolitan daily newspaper?

The unanswered questions are endless. So, too, are the pitfalls.

Considering the opportunity for chicanery, the possibility of extremism, and the likelihood of abuse, the wiser course is to leave well enough alone. Any meddling with the First Amendment is a foolhardy expedition into a dark forest.

I would, therefore, counsel my fellow newsmen that if the Government protects you against performing the duties of citizenship, one day it will control you.

to the student : a commentary

Senator Jesse Helms of North Carolina is a man unusually qualified to speak about a federal shield law. He is both a legislator and a former journalist, and thus has a dual background from which to speak.

Unfortunately, the shield problem isn't as straightforward as Helms would make it seem. Other reporters, unlike Helms, have explained their problem to a grand jury—and gone to jail. Peter Bridge, reporting for the *Newark News,* refused to give a New Jersey grand jury information about an alleged bribe of a state housing authority official—information which he had not published. He spent three weeks in jail. William Farr, while on the staff of the *Los Angeles Herald-Examiner,* published information given him by one of the attorneys in the Charles Manson murder trial. Farr was protected by the California shield law, but when he left the newspaper, the judge called him into court and asked him to reveal his source. When Farr refused, the judge noted that he was no longer a journalist—and therefore not protected by the shield law—and cited him for contempt. Farr spent forty-six days in jail.

The California law was later revised to protect persons who were reporters when they received information, even though not reporters when asked to testify.

More than half the states in the union have shield laws, which protect reporters before state judges and local grand juries. But there is no protection in any state when the journalist encounters the federal judicial system. This is why some news reporters are calling for a federal shield law, which would cover the entire legal process.

There are two kinds of shield laws, however, commonly classified "absolute" and "qualified." Generally, an absolute shield gives the reporter an unconditional right to decline to reveal a source before any governmental proceeding—judicial, administrative, or legislative. A qualified shield either outlines clear procedures whereby the courts can revoke the shield, or specifies one or two distinct exceptions to the shield, usually involving libel or slander.

Why should news reporters refuse to reveal sources? In a statement to Congress, Stanford Smith, president of the American Newspaper Publishers Association, put it this way:

The heart of the matter is this: does the press, in going about the business of keeping the people informed, have the right to disclose sources of information when a newsman secures such information only after a promise of anonymity to the source? Do newsmen and their employers have the right to refuse to submit to subpoena of internal memoranda, reporter's notes and other unpublished material for the same reason?

We believe the news media do have such a right and that the public interest requires it. . . . What we are discussing here is the public interest in protecting the right of the press to operate in an atmosphere free from intimidation, free from the threat of incarceration and free, most of all, to accomplish its function of informing the people.

It's obvious that some news stories require that a source be kept confidential. The Watergate coverage may be the most universally known example. But is legal protection really necessary? Brit Hume, once an associate of Washington columnist Jack Anderson, researched the problem for an article for the *New York Times Magazine.* He found several examples of stories that were not made public because of potential legal problems. One will serve here:

Ike Kleinermann, a C.B.S. News producer, took a camera crew through the South recently to develop material for a documentary on the problems of children in America. He hoped to arrange an interview with a mother who could describe vividly how the welfare system, with its prohibitions against payments to families with working fathers, has encouraged the breakup of homes. He finally found just such a woman. She was a welfare client who spoke eloquently from experience of the system's inequities. She agreed to be interviewed on camera, but only with her face averted and with absolute assurances she would not be identified by name. She had been secretly harboring her husband in her home and feared this would be discovered if she spoke out publicly. Although promises to withhold names have traditionally been routine in journalism, Kleinermann called C.B.S. headquarters in New York to check. The matter was referred to the legal department, where the judgment was swift. Kleinermann was told not to give the requested assurance. The interview was canceled.

In this case a legitimate news story was never presented. Whether the woman was right or wrong, or whether people would agree or disagree, is immaterial. The crucial point is that people never had the chance to decide for themselves. The public was not informed.

Without a shield law any reporter who encounters a source who wants anonymity has to ask a simple question: Am I willing to go to jail? Although the actual instance may be rare, every promise to a source contains the possibility that the reporter will confront the bottom line. Either the reporter gives his word, and carries it through all the way, or he doesn't give it at all. There should be nothing easy or glamorous in the decision to protect a source; the cold realities of legal problems require that a reporter be honestly and completely committed.

What would you decide?

LLS

The White House and the Press

"The first duty of a newspaper to public opinion," Frank I. Cobb said in [*The New Republic*] over 50 years ago, "is to furnish the raw materials for it and the tools for its formation." And when newspapers—or media as we must now say—do their duty, they perforce come into conflict with government. For the governors want their constituents to get primarily that information which makes officials look good—pretty pictures that flatter. This conflict of interest between reporters and those reported on has an honorable lineage. It was anticipated by the Founding Fathers, even encouraged through protections given the press in the first amendment of the Bill of Rights—a safeguard as Frank Cobb wrote, that "reeks of sedition. In every clause it shakes its fist in the face of constituted authority and thunders 'Thou shalt not.' "

The running battle has changed only in form, not substance, with the ascendancy of television on one side, and even more centralized control of information by government on the other. Television has become the principal channel for distribution of national news, diminishing the influence of competing major metropolitan newspapers TV has helped destroy economically. Television has unique characteristics. A government official can sharply limit television coverage by refusing to go before the cameras, leaving the story without a picture and so dampening its impact. But television also has benefits to confer on a politician who wants, on his own terms, to speak directly to the people. It reaches more of them than any other single medium. The speaker cannot be cut off or interrupted by intrusive newsmen. No wonder TV is the President's favored means of communication with the voters.

Since television news gathering is far more costly than print, however, it does not and cannot give us the in-depth coverage of major stories that we expect from a good newspaper. And on a day to day basis, it cannot undertake investigative reporting. In addition, though it has given the country three daily national news sources, television carries a burden unknown to print: it is licensed by the government and thus responsive not only to rulings of the Federal Communication Commission but also, more than print, to review and threats of review by the White House and the Congress.

The growing power of television has been paralleled by centralization of news distribution by government. For example, the system of classifying official documents has been used by three successive administrations to limit what the public could know about the Vietnam war. Tighter control over what officials may say, the hiring of more professional public relations men who know the art of news packaging, further constrict the flow of competing and sometimes contradictory facts and opinions. While government has always dominated the media (names make news, and the bigger the names the bigger the news), the press for the most part has nevertheless been free to tell whatever story it was determined to tell. And while every administration has complained about "unfair" reporting, for the most part the press has carried the government story, and the few exceptions were not considered important enough to shout about—not until recently.

What has happened recently is the surfacing of a new and venomous attitude in the White House. These people *hate* what they call the liberal, elitist, Ivy League press. They hate it for disparaging Nixon and the ad-man mentality of his advisers. They hate it as an unsympathetic, alien excrescence. Vice President Agnew launched the attack in 1969. Then in 1970 Attorney General John Mitchell turned to the use of subpoenas, the most publicized going to Earl Caldwell of *The New York Times,* who had been writing on the Black Panthers at a time when the Justice Department was running grand jury investigations of the organization. Less publicized subpoenas went to television stations and the networks for news film, particularly film of civil disturbances.

Adverse publicity over the Caldwell subpoena forced the government to codify and publish its subpoena policy for newsmen, and since August 1970, when the policy was announced, 13 subpoena requests have been approved by the Justice Department. Only two of them were fought by the media. The government's subpoena strategy received an unexpected boost when the Caldwell case went to the Supreme Court, along with two others involving newsmen reporting on alleged criminal acts who later refused to testify before grand juries. The Court in early 1972 accepted the government's argument in a 5–4 decision that newsmen had no automatic privilege not to testify. The Mitchell subpoena precedent and the court decision encouraged state and local law enforcement officials and state legislative bodies to go after newsmen who refused to name their sources. Several were jailed and a few still face that prospect. But after a flurry of cases and almost unanimous press criticism, the practice has died down. As Frank Cobb noted, "nobody ever succeeded in bettering the weather by putting the thermometer in jail."

The press has been sufficiently alarmed, however, to beseech the Congress to approve a "shield" law granting newsmen immunity at both the federal and state level. We have some doubts about the practical benefits that would follow from its adoption. The issuance of subpoenas for newsmen is, in the first instance, as Nathan Lewin has written in [*The New Republic*], a reflection as much on the use—or misuse—of the grand jury system as it is an attack on the first amendment. It would do no harm for Congress to make known to federal and state prosecutors and judges that *it* looks with disfavor on the practice of subpoenas for newsmen, but Congress is not likely to say—nor should it—that no journalist may ever be required to give information to a grand jury under any circumstances. Moreover the myriad technical questions involved in drafting such legislation would eventually place before the courts such questions as who is a journalist. Finally we wonder how much *real* investigative reporting is being lost today because there is no shield law. On this question Assistant Attorney General Roger C. Cramton told a House subcommittee: "Anonymous informants have always been faced with the possibility that the pressure of events will lead to revelation of their identity or the much more remote possibility that a grand jury investigating criminal activity might require the reporter to divulge the identity of his source. Nevertheless, despite the existence of these risks, informants have not been deterred from providing information, tips and documents to the press." Indeed, reporters on *The Washington Post* and *The New York Times* . . . manage[d] to dig up the most damaging information about the Watergate bugging, and from sources in and around Mr. Cramton's department.

The defenders of full press freedoms may in fact be battling on a vacated front by lobbying in Congress to outlaw the subpoena of journalists. The administration's attack has shifted. The arrest of Les Whitten, Jack Anderson's top assistant, for receipt and possession of "stolen" property (documents taken from the Bureau of Indian Affairs, which Whitten says he was helping to return), is another form of harassment. Expansion of the laws on security classification as embodied in recodification of the criminal code, if successful, would give the administration still another weapon against information leaks in the foreign policy and defense areas. Elsewhere the claim of widened government privilege to hide documents from the public that is laid down (thanks to Justice Department intervention) in the new rules of evidence for federal courts would not only limit what can be produced as evidence in a trial, but also information that is now available to the press under the Freedom of Information Act.

Here are the fronts where the press should be fighting. For it protects its freedom in the last analysis by using it. Frank Cobb has the final word: "The American people cannot deal intelligently with any of these problems without knowing the facts, and they cannot know the facts until the newspapers brush aside the propagandists of contending factions to get back to first principles of newsgathering."

---

to the student : a commentary

This editorial from *The New Republic* deals with a central journalistic problem. When journalists attempt to report the news, they often run afoul of government officials' desire to present pretty pictures. Television has become the chief channel for national news, the editorial holds, yet unfortunately, television news is far more costly than newspaper reporting. Moreover, television carries the burden of government licensing.

Let's look first at the efforts of government officials to make their actions seem praiseworthy. When President Nixon sent American troops into Cambodia in 1970, so bitter was the reaction from the nation's campuses that the administration decided to counter it by inviting expressions of opinion from any American who wanted to call the White House. Early one morning United Press International (UPI) reporters in New York made four calls to the special White House number that had been set up to record the votes for or against. Two UPI reporters who announced that they wanted to cast votes favorable to the president's action were switched immediately to someone who answered "White House." The other two callers, who said that they opposed the president's action, never got past the switchboard. The calls ran:

UPI—"I'd like to register a vote for the President."

White House—"Yes, you certainly can."

UPI—"This is the White House, I hope."

White House—"Yes, where do you live?"

UPI—"New Jersey."

White House—"All right, thank you very much for your call."

UPI—"Listen, are you taking votes?"

White House—"No, I'm not taking votes. Are you taking votes?"

UPI—"I'd like to register a vote against President Nixon."

White House—"You're way late, where have you been?"

UPI—"You're not taking votes?"

White House—"I'm not taking any votes and haven't been taking any votes."

UPI—"I'd like to register a vote for President Nixon's policy, please."

White House—"You certainly can. Can I have your name, please?"

UPI—"James Coburn, Weehawken, New Jersey."

White House—"I'll take a message if you want to give me one. Give it to me."

UPI—"I don't want to say too much except that I am thoroughly in agreement with everything the President has said."

White House—"Okay, James, and we really appreciate that now, and I can tell you that he does too. Thank you very much."

UPI—"I understand you are taking votes and I'd like to say I'm against the President and Vice President Agnew too, and the policy. Can I register that please?

White House—"You want to vote on the President?"

UPI—"Yeah, I'm against the President and against what he has been saying."

White House—"This poll is being taken on the extension of troops into Cambodia and not on whether or not you're against the President."

UPI—"I'm against the extension of troops into Cambodia and against any more American troops going anywhere in southeast Asia."

White House—"Where are you calling from?"

UPI—"New York City."

White House—"From New York. Well, this office is closed here in Washington, it's almost six o'clock."

This is, of course, the kind of information the journalists attempt to gather. They must always be on the alert, suspicious of the motives of officials in order to report the way in which the White House information is gathered —and isn't.

Lawyers also create trouble for journalists. In 1968, the American Bar Association approved the "Standards Relating to Fair Trial and Free Press" recommended by an advisory committee headed by Massachusetts Supreme Court Justice Paul Reardon. The standards prohibit lawyers from releasing certain information when there is a "reasonable likelihood that such dissemination will interfere with a fair trial or otherwise prejudice the due administration of justice." In investigations and grand-jury proceedings, lawyers are to "refrain from making any extrajudicial statement, for dissemination by any means of public communication, that goes beyond the public record or that is not necessary to inform the public that the investigation is underway, to describe the general scope of the investigation, to obtain assistance in the apprehension of a suspect, to warn the public of any dangers, or otherwise to aid in the investigation."

The Reardon Report, as it has become known, includes many explicit provisions that have enraged journalists, especially the recommendation that courts use their contempt power to punish publications that judges believe violated defendants' rights to fair trial. Although the Reardon Report is not law, it influences the conduct of many courts.

The news media seem free to report almost anything because of the protection of the First Amendment. But what if it becomes a question of whether a defendant can receive the fair trial that he is promised by the Sixth Amendment? The conflict between the First and Sixth Amendments was sharply at issue late in 1975 in Lincoln County, Nebraska. Judge A. Ronald Ruff ruled that news reporters could attend a preliminary hearing, held to determine whether there was enough evidence to put Erwin Simants on trial for murder, but they could not report the testimony. The journalists protested strongly. Judge Ruff declared, "When the two rights come into conflict, the right of the free press must be subordinated to the right of due process." He was saying that the Sixth Amendment has precedence over the First Amendment. That, of course, must be decided by the U.S. Supreme Court, which held its first full-dress hearing in April, 1976.

This is but a small part of the issue. Although you are not expected to master it—some Supreme Court justices can't—this should give you an introductory view of one of the most complicated problems in American society.

WLR

study questions

1. Does the lack of a federal shield law prevent reporters from effectively carrying out investigative reporting? Or is it needed?

2. Should journalists be given special rights the rest of the public does not enjoy, such as the right to withhold information from a grand jury without fear of punishment?

3. Does the jailing of certain reporters on contempt charges for refusing to reveal sources constitute a threat to the freedom of the press?

4. Many journalists feel that if they invite the government to act as their protector, they will have opened the door for future government interference in the form of regulations and controls. Is this a valid argument against having shield laws?

5. Is it bad judgement for a reporter to promise confidentiality to a source involved in criminal or unethical activities? Are there conflicts between good news judgement and the performance of one's duties as a citizen?

6. Is there any justification for the government's use of subpoenas to force news reporters to testify in criminal investigations? Are news reporters obligated to aid the government in these investigations? If they are so obligated, how will this affect their functioning as effective reporters?

7. Do newspapers have any right to demand that others open themselves to public scrutiny when they themselves keep their business operations so closely guarded? Or is this confusing the journalistic and business functions of the newspaper?

8. Is there any justification for newspapers to so jealously keep secret their business operations?

9. Do the characteristics of the business aspects of a newspaper's function diminish the concept of the press as the safeguard of democracy and as the conscience of society?

10. Are there any changes that could be made in the business operation of newspapers that would improve the journalistic operation? Could the newspaper better serve the public under another system of operation?

maga-
5 zines

Magazine publishers continually ask: How can we continue publishing? Not only is television a new and powerful competing force, newspapers are gradually becoming more like magazines. The newspaper feature is growing longer and more complicated, with the writer combining many short interviews into longer, sustained stories. Why should anyone subscribe to a magazine when the newspaper seems to provide much the same diet?

Why a magazine can continue publishing is answered directly in the article entitled "Magazines in the Seventies: Whatever Happened to that Nice Old Edward Bok?" For most magazines, this is the age of specialization.

Still, many magazine editors are worried about how they will make the income match the payroll. Articles in the "Constraints" section deal with these problems directly.

These articles are your introduction to the glories and the problems of magazines. But the magazines themselves, in all their wonderful variety, will complete the picture of that world of publishing in a way that no other source can.

magazines

social force

Drawing by Opie; © 1959 The New Yorker Magazine, Inc.

"Pardon me, Sir, but I'm afraid we must ask you to leave!"

256

Theodore Peterson

Magazines in the Seventies: Whatever Happened to that Nice Old Edward Bok?

Bill Arthur was the last editor of *Look,* and he took its death as a personal sorrow. That first weekend after Gardner Cowles announced *Look* was to die, Bill moped around his home on Long Island. He brooded over the 27 years that he had devoted to the magazine, brooded over what was to become of his staff members suddenly thrown out of jobs. At length, for a change of scene, he pulled on a handsome new jacket and strolled to the beach to try to get some perspective. As he looked out over the sound, under a gray autumn sky, he reflected that change is a part of existence. Seasons change, times change. People change, institutions change, and sometimes they die. He began to realize that, in the history of mankind, *Look* was no more than a speck in time, a particle in the cosmos. And then, as he was pondering the insignificance of man and his magazines in the great order of things, a seagull winged close and spattered all over Bill's handsome new jacket. Dabbing at the mess with his handkerchief, Bill looked skyward and muttered, "Okay, God. I get the message."

That story should remind us that magazines, like men, are transients in this messed up old world and sooner or later must give up their seats on the park bench to newcomers. The world of magazines is a world of change, and like Bill Arthur, I would like to put that change in perspective.

The changes in magazine publishing got a big shove from Edward Bok, a chill, woman-hating, opportunistic public idol who in the thirty years before 1919 made the *Ladies' Home Journal* one of the largest, most successful, and perhaps most influential of magazines in its time. Bok introduced or pioneered in many of the conventions that magazine readers and publishers nowadays take for granted—a different cover design for each issue, color printing and color photography, stories that jumped from the middle of the book to the interstices between the advertisements in the rear, service to the reader. He and a few others—S. S. McClure, for instance, and Frank Munsey—pretty much invented the modern magazine.

257

If Bok were to return to publishing today, he would find much of the turf familiar. But parts . . . would drive the old Dutchman absolutely bonkers. And that is my theme, really: There has been a lot of recycling of ideas in magazine publishing, and fundamentally new ideas are rare. Yet the twists and turns given to some old ideas have made the magazine terrain quite different from what it was, say, even in the 1950s.

Before I move along to some aspects of magazine publishing in the seventies that I find intriguing, I would like to illustrate that point. A publisher of one of the major newsweeklies has started a magazine that is aiming at its audience through single-copy sales. It is a little more than a year old, and it is having a remarkable success. The editor is explaining why. The reasons, he says, are that "people like to read about people" and that they like brevity. He adds: "Almost every important story today is wrapped about a person or people. Where twenty years ago events dominated people, the reverse is now true. More than ever news publications are looking for the people behind the events."

Now, if you think that magazine is Time Inc.'s *People,* started a little more than a year ago as a newsstand-seller, you are about twenty-five years too late. The magazine was *People Today,* which *Newsweek* began in 1950 and which for many years has occupied an unmarked grave in that weedy place where departed magazines lie buried. Its basic pitch was not much different from that of Time's *People.* But *People* is crucially enough different and has enough good things working for it to make one suspect that it will have a longer and happier life than *People Today.* The old and familiar has taken a new turn, and so it is with much that is going on in magazine publishing today.

Take the first development that I wish to mention—the awesome spread of the special-interest magazine, the magazine of intensely concentrated editorial and marketing appeal. Scarcely a week goes by but what someone proclaims, with an astonishment that I find astonishing, that this is the Great Age of the Specialized Magazine. Indeed it is. Just look at the titles on the newsstand, and you will conclude that humankind has no itch, no inclination, no interest that some publisher out there is not trying to capitalize on. Just read the reports of advertising linage and dollar volume, and you will find that the great gains in recent years have gone to magazines that have sharply defined their audiences. . . . Magazines are specialized in one way or another, since the omnibus magazine died with *Life* and *Look.* (The *Reader's Digest* is an exception. But it seems divinely exempt from the rules that govern and the follies that bedevil mortal man.)

Yet magazines of specialized appeal are nothing new. If you had been around when the century turned, you could have read *Shooting and Fishing* if you were a hunter or angler, *Snap-Shots* if you were an amateur photographer, *Guide to Holiness* if you worried about your spiritual well-being, and *Cupid* if you were seeking a mate. Magazines have been specialized ever since Andrew Bradford started the first one in the Colonies.

But today's specialized magazines are profoundly different from their predecessors. Let's examine why and how they have changed since, say, about World War II.

They are different because many of the interests and activities that once were the province of the well-to-do elite have become democratized. Yachting is no longer a millionaire's luxury; pleasure craft on Lake Michigan are so numerous on some Sundays that one can walk from shore to shore without wetting his feet. Vacation trips to Spain or France or Guatemala are something that a secretary can aspire to. So it is with other things. *Business Week* provided the text for all of this in an article called "The Leisured Masses" back in September 1953. Leisure, it said, had become democratized as a result of the 40-hour week, the two-day weekend, the three-week vacation with pay and early retirement on pension. It concluded: "Nothing quite like it has occurred before in world history. Never have so many people had so much time on their hands—with pay —as today in the United States." Time Inc. had concluded much the same thing from a study of postwar markets that led circuitously to the creation of *Sports Illustrated.* Time found that discretionary income would shoot up faster than other items in the budget, and it assumed that Americans would use their free dollars for leisure. Despite the undeniable poverty in our midst, despite the erosions of inflation, ours is still a comparatively affluent society. People—at least the people whom magazines want to reach—have time to fill and the money to fill it.

Furthermore, the specialization of magazines is a reflection of what has been happening to all of the mass media to varying degrees—a narrowing or pinpointing or stratification of their audiences. Newspapers have circumscribed their audiences by geography. The large, omnibus metropolitan dailies are merging or dying; the suburban papers are flourishing like crabgrass on suburban lawns. The movies have sifted their audiences with a coarse screen. Once the whole family went to the Rivoli to see Betty Grable in *Moon Over Miami* or Will Rogers in *Steamboat Around the Bend,* and everyone was somewhat entertained and no one was offended. Now movie-makers are turning out productions for viewers interested in cinematic art and experimentation, social realism, and explicit depiction of sexual behavior in an eye-popping array of manifestations. Radio too has fragmented its audience. Once the whole family sat around its Philco listening to "Mr. Keene, Tracer of Lost Persons" or Jack Benny flacking for Jello. Now broadcasters offer us the choice of stations devoted almost exclusively to news and public affairs, classical music, jazz, rhythm and blues, country western, non-music Muzak and ethnic subcultures. I doubt that television can forever be immune to this fractionalization of audience. The mammoth audiences of our massiest of mass media, I suspect, will be broken into smaller bits with the spread of community cable systems, multiple-set homes and future technological developments.

Television and public education too, I suspect, have affected specialized magazines by broadening the interests and concerns of the reading audience. All of those football games on TV surely must be related to the multitude of sports magazines in recent years, and Julia Child surely must be accountable in part for bringing *Bon Appetit* and *Vintage* into the kitchen and dining room.

Being born into and growing up in such a world, today's special-interest magazines have differed from their earlier counterparts in two significant ways. For one thing, they have become ever more specialized. As more and more people come to share an activity or interest, some publisher is bound to explore its more arcane aspects. Caskie Stinnett of *Holiday* once told an anecdote that underscores just how specialized magazines have become. Several years earlier, he said, he and a few associates had attended a reception in Lisbon at which each was asked to identify his magazine. One of them facetiously said that he represented *Popular Wading*. The magazine specialized in shallow-water sports up to the knee, he explained, and focused on their medical aspects, including such ailments as "immersion foot." The host and guests thought it all hilarious. "But you know," Stinnett recalled, "I don't think anyone would laugh today. In fact, I'll almost bet that somewhere out there you could find a special-audience magazine for waders." . . .

A second characteristic setting today's special-interest magazines apart from their predecessors is that they have become essentially trade and technical publications for consumers. Trade and technical publications, as you know, are magazines like *Iron Age, Casket and Sunnyside, Tap and Tavern, Modern Packaging* and *Corset, Bra and Lingerie* that provide specialized information to help ironmongers, morticians, draftsmen and modern packagers to perform their useful occupational roles in society. They are a continuing source of information—often highly technical information, often information that one cannot get elsewhere—that enable their readers to pursue the goals and efficiency and profit. Consumer magazines have become trade and technical magazines but with a reverse twist: Instead of telling their readers how to save time and make money, they tell their readers how to fill time and to spend money. The great bulk of consumer magazines begun since World War II have been designed to help the reader cope with his increased leisure and his increased affluence. To that end, like trade journals, they have become a continuing source of information about almost infinite specialties; their information is often highly technical, often unobtainable elsewhere. *Wine World* suggests alternatives to Mogen

David, and *Sphere* describes the meals to accompany them. *Weight Watchers* and *Smoke Stopper* help to curb our excesses. *Ohio Motorist* tells us of the sights to see in Chillicothe and Bucyrus. *Street Chopper* tells us of the wonderful fun we can have on our motorbike. *After Dark* guides us in where to go and what to do after sundown, and *TV Dawn to Dusk* suggests one way of spending our time if we must stay at home. *Pool 'n' Patio* tells us how to get the most from our home pool, and *Official Karate* instructs us in how to make even Charles Atlas seem to be a scrawny-chested weakling. *New York* tells us how to survive in Fun City, *Sunset* how to live graciously west of the Rockies. And *Backpacker* tells how we can escape from it all.

Those, then, are the two characteristics that distinguish contemporary special-interest magazines—their finely tuned specialization and their role in how readers spend their time and money. Size of circulation is no guide to whether or not a magazine is specialized, for magazines with their editorial focus sharpened to pin-point size can amass tremendous sales. *TV Guide* performs a narrow function, but its circulation is more than nineteen million. *Workbasket* comes out strong for little beyond knitting, tatting, crocheting and embroidering, but it has a distribution of more than two million. *Gourmet* and *Weight Watchers* are fighting it out with the score 557,000 to 552,000 in favor of eating.

Of all the magazine phenomena in recent years, one catching many people by surprise has been the proliferation of the sex-oriented magazines —the skin books or girlie books, as the trade calls them. Certainly it caught Hugh Hefner by surprise, out there at Mansion West amidst his llamas and cockatoos. The sex-oriented magazines have become so much a part of the publishing scene and so interesting a cultural phenomenon that they deserve at least some comment. A while back one of the newsweeklies reported that *Playboy* and *Penthouse* alone accounted for about 20 percent of all U.S. single-copy sales. They may have in some markets, but last year *TV Guide* alone had a greater single-copy sale than the two combined. Even so, *Playboy* and *Penthouse* together sold more single copies than the combined total of such upright citizens as *Reader's Digest, Better Homes and Gardens, McCall's, Ladies' Home Journal, National Geographic, Good Housekeeping, American Home, House and Garden, Parents', Time, Newsweek, U.S. News, Sports Illustrated, Business Week, Popular Science, Popular Mechanics, Esquire, New Yorker* and *Boys Life.* If *Fortune* can examine Robert Guccione and his *Penthouse* and if virtually every publication this side of *Our Sunday Visitor* can speculate on Hefner's psyche and finances, well, certainly we can afford to give them a few minutes.

Sex-oriented magazines are nothing new. The 20s and 30s had their share of racy magazines, which bore such titles as *Hot Dog, Artists and Models, La Vie Parisienne* and *Capt. Billy's Whiz Bang* and which trafficked in the simple sex and barnyard humor that Boy Scouts sniggered over when the scoutmaster was out of earshot. The 40s and 50s had that kind of magazine, too, but that period was really characterized by magazines that seemed to have been edited by abnormal psychology majors who dug Freud, Krafft-Ebing and Stekel, for many of them explicitly or implicitly dealt in masochism, sadism, and fetishism. If you wanted female nudity, you bought an art studies magazine or maybe a nudist magazine. If you wanted the male physique, your best bet was *Physical Culture.*

And then, in 1954, along came Hugh Hefner. His prototype for *Playboy* was the *Esquire* of the 30s; publicly at least, he never associated his magazine with the skin-books and the voyeurs who bought them. Publicly his aim was to liberate his fellow Methodists from their repressions and to instruct the urban male in the Good Life, of which sex was but a part. In fact, his genius was in coupling sex with upward mobility and in making it respectable. His *Playboy* anticipated and contributed to the revolution in manners and morals in the 60s, and it benefited from the Supreme Court's grappling with, liberalizing, and eventually confusing the definition of obscenity.

Playboy at age 21 was fat, wealthy, and the patriarch of the genre. The irony is that it became so successful, so profitable that it is responsible for the wave of competing magazines which swept the newsstands in the late 60s and early 70s—*Penthouse, Playgirl, Coq, Viva, Gallery,* and all the rest.

The present-day skin books have five characteristics that distinguish them from their predecessors of a less enlightened era.

First is their utter lack of inhibition. Until the late 60s, *Playboy* for all its daring subjected even its Playmates to discreet treatment by airbrush. Today *Playboy* and its cohorts run acres of bare flesh in glorious four-color and among them are unobscured patches of the pelvic regions of males and females alike. In stark detail the magazines depict an astounding assortment of sexual acts and postures, some of which would tax the agility of the best trained gymnast. They advise their readers on sexual problems, sexual customs, sexual experimentation, sexual prosthesis and accessories. And they do all of this, usually, with intellectual pretension.

Second is that the magazines have become respectable. In keeping with their intellectual pretensions, they turn to respectable and well-known public figures and authors to sit for interviews or to contribute to them— John Kenneth Galbraith and J. Paul Getty to *Playboy,* J. P. Donleavy and Pietro di Donato to *Viva,* John Updike to *Penthouse. Playgirl* even had a Ph.D. in Hispanic studies— a William Lewis—for one of its frontal nudes. But there is more to their respectability than that. You will find the magazines displayed in airport terminals, drugstores, supermarkets and shopping centers. They just about have to go on display in those public places if they expect to achieve and maintain their large circulations, for they depend heavily on single-copy sales—*Playboy* for about two-thirds, *Penthouse* for perhaps 99 percent.

A third is that they are big business. Hefner's personal fortune is estimated at $200 million, which since the founding of *Playboy* works out to an average take of about $10 million a year for him alone. *Penthouse* reported profits of $3 million on revenues of $31 million in 1973. In the first half of 1974, it reported revenues of more than $20 million, but it did not disclose its profit figure. *Playgirl* claims to have made a profit from its first issue, a remarkable circumstance if true.

A fourth is that they engage in a form of editorial incest. As I have already mentioned, *Playboy* is the father of them all, and they all share a family resemblance. Besides that, editors and key staff members move from one magazine to another—from *Playboy* to *Gallery* to *Touch;* from *Playboy* to *Gallery* to *Coq;* from *Voir* to *Gallery* to *Playboy;* and so forth. One magazine, staying close to home, set up its offices just across the street from the Playboy Building.

A fifth is that the magazines have at last concluded that sex involves both males and females. Women never had sex-oriented magazines of their very own until Helen Gurley Brown made publishing history by reviving a moribund *Cosmopolitan* magazine on the premise that single girls know about sex. *Playboy* from its start has been a magazine for men—a magazine that treated women as objects, like hi-fi sets and sports cars, as a score of critics have complained. Now women no longer have to sneak looks at *Playboy,* for they have magazines of their own. They have *Playgirl,* a kind of mirror image of *Playboy,* which runs photographs of nude males in its gatefold and which in its first six months picked up a circulation that it had taken *Playboy* two years to attain. They have *Viva,* which Robert Guccione described in over-ripe prose as "a lusty, real, indefatigable, down-to-earth, fetching, bright, sexy, uncompromising woman." And they have, on an equal, coeducational basis with men, such go-between, swapping-mart magazines as *Adam,* which, owing much to the invention of the Polaroid camera, carries photographs of naked correspondents from various parts of the U.S. who wistfully describe themselves and their longings. . . .

A good question is whether or not the market is saturated with these magazines. Trade publications—and even civilian ones—from time to time record the vicissitudes of Playboy Enterprises and note that this publication or that has slipped in advertising or circulation or both. Predicting their future is a chancy business. One wonders, for instance, what editorially they can do next: What sexual wonders remain to be disclosed? Yet it seems too early to start numbering their days. All evidence indicates that *Playboy* and the London Playboy club remain Hefner's two big money-making ventures. . . .

Moreover, the drops in circulation are explainable by something other than mass defection. To get their large circulations, *Penthouse* and its brothers and sisters have flooded newsstands with copies in the knowledge that some would come back unsold. The number of copies that newsdealers returned might be high—for the early *Penthouse* the figure was as high as 40 percent—but so was circulation. Surely some drops in circulation can be attributed to a curtailing of this wasteful practice in a time of spiraling costs. Furthermore, the mortality rate among the sex-oriented magazines seems no higher than for conventional magazines.

Whether or not the genre is hale and hearty, I do not know, since most of the magazines are published by privately held companies that can keep their health as secret as they wish. I am simply saying that it seems premature to predict their ruin.

Earlier I said that *Esquire* was the model for Hefner's *Playboy. Esquire* in the 60s had other influences on magazine journalism that I would like to remark on. Recently I got a letter from Robert Sherrill, formerly of *Esquire,* in which he commented on the *Esquire*-ization of magazines generally in the recent past. Just what he meant by that remark, I am not quite sure, but he did set me to thinking about two influences of *Esquire* on other magazines since the 60s.

One has been in attitude. That is a hard thing to define and to explain, but there are clues to what I mean in the charming title of an *Esquire* anthology of the 60s—*Smiling Through the Apocalypse*—and in some observations that Harold Hayes, then editor, made in his introduction to the book. The editorial attitude of *Esquire,* according to Hayes, arose in reaction to the banality of the late 50s. It took shape, he said,

as we went along, stumbling past our traditional boundaries of fashion, leisure, entertainment and literature onto the more forbidding ground of politics, sociology, science and even, occasionally, religion. Any point of view was welcome as long as the writer was sufficiently skilful to carry it off, but we tended to avoid committing ourselves to doctrinaire programs even though advised on occasion that we might thereby better serve the interests of mankind.

What evolved was an attitude of wry skepticism that while not really anti-establishment was certainly not pro-establishment, an attitude without commitment, one which saw all ideologies up for grabs. Hayes put it this way:

For a while we called ours an effort toward a rational view, then satire and then irony. But only humor—of a most complex, often unfunny sort—is sufficiently flexible to cover the larger part of our effort, from black wit to custard-pie burlesque.

The local magazines must begin with the *New Yorker*. The *New Yorker* observed its fiftieth anniversary—note that I said observed, not celebrated —in 1975, and that is an old age for any magazine. Some people probably would say that the *New Yorker* has always been an old magazine, even in its youth. It is easy to poke fun of the *New Yorker*, for it can be an exasperating magazine. Eustace Tilley on its cover symbolizes a supercil- iousness that cannot be explained by William Shawn's shyness, for the magazine treats almost everyone outside of 25 West 43rd Street as if they were members of Pick and Shovel at Colorado A & M while they were tapped by Skull and Bones at Yale. Its unchanging, archaic format seems an affectation. Its articles invariably could do with a few hours of sharp editing, and its interminable sentences make Henry James and William Faulkner sound like disciples of Rudolf Flesch. It is a forbidding magazine, apart from its cartoons and fillers, one easy to put aside for a future reading that never comes.

But for all of that, like so much of James Thurber, it is a sane voice in an insane world. In articles by John Hersey and Rachel Carson, to drop but two names, it was reminding us of man's propensity for self-destruction long before today's generation of activists could spell "e-n-v-i-r-o-n- m-e-n-t," and it was among the first to expose the poverty within our affluent society and to question the morality of the war in Viet Nam. For all its faults, the *New Yorker* is a national resource.

Because of its supremacy in its field, the *New Yorker*, like *Playboy*, for many years made competitors redundant. Despite its Manhattan base, it usurped the local markets of most metropolitan centers. An advertiser wanting an elite audience in, say, Chicago could reach it more effectively through the *New Yorker* than through the many local Chicago magazines attempted over the past couple of decades. In Boston, Chicago, New Or- leans, San Francisco, Washington and other cities, publishers tried local magazines modelled upon the *New Yorker* but always without success.

The local magazines that existed before World War II were kept maga- zines, mistresses of Chambers of Commerce. Indianapolis had had one since the 1890s, Detroit and Philadelphia since 1908. A crop of them sprouted up across the land in the sunny boosterism of the 1920s.

After World War II, a new variety of local magazines began to appear —magazines that owed little to such local society organs as *American Sketch*, magazines that recoiled from the embrace of the Chamber of Com- merce, magazines that looked realistically at their communities. Even some of the kept magazines declared their independence. What brought about this resurgence of interest in the local magazine, it is hard to say. Ben Moon attributes it in part to the "urgent challenge of making the cities habitable" as residents and businesses fled to the suburbs, as the tax base of the cities narrowed, as central areas deteriorated into slums and as violence abounded. *New York,* in fact, has made survival in New York City its publishing premise.

Whatever the reason, one reassuring segment of magazine publishing in the 70s has been the local magazines. They have turned up in, among other places, Philadelphia, Washington, Boston, New Orleans, San Francisco and Atlanta. Jon and Abra Anderson tried one in Chicago, which however folded after a year.

The magazines have been of uneven quality; even *New York,* the most visible of them all, has had an uneven performance. Yet they have engaged in some gutsy reporting, the kind which one might hope the local dailies would do. The *Washingtonian,* for instance, critically examined the records of various federal judges. The *Philadelphia* magazine has reported on the black ghetto, bankruptcy frauds, a newspaper reporter who blackmailed businessmen and mismanagement of the Pearl Buck Foundation. It has won the distinguished reporting award of Sigma Delta Chi on three occasions, and it won a National Magazine Award for its comprehensive "uncoverage" of the Delaware River Port Authority in 1972. *Texas Monthly* in its first year of existence won the 1974 National Magazine Award for specialized journalism. It has explored the state's highway lobby, assessed the state's daily newspapers (and found them wanting), picked the state's ten best and ten worst legislators and undertaken other provocative reportage.

New York grew out of the *Herald Tribune's* Sunday supplement. In the few years since the first issue appeared in April 1968, the magazine has had an undeniable effect on magazine journalism. Just as the local magazines of the 30s took the *New Yorker* for their model, many of today's local magazines look to *New York* for inspiration. A. Kent MacDougall in a piece in the *Columbia Journalism Review* dissected the magazine and summarized its strong and weak points. He noted that it had carried some of the most talked-about examples of the New Journalism—Tom Wolfe's "Radical Chic," Gail Sheehy's "Redpants and Sugarman," Aaron Latham's "An Evening in the Nude with Gay Talese." He added:

But all is not prosperity and respectability. If *New York* has helped popularize the New Journalism, it also has helped discredit it by publishing fiction disguised as fact. If it has provided a showcase for good writing, it also has alienated good writers with callous editing and parsimonious pay policies. If it has encouraged the women's liberation movement, it also has published photographs and articles that feminists denounced as sexist. If it has run many serious, well-documented articles, it also has run many superficial, hyped-up pieces. Along the way it has received two dozen law suits charging libel, invasion of privacy and plagiarism.

. . . It is time for me to stop, but before I do I would like to restate a theme that I hope has been apparent in what I have been saying—that much of magazine publishing in the 70s has consisted of applying old and familiar ideas to new and unfamiliar circumstances. What Edward Bok would say about such women's magazines as *Playgirl* and *Ms.*, I can imagine just as I can imagine what *Playgirl* and *Ms.* would say about Edward Bok. Back in 1890, speculating on the magazine of the future, Bok did say that the successful one would be that which "proves most helpful to its readers." Most of the magazines that I have been talking about have been heavy on providing the reader with some help that he needs. That much, at least, Bok would have appreciated and approved of.

to the student : a commentary

As you probably noticed while reading Theodore Peterson's speech, he is not at all deanlike. Although he is the dean of the College of Journalism and Communications at the University of Illinois, his speaking style goes down as easily as any professional writer's. Peterson's significant book, *Magazines in the Twentieth Century,* traces the rocky path of many magazines that have died and others that have been born recently.

This is one of Peterson's most significant speeches. He has told us, wittily, how the magazines have been changing. But of course, he did not have time in his speech to deal with the wide range of magazines. For example, he has also published an article on the importance of the minority magazine—those dealing with literature and the other arts, opinion and criticism, politics and public affairs. Magazines such as *The Nation, The New Republic, The Progressive, National Review, Current History, The Atlantic,* and *Harper's* introduce ideas, weigh them, and if they have merit, feed them into the mainstream.

In "The Role of Minority Magazines," Peterson says,

A point commonly overlooked is that over the decades the mass media as a whole have taken on some of the tasks that the minority magazines once had to perform. Newspapers generally are giving significant events better coverage and more skillful interpretation than they were in the 1920s. Readers can find enough background and interpretation of public affairs in the *New York Times* each Sunday to last them for a week, and one need not be a capitalist to find enlightenment in the *Wall Street Journal.* Syndicated columnists along the political spectrum turn up on editorial pages the country over. Some magazines of relatively large circulation—*Mademoiselle,* for instance, and even *Playboy* —carry fiction of a sort that once would have nestled comfortably in the pages of the little magazines. And besides all that, both political parties and the majority of the electorate now take for granted a good many of the social gains that the political journals of an earlier day vigorously campaigned for.

The thrust of each of the mass media is different. Radio and television are primarily useful in signaling events, providing the immediate—and sketchy— reports that announce happenings. The nature of most programs requires that broadcast journalists skim the top of the news, working with the headlines, the leads, and the bulletins that alert the public. Av Westin, a news executive of the American Broadcasting Company, has said: "I think television news is an illustrated service which can function best when it is regarded as an important yet fast adjunct to the newspapers. I know what we have to leave out, and if people do not read newspapers, news magazines, and books, they are desperately misinformed."

Newspapers cannot compete with radio and television for rapid transmission, and they cannot compete with television in the sheer impact of seeing and hearing news in the making. But a newspaper is available at any time, and it can provide a vast range of information on many subjects. The importance of the newspaper has been best described by a man who was interviewed during a newspaper strike: "I don't have the details now; I just have the result. It's almost like reading the headlines of the newspaper without following up the story. I miss the detail and the explanation of events leading up to the news."

In some aspects, magazines are even more limited than newspapers. Most magazines contain a relatively small number of articles that treat their subjects in depth. Even the news magazines, which attempt to cover wide ranges of subjects in some detail, do not publish as much information in their weekly issues as can be found in a single issue of a large daily newspaper. Like the authors of books, those who write for magazines can seek out the unreported, flesh out the information that has been presented only in silhouette in broadcasts and newspapers, and report matters missed by faster media in the rush of meeting deadlines. The writers of magazine articles also take advantage of their widely spaced deadlines to fashion articles that usually have more flavor, grace, and unity than most writers for radio, television, and newspapers have time to achieve.

The large magazines, with this grace and flavor, are slowly crushing some of the minority magazines, which used to be the source of much of the best magazine writing. There was a time when a mass magazine writer like Quentin Reynolds considered it perfectly natural to fashion an article on Joe Louis, then offhandedly head for Havana to spend a couple of weeks covering the New York Giants' training camp, splicing in a piece in the same period on Cuban dictator Fulgencio Batista. During one year he turned out thirty-six widely diverse articles for *Collier's*—three in a single issue—and maintained a lively social life. In those days, when a facile writer was deemed to be able to handle almost anything, the difference between writing about boxer Max Baer and Winston Churchill was primarily geographic. As Reynolds said, "It was easy to read—and easy to forget." But readers seldom forgot the articles in the minority magazines.

What can the editors of minority magazines possibly do to keep their publications alive in a time of increasing costs? I have no easy solution for these editors in their contest with the specialty magazines. The challenge to the minority magazines might be met with the story told some years ago by Frank Walsh. He had written a series of syndicated articles for the Hearst newspapers, which had a circulation of ten million. He had *never* met anyone who had read his articles. But as soon as *The Nation* had published a single piece by Walsh on the same subject, senators, lobbyists, editors, and many other influential people called him.

That's the strength of the minority magazine. It needs your support.

WLR

study questions

1. Peterson devotes much of his speech to such publications as *Playboy* and *Harper's*, magazines that might easily be called "special interest" rather than "mass." How would you define a special interest magazine? A mass magazine?

2. The death of many publications normally considered mass magazines—*Look, Life, Saturday Evening Post*—is most often blamed on television. What other factors could have been involved?

3. As Peterson has said, "Over the decades the mass media as a whole have taken on some of the tasks that the minority magazines once had to perform." How is this done? For example, read the twenty-year-old issues of the *New York Times Magazine,* then contrast those with the more recent issues. Are the more recent issues longer than they have been? Are the articles in greater depth, more likely to please a specialist?

4. Can the editors of minority magazines please *you?* Which of the magazines are more likely to be publications that you will read after college?

magazines

constraints

John Fischer

The Perils of Publishing: How to Tell When You Are Being Corrupted

A young man walked into my office a few weeks ago and announced that he was ready to sell out. What he wanted, I discovered eventually, was a job. He had been out of college for about a year, making the scene, as he put it, around New York. Recently his parents had stopped sending him money; so now strictly for want of bread, he had to go to work.

Publishing, he confided, struck him as less distasteful than any other occupation he could think of. Consequently he was prepared to sacrifice his integrity to the sordid demands of book or magazine publishing—he didn't care which—but since he valued it highly he trusted that *Harper's* would pay him handsomely for it. In our further conversation it turned out that he had nothing else to sell, such as a marketable skill. Like many students who have a hard time deciding what to do with their lives, he had majored in English literature. He knew virtually nothing, it seemed, about the contemporary world, aside from rumors he had picked up from other students and his teachers, most of them almost equally innocent. He was convinced, however, that work in almost any business firm was certain to be both dull and debasing, and that corporations were by definition corrupt institutions. Only after much anguished wrestling with his conscience had he decided that it was better to let himself be co-opted and corrupted than to starve.

Corrupted how? On this point he was a little vague, but he assumed that he would have to write and publish lies at the behest of advertisers—probably cogs in the military-industrial complex—or on demand of the Establishment characters (whoever they might be) who owned the joint. I never was able to persuade him that this danger was illusory. Neither could he comprehend that a man so ready to surrender his own convictions would be of no use to a publisher.

Corruption is a real danger to a publisher, but it rarely comes on in the simple guise of bribery or coercion. All during World War II, I kept alert for some beautiful blonde spy in a black satin dress who might try to worm her way into my confidence; but none ever did. Nor in more than thirty years of editing and publishing have I ever been offered a bribe, or a promise of advertising in return for editorial favors. On the one occasion when I was offered money—a dazzling sum—for partial surrender of the editorial control of this magazine, the man who tendered it had no thought of bribery. On the contrary, his motives were lofty and (as I shall explain in a moment) he sought to gain nothing but the public good, as he saw it.

Coercion is seldom a bother, either. A long time ago when I was editing the undergraduate daily at the University of Oklahoma, I was threatened by a gang of campus toughs—a cross between a secret fraternity and a juvenile Klan—which wanted to suppress news about a local abortion mill. As a consequence I borrowed a .32 Colt from a friendly deputy sheriff, and for a few weeks after the first of the anonymous telephone calls I actually wore it in a spring-clip shoulder holster while walking home from the print shop in the early hours of the morning. Nothing ever happened, so the gesture probably was unnecessary—if not a little silly—although Oklahoma was a rough place in those days and I did not feel overly melodramatic at the time. Never since then has anyone tried to coerce me, if you don't count the occasional poison-pen letters which are a standard occupational annoyance.

The legend that advertisers dictate the policy of newspapers and magazines is deeply embedded in American folklore, and apparently has become an article of faith with the New Left. In fact, advertisers seldom attempt anything of the kind, and virtually never succeed. Only three times in fourteen years of editing this magazine did I run into anything that could be called advertising pressure, and in each case it was trivial. A European travel bureau once canceled a small advertising schedule because we called its country's dictator a dictator. The tourist agency of a New England state did the same, when the late Bernard DeVoto noted that billboards were ruining the state's once lovely countryside. And the Knights of Columbus withdrew its advertising because its then Supreme Knight resented our publishing an author who had criticized Senator Joe McCarthy. It may be significant that none of these instances involved a corporation. There may be businessmen who refuse to advertise in *Harper's* because they don't like its editorial policy—but if so, they don't tell the editors. My impression is that most of them, and their advertising agencies, couldn't care less; what they are interested in is the size and character of a publication's audience, since they want to place each advertising dollar where it will produce the maximum results.

A notable case history of the relationship between a publisher and a powerful corporation began on December 4, 1899, when Harper & Brothers went into receivership. It had been bankrupted by a depression, loose management, and the withdrawal of capital on the death or retirement of some of the partners. In desperation the remaining partners turned to J. P. Morgan, the nation's leading financier and also the Boss Demon in the hagiography of all sound liberals at that time. He bailed the firm out with a big loan, put his men on the board of directors, and helped reorganize the management. As a natural result, according to the conventional wisdom, the company's books and magazines should promptly have become mouthpieces for political reaction and The Trusts.

It never happened. So far as I can discover, J. P. Morgan & Co. never tried to exert any editorial influence whatever during the following quarter of a century when it held the financial strings. On the contrary, the Harper firm continued to publish a lot of authors who must have given old Mr. Morgan acute colic—for instance, Henry Demarest Lloyd, whose *Wealth Against Commonwealth* was one of the earliest and most effective salvos of the muckraker era. Another example is William Dean Howells, for twenty years (Morgan years, all of them) the writer of this column; his editorials now sound painfully genteel, but in his day he was considered a pioneering social critic. Moreover, *Harper's Weekly* first proposed the Presidential candidacy of an unorthodox academic, Woodrow Wilson, whose political ideas tasted like rat poison to Wall Street; and the house published sixteen of his books without a peep from the Morgan partners.

These facts are worth mentioning only because they are, I believe, quite typical of American publishing in general. It is true that some of the weaker newspapers do run publicity stories for big advertisers, particularly in their real-estate sections. A few travel writers will accept free plane trips and hotel accommodations with the tacit promise of saying something nice in return. And I have heard rumors that certain women's magazines will gush a little more breathlessly over a new fashion if a plump advertising contract is in prospect. Fifty years ago, according to old timers' tales, all these forms of payola may have been fairly widespread. But today I am convinced that they are relatively rare. The truly serious dangers of corruption are more subtle and harder to resist.

The most insidious is built into the power, such as it is, of the editor. In comparison with elected officials, corporate managers, or university deans, an editor commands only a small quantum of power—usually far less than he thinks. To writers, however, it is a power of considerable significance, because he stands like a gatekeeper between them and their audience. Every day he confers on a few of them access to the printed page, and turns away hundreds of others. His decisions, moreover, are essentially authoritarian. However carefully he listens to the view of his associate editors and literary advisers, in the end every editor in chief—of a newspaper, magazine, or book publisher—has to make up his own mind what to print. As our libel laws so pointedly demonstrate, the final responsibility cannot be delegated. Neither can it be diffused among any sort of democratically constituted group.

The authority of any editor, even of the most ephemeral publication, tends to corrupt, just as surely as the more awesome forms of political and sacerdotal power which Lord Acton had in mind when he wrote his famous letter to Bishop Creighton. For the editor can, in some petty measure, help his friends and hurt his enemies. Indeed, he is under constant pressure, or temptation, to do both.

For example, one of the duties of a magazine editor is to cultivate the friendship, or at least the goodwill, of authors. A lot of them write books as well as articles; and when they do, they are quite likely to hint that they would appreciate a friendly review. Or, at least a review. Since some 25,000 books are published in this country every year, and since no publication can cover more than a tiny per cent of them, the pressure for review space can become pretty stark. Some authors, or their agents, put it bluntly: If the magazine doesn't come up with a good review, I'll never submit another manuscript.

A few years ago I turned down an essay by a distinguished professor of literature, because it struck me as tedious and pedantic. Next week a letter arrived from one of his former students, a writer whom I had been trying hard to persuade to contribute to *Harper's*. He pointed out that the professor was on the verge of retirement; that publication of the essay would brighten his declining years; that *Harper's* had printed worse stuff; that any editor with a spark of kindliness in his breast would do the decent thing; and that if I didn't reconsider my decision he would never speak to me again. I didn't, and he hasn't. . . .

. . . An editor would be less than human if he didn't have an impulse now and then to slug somebody—an impulse which can be especially dangerous for inexperienced editors who have not yet learned how hurtful the printed word can be. A precocious friend of mine once became sports editor of a small New Jersey paper just after his graduation from high school. One of his first columns was a funny but scathing attack on the local basketball coach, who had a few months earlier dropped the author off the high-school team. It was, I think, intended in a spirit of mischievousness rather than malice; at any rate my young friend was drenched in remorse when it resulted in the coach's losing his job.

More often than I like to admit, I suspect that my opinion of a manuscript may be colored by my dislike of the jerk who wrote it. In such cases, I have come to believe, one ought to depend heavily on the judgment of colleagues who don't know the man. It would be better yet to stick firmly to a cardinal rule of publishing: When you are wearing your editor's hat,* you have no friends and no enemies. Unhappily, I'm not always sure that I have that much strength of character.

(I should note that this rule evidently does not apply to Little Magazines and some scholarly quarterlies. On the contrary, their chief function often seems to be the evisceration of the editor's enemies.)

Another temptation lives permanently just down the hall from the editor's desk, in the offices of his colleagues who are responsible for manufacturing and selling the publication, and producing enough revenue to keep it alive. Nearly every day one of them is likely to try to persuade him to short-ration the readers just a little bit.

This doesn't mean that they are wicked fellows. Usually they are just as honest as the editor, and his close friends to boot. But their jobs are quite different from the editor's, and inevitably they sometimes conflict. For instance, it is the duty of the manufacturing man—whether on a periodical or in a book publishing house—to get the end product at the lowest possible cost. This can be done in a lot of ways: by narrowing the margins of the printed page an eighth of an inch, by using paper a few pounds lighter per roll, by squeezing another hundred words on the page, by cheapening the binding where hardly anybody would notice. Probably no one of these changes would matter much; but if the editor keeps going along with these suggestions, in a spirit of amiable cooperation, he will find one day that he is turning out a shoddy product—and the fault is his, not the manufacturing department's.

In similar fashion, a magazine's advertising salesmen always want a publication which will be more interesting to their potential customers. They are not even aware that the advertisers' interests, or the salesmen's own, may be considerably different from those of the particular readers whom the editor is trying to reach. Consequently a salesman's suggestions are offered in good faith, and with a deep conviction that all he wants is a better magazine. The editor, however, had damn well better examine every one of them as carefully as a horse trader looks at an old mare's teeth. The tip-off is the fact that most advertising salesmen refer to their publication as "a consumers' book." When the editor begins to think of his readers simply as potential consumers of advertised products, he is in bad trouble; and so, in the long run, is the publication.

---

*This is not merely a figure of speech. George Leighton, a one-time associate editor of *Harper's*, had a railway conductor's cap with a brass plate in front bearing the inscription "Editor" in two-inch letters. He was wearing it on the hot July day when I first met him. Since his cubbyhole was not air-conditioned, he had stripped off his shirt and undershirt; and sitting behind his desk, at first glance he looked naked except *for* his editor's hat. That ended any suspicion I might have had about publishing being a conformist profession.

A book salesman, naturally enough, is apt to argue for a jacket design just a trifle sexier than the text of the novel actually justifies. The newsstand dealer yearns for more sensational titles. The business manager's figures would look better if the editor would accept a lower ratio of editorial content to advertising. All of these people are doing their jobs as conscientiously as they know how. And the editor's job, a good deal of the time, is to resist them. I have been lucky, during most of my time in publishing, in having colleagues with whom such conflicts could be resolved on reasonable terms; but they are always there.

Robert Colborn, editor of *Science and Technology,* recently observed that conflict between the editor and his business associates "is present, open or concealed, on every magazine, the good ones and the bad ones. . . . It is simply a fact about the publishing business. Every business, of course, has to endure some sort of tension between its long-term health and its short-term advantage. But it is not as temptingly easy in most other business to forget what business you are really in. That easy confusion is what makes it constantly necessary, in publishing, for someone to guard the future of the business against its present. . . . To be guardian of the future is a permanent and important part of any chief editor's job. . . . He *must* be a tough, suspicious son of a bitch. If he isn't, he is cheating his employer and had better take up teaching or social work."

The trickiest booby trap in the editor's path probably is the Temptation of Good Causes. His friends, eminent citizens, and his own conscience exhort him without respite to give more of his space (always pitiably limited) to the promotion of some worthy cause. It may be peace or birth control or the American Cancer Society or the reelection of a statesman he reveres. The editor is genuinely interested in the subject; if he published one more article about it (even a piece that is not quite first-rate) he would be striking a blow for mankind. He also would gratify some influential people, and feed his own ego with that most intoxicating of hallucinogens: the feeling that he is an Important Influence. In this heady state of mind he is all too likely to forget that worthy causes seldom make interesting copy—and that a publication which harps on one subject too often is sure to sound like a stuck phonograph record.

Only once in my experience were these seductions accompanied by hard cash. It was proffered by—of all people—Dr. Robert Hutchins, sometime president of the University of Chicago and perennial guardian of the public morality. At the time he was head of the Fund for the Republic, which he described as "a wholly disowned subsidiary of the Ford Foundation," devoted to furthering the ideals of a democratic society.

Over lunch Dr. Hutchins explained that the thoughts of the Fund's staff and its grantees were not getting the public attention they deserved. Indeed, the pamphlets it issued sometimes were ignored entirely by the

American press. To remedy this lamentable situation, he proposed that the Fund should take over each month a section of *Harper's*—say thirty-two pages—and fill them with articles of its own production. In return it would pay *Harper's* $500,000 the first year, and if the results were satisfactory the arrangement might be continued.

Did Dr. Hutchins mean that he would like to buy thirty-two pages of advertising space each month? No, no, that wasn't the idea. The space to be filled by the Fund would not be labeled as advertising. In fact, the name of the Fund would not appear at all. The articles it provided would seem to be a normal part of the magazine, so the readers need never know that they had not been developed by the regular editors. The impact, he suggested flatteringly, might be greater that way.

As I remember it, I assured Dr. Hutchins that I was in favor of both ideals and a democratic society, and probably would agree heartily with most of the causes he wanted to promote. But, I added, the primary responsibility of all editors was to their readers. In good conscience, therefore, an editor could not surrender control over the editorial content of his publication, even for the best-intentioned of purposes. Neither could he offer the readers somebody else's product under the guise of his own.

All this sounded pretty stuffy, I'm afraid; but I still believe that the role is a sound one. It is some protection, moreover, against all of the dangers mentioned earlier. So long as an editor remembers that he is working, first and last, for his readers—who are, ultimately, the people who pay him—he usually should be able to resist most temptations, even those of his own ego. And in so doing, he will best serve the long-run health of his publication and the financial expectations of its owners.

---

to the student: a commentary

Like most of John Fischer's writing, this article's argument is almost irresistible. However, you must recognize that he was editor, for fourteen years, of *Harper's*, a minority magazine. Although this position exposed him to the pressures that other editors face, by no means did he face temptations of such intensity as those confronting mass magazine editors. Unlike many other magazines, *Harper's* is not thought of as a money-making proposition.

Several editors of mass magazines have had bitter experiences with advertisers. Decades ago, the advertiser emerged as the man who pays most of the bills; in effect, he rents the audience. Mass production and mass distribution required mass selling to bring together the buyers and sellers of goods and services on a nationwide scale. Advertising came to be the economic foundation of the magazine—and a constant worry to the business office, and almost surely to the editor.

One problem can be illustrated by *Look,* which died several years ago. The advertising salespeople brought in full-page ads for movies. That was, of course, advertising, but there was an editorial decision that made the magazine suspect: The ads were published in the same issue in which the magazine carried a gushing article about movies, or one in particular. The connection was obvious.

As Fischer points out, the authoritarian role of the editor tends to corrupt him. He has power because of what the writers submit, and thus he is likely to listen to those who want reviews of their books. Will he make certain that the reviewers praise the books? I think not. I have written nearly a hundred book reviews. In no case has any editor tried to determine my attitude. I was once asked to review *Travels With Charley* by John Steinbeck. I liked it for the first few pages, then came upon the description of Charley, the dog that was his companion. I wrote:

Steinbeck's companion, the "Charley" of the title, is a large poodle, friendly to the point of pacifism. He is an arresting dog, but his urinating habits are hardly cause for humble philosophizing. Steinbeck chooses to observe, however, that in this field, "the slow, imperial smelling over and anointing of an area, he has no peer. Of course his horizons are limited, but how wide are mine?" Later, "There Charley could with his deliberate exploring nose read his own particular literature on bushes and tree trunks and leave his message there, perhaps as important in endless time as these pen scratches I put down on perishable paper." Thus humility becomes absurdity.

No one has ever asked whether I like a book: they just tell me when the review should be submitted. And the magazines for which I have written cover a wide range: *Saturday Review,* the *New York Times,* the now-defunct *Reporter, Journalism Quarterly, Ramparts,* and several others. Of course, I cannot know how much the editors writhe over some of them. But they publish them.

There is a lesson in considering the stance of the editor of *Saturday Review,* Norman Cousins, after publishing the review of *The Unicorn and Other Poems.* The book was written by the famous poet, Anne Morrow Lindbergh, the review by John Ciardi, the poetry editor of the magazine. Ciardi began his review:

Anne Morrow Lindbergh's great personal distinction, together with the popularity of her six earlier volumes, some of poetry and some of prose, made it clear from the start that her latest volume of verse, "The Unicorn and Other Poems," would sell widely. Poetry nevertheless is no reliable consort of either personal distinction or of bookstore success. Everyone is in trouble when he looks at the stars, and under the stars I am as humanly eager to grant Mrs. Lindbergh the dignity of her troubles as I am to enjoin my own.

One of my present troubles is that as a reviewer not of Mrs. Lindbergh but of her poems I have, in duty, nothing but contempt to offer. I am compelled to believe that Mrs. Lindbergh has written an offensively bad book—inept, jingling, slovenly, illiterate even, and puffed up with a stereotyped high-seriousness, that species of esthetic and human failure that will accept any shriek as a true high-C. If there is judgment it must go by standards. I cannot apologize for this judgment. I belive that I can and must specify the particular badness of this sort of stuff.

Ciardi ended his long review with, "Who will forgive Mrs. Lindbergh this sort of miserable stuff?"

The biggest storm in the long history of the *Saturday Review* gathered rapidly. Hundreds of readers wrote to the magazine to protest the review. Exactly four readers wrote in support of Ciardi. The most significant action was taken by Cousins in the next issue. His editorial ran:

In fairness to Mr. Ciardi, before he is gobbled up alive by our readers, some points ought to be made clear. First, he did inform the editor, before the latter went abroad (there being no connection between the two events), of his intention to write a highly critical review of Mrs. Lindbergh's book. Mr. Ciardi was told that so long as he was Poetry Editor he would continue to enjoy the same authority over his department possessed by other members of the staff. He would have direct access to the columns of the magazine. We would stand behind his right to unobstructed critical opinion; but this did not mean he could count on our automatic support for his views. . . . This editorial is not intended to chastise Mr. Ciardi. From the moment he joined *The Saturday Review* staff he added real salt to our stew. We have never caught him in an ambiguous moment. He lives as he thinks and writes, with vast energy, freedom, conviction. He has won the very real affection and respect of the entire staff. We believe that in the months and years ahead his relationship with our readers will be no less rewarding to them and to him.

Fischer is probably more right than wrong in his judgment that an editor is likely to be corrupted. Unlike Fischer, most editors feel a continuing tug. Many of them yield.

WLR

Dave Noland

Flying Pussycats

At one time I was editor of *Air Progress,* the second largest consumer magazine for private pilots and flying buffs. We had been working for several months on an article about "product liability" lawsuits involving light-plane crashes, a delicate subject for the manufacturers. The landmark case is a suit in which $19 million was awarded to the family of a man killed in the crash of a Beechcraft Baron. The jury concluded that faulty fuel-tank design had caused the crash, and awarded $2 million in damages. The jury also decided that Beech Aircraft Corp. had known about the problem for years, ignored it and had misled the court and the Federal Aviation Administration. For this, the jury levied $17 million in punitive damages, which, by law, cannot be insured. The $17 million has since been ordered reduced by an appeals court, and litigation continues, but if the final judgment is anywhere near $17 million, the second largest company in the industry will go belly up.

Obviously, to discuss aircraft product liability without mentioning Beech would be like discussing Watergate without Nixon. The author of the article, Keith Connes, banged on Beech's door for months trying to get its side of the story. Beech stonewalled; company policy was to say nothing at all about the matter. *Air Progress*'s new publisher, Tom Guthrie, read Connes's manuscript and quickly saw that Beech would hardly be pleased. He had just signed Beech to a $55,000 advertising contract. The figure represented better than 20 percent of the magazine's projected ad revenue for 1975. Guthrie delayed publication of the article for six months, then, over my strong objections, showed a copy of the manuscript to Beech ad manager Jim Yarnell. When Guthrie returned from his meeting with Yarnell, he told me the article would be killed. "Editorial integrity is fine," Guthrie said, "but just try and feed your kids with editorial integrity." I resigned as editor.

My experience is by no means unique. On the contrary, it is a prime example of the aviation press's fawning acquiescence to the pressures of big advertisers. The three major flying magazines—*Flying* (circ: 400,000), *Air Progress* (175,000) and *Pilot* (175,000)—have a combined circulation that rivals *The New York Times* (and, of course, considerably more influ-

Reprinted by permission of David Noland from *MORE,* November 1975.

280

ence among private pilots), but they pay only the mildest lip service to the standards of journalism. The light plane builders are in many respects a miniature version of the auto industry, dominated by a Big Three—Cessna, Beech and Piper—centered in one city, Wichita. It's a small, close-knit group and the companies consider the magazines part of the family, virtual extensions of their public relations departments. As in most conservative midwestern families, unruliness is not tolerated. An editor who publishes nasty words about an airplane is likely to get an angry phone call from the company president—or worse.

Jim Holahan used to be editor of *Business and Commercial Aviation,* a trade book and sister magazine to *Flying* in the Ziff-Davis Publishing Co. stable. Holahan also wrote an article reporting the facts of the Beech fuel-tank lawsuit. Ed Muhlfeld, publishing director of *B/CA* (he's also responsible for *Flying*) had written a memo to Holahan, asking that all copy concerning the Beech litigation be cleared with him first. Holahan, relying on previous promises from Muhlfeld of total editorial control, ignored the memo. The story was eventually killed in page proofs by Muhlfeld, and Holahan left soon thereafter, another victim of the Beech advertising department. Beech has continued to advertise heavily in *B/CA*. Holahan is now editor of *The Aviation Consumer,* a struggling newsletter that accepts no advertising.

When an inattentive publisher does allow a few words into print that Beech considers inappropriate, the fireworks can be spectacular. In 1967, *Pilot* printed an article critical of the Federal Aviation Administration for spending $200,000 on Beechcraft Queen Air twin-engine executive aircraft. *Pilot* editor Max Karant suggested that the money would have been better spent on a larger number of single-engine planes. Beech president Frank Hedrick called Karant, chewed him out for being anti-Beechcraft and cancelled all advertising. The Beech advertising ban on *Pilot* has continued until this day, despite the fact that most manufacturers consider *Pilot* a "must-buy" ad medium. The cost to *Pilot* has been literally millions in lost ad revenue.

Pilot continues to try and get those ads back. A recent *Pilot* article on the Beechcraft Sundowner (a sickly performer widely regarded as one of the worst on the market) lavished praise on the aircraft because it proved to be as fast as the owner's manual had promised. The article failed to mention, however, that the handbook speed was nearly 30 mph slower than the speed achieved by the Grumman Traveler, the Sundowner's direct competitor. Indeed, the Sundowner is far slower than any airplane in its class, a fact the enthusiastic *Pilot* writer neglected to mention. He also failed to report that Beech had just lowered its speed claims, since the Sundowner had been infamous for falling short of its original handbook figures.

The editors of the other flying magazines have of course taken heed of Beech's actions. All have scrupulously avoided any mention of the fuel-tank lawsuit. The only reference to it in the aviation press was a couple of sentences in an *Air Progress* pilot report on the Beechcraft Debonair, which originally had the same faulty fuel tanks. In fact, the only publication to report the suit directly has been *The Wall Street Journal,* which ran a front page investigative story. Beech, of course, was outraged and threatened libel suits and ad cancellations; the *Journal's* reaction was a polite, "So who's stopping you?"

Beech, although certainly the most blatant wielder of its advertising dollar's influence, is by no means the only one. For example:

• In 1973, *Air Progress* evaluated the American Yankee, a sporty two-place trainer. The author wrote ecstatically of the plane's snappy handling characteristics, and bluntly stated he'd much rather fly a Yankee than its nearest marketplace competitor, the Cessna 150. His only criticism was of the airplane's flap system, which he labeled "Mickey Mouse." American Aviation, ignoring the overall praise of the plane, pulled six months' worth of ads because of the criticism of the flaps. Cost to *Air Progress*: $10,000. Three months later, the same author interviewed the designer of the Schweizer Teal amphibian aircraft. The builders of a rival amphibian, the Lake LA-4, promptly dropped a scheduled one-year ad contract. Cost to *Air Progress*: $20,000. Ed Tripp, publisher at the time, never mentioned these cancellations to the writer, although the lost accounts added up to 10 per cent of the magazine's annual ad revenue. Tripp usually made it a practice to isolate the editorial staff from advertiser pressure, a major factor in *Air Progress's* relative credibility at the time.

• *Private Pilot,* a low budget, low circulation magazine, has on two occasions printed photos of Maule utility aircraft on its cover. Nothing unusual there, but then the reader turns the magazine over to find the same picture on the back cover—as an ad for a Maule dealer. Such blatant ad-for-editorial tradeouts are commonplace among the lesser magazines, which must hungrily scratch for every ad just to survive. Such deals are usually struck with the smaller companies, such as Maule and Lake Aircraft, a Texas amphibian builder.

• *Pilot* editor Max Karant wrote an article criticizing a cutback in service by Exxon to its aviation customers amid record profits. The advertising department raised hell and snipped out the comment as the magazine went to press because it was trying to persuade Exxon to advertise its aviation fuel in *Pilot.* "This sort of intimidation goes on all the time," says a writer for one of the big three magazines. "Jesus, what whores we are."

Stephan Wilkinson, former executive editor of *Flying,* says, "There was a constant battle at *Flying* to remember that we were in the magazine business instead of the airplane business. Sometimes we lost the battle.

There was a general feeling among the staff that the manufacturers needed help selling their turkeys, and that it was our job to help them out. . . . We felt there was no such thing as a bad airplane. By definition they were all marvelous devices."

And apparently all *equally* marvelous. A recent *Flying* article was billed as a side-by-side flyoff between the Mooney Ranger and the Grumman Tiger, two airplanes noted for their high speed. Who would win the great match race? *Flying* readers never found out, for the editors decided that to name a winner also meant to name a loser, and *Flying* didn't like naming a big advertiser—in this case Mooney—a loser. "Well, yes, that was part of the reason," says editor/publisher Robert B. Parke.

Not that *Flying* doesn't occasionally get tough editorially. Its muckraking enthusiasm, however, is generally directed at nonadvertisers. The big, bad bureaucratic Federal Aviation Agency is always a tempting target, of course. And a recent *Flying* pilot report on the twin-engine Robertson/Cessna 414 took the airplane to task for its shortcomings under emergency single-engine conditions. Robertson is a small company that modifies Pipers and Cessnas for better takeoff and landing performance; the deficiencies pointed out in the article were unique to the Robertson-modified airplane. Robertson doesn't advertise in *Flying.* Cessna does.

A *Flying* writer once wrote in grisly detail about how the 400-hp Lycoming engine in a Piper Comanche failed time and again to start. After the article appeared, Cessna switched from the Lycoming to a Continental engine for one of its airplanes. Was Lycoming mad? You bet. Was Lycoming a *Flying* advertiser? Of course not. Was Piper, a major *Flying* advertiser, mad? Not at all, since the Comanche 400 had been out of production for several years, and there were no plans to resume selling it.

In another case, *Flying* sent Peter Garrison, a sarcastic but expert writer, to report on the McCulloch Gyroplane, an odd contraption designed by a fellow named Drago Jovanovich. Garrison panned the airplane, commenting that its designer "had a name like a Transylvanian pasta chef." Since McCulloch was not an advertiser, the article ran as written. (Jovanovich sued, and an out-of-court settlement was finally reached.) The point is that Garrison would never have been sent to evaluate a Beechcraft airplane, or to write, for example, that chairwoman Olive Ann Beech "had a name like a Sicilian fruit tree."

The paranoia of the industry sometimes strains credulity. *Air Progress* once slugged a picture of a new Beechcraft "Son of a Beech." (The plane looked like a miniature version of a larger Beechcraft, the Super King Air.) Beech ad chief Jim Yarnell responded with a pained letter to publisher Guthrie, entreating, "My God, what next?" American Aviation complained bitterly to *Air Progress* about a picture of a man lying down in the roomy baggage compartment of its Traveler model. According to American, people shouldn't be doing things like that, even on the ground with the engine off. A Mooney account executive once complained to an *Air Progress* salesman that a two-page color photograph of a Mooney in the magazine was displeasing to him—the angle of the sunlight showed up too many rivets and made the aircraft look mottled.

All the magazines regularly borrow airplanes (at no cost) from the manufacturers for evaluation flights. On one typical *Air Progress* trip, staff members made a round trip flight from Wichita to Haiti in a Beechcraft Baron. About 25 hours of flight time was put on the airplane, which would normally rent for $60 to $80 per hour. (Total: $1,500 to $2,000.) The magazines, of course, realize that if they stay in good graces with the manufacturers, free airplanes are more likely to be available. *Flying* regularly gets scoops on new airplanes, partly because of its large circulation, partly because the manufacturers are confident the magazine won't be too critical. Shortly after the Piper Seneca was introduced in 1972, *Air Progress* pointed out certain deficiencies (i.e., that it was slow, noisy, handled abominably and couldn't carry much load). When the improved Seneca II appeared in 1974, *Air Progress* wasn't given an airplane for evaluation until four months after *Flying* had the "scoop."

The journalistic dilemma of the aviation magazines is shared to some degree by all special interest enthusiast publications. Magazines about cars, boats, skiing, photography, motorcycling, skin diving, etc., all have a vested interest in promoting their thing and coddling advertisers, frequently to the detriment of the reader. But the aviation magazines are in a particular bind because the "family" is so small and the advertising so concentrated. *Air Progress,* for instance, carries literally 99-plus per cent aviation-oriented advertising. A recent issue of *Flying* contained only two pages of non-aviation ads. And despite a readership that is mostly affluent, male and youngish, efforts to bring in general advertisers usually fail because the cost per reader is so much higher than, say, *Reader's Digest* or *The Waltons.*

Given this advertising equation, there seems faint hope that the consumer aviation press will soon abandon boosterism. For pilots and other readers, the forecast is continued blind flying.

---

to the student : a commentary

Dave Noland, as a past editor of *Air Progress,* has the experience to know what he's talking about in faulting special-interest magazines, particularly the flying magazines, for bending to the pressure of advertisers. While Noland obviously argues for editorial integrity— feeling the magazine's duty is to serve the reader, not the advertiser—he is up against a typical response: "Just try and feed your kids with editorial integrity."

The crucial factor, of course, is an economic one. Nearly all of the advertising in flying magazines is connected with aviation, and the major companies buy a king-sized slice of those ads. Offending a single advertiser, as Noland pointed out, can cost a magazine as much as 20 percent of its annual advertising revenue.

There is no question that businesses have a right to withdraw advertising, or spend their advertising dollar selectively. They are quite free to express disapproval any way they like—it is, after all, *their* money. It is also not automatic that the advertisers are the bad guys and the magazines always a struggling voice of truth.

But truth is the central concern. If a magazine distorts, alters, or omits information in order to please advertisers, then the reader who expects an honest and reliable account for his money is being shortchanged with every issue. And most readers *do* expect an honest reporting effort. Would anyone subscribe to a magazine that promoted itself by saying, "We provide partial and incomplete coverage of the field"?

Free gifts and services given to journalists by business pose additional problems to nearly all journalists, not merely those who work for special-interest magazines. As Charles Long, editor of *The Quill*, once pointed out, a wide range of things can come under the heading of "freebie." "A freebie can be a large thing, like the invitation to fly to a product unveiling in Los Angeles or New York at the expense of the manufacturer. Or it can be relatively small and come after the fact, like a bottle of booze at Christmastide from a local somebody you've come to know on your news beat."

Long also considers many of the journalism contests another aspect of freebies. As examples of "industry-based, self-serving public relations contests," he lists the Thoroughbred Racing Association, American Bowling Congress, American Auto Racing Writers, National Association of Engine and Boat Manufacturers, National Association of Home Builders of America, National Association of Real Estate Boards, International Rodeo Writers Association, National Swimming Pool Institute, and Wine & Health Awards. These organizations offer cash and prizes, and it's questionable if they are free from ulterior motives.

Many news organizations have set strict policies regarding the acceptance of gifts. The Associated Press has told its sports writers not to accept complimentary tickets. Along the same lines the *New York Times* sent a memo to the staff: "We are of this day putting into effect a new policy with regard to complimentary tickets to sports events. From now on we will accept none. . . . If a member of the staff feels the professional need to be present at a sports event to which he is not in the possession of working press credentials the sports editor or his deputy will try to purchase a ticket for him —and the *Times* will pay for it."

In West Virginia, the *Huntington Advertiser* and *Herald-Dispatch* staff members are not permitted to accept any complimentary tickets, dinners, junkets, gifts, or favors; the list is so extensive that it even includes "tickets to circuses." The publisher of the newspapers has a simple reason for the rules: "It [is] incumbent on all journalists to consciously avoid any conflict which would give the public even the slightest hint that objectivity and/or integrity was being compromised. It's not enough for us to know we can't be bought—we've got to prove it."

That feeling is echoed in the code of ethics of the Society of Professional Journalists, Sigma Delta Chi. "Journalists and their employers should conduct their personal lives in a manner which protects them from conflict of interest, real or apparent," the code states. "Their responsibilities to the public are paramount. That is the nature of their profession."

The code of ethics adopted by the American Society of Newspaper Editors over half a century ago states that "Freedom from all obligations except that of fidelity to the public interest is vital."

Such statements obviously go against the actions of editors and publishers who seek to please advertisers at the expense of straightforward reporting. Whenever such concessions are made, advertisers and bookkeepers may be happy, but the reader is clearly being cheated.

LLS

study questions

1. Why should a magazine be fair and honest? What right does the reader have to expect a privately owned publication to serve his best interests with integrity?

2. The two magazines mentioned in this section, *Harper's* and *Air Progress,* are unusual magazines: elite on the one hand, and special-interest/enthusiast on the other. Consider a magazine like *Time* which is basically a news review aimed at a mass audience. What pressures do you think operate on its editorial staff? Is it more or less prone to corruption than a magazine like *Harper's* or *Air Progress?* Is *Time* more or less susceptible to advertising influence on editorial policy? Is there evidence of boosterism (for example, of the United States' position in world affairs) in its presentation of news and events?

3. If Fischer's description of the constant battle of the editor against subtle forms of corruption is accurate, what can a magazine do to protect itself from succumbing, other than hoping its editor has the strength of character to resist?

4. Will any assurance of journalistic and editorial integrity be possible as long as magazines rely on advertising for their survival, and as long as one man, the editor, is in a position of such authority?

film 6

Film is a slightly different form of mass medium than those usually lumped under the term. First, it isn't all that "mass," since the audiences are fragmented into groups ranging from a handful to several hundred people. By the same token, it is often dependent on group psychology to achieve its full impact: a funny film may not seem all that funny in a nearly empty theater.

In addition, the components of film have an extended life span. Radio and television (reruns aside) are broadcast and gone; newspapers live one day, magazines a week or a month; but movies can be shown in different places at different times, and are new in one place while old in another.

Film is as susceptible as any other medium, however, to charges of influencing its audience in sensitive areas such as violence, pornography, and propaganda. It has been subjected to a wide range of restrictive measures, from congressional hearings to internal black-listing to production codes. The articles that follow examine some of the contemporary issues—violence, minority stereotyping, ratings—along with an in-depth look at that ubiquitous constraint, economics.

film

social force

"I can't speak for the sex but the violence was terrific."

Richard A. Blake

Violence – The Price of Good Box-Office?

Edwin S. Porter, in 1903, revolutionized the motion picture industry with his eleven-minute masterpiece, *The Great Train Robbery*. No longer could the camera be a static observer of the vaudeville stage or a mechanized family album. Through an ingenious technique of cutting and splicing, Porter was able to tell three stories at once and create suspense of an intensity never before achieved.

The audiences who flocked to see *The Great Train Robbery* were unaware of the subtleties of editing and the historical value of this first great Western. What drove them to the nickelodeons was a fascination for the violence they shared with the characters on the screen. An engineer is struck with a shovel and thrown from a speeding train; a telegrapher is pistol-whipped into submission and bound hand and foot, only to be discovered by his horrified daughter; a passenger on the ill-fated train tries to escape and is gunned down in cold blood as he runs toward the camera; when the sheriff and his posse finally catch up with the robbers, there is a classic shoot-out in the woods and the bandits drop like John Ford Indians. All this bloodshed, pressed into eleven minutes of film, surely gives substance to the suspicion that even seventy years ago, violence meant good box-office.

Conflict resolved in death has been part of motion picture drama from the beginning. Generations of cowboys and cavalry officers, gangsters and detectives, Roman legionnaires and Green Berets have proved their manhood, extended the frontier and made the world safe for democracy by a ready use of guns, knives, fists and animal cunning. Even comedy specialized in slapstick, which is a kind of violent assault on the person: Chaplin's flat foot applied to the seat of the pants of his rival, the Three Stooges' constant slapping of one another, Woody Allen's penchant for disastrous accidents.

The restless nature of the medium demands a violent resolution of dramatic conflict because it needs visual material to express inner activity. In classic forms of drama, a soliloquy could open a character's inner workings, for the stage is the medium of character and spoken word. Stage is

Reprinted by permission of Richard A. Blake from *America,* 12 February 1972.

intimate: two or three characters at a time in a confined area, where personalities strike sparks against one another. Film, by contrast, is vast in scope and fits more easily with vast arenas of activity, like an entire battlefield or a chase in which the geography becomes an important element in the narration. Film is the medium of action and motion.

Conflict between personalities in film must be presented, not through the medium of spoken word and gesture as it is on the stage, but through the medium of physical activity. In this it is closer to dance and mime than to drama, for the body must function as the metaphor of interior action. Persons in conflict cannot speak about their hatred and anger, as they would on the stage; they must fight and maim one another. Conversely, fights and battles always appear awkward on the stage, because the medium is uncomfortable with such gross forms of physical activity.

Even though violence has been a mainstay of film art from the beginning, few would deny that the contemporary change in the style of violence has been startling. In the more traditional varieties of conflict, injury and death were part of the expected dance of life. Villains clutched their chest and grimaced their way painfully to death; heroes suffered flesh wounds and at times during convalescence an occasional blood-stained bandage reminded audiences that they were watching a flesh-and-blood hero, a man of mortal stature.

In the past few years, however, the style of suffering has changed. And perhaps *The Wild Bunch* marks the watershed more clearly than any other single screen event. Bullets, for director Sam Peckinpah, were not anonymous emissaries of good clean death, but machines that tear huge bleeding wounds in human beings. The traditional death by gunfire left the clutch-and-fall pattern and became a gorgeous slow-motion dance, much like the incredibly graceful replays of professional football, where the bone-cracking impact of athletes is transformed into the beauty of classical ballet. Women and children are caught in lethal crossfire, and where another director would have had them scurry to safety in terror, Peckinpah makes the audience endure the indiscriminate destructiveness of violence. The old mold was broken and film acknowledged that even women lose flesh when shot at short range with shotgun fire.

The *Wild Bunch* was acknowledged as a serious film, with a pertinent message for our time. Because of its critical reception, it made bloody violence respectable, and thus accessible to far less talented and honest directors. History repeated itself, for in 1964, *The Pawnbroker* featured a scene in which a young prostitute exposed her bosom in a dramatically powerful scene. The scene was indeed a shock at the time, but it did eliminate the barrier and allow an entire series of meretricious filmmakers to use the same device with no justification other than that a few nude scenes would sell tickets. What is amazing is that the cult of bloodshed seems to have infected every level of contemporary filmmaking. A slick superficial detective film, *Dirty Harry,* uses plot merely as a vehicle to transport the audience from one vicious beating or mutilation to the next. Clearly not out to exploit the new trend to graphic violence, Roman Polanski felt he had to drag out the final downfall of Macbeth, with a series of bloody combats and a surgical decapitation, with the head of the hero rolling crazily across the screen. Incidentally, each of these two films contains a gratuitous and now obligatory "nude scene."

Evaluating such films from an aesthetic and moral stance is a task that calls for more than an impressionistic sense of outrage or horror. Violence is indeed a sickness of our society. And responsible artists, if they are to give an adequate picture of our age or comment pertinently on our social ills, are perfectly justified—and perhaps even obliged—to show us the horror of human cruelty in a way that leads us beyond the point of cheering when the Japanese pilot is shot down or the Indians are impersonally ambushed and "wasted." An artist has the special obligation to reveal brutality in all its ugliness to a country and indeed a world that reduces institutionalized murder—Pakistan, Vietnam, Ireland—to a statistic or a part of the nightly television news.

Two points must be clarified at the outset. The use of violence, or for that matter erotic sexuality, in film is a matter for artistic discernment. Exploitation of such concerns in modern society is reprehensible and irresponsible, and few serious critics would be moved to defend or explain the common downtown "cheapies" in any other context than as a social phenomenon. In addition to presuming a responsible artist as filmmaker, a responsible adult viewing audience must be clearly kept in mind. And it must be clear that "adult" admits of many degrees. A professor of literature may find in Henry Miller or D. H. Lawrence a crucial statement concerning man's quest for love in post-Freudian society; his contemporary, an intelligent college graduate now in business or engineering, may find his undergraduate courses in literature weak preparation for such an experience and consequently be shocked at those "dirty books."

The analogy to controversial literature is not altogether satisfying, since film has traditionally been the art form of the people, especially the young and the working classes. It is still popularly regarded as an evening's entertainment, rather than an art form, and without the support of the people the industry would collapse. But although film-going elites are a distinct minority and filmmaking artists are touched by commercial necessity, still there is a possibility that this current use of violence and sexual exploitation may in many cases be a valid and artistic expression. To evaluate the uses of violence, the artistic statement as a whole must be weighed very carefully.

Sam Peckinpah, who began the trend toward horrifying violence with

The Wild Bunch, has surpassed his earlier works with *The Straw Dogs.* Despite the setting in present-day England, the film is another saga of the Old West. Peckinpah believes strongly in the frontier ethic, that a man proves his manhood by violent self-assertion, which becomes more difficult in this mechanized modern age. In *The Wild Bunch* the bandits ride into Mexico, searching for a new frontier territory where the law of fist and gun still rules and the automobile and steam engine are unknown. The anachronistic striving for manhood is suicidal, and at the end the wild bunch are torn to pieces by a machine gun manned by uniformed forces of civilization. They faced death rather than yield to the realities of modern society.

The hero of *Straw Dogs* is in precisely the opposite situation. He is a professor of mathematics who cannot cope with the violence of the American campus, and so he retreats backward from the frontier eastward to his roots in England where he is free to concentrate on his studies of abstract mathematical forms. Workmen from the village humiliate him for his inability to function in their world. As they keep him out on a hunting trip, again to prove his weakness, two of them return to his home and rape his wife. Later, the same band of workmen hypocritically hunt for a half-wit they claim has murdered a girl in the village. The hero gives refuge to the terrified man and the vigilantes attack the house in a traditional Western siege that extends back through countless circled wagon trains to the climactic scene in *Birth of a Nation* (1914).

The professor refuses to yield to their mindless blood lust and surrender the half-wit to them. He makes a moral decision for justice and stakes out his home as a private preserve. The evil that is personified in the attack party cannot be stopped by the forces of law and order which are powerless in the face of such evil, and the local magistrate is accidentally murdered by the attackers. In defending his home, the mathematician has only his own resources and manhood to rely on. Thus, in a series of brutal and graphic battles he systematically kills all of his assailants. At the end, as the last enemy is about to destroy him, his wife joins in the mayhem by pulling the trigger of a shotgun.

Evil and violence in mankind is a mutilating experience in society, as Peckinpah graphically documents in his film. Yet underneath the violence is the statement that man, as a rugged individualist, does have the power to make decisions and oppose the forces of evil in the world. He is capable of protecting the victimized, even at the risk of his own life—and he struggles to his utmost to preserve life.

What undercuts the moral statement that has been made through all the violence is the final scene, where the professor is driving the half-wit back to the town, where he will be taken to the authorities. He comments that he doesn't know where he is going, as though all that happened was a function of blind animal instinct rather than rational, moral, decision-making processes. Furthermore, the explicit dwelling of the camera on open wounds and bizarre deaths (one attacker is slowly decapitated when the professor pushes his head into a trap) gives more than a suspicion that Peckinpah, and his intended audience, may be fascinated with the spectacle to the point of enjoyment. But the film is the statement of an artist, and has all the loose ends of human experience and artistic expression. It does not have the clarity and precision of mathematics. But under the ambiguity is a moral statement and despite the reservations one might have about the frontier ethical concept of manhood, the action of the hero is admirable.

Another . . . film, which lacks the moral complexities of *The Straw Dogs,* but by the fact of its apparent simplicity is infinitely more pernicious, is Mark Rydell's *The Cowboys,* another study of frontier *machismo* with John Wayne. At first the cross-country cattle drive with John Wayne and his team of young boys is charming. They are learning the frontier virtues of self-reliance and courage from the master. Wayne is a simple man, stiff and unforgiving to liars, unsympathetic to debtors and the weak. Finally, in a meeting with rustlers, Wayne surrenders the herd to protect the "boys." In a bloody fist fight with the longhaired bandit, he proves that the "Duke" is still the better man. Humiliated, the bandit shoots him in the back and rides off with the herd. After burying Wayne, the boys concoct a revenge plan and assert the meaning of manhood on the frontier by an improbable shoot-out with the rustlers. When the last of the villains has been ambushed and shot, the boys walk calmly through the piles of mutilated bodies with no emotion and watch calmly while one of their number frees a horse which drags the longhaired bandit to his death. By ignoring his pleas for mercy they have proved themselves men in the Wayne tradition.

At this point the director had a choice; he could lament the fact that the presence of evil in the world is ultimately corruptive of the young or he could applaud their Bar-Mitzvah of the spirit. He chooses the latter. By shooting upward at their cold emotionless faces, he adds stature and power to their images, then he cuts to the vast open plain before them, indicating that now they are one with the majesty of America. Wayne, likewise, was buried in the plain, which we are told took care of him in his youth and will look over him in sleep. When the boys return to put a monument over the grave, they cannot find the marker. Wayne, too, is one with the plains, unconfined by the geography of the grave. Despite the triumph of good over evil and the simple resolution of conflict, the moral statement in *The Cowboys* is far more dubious than that of *The Straw Dogs.*

Stanley Kubrick's . . . film, *A Clockwork Orange*, is equally noteworthy for its graphic violence (and crude sexuality), but it veers away from the theme of frontier morality and *machismo* through mayhem. In *Space Odyssey: 2001*, Kubrick was concerned with the power of machines and technology to depersonalize man. In *A Clockwork Orange*, the attack upon humanity comes not from machines but from the social institutions and theories of social control. In such a sterilized society, Alex and his friends chose the path of mindless rebellion: they rape and murder for entertainment. Human wisdom eventually conquered Hal, the computer in *Odyssey*, and in *Clockwork* man's ability to rebel triumphs.

In addition to rape and murder, Alex, the young hero, likes Beethoven; all three are taken together as signs of his ability to react humanly to his environment. When society sentences him to the dehumanizing environment of the prison, he proves too strong and eventually he is subjected to therapy that will make him a "productive" member of society: All three delights of his life are systematically removed and he becomes preconditioned in his responses to the world and society around him. In this dehumanized state, social institutions conspire to destroy him: the police brutally beat him and political leaders exploit him for their own advantage, for he is a helpless robot. Driven to attempt suicide, Alex discovers that the human body, like the spirit, refuses to die. During convalescence, he realizes that he is again human: his thoughts turn to lust and violence, and finally a huge stereo set is wheeled in and he can again take delight in "Ludwig Van." The perverse resurrection of the human spirit is imaged in a final fantasy sequence where Alex is engaged in violent sexual activity in an open grave while the social gentry, costumed for the Ascot, stand at the margins of the tomb politely applauding. Kubrick tells us that man must revel in his capacity for evil if he is to be truly human.

Kubrick pretentiously claims that Alex is a character like Richard III, whom the audience sympathizes with despite his palpable evil. This is not true. Alex is a horrifying metonym for humankind, for he is one-dimensional. He is incapable of receiving or giving love and is completely dedicated to his own interests. His freedom consists solely in a capacity for evil (with Beethoven as his one redemptive trait). Freedom surely means a capacity for love as well, but Kubrick is not interested in that question. He has made a profoundly moral statement about one facet of mankind and has issued a salutary warning about the impact of social institutions on man's life. The brutal beatings and senseless rapes are an exploration of the id, when the planned society strives to function as the universal superego.

These three films illustrate the difficulty a critic finds in evaluating the new violence in today's films. The two which are much more graphic in their use of sex and violence are by far more profoundly moral artistic statements. The apparently harmless film is ethically poisonous. Each of the three is a demanding experience that grips the human sensitivities and sends a movie-goer looking frantically for a theatre where *The Boy Friend* is playing.

---

to the student: a commentary

Richard Blake, a Jesuit priest and associate editor of *America* magazine, takes an unexpected approach in his analysis of three modern films; he looks for artistic justification for the violence portrayed. Responsible artists, Blake says, have a special obligation to reveal brutality in all its ugliness to a world that has institutionalized murder. He acknowledges the possibility for exploitation, but points out that one must presume both a responsible artist and a responsible audience.

One might agree that some films have a legitimate use of violence, but one must also admit that in most films violence is gratuitous, thrown out to the audience like chunks of raw meat. Since we are now subjected to graphic violence, we should consider how they affect us. Are they likely to increase our tendency to resolve conflict by violence? Are they providing models for us to imitate?

Such questions are so broad that they are often ignored, bypassed in favor of topics such as "artistic intent." Yet who has not felt the visceral response of an audience as the hero finally "wastes" some particularly grim villain? Audiences have been known to scream approval as the star of *Magnum Force* methodically cripples a killer. Are such scenes merely cathartic, temporarily cleansing us of darker emotions, or do they prime us for violent action? Can they also serve to make us callous, bringing us to a point where death and destruction, filmatic or real, becomes part of our expectations of how things are?

The National Commission on the Causes and Prevention of Violence was willing to reach some conclusions on such questions. The Task Force on Mass Media and Violence listed "hypotheses" they said were "clearly consistent with and suggested by established research findings and by the most informed social science thinking about the long-run effects of exposure to mass media portrayals of violence." The Task Force said that "persons who have been effectively socialized into the norms for violence . . . would behave in the following manner:

a. They would probably resolve conflict by the use of violence.
b. They would probably use violence as a means to obtain desired ends.

c. They would probably passively observe violence between others.

d. They would not be likely to sanction or punish others' use of violence.

e. They would probably use a weapon when engaging in violence.

f. If they were policemen, they would be likely to meet violence with violence, often escalating its level."

The task force also flatly stated: "Audiences who have learned violent behavior from the media are likely to exhibit that learning (i.e., engage in acts of violence) if they encounter a situation similar to the portrayal situation. . . ."

There has been a long and sometimes bitter battle over the conclusions of the commission (as there has been with the later surgeon general's report on television violence), with many of the critics charging that there is too little empirical evidence to support the conclusions.

James Wilson, a Harvard professor who analyzed violence research, has said that

social science probably cannot answer the questions put to it by those who wish to rest the case for or against censorship on the proved effects of exposure to obscenity, media violence, scurrilous political literature, or whatever. . . . The irony is that social science may be weakest in detecting the broadest and most fundamental changes in social values, precisely because they *are* broad and fundamental. Intuitively, it seems plausible that the media and other forces have contributed powerfully over the last generation to changes in popular attitudes about sexuality, political action, and perhaps even violence. But . . . it is unlikely that this will ever be proved scientifically.

Are we then to be left to our own judgments on what level, or what uses, of violence will be considered tolerable? The uses of violence, Blake says, are a matter for artistic discernment. Shakespeare presented fifty-two violent deaths onstage, yet had another sixty-four take place behind the scenes. He did not have the advantage, however, of slow-motion or full-color close-ups. Perhaps he too, as director Roman Polanski did, might have had Macbeth's head rolling crazily across the screen.

We might ask of such scenes—and of those in the next "action-packed thriller" we see—just how much is enough?

LLS

Eugenia Collier

A House of Twisted Mirrors: The Black Reflection in the Media

We are surrounded by images. Our world is a house of mirrors in which we see on every side reflections of ourselves in various phases of our existence. When the mirrors are bent or dim or tinted, we see distorted images, and, if we are not aware of the flaws in the mirrors, then we think we really look like that; our concept of ourselves is severely damaged, and actions that flow from that concept are out of tune with reality. The popular media—music, literature, film, television—are important mirrors in which we see ourselves. On one level, the media are considered entertainment. But on a more profound, less obvious, symbolic level, the media are powerful conveyers of messages, insidious manipulators of our minds.

For those of us who are black, the messages of the media are particularly important—more so, I believe, than for whites. The realities of white Americans have already been defined. Whites themselves have defined their world and their place in it: white is right. The Western way is the way that counts. And since whites control most of this country's institutions, we (most of us) accept their definitions as right. Therefore, an aberrated white character on the media is considered simply a "different" individual, and no harm is done to the basic image.

But for blacks, the case is different. Ever since our arrival on these cold shores, we have been told that we are genetically inferior, that we are a problem, that our bondage is our shame. If white Americans admit our worth, most of them will face a terrible guilt that this country is now and has always been unable to face. And most of us blacks grow up convinced, often unconsciously, that we are a degraded people. Hence great numbers of us embark early on the sad and impossible task of eschewing our blackness and adopting attitudes, life styles, and value systems which are (or, at any rate, seem to be) white.

Reprinted by permission of Eugenia Collier and *Current History* from the November 1974 issue.

Given the peculiar mind set of both black and white Americans, the effect of a distorted image of blacks via the media can be crippling. A black man in a film is not merely a man who happens to be black. He is a "black man" who emerges from a distinctive tradition and whose responses reflect that tradition. A character who is stupid, weird, or way out reinforces both the prejudices of many whites and the negative self-image of many blacks. Thus he contributes to our enslavement and postpones our long sought and still elusive liberation.

It would behoove us, then, to examine the nature of the black image. . . .

It is in film and on television that the most damaging image is perpetrated. Both industries appeal to a mass audience. People who would never pick up a book go to the movies, and it is estimated that over 85 million people watch prime-time television nightly. Both industries are overwhelmingly commercial and are motivated by what will sell rather than by what will educate. And what will sell, regarding black people, is an image that will not rock any boats.

Film has generally followed the lead of fiction; so when blacks have appeared at all, there is the usual assortment of incomplete, unrealistic characters functioning in ways that do not challenge the myth of white superiority. Early films, in fact, treated blacks shamefully, showing us only as clowns, criminals, and generally subhuman types. Even the few sympathetic portrayals, like *Cabin in the Sky* in the 1940's, seldom rose above the stereotype. Now and then a sloppy sentimental piece like *Imitation of Life* would present a warped view of blacks who wanted nothing in this world but to be white and whose humanity (exceptional for blacks) made them deserving. During the 1960's this image was slicked up in the sophisticated Sidney Poitier flicks, in which black and beautiful Sidney proved his humanity over and over by being more intelligent and more sensitive than the whites in whose world he functioned, and sometimes by earning the pristine love of a self-sacrificing white woman. Check out *To Sir with Love, In the Heat of the Night,* and that horror story, *Guess Who's Coming to Dinner.*

The recent rash of movies about blacks has helped very little, despite the fact that certain blacks are having more to say about what goes into films. Melvin Van Peebles's *Sweet Sweetback's Badass Song* demonstrated that a lucrative market existed in young blacks who would stand in long lines and pay their money to see some black superstud beating up on whitey—especially if the stud had style. Perhaps more to the point, the new type of hero was challenging the system that has oppressed us for centuries, and there is an obvious psychological mechanism behind the response of young blacks. The damaging aspect of this type of hero is that his challenge is futile (what, really, did Sweetback win?) or that beneath his flamboyant style there are methods destructive to the black community (e.g., Superfly, the well-dressed pusher). This is a hero without humanity, and so he is ultimately a loser.

Several more serious films have distorted the black image in a more insidious way. *Lady Sings the Blues* created dreadful misconceptions about Billy Holiday—played up the sensational, omitted incidents that would have contributed to our understanding of her, added several out-and-out lies, even muted the raw tragedy of her last days. Another . . . film, *Conrack*, completely overlooked the culture of Sea Islanders in order to show how beautiful and generous and intelligent is the young white teacher who comes to bring enlightenment to the lowly. People have taken these films seriously and believe their distortions.

Nevertheless, some films have attempted to come to grips with a serious portrayal of blacks. For the most part they have been limited in their effectiveness by the American penchant for success and the happy ending. The best of these was undoubtedly *Sounder,* which showed not only the suffering but also the family solidarity, the spirit, and the ultimate triumph of a southern black family. Superbly acted, directed, and photographed, the film made an unnecessary bow to American slickness by forsaking the book written by William Armstrong in which both dog and father die and hope is very dim, and substituting the happy ending, with the father and dog in good shape and the boy going off to school and a Bright Future.

More recently *Johnny Tough* has attempted to examine the dynamics of a social climbing middle-class black family and an insensitive school system that ultimately destroy young Johnny. The attempt is undermined by a rather simplistic treatment.

A more popular film, *Claudine,* shows the cold inhumanity of the welfare system in its relationship to individual clients, and the necessity to cheat if one is to survive. Created mainly by blacks, it explores several themes meaningful to the black community. But there are weaknesses. Diahann Carroll looks and acts like a glamorous lady who has just stepped out of a milk bath, not like the impoverished mother of six. And there are other things about the film that smack of the old comfortable-for-whites image: the black hero hides out to avoid supporting his children; the black nationalist teenager has a vasectomy. Thus the black man is shown as a negative rather than a positive force to the black community.

Film, in general, has been more responsive to moneymaking than to truth, which could be a basis of art. Now and then a film like *Sounder* seems to promise a more honest portrayal, but most films fall victim to the slickness that plagues American popular art. The most effective film image of blacks has been projected in the documentaries on Malcolm X and Martin Luther King, which had limited runs and had neither the press nor the following of *Superfly*.

The key, of course, to black image in . . . film . . . is more black writers, directors, and producers, and freedom in which to work. For only the black artist can tell the story. Only the black artist. Truth, we know, is many sided, and it takes great courage to show a side that is unpopular, especially in the money-mad world of the mass media, a world whose distinguishing features are racism and artistic mediocrity.

In all the media, in fact, the pattern is painfully clear. The farther one travels from the black folk and the closer one gets to the American public, the more the black image is distorted. And this will be the case until blacks attain decision-making power in the mass media, and/or until the vast majority of white people are willing to accept the truth about blacks, which is also the truth about themselves. Neither possibility is imminent. Meanwhile, we—all of us—must continue to view ourselves through the twisted and contorted mirrors of the media. And accept the aberrations as truth.

---

to the student: a commentary

Eugenia Collier, who teaches in the African American studies program at the University of Maryland, Baltimore County, directly and bluntly confronts the problem of double distortions of blacks in the media. Stereotyped versions of black life are not only mainly the product of white writers and directors, but the product is sold to black viewers, who may themselves identify with the stereotype.

The effect of the distorted image, Collier says, can be crippling. Whereas unusual white characters will be considered merely unusual, unusual black characters will be considered typical blacks. Early films portrayed blacks with the worst kind of stereotypes; more recent films provide a commercial polish that, while successful at the box-office, is still ultimately a negative stereotype.

Collier has accurately judged the treatment of blacks in early films. The three best remembered black film stars of the first half of the century, as writer Stephen Fay said, are Buckwheat, Farina, and Mickey Mouse.

While it could hardly be contested that Buckwheat and Farina, those endearing ragamuffins of the "Our Gang" series, were popular black screen personalities, some might challenge the legitimacy of including Walt Disney's renowned rodent in the thin ranks of Negro film stars on the grounds that Mickey (though black), was not human. Indeed he was not human—a characteristic which makes him eminently qualified for membership in any grouping of Negro screen actors, none of whom was human.

There is still an odious trend in cinema, Fay added, to avoid depicting the black man as a human being. The same criticism has been leveled at the rash of recent movies aimed directly at the black audience. The switch from Stepin Fetchit to Super Nigger is only proof that the black film stereotype has come full circle, according to Junius Griffin, president of the Hollywood NAACP. *Superfly,* he says, "is an insidious film which portrays the black community at its worst. It glorifies the use of cocaine and casts blacks in roles which glorify dope-pushers, pimps and grand theft."

Another huge box-office hit, *Shaft* (along with the predictable sequels), has been called "James Bond in Blackface." It has been criticized as yet another fantasy that steers clear of reality. The black director of *Shaft,* Gordon Parks, firmly defends the film. "I think the black is entitled to have a black hero, and I would rather have any kid admire Shaft instead of James Bond. Shaft can be accepted as a good guy who's for law and order. What got to black audiences about *Shaft* was that for the first time on screen they saw a black man winning. No matter how fictional, that's important."

"The Hollywood studios have been remiss in not providing black heroes," Parks added. "Now that they see black audiences want such films, perhaps they will take another step and present real-life black heroes. We needed a *Shaft* before any studio would make a film about Frederick Douglass."

Parks's interpretations may be both self-serving and inaccurate. Black audiences, like audiences everywhere, seem to have a marked preference for sex and violence. An excellent documentary on Malcolm X, which put together film clips of his speeches and interviews, died at the box-office. Such films as *Sounder* and *The River Niger,* which at least took a stab at realism, did reasonably well, but they don't come close to the commercial success of Super-Black films. *Shaft* raked in some $15 million; *Sweet Sweetback's Badass Song* grossed more than $12 million; and *Superfly* took in more than $1 million in one week at two New York theaters alone.

Such success has spun off a growing list of black-oriented films, many of which are remakes of Grade B white films. *Blacula, Blackenstein, Black Bart, The Werewolf from Watts, Blackfather, Black Christ, Black Gunn, Black Girl, Trick Baby, The Nigger Lover,* and *Sundown in Watts* are only some of the drive-in quality movies designed for a slice of the black market.

Actor Jim Brown says that

the problem lies with the Hollywood studios, who are in too much of a hurry to grab the black dollar. They color all the old white formula films black, and then claim that they represent the "black experience." *Cool Breeze* was just a re-make of *The Asphalt Jungle*. *The Lost Man* was a black version of *The Informer*. *Cotton Comes to Harlem* and *Come Back, Charleston Blue* feature Keystone Kops in blackface. Putting Sidney Poitier into *Buck and the Preacher* doesn't change the fact that the film is a John Wayne type of formula Western. Sure, these pictures sell and provide jobs for blacks. They also provide entertainment that blacks can enjoy. But they should be recognized for what they are.

Where does that leave future black films? If there is some agreement as to what should *not* be done, is it possible to say what ought to be done? One possible answer is suggested by writer David Denby:

Perhaps the best direction for black cinema, and also the one that would satisfy the conflicting demands being placed on it, would be to deal with the ordinary heroism of black life, the struggle simply to survive in America with dignity and selfhood intact. The film-makers certainly have the attention of the public, and they should be able to take a few chances. If that public is cheated of the quality its enthusiasm deserves, black movies will be remembered only as another form of exploitation and betrayal.

LLS

---

study questions

1. Does film truly distort reality, presenting us with a twisted and misleading reflection of the world we live in? Give reasons for your answers.

2. Professor Collier raises the question of stereotyping. Do you think that films present stereotyped characters rather than portraits of true human personalities? If they do, how might this affect our interactions with other people? How would this change our expectations of others, of how we think they should act? How might this influence our images of other groups within our society of whom we have no direct experience?

3. How have films distorted your perception of reality? Can you think of an instance in which your direct experience of something has not coincided with the way in which the media have presented it? Can you think of any misconceptions under which you may presently be acting as a result of secondhand knowledge through the media?

4. Is film really anything more than "an evening's entertainment"? Is it mere pretentiousness to try to elevate it to an art form and to expect it to serve the social function of art? Why?

5. If such films as *Superfly, Jaws, The Texas Chainsaw Massacre,* and *Dirty Harry* draw large audiences and make money for their distributors, doesn't the responsibility for the predominance of such films rest with the public? What kinds of movies does the public choose? What are your reactions to these choices?

6. People have always sought film as an escape from their everyday lives and the all-too-real world. Is this a valid social function, or are its harmful effects such that it serves no good purpose at all?

7. Richard Blake defends certain instances of violence and sex in films on the basis of their "redeeming social value." Does a film that twists reality have any redeeming social value?

film

constraints

MISS PEACH by Mell Lazarus, Courtesy of Mell Lazarus and Field Newspaper Syndicate.

The Family Movie Could Be an Energy Saver

Wouldn't it be fun to be able to take the family to an entertaining movie on Friday or Saturday night for a change, a movie that would not cause embarrassment or something close to nausea? With all the technological improvements of modern cinema production, color, wide screen, anamorphic lens, and synchronization of sound, why are producers unable to duplicate the audience attraction of pictures like the western classic Stagecoach, Swiss Family Robinson, Going My Way, Around the World in 80 Days, and The Sound of Music—to mention a few distinctly enjoyable films?

Now that gasoline for the family car needs to be conserved, there is an opportunity for the local motion picture theater to capitalize on family attendance. One enterprising theater manager recently undertook a promotion campaign that offered a special admission price for each car load of six persons who drove in from out of town. Although there has been a reported resurgence of interest in going to the movies, it is still well down the list of favorite ways of spending an evening, ranking below watching television, reading, dining out, and engaging in family activities at home. The public's expressed film preferences in a 1974 Gallup poll ranked comedy first, followed by drama, western, suspense film, love story, musical, science fiction film.

Whether the trend of increased interest withers and dies or expands to a really impressive turnout of patrons will undoubtedly depend to a great extent on the number that are produced of what are characterized as "family films." At present they are few and far between, although one trade journal publishes a letter from a reader commenting that "There truly seems to be a hunger for decent entertainment for growing families."

The motion picture industry for the most part tends to take the position that family pictures don't sell; that the audience turnout is poor; and that most people find family pictures boring. On the other hand, one producer has pointed out that exhibitors have a tendency to blame the failure of a poor quality film on the fact that it is a "family picture," instead of recognizing that even the sex and shock pictures that are currently paying off handsomely have in some cases also been financial flops. As one critic put it: "To make the top of the best money-making films with quality, you have to spend a lot of money, and the risk of failure is great. With sex films (or horror or cheap violence), there is little investment, high chance for good profit and an outside shot at a killing."

That there is meager family attendance at neighborhood movie houses is not surprising considering the currently fashionable trend, characterized by one newspaper headline as the "shock and scare" season, "rudely slamming through taste barriers." Distaste for the "sexploitation," "porno" films, and "skin-flicks" has been intensifying for some time. Even back in May, 1971 the Motion Picture Herald commented:

What was once exciting and titillating and novel is rapidly becoming, by repetition, dull and boring and monotonous—and most important—no longer salable. Of course, there always will be a hard core of pornographic purveyors. . . . But the day of the fast-buck "porno" boys is fast going. . . . It is our belief that the pendulum may well swing the other way—although not all the way, certainly—and the day of the romantic, sophisticated but "clean" dramatic rendition on stage and/or screen may be fast returning.

The neighborhood disapproval and condemnation of the motion pictures rated X according to the voluntary rating system of the Motion Picture Association of America has led to some disillusionment with the whole MPAA technique of providing guidance to the public in evaluating the suitability of particular films for viewing by young people and children. The MPAA Rating Program provides four classifications:

X—persons under 17 not admitted
R—restricted, with persons under 17 not admitted unless accompanied by
    parent or adult guardian
PG—all ages admitted (parental guidance suggested)
G—general audience

Two church groups that supported the association's project originally felt obliged in 1971 to take the position that:

The basic criterion for evaluation of the rating program is whether it protects the young from material beyond their ability to cope. We believe that the ratings at present do not take into account sufficiently the total context of a given film, that they place too much weight on overt visual sex, and not enough on the implicit exploitation of sex and the overall impact of violence and other anti-social aspects of the film on the child. In addition, overt sex is now finding its way into the "GP" (All Ages Admitted, Parental Guidance Suggested) films.

As readers of CR's Ratings of Motion Pictures have observed, there are very few films that merit our AYC classification as suitable for family viewing. The industry's PG rating has proved quite unsatisfactory to careful parents since films so designated have often been a cause of embarrassment. According to a report in Variety, trade journal of the amusement world, almost 75 percent of the films made over a recent 5-year period were in the combined PG and R grouping. Parents generally are not acquainted with the criteria used to arrive at a PG rating and do not realize that there is little or no attempt to evaluate the content and to judge whether the theme is within the emotional maturity and intellectual comprehension of a teen-ager. Indeed, some critics have even raised a question about the propriety of an R classification for The Exorcist, which has been playing to packed houses.

This 2-hour film was described by Cue Magazine as: "A hair-raising spine-tingler in the horror genre. Sweet young girl turns into a monster with signs of possession by the devil, as anguished mother turns to exorcism. Shocking, shattering scenes as twisted child spews profanity, grows violent, and battles priest trying to drive out the devil. . . . Rated R— children under 17 admitted only with parent."

In Washington, D.C., the morals division of the police department warned the management of the theater that arrests would be made if more tickets were sold to minors, after nearly every reviewer in town indicated that The Exorcist was not for children. An X rating would certainly have kept the film out of many a theater across the United States and would have greatly reduced its potential profit.

One critic, Roy Meacham, whose outspoken observations have been credited with helping persuade the Washington, D.C., police to bar the film to viewers under 17 years of age, pointed out that:

Blood and gore and amorality are not among the standards that the MPAA's review board uses to restrict children from the movies. . . . But although . . . [the MPAA's] system couldn't protect them [the motion picture companies] when the movie producers went overboard on sex, they have greater hopes that violence may be their new savior. . . .

Recapturing the lost movie audience will not be easy. The family trade has deserted the neighborhood theater because what its members enjoy and what the critics acclaim as representing the artistic freedom of "responsible artists to create films on mature subjects employing adult treatment" are usually not compatible. After one or two embarrassing experiences of taking the family to see some favorably reviewed "adult" film, further attendance is likely to be curtailed and viewed with disfavor. As one church newsletter (in another connection) put it: "To dignify such shows with arguments about creative freedom, contemporary relevance or maturity is nonsense. . . . Exploration of 'mature' subjects must be seen for what it is: a specious attempt to exploit sensational material under the guise of creative freedom and social relevance."

Considering the deference paid to the cause of freedom of speech and expression in the United States the exhibitor who schedules for his neighborhood theater the showing of such R-rated films as The Exorcist, Serpico, That Man Bolt, or Thieves Like Us may not be subjected to a campaign of disapproval from irate parents. On the other hand he is not likely to build a growing audience for regular movie patronage that all exhibitors, even those in big cities, would like to secure once more. Except for checking the classification in our ratings of motion pictures (or that of some of the critical sources used), which may not be in hand when a particular film is being shown at a convenient theater, how can discriminating parents evaluate its desirability for family attendance when even the G rating (acceptable for family viewing) of the MPAA has sometimes been found wanting?

In view of a market survey of movie-going newspaper readers indicating that 89 percent checked the movie information in their daily papers before deciding to go, perhaps concerned groups could persuade their local editors, advertising managers, and theater exhibitors to emphasize some definite and accurate classification in the advertising of the motion pictures scheduled for current viewing. The exhibitors themselves, who frequently complain that there is little or no attendance at pictures rated G for family viewing, might be well advised to stress this classification.

Of course, it is essential to keep in mind that a G rating will not make a poor picture popular and that regular family trade cannot be built on popcorn and candy alone or on the desirability of conserving gasoline. What is needed is more good family pictures.

to the student: a commentary

The editor of *Consumers' Research Magazine* laments the lack of good family movies and criticizes the film rating system. Perhaps many of you disagree with the views expressed in this editorial, or perhaps you find fault with the film rating system for different reasons.

I'm reminded of the time when I was lecturing a college class on movie ethics. I gave a sentence or two to the fact that the movie ratings—X, R, PG, and G—seemed to be working. As I started to move on to a specific question of ethics, however, I was interrupted by something like a roar. Although everyone in the class was at least eighteen, *all* of them were bitter at the memory that they were excluded only a few years ago. "How could they close us out?" one asked, almost shouting. A bit taken aback, I responded finally with a question: "Would you like your nine-year-old sister to go to anything? *Any* movie?" Well, no, they responded, but somehow the age will have to be lower than it is. Luckily, I had asked perhaps the *only* question that would cause them to pause. Those who had younger sisters halted, then decided that thirteen was the only reasonable limit.

When we consider the current movie ratings, perhaps it is necessary to think a moment of the history of movie regulation. In 1896, just two years after the first public commercial showing of movies, May Erwin planted a healthy kiss on John Rice in *The Widow Jones.* That kiss was called "no more than a lyric of the stock yards," and "absolutely disgusting." Some of those who feared that moral chaos might result from showing such intimate moments called for police interference.

By 1921, thirty-seven state legislatures were considering some form of legislation. The motion picture industry decided to form a new agency to be headed by an outstanding public figure. Will H. Hays resigned as postmaster general in 1922 and was brought into the movie industry to give it the stamp of respectability and the atmosphere of conservative elegance that seemed to characterize the administration of President Warren Harding. With many political friends in influential positions, and with a large operating fund from the industry, Hays warded off the most serious threats of governmental censorship while improving Hollywood's image. Other respected figures of the industry went on the speaking circuit, talking to civic groups, editors, and legislators. Movie titles were made less sensational. The Hays office began to give advice to producers on what material might be offensive to some groups.

In 1934, the Catholic Legion of Decency organized a nationwide boycott of objectionable films. That resulted in setting up an enforcement mechanism, the Production Code Administration, with provisions for issuing official certificates of approval and with a $25,000 fine for the release of films without approval. The code, with minor revisions, remained in effect until September

1966, when a new production code was announced. The new president was Jack Valenti, who had been an assistant to President Lyndon Johnson.

Valenti announced a new code that would "encourage artistic expression by expanding creative freedom and . . . assure that the freedom that encourages the artist remains responsible and sensitive to the standards of the larger society." He also added: "This is self-restraint, self-regulation, and self-discipline. We want to make clear that expansion of the artist's freedom doesn't mean tolerance of license."

Actually, the Motion Picture Association of America became convinced that its code was almost useless. Replacing the strongly detailed provisions for production standards were:

The basic dignity and value of human life shall be respected and upheld. Restraint shall be exercised in portraying the taking of life.

Evil, sin, crime and wrong-doing shall not be justified.

Special restraint shall be exercised in portraying criminal or anti-social activities in which minors participate or are involved.

Detailed and protracted acts of brutality, cruelty, physical violence, torture and abuse shall not be tolerated.

Indecent or undue exposure of the human body shall not be presented.

Illicit sex relations shall not be justified. Intimate sex scenes violating common standards of decency shall not be portrayed. Restraint and care shall be exercised in presentations dealing with sexual aberrations.

Obscene speech, gestures or movements shall not be presented. Undue profanity shall not be permitted.

Religion shall not be demeaned.

Words or symbols contemptuous of racial, religious or national groups shall not be used so as to incite bigotry or hatred.

Excessive cruelty to animals shall not be portrayed and animals shall not be treated inhumanely.

Later, in 1968, the motion picture industry all but threw up its hands. The latest productions were ignoring even the relaxed standards set by the new codes. So industry leaders formalized a series of labels designed to guide parents toward suitable movies. In effect, the code began to adapt itself to the practice of producers rather than prescribe their conduct.

Where do you stand regarding movies? Perhaps you need to listen to a Hollywood scriptwriter when he was trying to wrestle with the codes. This was in 1956, when the scriptwriter dreamed:

There'd be motion pictures in which a married man would have an affair with his secretary and return to his wife with his marriage enriched; a husband and wife would quarrel, get a divorce, their friends would conspire to get them together again, and it wouldn't work, because the couple genuinely disliked each other; an unmarried woman would fall in love with a man, live with him for two years, and leave him because she's met someone else, and the left-behind lover would go out and celebrate with his friends because he'd been tiring of her; a married man would visit a call-girl one night and nothing —but absolutely nothing, not even pangs of conscience—would happen later; a married couple would decide they didn't want children, and they wouldn't have any, and they'd be quite happy; a fortune hunter would have a choice between a lovely but poor young girl and a bitchy but rich heiress, and he would marry the heiress, fade-out the end; a doctor would give up his small-town practice to become a Park Avenue doctor, meet a rich girl, build up a lucrative practice, never go back to the home-town, and become one hell of a happy guy. The possibilities are endless!

To get a clear view of today, match the movies you have seen against the prescription the scriptwriter has presented. Perhaps that will tell you how good the movies are today.

But finally, what of your nine-year-old sister?

WLR

M*A*S*H Notes

The right idea at the right time has always proved invincible. Thus the new era of motion-picture production began when in 1951 Arthur Krim moved into an old and not so glamorous office building at 729 Seventh Avenue in New York City as president of United Artists. Krim was the right man with the right set of ideas at the right time. His talents encompassed the brain of a big-time lawyer, the gambling instincts of a businessman and the sense of showmanship without which no man can compete with the moguls of Hollywood. His ideas were largely dictated by the harsh reality of United Artists' financial statements which at that moment totaled up to one important bottom line: very little cash. His inventive mind turned this condition into a virtue by enabling stars, directors and producers to get ownership participation and profit percentages instead of cash. Magically, at that very moment, the Hollywood establishment, the so-called majors, MGM, Twentieth Century-Fox, Warner Brothers, Columbia, Paramount and Universal International, in a program of misguided economy, decided to discontinue their policy of keeping actors and directors under long-term exclusive contracts. Their mistake provided Krim with the all-important, perfectly timed opportunity of hiring on the open market stars like Clark Gable, Jane Russell, Tyrone Power, Gary Cooper and directors of the caliber of Billy Wilder, Willy Wyler and George Stevens. The Hollywood establishment was caught napping when United Artists gave these god-lings of the silver screen something they had never tasted before—a piece of the action—the feeling of ownership and a sense of adventure. Artists who had lived their sheltered existences behind their Bel-Air walls, while their business managers had taken care of every worldly transaction from hiring a maid to investing in real estate, were suddenly exposed to the appeal of becoming bosses, entrepreneurs and powerful forces in the business. Their appetites were whetted by the *fata morgana* of enormous profits and favorable loopholes in the laws governing personal income taxes and capital gains. The fact is that many of these high expectations remained unfulfilled, but no matter how unprofitable each single film proved to be, the general result was a flow of product that provided United Artists with much-needed merchandise. As the major motion-picture companies

Reprinted by permission of Ingo Preminger from *Esquire,* August 1970.

turned over production to outside talent, producers, directors and stars became co-owners and partners in the profits.

In this connection, a new look at the term "profits" is appropriate. The concept of profits as the difference between incoming and outgoing moneys has to be understood in the new context where one of the partners in the profits also receives a fee for his efforts as a distributor. The distributor enjoys the privilege of deducting and collecting his fee off the top for his own account, before any funds are used toward repayment of expenses, including the cost of the making of the picture. The felicitous position of the distributor is responsible for the production of films that promise huge grosses and distribution fees, but offer very little chance of ever showing a profit. High costs of negatives of the film and the costs of distribution just keep eating up all the money coming in from the play dates, with the result that the artist rarely collects any profits, while his partner the distributor receives huge distribution fees. It came as no surprise when percentages of grosses rather than profits started to appear in production-distribution agreements, thereby exposing the emptiness of a word that had served its purpose successfully when the game first started.

The rest of the distributors soon followed the example set by United Artists and, ironically, in a few years the bargaining position of stars, directors, and producers became strong enough to demand not only ownership, control and participation in grosses and profits, but also an ever-increasing amount of guaranteed cash. Directors like Mike Nichols and stars like Richard Burton have received a guaranteed million dollars per picture, a marked increase from the years when MGM voluntarily gave up its exclusive hold on its players in order to avoid the burden of a weekly salary.

The process of turning more and more controls over to the independent producer led to the order of today which, with minor exceptions, makes all the major studios not the producers of films, but the financiers of the so-called "independent package."

A "package" consists of one or more of the following elements: the first is generally a story in some form—it may be a produced or unproduced stage play, a published or unpublished novel, a story written for the film medium varying from a few words to hundreds of pages, a biography, a song title, an idea, or even the rights to remake an old film. Package ingredients can also consist of one or more actors, a producer, a director, a screenwriter, a composer, a cameraman or other elements which can emerge in a business of ever-changing fashion and trends.

A current example of the birth of a new kind of package element is the advent of pornography as an important and much-sought-after box-office attraction. Coincidentally the new production code or rating is serving as a means to publicize a film's pornographic character under the guise of protecting the public. It has become quite clear since the introduction of the code that its warning against the low moral standard of a particular motion picture has turned out to provide the blessing of free advertisement to attract the prurient interests of the paying moviegoer.

Before the new production code, a picture either did or did not receive the Seal, expressing the approval by the Code and Rating Administration of the Motion Picture Association of America. This administration, also named the Valenti office after its presiding member, is appointed and salaried by the major distributors, and represents a tribunal of self-censorship, as if self-administered censorship were more desirable. The excuse advanced for this hypocritical posture is that it helps ward off outside censorship; a highly specious argument in the light of the many court decisions declaring that all censorship prior to the release of a film is unconstitutional.

The ... code, under the jurisdiction of the same administration, has created a situation where the classifications G ("All ages admitted. General audiences") and GP ("All ages admitted. Parental guidance suggested") are regarded as box-office poison. The R classification denotes "Restricted. Under seventeen requires accompanying parent or guardian," while an X rating stands for "No one under seventeen admitted" because of sex, violence, crime or profanity. The letters R and X on a theatre marquee and in a newspaper ad are precisely what attract people, given their healthy appetite for hard-core pornography. Thus the new code has become a powerful force on the side of the dirty picture.

The packager or the man behind the package is generally the producer, but very often stars, writers, directors and/or their agents assume the initiative and wheel and deal, each on his own behalf.

Two questions come to mind: why does the distributor not do the packaging himself, and how does the distributor decide which package is to be financed?

As a fair generalization I would suggest that the answer to the first question lies in a disinclination to assume leadership and responsibility; in short, in the hedonistic inertia of people whose major interest in life is to hold on to a steady and comfortable job. There are, of course, special circumstances and reasons, but analysis of these would carry us beyond the framework of this piece.

The answer to the second question may seem deceptively simple. One quick look at the package should tell the story and determine the decision of the distributor: more elements of proven box-office attraction will make the package more promising in terms of its box-office potential. ... For instance, Paul Newman should justify a larger investment than Rock Hudson, and Arthur Penn as the proposed director should fetch more enthusiasm from investors than Richard Fleischer. A best-selling novel like *Marjorie Morningstar* by its own often over-rated strength will create acceptance for its owner-packager over and above a relatively unknown and underrated literary work such as *Goodbye, Columbus.* And then, as a matter of course, two or three good elements should be more bankable than one; conversely, two or more mediocre ingredients may make up for the lack of one outstanding one. The bankable star, the actor who suffices as the only package element, owes his position to his popularity with audiences as a box-office magnet. No distributor will turn down a Steve McQueen picture, although turkeys like *The Thomas Crown Affair* have not fulfilled the promise of the star to sell tickets.

The bankable literary property, like a hit play or a best-selling novel, offers the nervous investor the assurance of box-office appeal with movie audiences because of the fame, direct popularity and wide appeal of the work. But again, the harsh reality of many disappointments like *Death of a Salesman, By Love Possessed,* and *In Cold Blood* proves there is no such thing as a guaranteed transfer of success from one medium to another.

However, most of the difficulties of judging packages arise through factors that just cannot be precisely and objectively determined. The estimated cost of the film is the first item that comes under scrutiny. The same package elements that will make a two-million-dollar film attractive will fail to support a film estimated to run into a negative cost of four million dollars. The distributor will have to be expert at appraising the accuracy of cost estimates not only in the light of the material but also of the individuals involved. There are slow directors and fast directors and they will film the same story at vast differences in cost; there are stars who are notorious for causing delays in production, and there is Frank Sinatra who will not repeat a scene, galloping through his pictures and earning dubious glory as the "one-take actor." Some producers are known as well-organized professionals who bring films in on schedule and within budget while others are muddled, incompetent, or, to be generous, tired.

And then there are the cases when the acceptance of a package by distributors can be a mere formality. These are the deals involving, as package ingredients, moviemakers of unquestionable and unanimously recognized excellence. A select group of producers and directors demand and obtain absolute control beginning with the selection of the subject matter, through the final cut of the film. They make the decisions concerning all phases of production, including casting, hiring of crews, construction of sets, selections of locations. Their announcement that they plan to make a picture brings all the distributors running to bid for the privilege of supplying the necessary and often undetermined amount of financing. These are the men one can borrow money on, the bankable moviemakers. These are the most powerful men in the American movie business. They, more than anyone else, with their almost uncontrolled power and influence, bear the responsibility for the shape of films to come and the future of the motion picture as an art form. They have the means to realize their creative dreams without the need for compromise in order to pacify some banker's objections. They have, or are supposed to have, the magic rapport with world audiences and the ability to execute their visions on film.

Strangely, these men are virtually unknown to the millions of moviegoers. With the exception of Alfred Hitchcock, our most prominent directors and producers do not enjoy the fame and notoriety of their stars, a poor testimonial indeed to the effectiveness of the costly press-agentry subscribed to by so many creative contributors behind the camera. A classic example was the late Jerry Wald, who made his own personal public relations his life's work.

To truly appreciate the fortunate position of the bankable moviemaker, consider the woes that befall the run-of-the-mill producer trying to get his projects financed, produced and released.

Our average Hollywood producer-on-the-make must first find a story and tie it up with an option for a limited time. This in itself imposes an ulcer-making deadline, beyond which he loses not only his option but his entire investment of money and time.

The next step will take him on a search for actors and directors to make the deal more attractive. But people of importance—and these are the ones that our producer-on-the-make is after—are not easily contacted. Their agents have built an almost impenetrable wall around them. Even the attempt to contact the artist directly is punishable by the eternal scorn of the agent. This, by the way, often turns out to be a blessing in disguise: the agent, once he is an openly declared opponent to a project, cannot hurt it as effectively as he normally would under the guise of benevolence and friendship. But whatever approach the producer chooses, he will soon find out that his phone calls are frequently ignored, and the most common reply is simply that the artist is unavailable for several years. If any of his prospects finally agrees to examine his project, our producer will learn the great eternal verity in the motion-picture business: Nobody Reads.

His difficulties are further multiplied and exacerbated by the natural and charming custom of the industry to avoid the truth even when it costs nothing. This creates an emotional climate of paralyzing uncertainty, and with nobody having honesty or guts enough to give our friend a definite "no" he will soon despair of ever tying all the strings around his package.

But some independent producers succeed in wrapping up the package and proceed to the next step: submission to the financier.

Backers come in all shapes and sizes. There are those who watch themselves operate, being mainly interested in making an impression, and those, the hard-nosed, greedy money machines, who have learned certain solid ground rules on which they base any decisions. Those in the first group, which would include a Joe Levine and a Bob Evans, see themselves as the Ziegfelds and the Thalbergs of today. They are more concerned with looking glamorous in making a deal than with creating every chance for a good picture. The second group would include Leo Jaffe and a David Picker who operate strictly by the record.

And with it all, more often than not the least reasonable methods are the ones rewarded by spectacular success. The production of *Lion In Winter*, for instance, came about fortuitously when Peter O'Toole, committed to do the title role in *The Ski Bum*, preferred to play a roistering King of England and Miss Hepburn was available.

We now find our man, package in hand, staring across the vast reaches of a neo-Mexican desk at the Hollywood representative of a national television network.

You thought we were talking about movies. We are. All three of the national television networks have now entered the business of theatrical motion pictures. The reason for their decision to produce yet another wasteland may be a desire to become primary owners of motion pictures for television release in the face of ever-increasing prices quoted by the old-time movie people or else simply the legitimate wish to expand into a related, potentially profitable and more glamorous field not subject to the dictates of Madison Avenue. Anyway, with the old-timers short of cash and long on unreleased product, it seemed like a good idea to tackle one of the well-heeled newcomers.

In the weeks leading to the appointment with the network representative our candidate will have endured many humiliations from a battery of secretaries attempting to make him divulge more of the exact nature of his calls. Would he not like to speak to an underling first, or send over his project for examination and meet afterward if the matter has any merit?

Too wise and experienced to fall for these traps, our man finally has his day with the top man—who, like all top men in the business, has to check with somebody else—and gets his chance to present his project.

Again, a quick "no" would be merciful. But the inflated euphemisms from the man behind the big desk usually culminate in the dramatic imperative "Let me have your script," followed by, "I will read it over the weekend."

Unfortunately, the weekend, with all its demands of society, friends, and family, hardly leaves the network executive enough time to peruse his scripts that are in production and which he must get to know somehow.

Thus the script sooner or later is handed to a *reader*, whose job it is to condense the contents of literary work into so-called synopses.

The reader's report and a synopsis are placed on several desks through-out the distributor's office. Every reader worth his meager salary knows that top executives, as they go up the ladder of success and influence, become less and less able to read more than two paragraphs. The destructive synopsis routine serves only to make the refusal of a package seem more reasonable without ever mentioning the truth, which is simply the low grade of the bankable elements. The key question is the killer: "Who is in it?" If Barbra Streisand had accepted the script, the distributor would have found out about its contents at the invitational World Premiere long after gambling his stockholders' money on it. In a business built largely on hunches and intuition, one looks in vain for a reasonable explanation for the old-fashioned reliance on star names to sell tickets at the box office. This in the face of the overwhelming commercial success of the starless *The Graduate* and such flops as *Doctor Dolittle* with Rex Harrison.

After his first defeat, a producer can take his package to other money sources and perhaps, against all odds, conclude an arrangement for the distribution and production of his project. During the interview with the top executive the deal is concluded with a handshake. However, only the basic points are discussed. An experienced packager knows that this summit meeting with its veneer of urbane sincerity, fair play and goodwill constitutes his last chance to nail down important contractual details in his favor, and, if at all possible, he will obtain a memo committing these vital points to paper as promptly as possible. In the weeks following the summit meeting, the legal department of the distributor and a "negotiator," mainly a former lawyer in charge of contracts, will try to renegotiate—"reneg" as the pros aptly call it—every advantage granted by the distributor. At this later stage the masks of fair play and integrity are dropped and the law of the jungle openly prevails. Our producer's bargaining position has deteriorated after his press agent has rashly wired the announcement of the deal to all the trade papers. The negotiator is aware of this and will push the hapless victim around to the extent that he dares, short of inviting a lawsuit.

Surely, you think, the foregoing must be exaggerated. The fact is that the whole truth is even grimmer.

Why then would anybody in his right mind endure the ordeal of independent production? For the same reasons that men become involved in other areas of American commerce and industry—only more so. Much more so. Here, success can arrive with the speed and the disproportionate impact of a jackpot. Glamour, recognition, V.I.P. treatment by airlines and restaurants, access to beautiful women, power to hire and fire, and all the other goodies offered by the Bitch are constantly waved before the twitching noses of ambitious men. The examples of so many rather undistinguished people who made it big are constantly encouraging the newcomer;

no credentials are necessary, fabulous careers by high-school dropouts are the rule.

However, a certain innate cunning or acquired dexterity is essential. For example, the astute packager will know that his preliminary amenities with, say, Marty Baum of ABC should touch on European cuisine and the better vintages, without of course overreaching his opponent's gastronomic horizons, while with Bob Evans at Paramount, formerly a pants manufacturer, comment on his sartorial splendor will not come amiss. In approaching Lew Wasserman at Universal, chitchat will get him nowhere, but he would do well to dress conservatively lest he be made to squirm under the cool eye of the man who made the slim black suit *de rigueur* for the minions of MCA and Universal.

In addition to a certain adroitness in contending with the moneyman's personal idiosyncrasies, the producer-on-the-make will pick and choose his words when making the pitch. It is sometimes of value to use some high-falutin and essentially fatuous expression from *Cahiers du Cinéma* while taking care not to overtax the buyer's often-restricted vocabulary. It seldom hurts to call a run-of-the-mill Western "mythic," or to say a humdrum project combines dramatic ideas that will ensure a wide-viewer commercial success.

We might add that the packager, operated by his press agent's strings, will have tried to bolster his social position and glamour by creating the impression of having the right contacts. It helps to drive up to the Bistro in a Rolls-Royce or leave The Factory at three A.M. supporting Lee Marvin. The gossip columns of the trade papers and the Los Angeles *Times* bloom with planted names of party givers and guests. Parties have their own built-in values. If you get ten points for an invitation to a Ross Hunter or a Ray Stark dinner, then it is certainly worth fifteen to have been asked to Duke Ellington's birthday party at the White House and at least fifty to have been seen hightailing up Benedict Canyon on the rear of Steve McQueen's motorcycle.

The chances of becoming one of the elite, one of the bankable moviemakers, are naturally even more remote than those of becoming an independent producer. In almost all cases one must have the talent and the skill of a director rather than only a producer.

In recent times only one producer has made it in this category without being a director. His name is Sam Spiegel, sometimes also known as S. P. Eagle. Spiegel is easily the most fascinating international film personality to come upon the scene of the American film business, although at this writing his career has hit another low in a series of many violent ups and downs. His production credits include *Tales Of Manhattan, On The Waterfront, The African Queen, Suddenly, Last Summer, The Bridge On The River Kwai,* and *Lawrence of Arabia.* He was also responsible for such beauties as *Melba, The Chase, The Happening,* and *The Swimmer.* An analysis of Spiegel's good and bad fortunes yields a valuable insight into what can make the same man a good or bad producer.

Spiegel's successes were the result of his skill or, as Hollywood publicists would call it, genius, as an operator, catalyst, matchmaker, impresario, promoter, talent scout, untiring salesman and astute negotiator. He is the Sol Hurok of the film business and should have stuck to that rather than assuming the role of Arturo Toscanini. He is a master in dealing with sensitive and difficult creators like John Huston, Elia Kazan, Joe Mankiewicz and David Lean. His persuasive tongue was instrumental in snaring stars such as Humphrey Bogart, Katharine Hepburn, Marlon Brando, Elizabeth Taylor, William Holden and Alec Guinness. He gave Omar Sharif his first chance and Peter O'Toole his role in *Lawrence of Arabia.* He even proved his astuteness as a matchmaker when the new United Artists was born. His incredible dexterity in handling people deserves credit in overcoming the resistance of such formidable and difficult characters as Charlie Chaplin and Mary Pickford, the former controlling owners of the company, thereby enabling Arthur Krim and his group to take over.

But success is not conducive to insight. When Spiegel looked back on an unbroken list of blockbusters, he mistook his skill and knowledge for artistic creativity. He thought he could do it all by himself. He believed the stooges, the yes-men, the publicity hounds who told him that he deserved all the credit for those great films.

An unpublicized but true episode illustrating Spiegel's fallibility occurred at a luncheon meeting at which he tried to interest a slightly awed but infernally bright young fellow named Mike Nichols in directing one of his ill-fated brainchildren entitled *The Happening,* while Nichols tried to interest Spiegel—with no success—in financing a little number called *The Graduate.* The Spiegel of old, the man who took Kazan's and Schulberg's word for *On The Waterfront,* would have been wise enough to trust Mike Nichols' artistic judgment, thereby adding fifty million dollars to his and his partners' fortunes.

Well, the result of Spiegel's over-stepping the limited functions of a producer were dismal and this is the lesson to be learned: In the harsh and unforgiving world of the cinema, where yesterday's success is dubious currency in tomorrow's market, the producer overrates his abilities at his peril.

Paradoxically, yesterday's success is responsible for the retention of several names in today's list of bankable moviemakers. Rightly or wrongly, banks and their alter egos, the distributors, hold on to their idols for years after the curve of their successes has turned downward. Billy Wilder, Alfred Hitchcock and Robert Wise can still write their own tickets, although their output in recent years generally met with disapproval by both critics and audiences.

The ever-growing desire to see movies, and especially good and exciting ones, has become a vital force, moving millions of customers—particularly the young—in all walks of life, toward the box offices of the world. In millions of homes the small television screen, first feared as a deadly competitor, has become a servant of the motion-picture industry and is offering still more entertainment on film.

Movies are the dramatic art form of our age. It is unfortunate that their creation is so often in the wrong hands. For a good film is stimulating and fulfilling; a bad one is socially damaging. As in Architecture—another area where Art and Industry meet to create Beauty—the classic simplicity of Frank Lloyd Wright's reaction to a bad building occupying a good piece of land is painfully appropriate whenever a good story such as *The Brothers Karamazov* or *The Sun Also Rises* is manhandled by a team of shoddy entrepreneurs: "Another opportunity missed."

---

to the student: a commentary

Ingo Preminger has had a long involvement with the motion-picture industry and was the producer of the highly successful movie *M*A*S*H*. The article is a personal view of the process of producing a movie, and Preminger has no hesitation in giving his opinions about either the system or individuals involved. The obstacles that face an average producer—one who does not belong to that select circle of bankable moviemakers—are explained by Preminger as he takes the reader step by step through the agonizing process of financing a movie.

These economic complaints are not particularly new. More than a quarter of a century ago, David Selznick, in a conversation with writer Ben Hecht, berated the result of mixing money and art: "There might have been good movies if there had been no movie industry. Hollywood might have become the center of a new human expression if it hadn't been grabbed by a little group of bookkeepers and turned into a junk industry."

Hecht, who wrote some sixty movies—more than half of them in two weeks or less—also faulted the economic decision-makers of the industry. "The persistent banality of the movies," he wrote, "is due to the 'vision' of their manufacturers. I do not mean by manufacturers, writers or directors. These harassed toilers are no more than the lowest of *Unteroffizieren* in movieland. The orders come from the tents of a dozen invisible generals. The 'vision' is theirs. They keep a visionary eye glued to the fact that the lower in class an entertainment product is, the more people will buy it."

Hecht was speaking of those he called "The Owners," the heads of individual studios that had strong control over every phase of movie production. In an age of "independent packages" such men have passed into the same land as silent films. But when they were in control, what were the major studios like?

MGM (Metro-Goldwyn-Mayer) was founded in 1924 by a merger of Metro Pictures, the Goldwyn Company, and Louis B. Mayer Pictures. During the thirties, MGM became the symbol of what was considered glamorous and opulent in motion pictures. Chase National Bank backed MGM and gave it the power to buy some of the largest talent available. MGM bragged of "More Stars Than There Are in Heaven," which wasn't that much of an overstatement. Under contract to MGM at one time were such stars as Greta Garbo, Clark Gable, Jean Harlow, Joan Crawford, Spencer Tracy, Nelson Eddy, and Jeanette MacDonald, and later, Mickey Rooney and Judy Garland.

Throughout its prestige years, MGM was ruled by Louis B. Mayer, who has been referred to as being "universally detested." The studio style he developed was mainly a form of glamorous escapism: romantic melodramas, ornate musicals, adaptations of prestige or period novels—which were all translated into terms of opulence and optimism. The two best-known examples of the Mayer studio style are *The Wizard of Oz* and *Gone With the Wind*.

Paramount Studios began in 1912 when Adolph Zukor, who ruled the company for more than forty years, formed the "Famous-Player's Company." Unlike MGM, the Paramount productions reflected not so much the owner but the character of the star directors. Cecil B. DeMille cranked out his flamboyant spectacles, such as *The Sign of the Cross* and *Cleopatra*. Josef von Sternberg created visually elaborate films, often starring his "discovery," Marlene Dietrich. Paramount developed a sophisticated, continental style, mainly due to Rouben Mamoulian and Ernst Lubitsch, who had charge of production.

Paramount's strong point was light comedy, ranging in style from the sophistication of Lubitsch to the slapstick antics of the Marx brothers and the stuffy humor of W. C. Fields and Mae West. Other Paramount stars included George Raft, Ray Milland, Fredric March, Claudette Colbert, Cary Grant, Bing Crosby, and Carole Lombard.

Fox Studios merged with 20th Century in 1935. The most important assets of the new company were director John Ford and the child star whose head sported exactly fifty-five curls—Shirley Temple. Apart from Ford's westerns and the saccharine films of Shirley Temple, 20th Century Fox exhibited a strong preference for musical revues. Its list of stars included Will Rogers, John Wayne, Alice Faye, and Spencer Tracy.

The last major studio was Warner Brothers, which had a notorious reputation for strict discipline. The studio claimed it worked on the principle of maximum economy of production consistent with quality. Warner Brothers was best known for its fast-moving gangster films, often starring James Cagney, and the elaborate musical extravaganzas directed and choreographed by Busby Berkeley. The studio also risked social subjects such as the agricultural depression (*Cabin in the Cotton*) and lynching (*They Won't Forget*). *Merrie Melodies* and Looney Tunes, which starred Bugs Bunny and Porky Pig, came from this studio too. Its stable of human stars included Paul Muni, Edward G. Robinson, James Cagney, Humphrey Bogart, Joan Blondell, Dick Powell, Ruby Keeler, and Bette Davis.

The era of the big studio, with its star system, The Owner, and production line scheduling cracked under the weight of financial problems, splintering into "independent packages." There are still problems of economics and quality, as Preminger points out, and they will probably remain as long as there are movies.

LLS

---

study questions

1. Does the rating system work as an effective method of controlling the type, quality, and impact of films? Why?

2. What is the purpose of movie codes and rating guides?

3. Do you think that anything more than lip-service is being paid to the motion picture code and rating system by the industry? Are they honestly applied, fairly enforced, and conscientiously followed?

4. Do you think there is a large untapped market for good quality family films? Or is this another "silent majority" fairy tale?

5. The concept of self-censorship and self-regulation in the film industry is based on the belief that the industry has a moral obligation to control its impact and influence on the public (especially on children and adolescents). Is this moral obligation valid? Why? Is it being met in a responsible and sincere manner?

6. What kinds of restrictions does the new economics of "package deals" and independent production have on the type and the quality of films being produced? Does it provide a greater potential for artistic quality, or does it worsen the existing problem of marketplace ethics?

7. The distributor's major criterion for accepting an independent package is, "Will it sell?" Is there much hope that any changes in the quality and nature of films will be forthcoming? Why?

ad-
ver-
7 tising

Advertising may seem a dreary subject to many readers. You may agree reluctantly with Frederick Gamble, the former president of the American Advertising Agencies, who said, "Advertising is the great accelerating force in distribution. Reaching many people rapidly at low cost, advertising speeds up sales, turns prospects into customers in large numbers and at high speed. Hence, in a mass-production and high-consumption economy, advertising has the greatest opportunity and the greatest responsibility for finding customers."

You may not be interested that 400,000 workers are hard at work selling through advertising, but you must think beyond advertising itself. Read about the effects of advertising on language. Think seriously about the personal article entitled "The American Obsession with Fun." Finally, try to decide whether the Advertising Council is selling lies or is merely trying to influence you.

If you want to become an advertising worker, you should be armed with all these articles when you are discussing jobs. But even if you are not interested in advertising, you cannot say, "This doesn't concern me." Unless you are planning to become a modern hermit, living alone on berries and fish, advertising influences you.

advertising

social force

James W. Tankard, Jr.

The Effects of Advertising on Language: Making the Sacred Profane

"Our Lord Jesus would look droll seated in a Cadillac, would he not?"—
Henry Miller, *To Paint is to Love Again*

A recent television commercial showed a group of blacks dancing in the background while someone sang: "Write on, brothers, write on!" The product being advertised was Write Brothers Pens, by Papermate.

The commercial illustrates a drastic change in the meaning of the phrase "Right On!" The expression first appeared six or seven years ago and was spoken most frequently by blacks, usually Black Panthers. At that time, Panthers were marching into the California Legislature carrying rifles and were engaging in fatal shootouts with the Oakland police. "Right On!" was not a phrase that a white person would have used lightly. Now, "Right On!" is used to sell ball point pens, and beer ("Schlitz Malt Liquor brewed to meet a man head on—Right On!"). And the Los Angeles Police Department is using the phrase on billboards in a recruiting drive in black districts.

The exploitation of sacred words and symbols for the purpose of selling things has become routine in American culture. Often these exploited words and symbols have referred to the most basic and significant experiences of life. As Hayakawa pointed out, "One reason for the obscurity of modern poets may again be that the familiar symbols of courtship, home, mother, nature, and love of country have been so completely appropriated for commercial purposes as to appear unusable to the unsponsored poet." The intent of advertising, according to Hayakawa, is to *poeticize* or glamorize the object for sale by investing it with desirable affective connotations suggestive of health, wealth, popularity with the other sex, social prominence, domestic bliss, fashion, and elegance.

Reprinted by permission of James W. Tankard, Jr., from *Journal of Popular Culture,* Fall 1975.

327

Recently, advertisers have found the counter culture a rich source of symbols and slogans to borrow and associate with their products. These advertisements and commercials are filled with the catchwords and imagery of flower power, the love generation, peace, revolution, drug hipness, ecology, interpersonal honesty, and self-awareness. The co-optation of these themes often is based on the familiar advertising techniques of investing brand names with desirable connotations, playing on words, and making slogans out of commonplace facts.

The use of the phrase "Right On!" in ball point pen commercials, for instance, makes a play on words at the same time that it associates the pen with revolutionary hipness. The "Bank Ins" for new students held in 1969 by banks in Chapel Hill, North Carolina, involved a similar kind of play on the counter culture's Love Ins and Be Ins (which were in turn based on the civil rights Sit Ins). Another play on the word *love* showed up in Zales Jewelry's "We're nothing without your love" buttons (imprinted with a flower and a two-finger peace sign) worn by salesmen in 1969.

The state of Virginia invested its name with popular connotations and at the same time made a slogan out of a commonplace fact with its "Virginia is for lovers."

The *love* theme has been for a long time a popular one for advertisers and other exploiters. Erich Fromm pointed out on a telecast of CBS Reports dealing with "You and the Commerical" that fear of not being loved is prevalent in many commercials. Fromm stated that a hidden theme in many advertisements is "here are the things which will make you loved." Since the Love Ins of 1967–68, the references to love have become less hidden. The U.S. Post Office released a Love postage stamp in 1973, and the U.S. Army began putting up recruiting billboards with the message, "A country needs love too."

Blatant association of *love* with a product has shown up in a number of other advertisements, as the following examples indicate:

"Canada Dry tastes like love."

"Dr. Pepper. You've got to try it to love it."

"Hello. I'm Catherine Deneuve. When somebody loves me, I'm always surprised. But I don't want to be told. I prefer gestures. Like—Chanel No. 5."

Olympic Gold Medal winner Mark Spitz: "You know what's a great feeling? Giving someone you love a gift. The Schick Flexamatic is a great gift."

A prince in an animated cartoon: "Here's a present for you." Girl in cartoon: "What is it?" Prince: "Eau d'Love." (By Love Cosmetics)

A beautiful woman in a trench coat stands alone in the fog on a waterfront. She says, "I like men. Even when they're unkind to me. But men are men. They need love. They need understanding. And they need English Leather."

A good-looking man says, "I know what girls need. They need love. And love's a little color." A girl appears, and the man starts applying make-up to her face. The announcer says, "Love's A Little Color isn't makeup. It's only a little color."

"Love is being a nurse. Learn all about professional nursing by writing. . . ."

Advertisers have seized upon a number of major counterculture themes besides *love,* as the following examples show:

Peace. Orange Crush is described in advertisements as "the peaceful drink."

A 1970 television commercial began with a scene of a girl combing her hair. The off-screen announcer said, "The great American Tug of War goes on." A peace symbol (the nuclear disarmament pin) was superimposed over the girl. The announcer said, "Peace comes to the great American Tug of War, with Alberto VO5 Shampoo." The final shot showed the girl giving the V-for-Peace sign.

Drugs. A radio commercial during the Newport Jazz festival in July of 1971 implored listeners to "Take a trip with Bali Hai. Go downtown right after lunch. Get the wine with the tropical punch."

Ads in *Life* magazine for Johnson's Baby Oil featured fetching pictures of Ali McGraw and captions reading, "Turn on a tan with Johnson's."

A Seven-Up commercial on the radio was clearly aimed at "heads." It began with the statement, "And now, another turn on, from the Uncola." There were about 20 seconds of the sounds of bubbles fizzling. Then the announcer came back and said, "Another turn on, compliments of the trend, the Uncola."

Some cigarette commercials, before they were banned from television, were showing hints of an appeal to marijuana smokers. A Newport commercial, for instance, showed a man operating a jackhammer and singing, "I know it can't be true, but this jackhammer seems smoother too." (Translation: Newport gets you high.)

Magazine ads appeared for a while for a new cigarette called New Leaf with Wintergreen. The cigarette packages bore a picture of green leaves that looked suspiciously like marijuana, and the ads proclaimed, "It gives you a Tingle."

Ecology. The oil companies were some of the first to exploit the ecology theme, with Amoco's "What can one man do, my friend, what can one man do?" one of the more pervasive examples.

Crest toothpaste also incorporated the ecology theme into a television commercial during the 1971 Miss U.S.A. pageant. The spot opened with a beautiful outdoor scene, and then an announcer said, "You can plant another tree for us, but you can't replace your permanent teeth. Conserve your natural resources." The implication was that by buying Crest one would be doing something to help preserve the world's ecology.

Natural foods. A television commercial for Grape Nuts features Euell Gibbons, the author of *Stalking the Wild Asparagus*. "Hi, I'm Euell Gibbons," he says. "I've spent years learning about natural foods. Ever eat a pine tree? Many parts are edible. . . . Natural ingredients are important to me. That's why I make Grape Nuts part of my breakfast. . . . I call Grape Nuts my Back-to-Nature cereal."

Interpersonal honesty. Authenticity was a virtue valued quite highly in the counter culture in the late 1960s.

Advertisements soon reflected the trend: "It's the real thing—Coke is. . . ."

A radio spot for a hip clothing store in Austin, Texas, made this direct appeal to listeners: "Do you ever find yourself evaluating people by the way they look? If you're doing it to them, you can bet they're doing it to you. It's a shame it has to be that way, but as long as it is, you might as well do it right. . . ."

Self-knowledge. The importance of knowing yourself was another theme stressed in the counter culture, with drugs and mysticism two possible paths to self-understanding.

One advertisement suggested that a certain small cigar might be another route to the same goal: "Tijuana Smalls—you know who you are."

Women's Lib. An ad in *Life* magazine was topped with the caption "Liberation" and showed a picture of a beautiful woman with a flamboyant scarf around her head sitting at a typewriter. The copy began: "Slipstick is a revolutionary instrument you use like a pen to correct typing errors."

And Virginia Slims, of course, made Women's Lib the basis of its "You've come a long way, baby" campaign.

The influence of the counter culture also led to some right wing anti-flower-power themes appearing in other commercials. At a time when the Love Generation was stressing hitchhiking as a means of transportation, for instance, a television commercial by Union Carbide suggested, "Never pick up a stranger, pick up Prestone Antifreeze."

And Kimberly Clark reacted to the criticisms of the American establishment by producing Kleenex Americana tissues, with patriotic themes on the boxes.

The co-optation of counterculture themes by advertisers became so offensive several years ago that some underground newspapers started refusing to run certain ads. Ronald Lichty of Underground Press Syndicate reported:

Advertising in the underground press has always *implicitly* ripped off youth culture and still does, but several years ago a number of advertisers, including Columbia Records, became disgustingly explicit in their exploitation. One of Columbia's ads at that time stated, "The pigs can't bust our music." While UPS did not issue a statement on advertising, these ads did raise considerable discussion among underground papers and a number of them refused to continue running the ads. Advertisers got the message and designed their ads to be less blatant.

Paradoxically, representatives of the counter culture do at times themselves participate in the rip-off of the underground. Paul Krassner, editor of *The Realist,* reported in his publication that he was persuaded by the J. Walter Thompson agency to interview a "spacey chick" for a Seven-Up radio commercial. Krassner did it, he explained, "because I was so desperately in debt." Krassner pointed out that he was joining the company of Cass Elliott, Johnny Winter, and Wavy Gravy, who did commercials for Tijuana Smalls; Sammy Davis, Jr., and Ray ("Take Care of Business, Mr. Businessman") Stevens, who did spots for the U.S. Air Force; and Muhammad Ali, who did a commercial for Brut after-shave lotion.

Underground radio stations also join in to the extent that they accept commercials deliberately designed to be indistinguishable from the rock music the station customarily plays. These commercials often seem to be aimed at the desire for escape through drugs. For instance, recent commercial ditties featured these lyrics: "Drink a little Ripple and you start to liking people real fine," and "The New Riders of the Purple Sage help you forget what a downright unfriendly world it is."

Underlying many of these exploitive commercial messages is a basic cynicism about human nature. Sometimes this cynicism shows through with amazing clarity. For instance, the following radio message implored listeners to put pressure on restaurants to install Seven-Up taps. It sounded like it was aimed at a bunch of gangsters, but it was aimed at members of the counter culture:

Undergrounders! Did you know that some restaurants still don't have the Uncola on tap? That's right, it's a tap gap. The next time you go to such a restaurant, tell them that the Uncola is prettier than Colas. And tell them that a restaurant with customers is prettier than one without any. They'll get the message, undergrounders.

What are the effects of the kind of co-optation of language that has been described, on society and on language itself?

Hayakawa suggested that advertising is one of the major forces in our culture contributing to *intensional orientation,* or "the habit of guiding ourselves by words alone, rather than by the facts to which words should guide us." Advertising, according to Hayakawa:

... can either increase or decrease the degree of sanity with which people respond to words. Thus, if advertising is informative, witty, educational, and imaginative, it can perform its necessary commercial function and contribute to our pleasure in life without making us slaves to the tyranny of affective words. If, however, products are sold largely by manipulating affective connotations ... the influence of advertising is to deepen the already grave intensional orientation widely prevalent in the public. The schizophrenic is one who attributes a greater reality to words, fantasies, daydreams and "private worlds" than to the actualities around him.

A comment made on the CBS documentary "You and the Commercial" by Ted Bates of Bates Advertising Agency showed that Hayakawa's diagnosis of the intent of advertising is largely correct. Bates said, "We don't buy the product. We buy the satisfaction the product will bring us. And that's what the commercial should portray."

Another effect of the co-optation by advertising of valued symbols and slogans is a debasement of language itself. What happens to the meaning of a word with very special significance, such as *love,* when it is put into the context of selling something? Certainly it can only be to cheapen the word, and to increase distrust between people, because the most sacred words we have are being used to get something from us.

Ezra Pound cautioned, "If a nation's literature declines, the nation atrophies and decays." Pound defined literature as "language charged with meaning." The use of significant words by advertising appears to bring about an opposite state—language decimated of meaning.

This use of language appears to be what Eduard Goldstucker, Visiting Fellow at the Center for the Study of Democratic Institutions, was referring to in his article "Is There Any Future for Art?" when he wrote:

The sacral and magic patina has been almost worn off the coin of words by their too frequent, too often deceitful, use. It has become more and more difficult to bring an audience to that temporary suspension of disbelief which is the fundamental condition of all storytelling and, indeed, of all mythmaking. Audiences have been disappointed and disillusioned too often; they are now profoundly skeptical.

What, if anything, can be done to reduce the harmful effects of advertising on language? Several authors have suggested that the misuse of language, to which advertising is a major contributor, be viewed as language pollution. According to Postman:

A healthy semantic environment is one in which language effectively serves the purposes of the particular context in which it is used. "Effectively" means here that language is useful in helping people understand what their purposes are, what functions their activity serves, and what needs they are trying to satisfy. The semantic environment is polluted when language obscures from people what they are doing and why they are doing it.

Postman suggests, perhaps not entirely facetiously, that TV newscasts should end each night with an estimate of the day's language-pollution index.

Not all advertising serves to pollute the semantic environment. Some advertising meets Hayakawa's goals of being informative, witty, educational, and imaginative. Volkswagen ads have been recognized for some time for their honest, low-key presentation of product information. Polaroid advertised its new SX-70 camera with a 13-page layout in *Newsweek* that told how the new invention worked and showed examples of the kinds of color photographs it produces. The makers of Health-Tex Stantogs, clothes for children, have presented television commercials and magazine ads for children that "try to answer tough questions," such as why do people have different skin colors.

Perhaps as the public becomes more aware of the negative effects of symbol-manipulating advertising and voices that criticism, advertisers will respond with more advertisements that aren't, in Fromm's words, a "peculiar mix of fantasy and reality."

In the meantime, the audience can only reply to much advertising with the wise counsel of Schlitz Malt Liquor: "The bull on the label tells the whole story."

---

to the student : a commentary

James Tankard, professor of journalism at the University of Texas, focuses sharply on how advertising affects language. When we think about the way language is corrupted, as Tankard has stated it so clearly, we are at the beginning of a vast territory. Language has been cheapened resoundingly by the way we use it. Consider the difference between the following two items: Lincoln's Gettysburg Address and a parody by White House correspondents on President Dwight Eisenhower's speaking style.

Fourscore and seven years ago our fathers brought forth on this continent a new nation, conceived in liberty, and dedicated to the proposition that all men are created equal.

Now we are engaged in a great civil war, testing whether that nation, or any nation so conceived and so dedicated, can long endure. We are met on a great battlefield of that war. We have come to dedicate a portion of that battlefield as a final resting place for those who here gave their lives that that nation might live. It is altogether fitting and proper that we should do this.

But in a larger sense, we cannot dedicate —we cannot consecrate—we cannot hallow—this ground. The brave men, living and dead, who struggled here, have consecrated it far above our poor power to add or detract. The world will little note nor long remember what we say here, but it can never forget what they did here. It is for us, the living, rather, to be dedicated here to the unfinished work which they who fought here have thus far so nobly advanced. It is rather for us to be here dedicated to the great task remaining before us—that from these honored dead we take increased devotion to that cause for which they gave the last full measure of devotion; that we here highly resolve that these dead shall not have died in vain; that this nation, under God, shall have a new birth of freedom; and that government of the people, by the people, for the people, shall not perish from the earth.

I haven't checked these figures but 87 years ago, I think it was, a number of individuals organized a governmental set-up here in this country, I believe it covered certain Eastern areas, with this idea they were following up based on a sort of national independence arrangement and the program that every individual is just as good as every other individual. Well, now, of course we are dealing with this big difference of opinion, you might also call it a civil disturbance, although I don't like to appear to take sides or name any individuals, and the point is naturally to check up, by actual experience in the field, to see whether any governmental set-up with a basis like the one I was mentioning has any validity and find out whether that dedication by those early individuals will pay off in lasting values and things of that kind.

Well, here we are, at the scene where one of those disturbances between different sides got going. We want to pay our tribute to those loved ones, those departed individuals who made the supreme sacrifice here, on the basis of their opinions about how this thing ought to be handled. And I would say this. It is absolutely in order to do this.

But if you look at the overall picture of this, we can't pay any tribute—we can't sanctify this area, you might say—we can't hallow according to whatever individual creeds or faiths or sort of religious outlooks are involved about this very particular area. It was those individuals themselves, including the enlisted men, who have given this religious character to the area. The way I see it, the rest of the world will not remember any statements issued here but it will never forget how these men put their shoulders to the wheel and carried out this idea.

Now, frankly, our job, the living individual's job here, is to pick up the burden they made these big efforts here for. It is our job to get on with the assignment—and from these deceased fine individuals to take extra inspiration for the same theories for which they made such a big contribution. We have to make up our minds right here and now, as I see it, that they didn't put out all that blood, perspiration, and—well—that they didn't just make a dry run here, and that all of us here, under God, that is, the God of our choice, shall beef up this idea about freedom and liberty and those kind of arrangements, and that government of all individuals, by all individuals and for the individuals shall not pass out of the world picture.

Is the parody laughable? Is it obvious that the parody is about twice the length of the original? These and other differences between the two speeches illustrate many of the ways in which our language has disintegrated since Lincoln spoke a little more than a hundred years ago. Note especially the way the specifics in Lincoln's Gettysburg Address give way to nebulous phrases, as the phrase "a great civil war" becomes "this big difference of opinion, civil disturbance you might say." When language becomes bloated, we are losing.

As we go deeper into language, consider what others say about the slow disintegration of language into noncommunication. Ludwig Wittgenstein, a great German philosopher, began his lifetime work by asking whether there is any relationship between the words we use and the fact that occurs. He asks us whether the reality is an infinite retreat from words that speak only of other words, never coming to grips with the facts. Gradually, the more he studied and wrote, the more optimistic Wittgenstein became. Still, he held that our words *inherently* have the power to describe much of the world. But what happens if we allow our language to become looser and less precise, with less a relationship to what happens and how we attempt to describe it?

There are, of course, many others who inquire into this relationship, especially George Steiner, who has written *Language and Silence,* a thoughtful and stimulating book. But you must at least hold fast to James Tankard's valuable thought. And you must also think of the comparison of Abraham Lincoln and Dwight Eisenhower. Is that what's happening to the language?

WLR

Ann Nietzke

The American Obsession with Fun

In John Barth's *The End of the Road,* Jacob Horner describes a dream he once had in which, after several futile attempts to find out the weather forecast, he learns from the chief meteorologist that there simply will not be any weather the next day. He tells us about the dream in order to explain a particular state of mind that he often experiences, a state he has come to call "weatherless." Though analogies between moods and weather are commonplace, Horner questions their appropriateness in his case because a day without weather is almost impossible to imagine, and yet he frequently has days without any mood at all. At such times Horner is without a personality, is nonexistent in his own mind, except in the purely physical sense. He compares himself to those microscopic specimens that must be dyed before they can be seen: Horner needs to be colored by some mood or other in order to recognize himself. On his weatherless days he sits blankly in his rocking chair, rocking sometimes for hours until some external event colors him back into being.

Throughout the book Horner suffers from varying degrees of weatherlessness, the most extreme being a trance-like state of complete immobility. His standard device for warding off emptiness of mind is to repeat over and over an advertising jingle from the 1950s: "Pepsi-Cola hits the spot./ Twelve full ounces—that's a lot." This jingle serves as the test pattern of his consciousness: As long as he can say it, he knows he still exists. Once, when the jingle failed him, he sat frozen on a bench in Penn Station all night long. By the end of the book the jingle has lost its effectiveness because Horner cannot even remember to say it at the right times. In the final scene he sits in his rocking chair, totally weatherless. When he gets in a cab and says, "Terminal," we know he will take the bus to the nameless "Doctor," recognizing himself to be a spiritual terminal case.

I have a friend, a teacher at a junior college in a large midwestern city, who sometimes suffers similar periods of weatherlessness. Her attacks are less severe and less pervasive than Jacob Horner's; I think they are, in part, just a defense against being overwhelmed by modern urban living. When

Reprinted by permission of Ann Nietzke from *Saturday Review,* 26 August 1972.

things become a bit too much, she simply tunes out temporarily while her strength, the strength necessary for living a feeling life, gets replenished. Nevertheless, finding yourself in the company of someone who is in no mood at all, whatever the reasons behind it, is an unsettling experience. You just plain don't know how to act, since nothing you say or do seems to matter. There is nothing to interact with, no mood, emotion, or viewpoint to oppose or complement. You can't cheer your friend up, because she's not sad; you can't convince her of anything, because she's all too agreeable; and you can't make her feel better, because she doesn't feel bad. A few years ago, when I was visiting my friend during one of her weatherless bouts, I became exasperated and then saddened by my own helplessness in the situation. But as the weekend wore on, my sadness, interestingly enough, dissolved itself into moodlessness, too, so that finally the two of us sat there staring vacantly into space and feeling quite at home with each other. The only thing to do on such a weatherless Saturday night, of course, was to look at television.

At that time Pepsi had just begun a new series of commercials, which must have proved very successful since it is still being used almost three years later. The main theme, familiar to everyone by now, is in the refrain: "You've got a lot to live,/And Pepsi's got a lot to give." That night, after hearing those words, my friend turned to me with the first spark of life I had seen in her eyes all weekend. "Don't you just *love* that?" she said. And I had to admit that I did. The tune and the words together conveyed a spirit of vivacity and affirmation that was somehow irresistibly appealing. The rest of the evening and all the next day we couldn't get the song out of our minds. We sang it aloud, together or solo, and, like Jacob Horner, we found ourselves intoning it under our breath, tapping a foot or waving a hand breezily through the air to mark the time. The thing had gotten through to us and in some mysterious way filled the emotional vacuum we were in.

Well, the coincidental relationship among my friends and me and Jacob Horner and weatherlessness and Pepsi-Cola ads all came together in an intriguing way when I recently reread Barth's *The End of the Road*. I began to listen carefully to Pepsi ads and then to Coke ads, and, as is usually the case when advertising is analyzed, I learned much less about the products than about the public for which the ads are designed. As almost any American can tell you, "Pepsi helps you come alive" and "Coke is the real thing." These slogans seem simple enough, but a close look at what they imply leads us into some sociopsychological considerations that are not simple.

When I was trying to help my friend that weekend, I didn't yet understand that moodlessness is a kind of death, that "aliveness" of some sort might be just the thing required to dispel it. Of course, even if I had realized this, I don't know specifically what I might have done for her, but I think it helps explain our response to the Pepsi commercial. In its various ads on radio and TV, Pepsi uses two main stanzas, always followed by the refrain, "You've got a lot to live,/And Pepsi's got a lot to give."

It's the Pepsi generation
Comin' at ya, goin' strong.
Put yourself behind a Pepsi—
If you're livin', you belong.

There's a whole new way of livin'—
Pepsi helps supply the drive.
It's got a lot to give for those who like to live,
'Cause it helps 'em come alive.

On television the music accompanies scenes of people having good times. Not all the people look young, but we're made to realize that they all are "young in heart," that they are "living" and so are members of the Pepsi generation. On radio rock-'n'-roll stations various well-known recording stars sing the lyrics. I was particularly struck by the idea of deadness that underlies "coming alive" when I heard Johnny Cash sing about it in his most spiritless style.

The relationship depicted in the ads between being "alive" and having fun is psychologically a sound one, and it is in the sexual experience, of course, that the two are most closely related. Alexander Lowen, a medical doctor who has written a book on the subject of pleasure, believes that "the foundation for a joyful life is the pleasure we feel in our bodies, and that, without this bodily pleasure of aliveness, living becomes the grim necessity of survival." Every imaginable kind of product is advertised as holding the key to fun, good times, and sexual fulfillment. But, as Dr. Lowen points out, the American obsession with fun probably betrays a lack of true pleasure in our lives. Similarly, one reason the advertising business relies so heavily on sexual appeals is not that America has become sexually liberated, but rather that many people are so out of touch with their own bodies that they derive little pleasure from them and will therefore seek the missing pleasure through the use of products which, in one way or another, promise to replace it.

Lowen suggests that the common element in all neurotic-behavior patterns is a diminution in the sense of self, which includes "a loss of the feeling of identity, a reduced awareness of one's individuality, a decrease in self-expression, and a diminished capacity for pleasure." Certainly Jake Horner and my friend exhibited all of these symptoms in their states of weatherlessness, though they were chronic for him and temporary for her.

What is frightening to contemplate is that anyone who spends as much time watching television as the average American does must, almost by definition, exhibit these symptoms to some degree. For, if he were fully aware of himself as an individual, he would not constantly want to be treated as part of an audience. If he felt the need for self-expression, he would want to put himself in a situation that would give him a chance to fulfill it. And if he had a real capacity for pleasure, he would engage in pleasurable activities himself, not watch others so engaged on television. This is not to say, of course, that TV causes neuroses, but only that the neurotic as described by Lowen would naturally be drawn to watching it. And advertisers, to be sure, take full advantage of this fact.

My friend and I knew instinctively to turn on the television that weatherless Saturday night, although neither of us is an avid viewer. I would venture to guess that the difference between us and many full-time TV addicts is that we were quite conscious of our moodlessness because, for us, it is a sometime thing. Those who lack the strength to live lives of feeling, and in whom the sense of self is always ill-defined, are no doubt much less conscious of that state, although they may vaguely sense that something is missing from their lives. The price they pay for avoiding the pain of being fully alive is that they are excluded from the pleasure of it as well. They are, therefore, always tempted by any promise of pleasure, hoping that perhaps this time it will not elude them.

I understood the most sinister aspect of the phenomenon Vance Packard termed "hidden persuasion" when I began to consider what it might mean to be weatherless most of the time and not even realize it. There is nothing obviously "hidden" about what the Pepsi ad is saying; in fact, upon close examination it is hard to believe how straightforward the words are. But the psychological success of the commercial depends upon a lack of self-awareness in the viewer. For while it gives the impression of appealing to the "living" and those with a "zest for life," the ad is actually aimed at the "dead" who experience so little pleasure that they need something to help them "come alive." Thus, on the conscious level the ad provides support for the viewer's illusion that he is "alive" and capable of enjoying things and himself, while at the same time, on a deeper level, it is touching that vague sense of deadness that so many people experience. Even if the "dead" viewer were to take part in all the fun-filled activities shown in the ads, he still would not be capable of having any real fun. That is too terrible a thing for him to face consciously; it is easier to accept the notion, however irrational, that Pepsi might make a difference ("Put yourself behind a Pepsi—/If you're livin', you belong"). The point is that the persuasion depends, not on something hidden in the commercial, but on something the viewer has hidden from himself.

The neurotic, with his diminished sense of self-identity, has no way of really knowing when he is fooling himself. Because he feels that at the center of his being there is only emptiness rather than an integrated personality, he lives with a permanent sense of unreality. It is this realization that brings many neurotics to the analyst's couch, and, of course, the realization itself is a step in the right direction. For most, however, the realization probably never crystallizes; they go on existing with their weatherlessness and a vague awareness that their lives are unfulfilled.

At its deepest level the Coca-Cola pitch for "the real thing" appeals to this neurotic sense of unreality:

It's the real thing, Coke is.
That's the way it should be.
What the world wants to see
Is the real thing.

It's the real thing, Coke is.
In the back of your mind
What you're hoping to find
Is the real thing.

On one level of interpretation, Coke is held up as something genuine in a world of automation and imitation. (Interestingly enough, Coke became "the real thing" only after 7-Up billed itself as the "Uncola"—apparently in an attempt to imply that 7-Up is not a genuine soft drink.) It becomes associated in our minds with a nostalgia for the superior products of the past—"real" bread, "real" ice cream, "real" cars, "real" wood, etc. And, of course, people who are living imitation lives will be doubly attracted by the idea of "authentic" products.

The other meaning of "the real thing" is *love,* and this association is conveyed partly through the pleasant, soft-rock style of the song in the commercials. In the back of our minds we are all looking for the real thing —genuine affection—and would be ready and willing to buy any products that might help us find it.

A more complex and subtle use of the concept of love lies behind the familiar Coca-Cola commercial in which young people from all over the world are brought together on a hilltop in Italy, where they sing (in perfect harmony):

I'd like to teach the world to sing
In perfect harmony.
I'd like to buy the world a Coke
And keep it company.

I find the appeal of this ad, the music combined with the idea of buying the world a Coke, almost irresistible, a fact that disturbs me when I consider its implications. For one thing, the ad embodies the all too American theory and practice of *buying* good will, friendship, or even love. This notion is so pervasive at every level of our society that it is pretty much taken for granted—and for some reason has always been neatly associated with Coca-Cola. I remember that when I was in junior high school, if a guy bought me a Coke it was the first sign he was "interested" in me; later, if the relationship turned out be "the real thing," he might ask you to go steady with him. The ad illustrates perfectly, if unintentionally, how this economic aspect of courtship is projected onto the global plane in American foreign relations. We are always happy to buy the world a Coke if we believe that this will keep it in our "company" rather than the Soviet Union's or China's. (I am incidentally reminded of that outrageous scene in *Dr. Strangelove* in which Peter Sellers is begging Keenan Wynn to shoot open the coin box of a Coke machine so he can get a dime to call the President and explain why the world may be about to end. Keenan Wynn reluctantly complies with the request, saying, "Okay, but you're gonna have to answer to the Coca-Cola Company for this.")

Of course, this kind of sociological analysis is somewhat remote from the ad's ability to touch people emotionally. On a more personal level, I think it appeals to that sense of community that many of us long for but so rarely experience in contemporary urban life—in fact, may have lost the knack to experience. The irony about an idea like buying the world a Coke and keeping it company, though, is that it is so abstract it can be employed only in the mind, which means everyone has to experience it alone.

Still, the ad always puts me in a mood of buoyancy and good will, although then I don't quite know what to *do* with these feelings. The words and music inevitably make me smile and think any day now I will begin to show the world all the love I have in my heart, but, needless to say, I never do. Unfortunately, the "world" is made up of individual people, any one of whom is much more difficult to love than is mankind in general. I can sit alone and respond to that ad with a sense of joy; but later that same day, if I see an acquaintance who doesn't see me in the supermarket, I may still duck down some aisle and linger behind the shelves until he or she is out of sight. It is not that I dislike the person but that I wish to avoid the degree of involvement required for even the most casual conversation. What makes the jingle in the Coke ad so appealing is that it allows you to participate momentarily in a kind of love that is not dangerous or painful to you, a kind that makes no demands. Actually, loving another individual (the *real* "real thing") always involves the terrible risk of being hurt, which simply does not enter into the notion of buying the world a Coke and keeping it company.

The other day I noticed in a magazine advertisement that the Pepsi-Cola Company has come up with a new slogan: "Pepsi people—the smilin' majority." My first reaction was to connect the slogan with those signs and buttons and bumper stickers cropping up all over that remind people to smile, as if it were something to be done on cue. That in itself is a little scary. Then I remembered a couple of people I've known who smiled almost constantly, even when they didn't mean to or perhaps even when a smile was most inappropriate. The thought of them led me to recall a theory about the development of the human smile that some cultural anthropologists have expounded—that a smile actually represents a passive defense against the threat of aggression, a symbolic baring of the teeth to demonstrate that they will not be used in hostility. Like the smile, a lot more than meets the eyes lies behind those seemingly innocent soft-drink ads.

---

to the student : a commentary

Ann Nietzke, a free-lancer, writes with a gentle grace that almost hides her pointed statements about the use and meaning of television advertising. With smooth elegance she draws the reader into an analysis of commercials, slowly displaying an interesting way to look at the message within the message.

The need, the "neurosis," of the audience is shown by the vast amount of time people spend watching television. If an individual is fully aware, Nietzke says, and has any capacity for pleasure or self-expression, he would not want to be part of any audience. He would be doing things, not watching others do them.

According to research published in 1976, George Gerbner and Larry Gross found that one-third of the adults they sampled watched four or more hours of television per day. They also found that nearly half of the twelve-year-olds they surveyed watched an average of six or more hours per day. That adds up to a great many people who watch rather than do. If it is the images of activity that people look for in commercials, just what is presented to them?

It may be interesting first to divide such commercials into those directed at men and women. The beer commercials are probably the most "activity" prone of the male ads. The range of seemingly exciting male pursuits displayed on the screen is extraordinary. One has a group flying hang-gliders, another shows motorcycle racing, still others depict snowmobiling, auto racing, log-rolling, skiing, and anything else faintly macho. Some show worldly activities, where men live with gusto while sailing ships, climbing mountains, and playing baseball in exotic lands. Others emphasize local, weekend activities where men play a neighborhood football game, fly model planes, or play other man/child games.

The weight of "activity" ads aimed at women seem to fall into "sex" product categories like perfume and nylons. Women are seen stepping from Rolls Royces, turning heads in restaurants, holding court at cocktail parties, and strolling moonlit beaches. Some commercials, belatedly aware that a large number of women work, jam together a complete action-packed day that shows a woman working (with an increasing number of them in obviously managerial positions), going out to dinner, and then dancing until dawn.

An occasional activity commercial will throw in a twist on the sex role portrayals. The most striking example is the beer commercial in which one member of a group of motorcycle riders is sent to get refreshments. This helmeted, overall-covered person rides long and hard to get the right product. When the correct beer is approvingly delivered, the helmet comes off and —gee, surprise—it's a woman.

The obvious thing about such commercials, to return to Nietzke's point, is that no one is ever shown watching television. With all those people, whether worldly or average, running around doing interesting things, one could easily wonder if anyone ever stays home.

In reality a great many people do stay home, some spending as much as half of their non-work hours parked in front of the set. Approximately twelve minutes of each of those hours are devoted to commercials—many of which promise, for $1.89, the ability to live with Gusto a life of Sheer Energy.

How much of that, for you, is the real thing?

LLS

---

study questions

1. If you are twenty-five or under, the agencies handling the bulk of the advertising you are exposed to think they have your number. They think they know what you want and, says Tankard, how to maneuver you into wanting what they have to sell. Do they? Does Madison Avenue affect your life? Do you care? Do "hip" sales campaigns—or those oriented generally in the direction of "youth"—appeal to you? Why?

2. A little psychology, like a little knowledge, can be a harmful thing. Research the meaning of the words "neuroses" and "neurotic." Does Nietzke use these concepts correctly? If so, the implication is that vast numbers of Americans, perhaps a majority, are neurotic, since mass advertising must aim at a sizable group to be effective. Which do you think came first: the public's dependence on products for "fun" and "love" or the predominance of messages selling consumption as the road to happiness? If from childhood we're told that success, popularity, and sex appeal depend on our buying habits, might not many people come to believe this? Is it possible that the *advertisers* are neurotic?

advertising

constraints

"A quart is a quart, damn it! How can it be a big, jumbo quart?"

Bruce Howard

The Advertising Council: Selling Lies...

What do you think you could do with half-a-billion dollars worth of free advertising a year, especially if you were charged with using it to serve the public interest?

Would you use more than $15 million to "rally the country behind the President's [anti-inflation] measures"? Would you use $40 million to tell the nation that the man on the street starts pollution, and not the smoke-belching, poison-pouring industries? Would you use more than $10 million to encourage factory workers to be more "productive" for their employers? And how much would you devote to advertising that marijuana leads to a "loss of desire to work, to compete, to face challenges" and to a "compulsive" drug use?

Well, someone does have half-a-billion dollars in advertising at their disposal, practically all the free ads available in America, and those are some examples of how they use it. If you watch TV (especially late night) or read magazines . . . you've seen their work many times, always ending up with the logo of the Advertising Council.

The council is a non-profit corporation funded and directed by America's bonafide Captains of Industry. It produces those campaigns and dozens of others like them "in the public interest" on behalf of industry and the executive branch of the federal government. The Ad Council is by far the largest advertiser in the world. Since its formation in 1941, the council has used more than $7 billion worth of free "public service" advertising donated by television, radio, newspapers, and magazines.

Unfortunately, what the public thinks is good for it is not always the same as what the directors of the Ad Council believe. The board of directors of the Ad Council is a who's who of big business, including the media (NBC, CBS, ABC, Metromedia, Time Inc., etc.), the advertising agencies (J. Walter Thompson, which was so helpful in shaping the mentality of the Nixon men at the White House, Young & Rubicam, etc.), and the nation's major advertisers (Proctor and Gamble, all the Generals: Motors, Mills, Electric, Foods, and others). No public interest groups are represented on the Ad Council's board.

Reprinted by permission from *Ramparts,* December 1974.

347

Describing itself as "free enterprise's effective communication machine," the Ad Council has managed to monopolize more than 80 percent of the scarce public service time on network television, and the lion's share of free space and time in local television, radio, newspapers, and national magazines. In the past 30 years, the Ad Council has virtually created the landscape of public service advertising in America—traffic safety and seat belts, the United Way, the Red Cross, and, of course, that masterful cartoon conscience, Smokey the Bear. But as is often the case when General Motors and its colleagues get together to help the American people, there is more than meets the eye in the Ad Council's good will.

Who counsels the council

A closer look at the council's advertisements shows they are carefully designed to preserve the status quo and promote the image and interests of big business and big government. What makes the situation worse is the sorry scarcity of free public service time and space. The powers that run the Ad Council are the same ones that glut prime time with their paid ads. The media dregs, scraps—the gaps in the back pages, pre-dawn and late-night television spots—are then thrown to public service ads. But the big advertisers are not prepared to let even these scraps go to their own critics.

Says Thomas Asher, executive director of the Media Access Project, a public interest law firm in Washington, D.C., "The community forces are forced to capture attention with extraordinary protest activity because they are muscled out of the public airways and print media by the Ad Council. The council then flacks for the power brokers of business and government, who already have ready access to the media in advertising and news broadcasts."

In a sizzling exposé in [*More*] magazine in March 1972, Tom Asher went public with his long-time war against the Ad Council tyranny, but even with continued pressure from Asher, Congressman Benjamin Rosenthal (D-NY), and a scattering of other Congressmen and public interest groups, the public service announcement (PSA) situation has only slightly improved.

The main problem, they say, is that there is so precious little public service advertising, mainly because it is not required by law. No money-making operation, including the media, goes out of its way to provide free services. Magazines and newspapers are under absolutely no legal obligation to run free ads, and many in fact donate little or none.

Broadcasters, on the other hand, are required by the Federal Communications Commission (FCC) to state the number of public service announcements (PSAs) they have run in a sample week, and the number they intend to run in an average week in the next three years. Although the FCC sets no minimum number for PSAs, it could deny a license renewal if the local station were deemed not to have fulfilled its obligation to serve the community. So far, though numerous community groups have submitted challenges, no station has lost its license because it ran too few PSAs. As a result, stations donate less than three percent of total air time for PSAs. It is this fraction that the Ad Council has effectively tied up.

On network television, the Ad Council's spots account for more than 80 percent of all PSAs. (In addition to the 25 major campaigns the Ad Council produces, each month it distributes a bulletin to local stations listing the other campaigns it "endorses." Network executives acknowledge that such endorsement is a virtual prerequisite for being aired.) Using the anti-trust lawyer's rule of thumb for monopoly—control of two-thirds or more of a market—the Ad Council has clearly monopolized the public service market.

The situation on the local level is a little better, but not much. Local stations run PSAs in addition to the ones that come down from the network, and many station managers like to use locally oriented ads. But the ubiquitous Ad Council still swamps local stations with its national ads, arguing that they do have "local import." Interviews with station managers indicated that they use many of the Ad Council ads instead of local ones because a) they are more professionally executed than local ads; b) they are bland, and do not arouse viewers to complain or demand response time; c) local groups would often need to use the station's own facilities, personnel, and art departments, because they cannot afford to produce their own ads; and d) the board of directors of the council includes the networks, the advertising agencies, and the major advertisers. When Proctor and Gamble and the parent network, et al. ask for free time, well, it's hard to bite the hand.

"The public conscience"

Besides the industries and agencies on the board of directors, the Ad Council also has an Industries Advisory Committee and a Public Policy Committee. The latter consists of 27 people who, according to an Ad Council promotional leaflet, "represent the public sector [and] act as the council's 'public conscience.' " The committee has the same power that most citizen advisory committees have in corporations run by a board of directors composed entirely of businessmen: little or none. Its impotence is made evermore ironic by the high profile the Ad Council attempts to give it.

The Industries Advisory Committee, on the other hand, is in charge of raising money for the council, and it has the power that most revenue-producing branches have in corporations run by a board of directors composed entirely of businessmen. Thus the Ad Council has a nice Freudian triumvirate—a superego-public conscience, a single-minded id (the Industries Advisory Committee), and an ego (the decision-making board of directors) that, in this case, curiously resembles the id.

Helping the White House win

A fourth and not so silent partner of the Ad Council's board is the federal government, which often uses the council as a flack for its various projects. Although the White House is not represented on the Ad Council's board of directors, the businessmen's group has been patriotically receptive to White House politics. Curiously, the Ad Council by-laws say that it will "accept no subsidy from Government and (will) remain independent of it" and will "remain non-partisan and non-political."

Of the council's 25 major campaigns each year, more than a third are usually associated with boosting and popularizing government projects. The campaigns range from peddling low-interest U.S. Government Savings Bonds, to pushing recruitment for the National Guard and the Armed Forces Reserve, to promoting the Justice Department's incredible anti-crime campaigns in 1971–72.

An Ad Council release describes one of these: *"Help Prevent Crime. This campaign thus far has concentrated on auto theft prevention; the advertising urges motorists to fight juvenile delinquency and prevent crime by locking their cars and taking their keys."*

And we thought the roots of crime were troubling and complex. Not at all. You can forget about bad schools, bad drugs, bad housing, unemployment, and despair. Just don't forget your keys.

When the Ad Council is not distracting the public from the problems that the government should be dealing with but isn't, it is promoting the counter-productive efforts the government does mount—the war on marijuana, the Vietnam War, the WIN program.

One Ad Council cheerleader campaign for the White House was challenged by citizens. President Nixon decided that the nation needed to hear more about the plight of the American prisoners-of-war in Southeast Asia. With secret financial support from the Republican National Committee, an organization called the National League of Families of American Prisoners and Missing in Southeast Asia asked the Ad Council to sponsor a "Write Hanoi" campaign. The campaign was announced, and then mysteriously dropped. The Ad Council then designed a new campaign that deleted the letter-writing pitch. On April 14, 1971, the White House sent the council a telegram of support.

Four months later, an anti-war group of POW families called Families for Immediate Release, which was angered because the campaign implied support for continuing the war, began asking television stations for equal time to rebut the council's ads. The Ad Council campaign began officially in March 1972, but few stations carried it because of the equal time demands of the Families for Immediate Release.

. . . [T]he Ad Council . . . launch[ed] another outrageously partisan effort on behalf of the Ford White House. On Sept. 27, [1974,] President Ford met with Ad Council president Robert Keim to promote his Whip Inflation Now (WIN) campaign. In an election campaign season when many Republican candidates were running on Ford's WIN program, and many Democrats were running against it, the Ad Council began pushing the campaign. The council designed the WIN buttons, and distributed plans for reproducing them free to businesses around the country.

Keim gushe[d] with enthusiasm when he [spoke] of the council's WIN project. "It will be a special drive. [It will] rally the country behind the President's measures." [Said] Lewis Shollenberger, vice president of the Ad Council, and the man working with the White House on the WIN project: "Normally it takes six months to get a campaign moving, but we're trying to get this one rolling in six weeks. We're going all out. This will be one of our greatest efforts ever."

Russell Freeburg, President Ford's special assistant coordinating the WIN campaign, defended the "cooperation" of the Ad Council. "The President is President of all the people," Freeburg said while his boss was campaigning for Republican candidates in the Midwest, "and he is trying to solve inflation. Sure, if he solves inflation, it will help him politically, but if the Democrats would rather have us go down the drain so that they can win the next election, well, that's pretty short-sighted."

On the other hand, Freeburg [was] being a little short-memoried. He [said] that the Ad Council WIN media blitz will be based on "inflation-fighting" points in Ford's Kansas City speech of October 15, 1974. But he [did] not mention that this speech was considered so one-sided that the Democrats were given a free half-hour during prime time television to respond to it. . . .

Amotivational syndromes

The Drug Abuse Program produced by the council was also directed almost entirely by the White House, in flagrant violation of the council's by-laws. After requesting the Ad Council to handle the program, and then advancing the council $150,000 for the initial out-of-pocket expenses, the White House went on to design and direct the campaign, which was officially sponsored by the National Institute of Mental Health under HEW.

In June, 1969, Charles B. (Bud) Wilkinson, special consultant to President Nixon, wrote "A Supplement to the White House Proposal to the Ad Council for a Major Campaign on Drug Abuse." In it, he said "The White House will continue to assume a strong leadership role in the campaign, and the National Institute of Mental Health has been designated as the contracting agency. It was agreed that the coordinated Federal campaign would be conducted in cooperation with the National Coordinating Council for Drug Abuse Education and Information and the new campaign will build from the base established in the National Institute of Mental Health public service program. The development of the campaign and its execution will be subject to review at all stages by a committee composed of one of the designated representatives of each of the three government departments, and the National Coordinating Council under the chairmanship of a White House representative." Notice that there is no mention of the Advertising Council, which is supposedly running the campaign, and which is "independent of the Government."

By the way, it was this campaign that warned of the "social maladjustment" and the "amotivational syndromes" of marijuana, while adding that "not everyone who uses a mind-altering chemical becomes dependent upon it. Alcohol is one common example of this point . . . The majority of persons who drink do not harm themselves or those around them." Before you ask, the president of Joseph E. Seagram and Sons, Inc. is on the council's board of directors.

Tin can ecology

But the Ad Council is best known for its campaigns on behalf of non-profit organizations, many of which happen to be funded and directed by big business. The classic example of this is the council's $40 million a year campaign for Keep America Beautiful, Inc., an anti-litter organization directed and funded by the American Can Company, and other manufacturers of cans and bottles, beer and soft drinks, and steel, glass, and aluminum, all of whom are distressed by the litterbugs who pollute America's environment.

The KAB ads are the best produced and most controversial ones run by the Ad Council. The KAB ad portraying the Indian who sheds a tear when someone throws a bag of litter at his feet won two Clio awards for the best television commercial.

At the same time, however, the Sierra Club and four other environmentalist groups have resigned from KAB's citizen advisory council because

KAB has been actively opposing the only proven curb of litter—legislation that requires the use of returnable beer and soft drink containers. Oregon passed a so-called bottle bill in 1971, and has since reported an 80 percent decline in the number of cans and bottles littered in the state. Similar legislation is also supported by the Environmental Protection Agency, the Federal Energy Office, and the League of Women Voters because it would save energy and valuable resources, control litter, and reduce prices for consumers. Such savings for the consumer, however, would cost the canners, bottlers, and steel, glass, and aluminum manufacturers who run KAB millions of dollars in profits. And so KAB, the avowed leader in the war on litter, opposes the only legislation likely to do the job.

Although this controversy has been brewing for years, the fight shifted to high gear in January 1974, when KAB president (and former executive for the brewing industry) Roger Powers testified in the California State Legislature against a bottle bill there. Soon thereafter, the Sierra Club, the Izaak Walton League, the National Parks and Conservation Association, the Outdoor Writers Association of America, and the Wilderness Society resigned from the KAB advisory council.

In its letter of resignation, . . . the National Parks and Conservation Association wrote: "In fact, it seems that the KAB, Inc. is using its achievements in litter prevention education to cover its support for the container industries' efforts to oppose beverage container refund-deposit systems to restrict litter."

In its . . . letter of resignation, the Sierra Club asked if KAB was not "merely a front for container manufacturers." . . .

Infamous "Iron Eyes"

KAB's commercials, even one starring the infamous "Chief Iron Eyes Cody," as Ad Council execs call him, subtly promote the industry's war against returnables. Says Pat Taylor, a lobbyist with an environmental group in Washington, D.C., called Environmental Action, and a leader of the pro-bottle bill forces: "The commercials try to create the myth that people are to blame for litter, and not the industries that push the throwaway containers, and thus people should be made to change, and not industries. KAB argues against bottle legislation that's been proved to cut litter, and then it spouts its slogan 'People start pollution, and people can stop it.' "

More important, perhaps, is the KAB role in the "one-from-column-A, one-from-column-B" effect that frustrates so many community groups trying to get public service time. That is, most station managers try to spread out their PSA time among as many issues as possible, partly so that when someone asks "What about problem X?" they can point to the anti-X ads they already ran. Environmentalists trying to get their own PSAs aired have complained that many stations have cited the KAB ads in rejecting the requests.

There is reason to believe the Ad Council knew it was pre-empting serious environmental concerns when it decided to produce the KAB campaign. In 1969 a subcommittee of the council's Industries Advisory Committee was formed to "advise how the council should proceed on the anti-pollution campaign." The subcommittee was composed of the chairmen of Allied Chemicals, Bethlehem Steel, Kraftco., American Can Co., and U.S. Steel—all of them intimately knowledgeable about pollution. The subcommittee carefully reviewed all the sources of pollution in the country, and through a stroke of group-think genius, decided to focus on the real colossus of environmental destruction—litter-bugs. The principle is rather elegant: if everyone is responsible, no one is responsible.

The Zen of agribusiness

The Ad Council has produced dozens of other campaigns that serve the interests of big business. In the Minority Business Enterprise, for example, business takes a modest bow for its determined struggle against racism. One ad featured a full-face shot of General Motors board chairman James M. Roche, with the headline "Here's why Mr. Roche of General Motors thinks investing in minority business is just plain good business." The ad copy praised GM for accepting Federal money to set up "one of the first Minority Enterprise Small Business Investment Companies (MESBICs) to be licensed by the Small Business Administration." As [*More*] magazine reported in March 1972, "The MESBIC program is little more than a charade that finances big business subsidiaries that serve as decoys to industry's often discriminatory hiring and promotion practices." Nevertheless, underneath Mr. Roche's beneficent visage was the information that the ad was "donated for the public good." What's good for General Motors . . .

In the JOBS campaign, sponsored by the National Alliance of Businessmen, we learn of the accomplishments of business in hiring the poor, a success that seems all the more magical since it is achieved while unemployment rates still soar. The Technical Education and Training Campaign, run for the U.S. Office of Education and the Manpower Institute, encourages students to take up technical training because "technicians earn . . . as much or more than the average college graduate." Although this may be true for people just out of school, it is doubtful that it holds in the long run.

Even our furry fire fighter, Smokey the Bear, is not a total innocent.

Environmentalists view forest fires as far less severe a threat to America's timber resources than clear-cutting and indiscriminate logging by paper and wood products companies, but the ads instead say careless people destroy forests, not careless industries.

The Smokey campaign, by the way, is coordinated by James M. Montgomery of the Gulf States Paper Corporation. Meanwhile, when the Sierra Club approaches a broadcaster with environment ads, they are told "Oh, forests, we got them covered with Smokey the Bear."

Perhaps the most blatant pro-business ad campaign by the Ad Council is the productivity program ('How would you like to sign the work you do?"), which urges laborers to work harder for their employers. As yet, there is no council campaign urging employers to pay their employees more. Such "Work! Work!" campaigns cost thousands when attempted by individual factories and industries, and are usually prevented by watchful unions who know from experience what a "speed up" drive can mean. But, thanks to the Ad Council, the campaign is carried multi-media, nationwide, and free, "as a public service."

But the masterwork of all Ad Council manipulations has to be its Food, Nutrition, and Health campaign, which is sponsored by HEW, the Department of Agriculture, and the Grocery Manufacturers of America, Inc. It is coordinated by an executive of General Foods Corp. The ads urge viewers to send in for a free booklet entitled "Food Is More Than Just Something to Eat."

The booklet neglects to mention that Americans eat too much cereal, sugar, potato chips, processed foods, etc. Rather, the helpful manual chirps "Fresh or frozen? Canned or dried? Instant or from scratch? Which foods have the nutrients? Which do not? They all do." The message is don't worry, it's all good: The Zen of Agribusiness.

Robert Choate, director of a group called Children, Media and Merchandising in Washington, D.C., tried to distribute ads to show the other side of the nutrition debate, but without much success. "We produced the ads that said Americans ate too many snack foods, but the networks wouldn't let them on. They said they were too controversial. The local stations wouldn't touch them either, or else ran them at 2 A.M."

And finally, the Ad Council produced a campaign for the National Safety Council (funded and directed by Ford, GM, et al.) which pushes the use of seat belts. The Insurance Institute for Highway Safety conducted a study in 1972 that showed commercials asking people to use seat belts were totally ineffective. The report concluded, "The television messages had no effect whatsover on use."

Why did the Ad Council continue to squander free advertising on the seat belt campaign after it received the institute's study? The answer lies in the . . . 1974 *Status Report* of the Safety Institute, entitled "Auto Makers

Renew Passive Restraint Attack." The report describes how the auto industry, which has near control of the Safety Council, as well as a hefty representation on the Ad Council's board, has been actively lobbying against the replacement of seat belts by "passive restraints," such as automatically inflatable air bags.

The Ad Council abuses public service time: 1) by giving the impression that business and government are doing their job to help America (Minority Business Enterprise, JOBS, Jobs for Veterans, etc.); 2) by diverting attention towards window dressing solutions to serious problems (seat belts rather than unsafe cars, litter rather than institutionalized pollution, locked cars rather than sources of crime); 3) by using its prestige and economic clout to corner scarce public access; 4) by filling public service time with ads that are so bland as to have no impact on the status quo; and 5) by foisting the responsibility for government- and business-caused problems onto the individual, thus reducing social and political problems to the level of personal failings.

Such policy is actually the modus operandi of advertisers, networks, and stations—to maximize their profits, they have decided to use television as almost a purely entertainment medium. Disturbing documentaries, scathing exposés, and truly intelligent programing are kept to a minimum—the top priority is the continued blissful narcosis of the viewer. Television makes money by getting viewers to purchase advertisers' merchandise, and marketing science shows that anything above mild arousal is not conducive to a buying mentality. So with the slick, bland Ad Council advertisement, the broadcasters get the best of both worlds—the viewer is not aroused or offended by a serious, productive use of the PSA time by public interest groups, and the PSA commitment to the FCC and the community is numerically filled.

"Corrupting the intent"

The networks and broadcasters put up with and support this waste of their PSA time because they do not want to offend their viewers or their advertisers. For this reason, controversial PSAs are never aired by networks and most local stations. "If we accept yours," they say, "we'd have to let the other side respond." (For years Planned Parenthood was denied public service space for this reason.)

But according to the FCC, controversiality is not grounds for rejection. Said an FCC spokesman, "There's no reason why a PSA ad can't be controversial. If a controversial ad runs, and someone demands a chance to respond, then let him respond." Unfortunately, while controversiality is not good grounds for rejection, the networks and stations do not legally need any grounds at all. They can reject any ad for any reason they want.

This is the first aspect of the system that critics would like to change. "Let's open the public ads to the public," says Asher. "Let's air all the opinions, and especially those of the people who don't have access to the media already. If things get controversial, then the system's working. Just try to keep a balance."

"The problem now," he says, "is that we have one-sided controversial ads that are being passed off as non-controversial. Viewers are getting the establishment view, bland maybe, but establishment." . . .

---

to the student : a commentary

Writer Bruce Howard takes a definite and angry stance toward the Advertising Council, making a broad range of charges regarding misuse and bias. Howard's argument is an interesting one, and it is easy to agree with him on several points. There is, however, a certain amount of contradiction in what he says. On one hand he grants to the council the power to persuade and divert the public on important issues, yet on the other he quotes a report that says the Ad Council's seat belt campaign "had no effect whatsoever." And few people who recall the WIN promotion remember it as anything but a total flop. It should be fairly clear that one cannot talk about the council's advertising—or anyone else's for that matter—in terms of directly effective propaganda.

As Professor Stephen Greyser of the Harvard Business School put it:

Underlying a substantial amount of the criticism of advertising's persuasive powers is an assumption that advertising is extremely powerful. Indeed, attitude surveys show that both the public and the private sectors attribute considerable power to advertising in affecting consumer needs and wants. Many an advertiser, as he viewed the wreckage of a product failure which had heavy advertising support, has wished that this were so. The myth of the defenseless consumer is one of the most enduring outputs of the social critics of advertising.

Yet a substantial body of consumer behavior research tells us that the consumer is hardly a helpless pawn manipulated at will by the advertiser. We know, for example, that almost all consumers are very selective in what advertising they pay attention to, perceive, evaluate, and remember—let alone act upon.

This, of course, does not negate the *possible* impact of advertising, and Howard's concerns certainly deserve attention. But it does mean that one should be careful about attributing to any advertising the power of the "magic bullet." The "magic bullet" is a phrase social scientists have used in deriding the simplistic approach to propaganda campaigns. The "bullet" can be any piece of information that is "shot" into a mass audience and has a direct and predictable response. As Greyser points out, it just doesn't work that way.

Commercials, most people would readily agree, contain a certain amount of puffery; we expect them to exaggerate. We should watch for what Greyser calls the "various subcategories of truth" within commercials, because commercials do not usually deal in stark realities. Greyser asks four basic questions to identify such subcategories.

Literal truth: *Is the claim substantiable?* Here he says that many commercials may on the surface seem straightforward, but are often far from it. What about the "research" behind all those tests offered as definite proof of a product's value? Do they tell you the size of the sample—either of people or products—when they make their claims? When "four out of five doctors recommend," how many are they really talking about? And can the test results be considered definitive? How much is "more" or "better"? Another aspect of this is that some of the research claims deal with a minor part of the product, ignoring central questions about value or performance.

True impression: *Despite literal truth, ·is the impression true?* In this category Greyser asks about the suppression of relevant information. Does the claim apply to all models? Is the product in limited supply? Are there things about the product we should know, but about which the advertiser has reservations? No advertiser is going to carefully point out the weak points of his product, of course. But there are cases where the public has left them no choice, as in the mandatory health warnings that go with all cigarette advertising.

Discernible exaggeration: *Aside from the absence of literal truth, is the exaggeration or puffery discernible as such?* Greyser says that "we must concern ourselves with the notion of a reasonable man. All of us presumably would agree that people who actually believe a specific soap powder can truly 'make their washing machine ten feet tall' need a different kind of help than can be provided by the Federal Trade Commission. But where does one draw the line?"

This area, not unreasonably, should be of some concern when it comes to children's advertising. Can they distinguish obvious exaggeration? Take, for example, the presentation of one of a group of toys called "Hot Wheels," which at one point was being heavily advertised on children's programs. The commercial showed a toy car racing over sand dunes and leaping through the air. The presentation made full use of filmatic techniques, using slow motion, stop-motion, and a variety of camera angles. There were also some quick cuts to joyfully screaming children.

What was the product really like? It was a three-inch plastic toy with about two feet of attached cord. Push a button at the end of the cord and the car stood on its rear wheels. That was it. It did nothing else. The difference between the image and the reality was quite large, but how many children watching the commercial would know that?

False impression: *Does the ad actually include material that suggests a false impression?* In this category Greyser places advertisements that imply uniqueness, or fall back on imagery and allusions. The products that often use this approach can range from perfume to floor wax, gasoline to beer. It is, as a matter of fact, those products with little differences between competing brands that often resort to this tactic. Consider the images sold with "rugged" after-shave lotion, or the "excitement" portrayed in many of the beer commercials.

Different degrees of deception are thus involved in advertising. Howard charges the Advertising Council with using most of the public service campaigns to support institutional, "establishment" bias. His views deserve serious consideration. But it should be remembered that the issue is a complex one, worthy of more than easy answers.

LLS

study questions

1. How do you feel about the captains of industry and commerce controlling not only the bulk of commercial advertising, but the PSA market as well? Does the explanation of the PSA situation fit your definition of Big Brother propaganda?

2. What does the cooperation of three of the most powerful American institutions —the media, industry, and the federal government—evident in the makeup of the Ad Council, tell you about the "adversary" or "regulatory" relationships presumed to exist among them?

index